USING QEMM

PHILLIP ROBINSON

USING QEMM

Get the Most out of Quarterdeck's Best-Selling Memory Management System

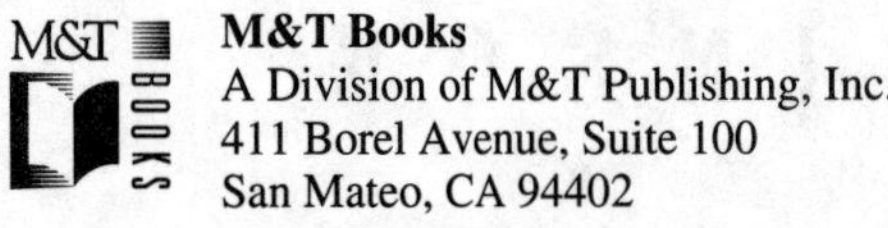

M&T Books
A Division of M&T Publishing, Inc.
411 Borel Avenue, Suite 100
San Mateo, CA 94402

Printed in the United States of America

Library of Congress Cataloging-in-Publication Data Available from Publisher

Robinson, Phillip
Using QEMM: managing memory with the best-selling memory management system / Phillip Robinson.
p. cm.
Includes index.
ISBN 1-55851-295-0
1. Memory management (Computer science) 2. QEMM. I. Title.
QA76.9.M45R66 1992 92-36576
005.4'3--dc20 CIP

95 94 93 92 4 3 2 1

Technical Editor: Steven Fisher
Production Supervisor: Cindy Williams
Art Director: Margaret Horoszko
Cover Design: Lauren Smith Design

Contents

Acknowledgments

Thanks to everyone at and around Quarterdeck who helped inform me. The key figures were Charles McHenry, Bob Perry and Orla Buckley.

Thanks to the M&T Books people, especially Brenda McLaughlin, Meredith Ittner, and Cindy Williams.

And thanks to all my friends who pretended I was a "writer" even though I was really just an "explainer".

Why This Book Is for You

If you want to gain full control of the memory in your PC, you'll need QEMM, the bestselling memory management tool from Quarterdeck, and this book.

Using QEMM is a concise, comprehensive and useable guide to using QEMM to maximize the memory in your PC. It covers the fundamentals including installation, step-by-step instructions for beginners and numerous tips for experts.

- Beginning PC users will learn more about memory and how QEMM works to maximize it.
- QEMM users, having trouble, will learn how to get QEMM to work.
- Intermediate and advanced computer hobbyists will learn how to fine tune their PCs with QEMM's many options.

Memory is at the heart of everything a PC does. As programs grow more powerful, they demand more memory and more cooperation with other programs' use of memory. This book will help you create the best system for your PC, tailor memory to your particular uses, and get the most from QEMM.

QEMM

QEMM is a memory management program for PC-compatible personal computers with 386 or 486 processor chips. It lets all other programs run more efficiently. Its cousin program QRAM does the same thing for PC compatibles with 8088, 8086, or 80286 processor chips. Both QEMM and QRAM install automatically, so beginners who care only about getting their programs installed won't desperately need a manual or a book such as this.This book is for beginners who want to understand what QEMM or QRAM is doing, any computer user who has trouble getting QEMM or QRAM to work, and intermediate or advanced computer hobbyists or professionals who want to fine-tune a PC with QEMM or QRAM's many options. In this book you'll find a complete listing and explanation of those options, along with examples of their use in customizing QEMM or QRAM to help programs such as WordPerfect and Excel, environments such as Windows and DESQview, systems such as PS/2 and Compaq, and peripherals such as hard disks and network adapters.

QEMM's Importance

You might think that the most common program for the IBM PC and compatible personal computers are the leading spreadsheet—Lotus 1-2-3—or the leading word processor—WordPerfect. Not so.

In fact, the most common programs are the operating systems—the fundamental software that animates every PC and compatible. Number one on this list is DOS, the Disk Operating System from Microsoft that appears under names such as MS-DOS and PC-DOS. Number two is Microsoft Windows, a program that adds to DOS, giving the PC an easy-to-use display of menus and graphic icons.

But there's another operating system program at the top of the best-seller charts —QEMM-386. Officially pronounced "Que-Ee-Em-Em" (though typically rendered as “Quemm”), the Quarterdeck Expanded Memory Manager-386 manages the memory inside any 386- or 486-based PC running DOS or DOS and Windows. Another version of QEMM, called QEMM-50/60 for PS/2 Models 50 and 60 computers, is nearly identical to QEMM-386. Throughout this book I'll call both just QEMM, except for the points where QEMM-50/60 differs.

Managing memory is no small job, nor are the results trivial. Memory is at the heart of everything a PC does. As programs grow more powerful, they demand more memory and more cooperation with other programs' use of memory. QEMM is the moderator, controlling what program gets how much memory, when, and where. The result is that QEMM lets DOS and Windows run more programs faster. Without QEMM many PCs would be crippled. (Owners of older systems compatible with IBM's PC, XT, or AT can use QEMM's sibling program QRAM for many of the same tasks.)

What QEMM Does

QEMM-386 is a memory management utility program—a memory manager, for short. It works with any PC compatible that runs DOS and has a 386 or 486 processor chip, such as the 386SX, 386DX, 486SX, i486DX, or compatible. (If you have an older PC, such as the 8088-based PC or the 80286-based AT, you can use the related QRAM program.)

QEMM is the software brains for the memory management circuits on these chips. It can map memory to make more available for DOS and Windows applications. It can improve the performance of Quarterdeck's DESQview multitasking utility. The latest version of DOS (DOS 5) can do some of this through its utilities called HIMEM.SYS and EMM386, but these fall far short of QEMM's power. In fact, sales of QEMM lagged just before DOS 5 appeared because rumors suggested the new operating system would include some memory management abilities. After DOS 5 appeared and it became clear that it couldn't do as much as QEMM, QEMM sales boomed. This book includes tips on using QEMM with and without DOS 5.

QEMM works with IBM's, Compaq's, and Microsoft's DOS from version 3.0 to version 5.0. It is compatible with DR-DOS 5.0 and 6.0, which are DOS competitors. It works with Microsoft Windows 3 in all three Windows modes: real (for Windows 3.0), standard, and enhanced. (It does need a special setup to run optimally with standard and enhanced modes, as explained in the chapters on

QEMM-386.SYS and Windows.) QEMM even works with DOS-extended programs—those written with a special programming tool called a DOS Extender to get at more memory than normally allowed. Windows in standard or enhanced mode is a DOS-extended program.

QEMM is not really a single program. It is a collection of utilities with a variety of routes to conserve and manage memory. Manifest analyzes your PC to find out how much memory you have and how it is employed. QEMM.SYS manages extended and expanded memory, the two quite different types of memory in today's most powerful PCs. LOADHI finds unused memory, enlarging the space for application programs such as Lotus 1-2-3 and WordPerfect. VIDRAM borrows unused memory from hidden areas in the PC. And OPTIMIZE automatically tests and configures your system to use LOADHI and QEMM.SYS.

Who Needs QEMM?

You may be happily computing on your PC, running your word processor, spreadsheet, or other application program. Perhaps you've never bumped into an error message telling you there is "too little memory." Maybe you're too busy to worry about improving your PC's performance, or you're content with its speed at getting and saving information and at calculating, spell-checking, or doing whatever else your application does. If so, you don't need QEMM or QRAM—yet.

But that description applies to few PC users. Most users would love to have their PC run faster. Many would like to change from one computer task to another more quickly. A fair number must decide which programs to use and which to avoid, because their computer just doesn't have enough memory for all of them.

These are the people who need QEMM or QRAM: most PC owners, from those just out of basic training to those with a decade of PC tinkering under their belts. That wide audience is a key to QEMM's best-seller status.

Who Needs This Book?

As with many computer tools, simple installation of QEMM is relatively routine. You can reap some of its benefits without any reading or study. However, to create the best system, to tailor memory to your particular uses, to get the most from QEMM, or simply to make QEMM work when troubles arise, you need some understanding of memory and QEMM. This book explains both.

You can install QEMM in minutes by running the automatic INSTALL program. This will not only copy QEMM to your system but also run a utility called OPTIMIZE to set up the optimum options for your particular PC. The result will be more memory for your programs to use.

However, QEMM offers hundreds of options you can use to go beyond what OPTIMIZE offers. These options fit QEMM's memory management to your individual programs and peripherals. And they're free—all you need to do is learn about QEMM and memory to put them to use. That's what this book is all about. The first few chapters give quick descriptions of QEMM and QRAM installations. The rest of the book goes into detail about squeezing the most from QEMM and your PC. Those without time or desire will think of this as fine-tuning. Those who must understand everything in their computer will consider it primary education. The rest of us will fall in between—satisfied at first with the automatic optimization of QEMM but soon looking to test QEMM's options for improving performance and avoiding memory conflicts.

QEMM can allocate expanded and extended memory to a program as it requests, allocating amounts dynamically without needing any immediate advice from you. But it follows your instructions for precise allocations, offering a wealth of opportunities to those with memory expertise. (Some competing memory managers force you to restart the PC for each allocation change.)

QEMM finds unused memory between 640K and 1024K. (DOS 5 does this too, but not as well.) This area is reserved for operating system software, but large portions of it are often left unused. QEMM can place many of the various pieces of software typically trapped below the 640K line into this unused high memory. These pieces are device drivers, task-switchable utilities, TSRs, network drivers, keyboard drivers, mouse drivers, and disk caches.

QEMM also can free the memory often occupied by system ROMs (Read Only Memory chips), Video ROMs, and other adapter ROMs to use as high RAM (Random Access Memory). All told this can make as much as 256K more RAM that would have been wasted otherwise.

If you want full control of the memory in your PC you need both QEMM (or QRAM) and this book. It will speed any computing you do, and some QEMM fans even think full understanding and customizing is fun.

What Background Do You Need to Read This Book?

You can read this entire book without any PC experience. However, you'll find it an easier go if you have some DOS experience—not a lot, just the knowledge of basic commands for changing directories, viewing batch files, and copying files from one disk to another. You can get this from any DOS book or manual, or from a couple of minutes with a DOS-wise friend.

How This Book is Organized

This book has three sections:

I. Quick: getting started with QEMM and QRAM (Chapters 1 and 2)
II. Complete: thorough explanations of QEMM and QRAM (Chapters 3 through 14)
III. Experience: special fixes and solutions for best QEMM and QRAM use with particular software and hardware (Chapters 15 through 21)

Section I gives you the basics, the minimum you need to know to get QEMM or QRAM running.

- Chapter 1, Instant QEMM, Instant QRAM is a guide to getting QEMM or QRAM on your PC, working, without any extra bother.
- Chapter 2, Quick Fixes is a list of the ten most common questions Quarterdeck tech support receives, and the answers to those questions.

Section II gives you all the thorough descriptions of the QEMM and QRAM utilities and of their options. Along with these it explains memory terms and how you can learn what memory is in your PC.

- Chapter 3, QEMM and QRAM—Inside Summary, briefly tells you what each part of QEMM or QRAM does and how you choose and use them, then directs you to the other chapters of Section II for details.
- Chapter 4, How Memory Works, is a thorough introduction to memory. Before you grasp any of the sophisticated QEMM options you'll need to understand memory.
- Chapter 5, MANIFEST, tells you how to use the MANIFEST program to see what memory is in your PC, and what is in that mem-

ory. You can only use QEMM or QRAM well when you can see what they're doing.

- Chapters 6 through 14 list and explain all the options for QEMM and QRAM utilities: QEMM386.SYS, QEMM.COM, QRAM.SYS, QEXT.SYS, OPTIMIZE, LOADHI, BUFFERS.COM, FILES.COM, FCBS.COM, LASTDRIV.COM, VIDRAM, EMS2EXT.SYS, EMS.SYS, and EMS.COM.

Section III is a collection of tips and traps for using QEMM or QRAM with various other programs and hardware.

- Chapters 15 through 20 cover QEMM and QRAM with DOS, DESQview, Windows, Networks, Applications (such as Lotus 1-2-3 and WordPerfect), and Hardware.
- Chapter 21 tells you how to learn more about QEMM or QRAM, by contacting Quarterdeck or others who use QEMM or QRAM.
- Appendices A and B, QEMM Installation and QRAM Installation, are detailed guides to the choices and options when installing.
- Appendix C, Installation without a hard disk, tells you how to install QEMM or QRAM on a PC on a system that only has a floppy disk drive.
- Appendix D, Troubleshooting, tells you how to approach a problem between QEMM or QRAM and your programs or hardware.
- Appendix E, What to know before contacting Tech Support, is a list of those things you should write down about your PC and your programs to get the fastest and most accurate help from a Quarterdeck tech support expert.
- Appendix F, Hexadecimal Numbers, explains how memory addresses are counted, and how to understand all those Hexadecimal terms in memory maps.
- Appendix G, DPMI Host explains the use of the companion program QDPMI which provides DOS Protected Mode Interface support for QEMM.
- The Glossary defines memory and QEMM terms.

Tips and Traps Icons

Throughout the book you'll find special "tips" and "traps" marked with icons.

Tip icon—This marks a method that can save you more memory or make memory management easier.

Trap icon—This marks a dangerous or troublesome spot where using the wrong option can cause conflicts from slower performance to crashing your computer.

Latest Versions

QEMM, QRAM, and all their utilities have evolved through a number of versions, as do most PC programs. This book focuses on the latest versions but mentions some specific changes and problems with recent previous versions.

The current versions are

QEMM-386 ....version 6.0
QEMM-50/60................version 6.0
QRAM ....version 2.0
Manifest.........................version 1.1
DESQview......................version 2.4

Get the latest version of QEMM or QRAM—that's the best advice you can have.

If you have any QEMM version before 6.0, you could have trouble with some PC's BIOS (the fundamental program on a chip inside the PC) and with the advanced options in some disk cache utilities. Chapters 23 and 24 explain these in more detail.

An upgrade will cost only $20 to $30 and will come with an upgrade booklet. (A new manual costs $20 or $30 more.) QRAM 2.0 and QEMM 6.0 added support for DOS 5, Windows 3, and DR-DOS 6.

SECTION I

Quick: Getting Started
with QEMM and QRAM

Instant QEMM or QRAM

This short guide tells you how to install QEMM or QRAM. For more detailed installation instructions, covering all the installation options, see Appendices A and B.

To installQEMM or QRAM, take these six steps:

1. **Choose QEMM or QRAM.**

   QEMM is for PC-compatible computers (including PS/2s) running the DOS (or compatible) operating system with a 386 or 486 (or compatible) processor. (If you have a PS/2 Model 50 or 60, you should get the special version called QEMM-50/60.) QEMM works best with a hard disk but can run on a floppy-only system (see Appendix C if you only have a floppy).

   QRAM is for PC-compatible computers running the DOS (or compatible) operating system with an 8088, 8086, or 286 (or compatible) processor; that means PC, XT, and AT compatibles. Also, if you have a PS/2 model that's compatible with those, QRAM's for you. It works best with a hard disk but can run on a floppy-only system (see Appendix C).

   Get the latest version of whichever you choose—call Quarterdeck to make sure yours is the latest (310-392-9701 in the US, see Chapter 21 for other locations).

2. **Put as much memory in your PC as possible.**

   If you cannot plug in more, or you don't have time yet, go to step 3. Otherwise add it when you can and then rerun your QEMM or QRAM installation.

   Most 386 or 486 PCs come with at least 1MB of memory. Install more if you can afford it (memory costs about $40 a megabyte): 1MB more for any use, 2MB more if you'll use DESQview, 4MB more if you'll use Windows. For 8088 and 8086 PCs, make sure you have at least 640K of memory, and then add memory with an EMS 4.0 expanded memory board. For 80286 PCs have 640K of memory, and then add an EMS 4.0 expanded memory board if you plan on multitasking (especially with DESQview). Otherwise, add extended memory. Chapters 2 and 3 give you more details on adding memory to PCs.

3. Install QEMM or QRAM (whichever you chose in step 1).

Start your PC. When the DOS prompt (probably C>) appears, put the QEMM or QRAM disk into the floppy drive. Then type

```
a: install
```

and press Enter. (If you're using the B floppy drive, type b:install.) Press Enter each time you're installation program asks a question. This means you accept the default (automatically chosen) decision. The installation program tries to make the best decisions after it studies your particular PC. This program automatically copies QEMM or QRAM to your hard disk, runs the OPTIMIZE utility to see how best to use QEMM or QRAM for your PC's memory, and then puts appropriate QEMM or QRAM instructions into your DOS startup files. It will restart your computer with QEMM or QRAM running.

4. Use your computer.

With QEMM or QRAM installed, just go back to using your other programs. You can ignore QEMM or QRAM—they'll work in the background doing their job. Your programs could run faster. Also, there should be more room for more programs.

Once QEMM or QRAM is installed, you don't need to think about them. Just use your computer as you always have.

5. **Watch for trouble.**

   If your programs show troubles, your computer hangs (freezes and doesn't respond to the keyboard), or otherwise misbehaves, contact Quarterdeck tech support, as explained in Chapter 21.

6. **Learn more.**

   When you have time and interest, work through Chapter 2 (for QEMM) or 3 (for QRAM), Chapters 4 and 5 (to understand memory), and then the rest of this book to find better ways to manage your PC's memory. The QEMM or QRAM automatic installation does a decent job for almost any PC, but an interested human can do a better job in almost any case.

CHAPTER TWO

Quick Fixes: The Top Ten

Quarterdeck's technical support experts field many thousands of calls, letters, and faxes about QEMM and QRAM use. This chapter gives you the ten questions they encounter most often and the answers to those questions. If you're stuck when installing or using QEMM, your best bet is to check here first for a solution. Then look to the rest of this book. Then contact Quarterdeck (see Chapter 21).

Q: *What is QEMM Exception 13, and what does it mean for my life here and now?*

A: Exception 13 is the complaint you're most likely to hear from an 80386 chip when you run QEMM and DESQview. When a program

a. executes a "privileged" instruction or input/output reference and so violates protected mode, or
b. an application program has a bug or is running out of control

the 386 chip reports a "General Protection Fault" error, otherwise known as Exception 13.

What do you do? You can run Change a Program in DESQview and allocate more memory to the application that caused the error. If this does not cure the exception, increase the protection level of that application's window to 3. That won't cure anything, but it could provide you with more descriptive (and so, less annoying) error messages. Then you can figure out just what is going wrong.

Q: *How do I respond to that pesky "Unknown Micro Channel Adapter" message that appears when I start my computer?*

A: Call Quarterdeck. Why? Because QEMM needs to know some special information about any PS/2 or other Micro Channel Adapter hardware. (The Micro Channel Adapter is a sophisticated bus for plugging in additional circuit boards. IBM invented it for the PS/2 line of computers. Cards plugged into the Micro Channel often have their own intelligent on-board adapter hardware to coordinate their work with other Micro Channel cards.) Usually QEMM finds out what it needs to know from the MCA.ADL file, which was copied to your QEMM directory when you first installed QEMM. QEMM checks MCA.ADL when it initializes to learn what memory addresses the cards are using. However, if you have an adapter that's not in MCA.ADL, because the card is new or because Quarterdeck overlooked it, you'll see an error message from QEMM. Quarterdeck technical support personnel probably already know what to tell your QEMM from their experience helping others with this adapter. If not, they can probably figure it out from the adapter's documentation and software disk (which you should keep on hand when you call).

Q: *I ran OPTIMIZE and now I can't get on my network. How do I go on?*

A: You're almost certainly the latest victim of the old LOADHI-network adapter feud. LOADHI is trying to put some bit of software in the same memory that the network needs for its adapter. Removing the RAM parameter from the QEMM386.SYS line in CONFIG.SYS should solve the problem. Voila, back on the net.

Then you can read your network documentation (sorry about this painful advice) to learn the memory address range used by the network. Add the EXCLUDE parameter or the ARAM & AROM parameters (explained in Chapter 6) to the QEMM386.SYS line to tell LOADHI to avoid the network in memory.

If that doesn't work, or if you can't find the memory address in the network documents, try the QEMM analysis procedures mentioned in Chapter 6 to find out where that network is. Then EXCLUDE it.

Q: *Is that nasty rumor true that even with QEMM I can't multitask with DESQview on my 286 machine?*

A: No, put that one to rest. A 386, with extended memory and a memory manager such as QEMM, is great for multitasking, but DESQview can also multitask if you have an EEMS (Enhanced Extended Memory Specification) memory board or an EMS (Extended Memory Specification) 4.0 memory board (meaning one that is both EMS 4.0 hardware and software, not 4.0 software with 3.2 hardware). Naturally you also need to set up DESQview for multitasking and have programs that are comfortable with multitasking. But having the right memory hardware is the foundation.

Q: *What is VCPI, and why should I care?*

A: VCPI is the Virtual Control Program Interface specification, a bunch of rules that programs can follow if they want to cooperate in using the Virtual-86 mode of a 386 or 486 processor. Such cooperation is necessary if you have more than one program that wants to use extended memory without leaving DOS. QEMM-386 runs the processor in Virtual-86 mode, and it follows the VCPI. So QEMM can work along with programs such as Lotus1-2-3 Release 3 and Paradox 386 that use DOS extenders to reach extended memory. When an application with a built-in DOS extender wants extended memory, it looks to the VCPI server inside QEMM. The latest twist is the more advanced DPMI standard. This permits more freedom in using protected-mode programs, and can be had with QEMM when you add the companion program QDPMI, as explained in Appendix G.

Q: *Why am I seeing these "insufficient memory" messages when I try to install QEMM? Would a doctor help?*

A: QEMM accomplishes many tasks with extended memory, converting it into upper memory blocks for stashing drivers, pretending it is expanded memory for programs that want that, providing it to programs that can use extended memory directly (see Chapter 6 for details on these types of memory). If you don't have extended memory, or much extended memory, QEMM quails; it cannot load and tells you so with an error message.

A typical PC today comes with at least 1MB of memory that will normally be configured as 640K of conventional memory and 384K of extended memory. However, some systems have a Shadow RAM feature (see Chapter 4) to make them run faster, a feature that can eat up all that could-have-been-extended memory. Even with more megabytes, your PC may be telling the extra memory to set up as something other than extended memory. If you have this memory trouble, find out how much memory your PC has (watch the initial memory test on screen, ask someone knowledgeable, or use Manifest, as discussed in Chapter 5). Then check your PC's manual to see how it sets up memory, and if there's a setup program you can get into to move some memory to the extended column. While you're at it, think about getting a few megabytes more—they only cost about $40 each—so your PC has at least 2, better 4, best 8MB.

Q: *I made a few trifling, itsy-bitsy changes to my AUTOEXEC.BAT and CONFIG.SYS files. Does that mean I need to do any more QEMMing?*

A: Make a change to AUTOEXEC.BAT or CONFIG.SYS, run OPTIMIZE again: It's not just a good idea, it's the law. (OPTIMIZE will see your changes and try to raise any new bits of program into upper memory to make your system work better, more, dare I say it, "optimally.")

Q: *I'm a QEMM kind of person, but now I'm becoming a Windows worker too. How do I run QEMM and Windows 3.0 in that spiffy Enhanced-386 mode?*

A: Easy. Run the QWINFIX program you'll find in the QEMM directory. This runs automatically when you first install QEMM, but you'll need to run it manually if you put Windows on your PC after installing QEMM. To run it, from the DOS prompt, in that directory, type

```
qwinfix
```

and then press Enter. QWINFIX changes the Windows SYSTEM.INI file to make Enhanced-386 mode work smoothly with QEMM.

Q: *One of my programs is picky, wanting only extended memory. Is this a reasonable request, and how do I cater to it?*

A: Don't do it. That is, don't make any special concessions to this program. In this day and age most DOS programs that need lots of memory use extended memory and follow the XMS specification (see Chapter 4). QEMM automatically deals them extended memory as they ask for it, if it is available. You don't need to set any aside.

Programs that ask for non-XMS extended memory can make a lot of trouble in your PC, conflicting with other programs using extended memory. In most cases you should be able to ask the program's maker for a new version that adheres to XMS; almost everyone does. QEMM can allocate old-fashioned, non-XMS extended memory, but you're asking for exotic trouble when you start dealing with such anachronisms.

Q: *What's the best way to install QEMM to make best use of my memory—my PC's memory that is?*

A: Read this book. No, seriously, the best answer is the one computer experts give most often, "That depends."

Most people will do just fine with the default installation, the setup that OPTIMIZE creates. Your extended and expanded memory will be allocated to programs at their request, and as many of your drivers and utilities will be bumped upstairs to upper memory, freeing conventional memory for your main programs.

However, if you really want to tune and temper your PC, you should learn at least the basic options described in this book. Your brain can still do a better job applying QEMM's powers than OPTIMIZE can ever hope to do.

SECTION II

Complete:
Thorough Explanations of QEMM and QRAM

CHAPTER THREE

QEMM and QRAM
Inside Summary

QEMM and QRAM are actually collections of utilities to manage memory. This chapter tells you

What they're called
What they do
When to use them (their advantages and disadvantages)
How to use them

The rest of this section then delves into the minutiae of each utility and all the parameters you can bring to bear on memory problems.

QEMM includes these utilities:

INSTALL
OPTIMIZE
Manifest
QEMM386.SYS
QEMM.COM
LOADHI
DOS resource utilities (BUFFERS, FILES, FCBS, LASTDRIV)
VIDRAM
EMS2EXT.SYS, EMS.SYS, AND EMS.COM

QRAM includes a similar list of utilities, with a few replacements (and somewhat different responsibilities):

INSTALL
OPTIMIZE
Manifest
QRAM.SYS
QEXT.SYS
LOADHI
DOS resource utilities (BUFFERS, FILES, FCBS, LASTDRIV)
VIDRAM
EMS2EXT.SYS, EMS.SYS, AND EMS.COM

When to Use What

Here are the situations when you would want to use each of the QEMM or QRAM utilities.

INSTALL (QEMM and QRAM)

When you first get QEMM or QRAM

OPTIMIZE (QEMM and QRAM)

When you install QEMM or QRAM
After you add or subtract memory
After you add or subtract programs
After you add or subtract hardware

Manifest (QEMM and QRAM)

When you want to find more usable memory
When you want to fix some memory conflict
When you want to learn about memory

QEMM386.SYS (QEMM only)

When you first get QEMM (it automatically installs)
When you want to change parameters to fix a problem
When you want to fine-tune parameters to use more memory

QEMM.COM (QEMM only)

When you want to turn expanded memory use on or off

When you want to quickly know what is happening in memory (like a quick version of Manifest)

QRAM.SYS (QRAM only)

When you first get QRAM (it automatically installs)

When you want to change parameters to fix a problem

When you want to fine-tune parameters to use more memory

QEXT.SYS (QRAM only)

When you're using QRAM on a 286 PC and want to offer extended memory to XMS-supporting programs

When you're using DESQview on a 286 PC and want to load part of it into the HMA area of extended memory

LOADHI (QEMM and QRAM)

When you want to move TSRs, drivers, and other programs into upper memory (this happens automatically with OPTIMIZE)

When you want to change the OPTIMIZE configuration for loading TSRs, drivers, and other programs into upper memory to fix memory conflicts

When you want to improve the OPTIMIZE configuration for loading TSRs, drivers, and other programs into upper memory to free more conventional memory

When you want to know what drivers, TSRs, and resources have been loaded high

DOS Resource utilities—BUFFERS.COM, FILES.COM, FCBS.COM, LASTDRIV.COM (QEMM and QRAM)

When you want to move DOS resources into upper memory to free more conventional memory

When you change the number of DOS resources you're using

VIDRAM (QEMM and QRAM)

When you're running a program that only uses text mode

EMS2EXT.SYS, EMS.SYS, and EMS.COM (QEMM and QRAM)

When you want to allocate old-fashioned extended memory to a program that doesn't understand the XMS standard (EMS2EXT.SYS)

When you want to fine-tune a few very specific details of expanded memory use (EMS.SYS and EMS.COM)

Stepping Through QEMM

To get the most out of QEMM:

1. **Prepare.**
   Have a 386 or 486 system and at least 384K of extended memory. Also have a hard disk—which is not strictly necessary, but computing without one is impractical. Buy several megabytes more if you can afford them.

2. **Install.**
   Chapter 1 tells how. This will put QEMM386.SYS into your PC. It should also remove redundant memory managers such as HIMEM.SYS and EMM386.SYS from DOS and Windows.

3. **Use.**
   Run your regular programs with QEMM installed (to see if there are any conflicts). Adapt them to the new memory if necessary—such as changing a parameters setting in the program to tell it that expanded or extended memory is now available. If you have time, try as many features as possible. Otherwise just compute as you normally would.

4. **Troubleshoot.**
   If you find any conflicts—from the system crashing to program features not working properly—see Chapter 21.

5. Add.

Find and employ memory-using utilities such as a disk cache that can improve system performance. (Most versions of DOS come with a disk cache, as well as other speed-enhancing utilities such as RAM disks. Read the DOS manual or the documentation for any other utilities you can now run in the freed and managed memory.)

Find and add any peripherals or network connections you previously couldn't fit into memory.

Consider using an environment such as DESQview or Windows. These can take more memory than running DOS programs one at a time but offer smoother switching from one program to another.

6. Optimize.

Run OPTIMIZE after you add any new programs or peripherals. Also run the QWINFIX utility (see Chapter 17) if you install Windows after QEMM.

7. Borrow.

If the program you're running uses only text, not graphics, and you have an EGA or VGA adapter, you could use VIDRAM to borrow up to 96K more conventional memory. This can let more of your text-mode program load so it can run faster, or you can run more TSRs with it. If you use a text-mode program sometimes and graphics mode programs other times, you can create a batch file to automatically use VIDRAM only with the text-mode program.

8. Inspect.

Run QEMM.COM to see if there are unused areas of upper memory that you can use to relocate more TSRs and drivers from conventional memory. If this doesn't give enough detail, run Manifest.

Check in Manifest to see that your ROMs have been copied to RAM so they run fast.

Check in Manifest that your memory has been sorted for speed and used in that order.

9. Load high.

If you found unused areas in upper memory (in step 8), convert your DOS resource statements into QEMM resource commands (with BUFFERS, FILES, FCBS, and LASTDRIV), and then add LOADHI statements to CONFIG.SYS and AUTOEXEC.BAT to load those resources into upper memory.

If you found unused areas in upper memory (in step 8), add LOADHI statements to CONFIG.SYS and AUTOEXEC.BAT to load TSRs and drivers into that memory.

10. Nurse (old programs and new).

If you have old-fashioned programs that can only use pre-XMS extended memory, use EMS2EXT.SYS.

If you are programming or experimenting and want precise control of some expanded memory variables, use EMS.SYS and EMS.COM.

11. Toggle.

If you're not using expanded memory or loading high, use QEMM.COM to turn expanded memory management off or at least to auto.

12. Experiment.

Look through Section III and then through the parameters in each utility chapter for tips and traps relevant to your PC, programs, and peripherals.

Look through Section III and the utility chapters for parameters that you could try.

Back up your CONFIG.SYS and AUTOEXEC.BAT (as explained in the Section III overview), run the Analysis procedure, and try the tips and traps you've found, as well as the various parameters that might help.

13. Confer.

Talk (by phone or online) with other QEMM and QRAM users to share ideas and swap tips and traps. (Chapter 21 tells how to find such people.)

Stepping Through QRAM

1. **Prepare.**

   Use the QTEST program (from bulletin boards, CompuServe, or Quarterdeck) to test your system and to tell you what QRAM can do for you.

   Have an 8088, 8086, or 286 system with 640K of memory and an EMS 4.0 expanded memory board with at least 512K of expanded memory. These aren't truly the minimums, but they are practical minimums. If you can, plug 2MB more of memory chips into the expanded memory board. Also have a hard disk—which is not strictly necessary, but computing without one is impractical.

   If you can afford it, move up to a 386 or 486 system and buy QEMM.

2. **Install.**

   Chapter 1 tells how. This puts QRAM.SYS into your PC.

3. **Use.**

   Run your regular programs with QRAM installed (to see if there are any conflicts). Adapt them to the new memory if necessary—such as changing a parameter setting in the program to tell it that expanded or extended memory (on a 286) is now available. If you have time, try as many features as possible. Otherwise just compute as you normally would.

4. **Troubleshoot.**

   If you find any conflicts—from the system crashing to program features not working properly—go to Chapter 21.

5. **Add.**

   Find and employ memory-using utilities such as a disk cache that can improve system performance. (Most versions of DOS come with a disk cache as well as other speed-enhancing utilities such as RAM disks. Read the DOS manual or the documentation for any other utilities you can now run in the freed and managed memory.)

   Find and add any peripherals or network connections you previously couldn't fit into memory.

On a 286 PC, consider using an environment such as DESQview. This can take more memory than running DOS programs one at a time but offers smoother switching from one program to another. Don't use Windows—it just isn't fast enough without a 386 or 486 processor.

6. Optimize.
Run OPTIMIZE after you add any new programs or peripherals.

7. Borrow.
If the program running uses only text, not graphics, and you have an EGA or VGA adapter, you could use VIDRAM to borrow up to 96K more conventional memory. This can let more of your text-mode program load so it can run faster, or you can run more TSRs with it. If you use a text-mode program sometimes and graphics mode programs other times, you can create a batch file to automatically use VIDRAM only with that text-mode program.

8. Inspect.
Run MANIFEST to see if there are unused areas of upper memory that you can use to relocate more TSRs and drivers from conventional memory.

9. Load high.
If you did find unused areas in upper memory (in step 8), convert your DOS resource statements into QRAM resource commands (with BUFFERS, FILES, FCBS, and LASTDRIV), and then add LOADHI statements to CONFIG.SYS and AUTOEXEC.BAT to load those resources into upper memory.

If you did find unused areas in upper memory (in step 8), add LOADHI statements to CONFIG.SYS and AUTOEXEC.BAT to load TSRs and drivers into that memory.

If you're using DESQview, make sure QEXT.SYS is installed (with a line in CONFIG.SYS) and that DESQview is using 63K of the HMA. (Check in Manifest.)

10. **Nurse (old programs and new).**
   If on a 286 you have old-fashioned programs that can only use pre-XMS extended memory, use EMS2EXT.SYS.
   If you're programming or experimenting and want precise control of some expanded memory variables, use EMS.SYS and EMS.COM.

11. **Experiment.**
   Look through Section III and then through the parameters in each utility chapter for tips and traps relevant to your PC, programs, and peripherals.
   Look through Section III and the utility chapters for parameters that you could try.
   Back up your CONFIG.SYS and AUTOEXEC.BAT (as explained in the Section III overview), run the Analysis procedure, and try the tips and traps you've found, as well as the various parameters that might help.

12. **Confer.**
   Talk (by phone or online) with other QEMM and QRAM users to share ideas and swap tips and traps. (Chapter 21 tells how to find such people.)

INSTALL

INSTALL puts QEMM or QRAM into your PC by automatically creating a subdirectory for QEMM (or QRAM), then copying (and decompressing) the program files from the original QEMM or QRAM disk to your PC's hard disk. Finally, it runs the OPTIMIZE utility which tries to configure QEMM or QRAM in the best way for your particular memory and programs. Appendices A and B have details on the various parameters you can choose when installing.

OPTIMIZE (QEMM and QRAM)

OPTIMIZE looks at how much memory is in your PC, what types of memory it has, and at what TSRs, drivers, and other software your current CONFIG.SYS, AUTOEXEC.BAT, and other linked batch files want to load into memory. Then it experiments and tries to find the most efficient way to load that software into upper memory. When it comes up with the best way it can imagine, it puts the necessary statements to create that way into the CONFIG.SYS and AUTOEXEC.BAT files and then reboots your PC.

OPTIMIZE runs automatically as part of the INSTALL process, described above. You should also run OPTIMIZE every time you change the memory, programs, or hardware in your PC. Run it by typing

```
OPTIMIZE
```

from the DOS prompt (while in the QEMM or QRAM subdirectory). OPTIMIZE runs and asks you questions as it goes. Chapter 14 has details on those parameters and on the parameters you can automatically call for when starting OPTIMIZE.

Manifest (QEMM and QRAM)

Manifest operates completely independently of QEMM and QRAM. It can even be purchased as a separate program. Current versions of QEMM and QRAM come with a free copy of Manifest that installs along with the other utilities.

Manifest is a memory-analysis program. It looks into your PC and reports on how much memory is there, what programs are in that memory, how those programs are using memory, what other uses the memory could have, and so on. If you want to know how fast some area of memory is, whether a ROM is at a particular address in memory, and many other far more technical details, Manifest is the tool.

That means Manifest is vital to fine-tuning QEMM or QRAM. If you're going to find and employ bits of memory that OPTIMIZE didn't find, you'll need Manifest's help every step of the way.

To use Manifest, you get to the QEMM or QRAM subdirectory, then type

```
MFT
```

and press Enter. The Manifest display appears with a menu along the left side and more detailed submenus across the top. Move the highlighting up and down the left-side menu by pressing the UpArrow and DownArrow keys. This selects a category. Then select a topic within the category by moving the highlighting in the top menu: press the LeftArrow and RightArrow keys.

Probably the most popular category in Manifest is the First Meg, which tells you what is happening in that first, most-precious megabyte of your PC's memory, from 0 to 1024K. Chapter 5 has details on all the categories and topics of Manifest.

QEMM386.SYS (QEMM only)

QEMM386.SYS is the main driver, the utility program that manages expanded and extended memory for QEMM. In some ways it is QEMM, though surrounded by other dependent or related utilities. To use XMS extended memory, to use EMS expanded memory, to load high anything into upper memory, you need QEMM386.SYS installed. Older versions (before version 5.1) called this same file QEMM.SYS. The name was changed to avoid confusion with those versions of QEMM that did not support Windows 3.0.

When OPTIMIZE runs it automatically puts a QEMM386.SYS line similar to the following into your CONFIG.SYS file:

```
DEVICE=C:\QEMM\QEMM386.SYS
```

From there it loads into memory. The line can be longer, with several parameters following it. These parameters dictate just how extended and expanded memory will behave, what addresses in upper memory will be used for loading drivers and TSRs high, and so on. QEMM386.SYS has more parameters than any other QEMM utility.

Probably the most common parameter is EXCLUDE. This tells QEMM386.SYS not to map memory into some area of addresses. Typically you use this because those addresses are already in use, perhaps by a network adapter's ROM that OPTIMIZE didn't notice. If after OPTIMIZE installs QEMM386.SYS you have some trouble—from the PC not working to the network connection not operating—you might look to Manifest to see if some memory conflict was the source of that trouble. In Manifest you might see that a ROM was at addresses E000 to E8FF. In some cases Manifest might even miss this fact, and you'd have to turn to the Section III of this book, Quarterdeck's technical support staff, or the manuals for your various hardware add-ons (such as the network adapter) and programs to see what addresses they used. When you deduce that addresses E000 to E8FF should be off limits to QEMM use, you add the EXCLUDE parameter to the QEMM386.SYS line:

```
DEVICE=C:\QEMM\QEMM386.SYS EXCLUDE=E000-E8FF
```

See Chapter 6 for details on QEMM386.SYS parameters. There's a lot to learn there, and a lot to be gained in QEMM subtlety and memory freedom.

QEMM.COM (QEMM only)

QEMM.COM is not just another version of QEMM386.SYS. Instead it is a utility with only two purposes: to give a quick view of memory use and to turn expanded memory management on or off.

If you don't have the time to turn Manifest on, you can see what's in memory by changing to the QEMM subdirectory, typing the command

```
QEMM
```

and then pressing Enter. That gives you the summary of memory use. You can learn about other aspects of memory by typing TYPE, ACCESSED, ANALYSIS, or MEMORY after QEMM . You can use parameters with those various reports, too.

If you want to turn expanded memory support off, even with QEMM386.SYS already installed, just change to that QEMM subdirectory and type

```
QEMM OFF
```

You can then turn expanded memory support back on later by typing either

```
QEMM ON
```
or
```
QEMM AUTO
```

which lets expanded memory support turn on when some program requests expanded memory. (You cannot turn expanded memory management off if a program is using expanded memory or if upper memory is in use for loaded-high programs.)

QEMM.COM has parameters as well.Chapter 7 has details on the parameters for both uses of QEMM.COM.

QRAM.SYS (QRAM only)

QRAM.SYS is the main driver for QRAM, the utility program that manages expanded and extended memory for QRAM. In some ways it is QRAM, though surrounded by other dependent or related utilities. It is the counterpart to QEMM's QEMM386.SYS.

To use XMS extended memory on 286 systems, to use EMS expanded memory, to load high anything into upper memory, you need QRAM.SYS installed.

When OPTIMIZE runs it automatically puts a QRAM.SYS line similar to the following into your CONFIG.SYS file:

```
DEVICE=C:\QRAM\QRAM.SYS
```

From there it loads into memory. The line can be longer with several parameters following it. These parameters dictate just how extended and expanded memory will behave, what addresses in upper memory will be used for loading drivers and TSRs high, and so on. QRAM.SYS has more parameters than any other QRAM utility.

Probably the most common parameter is EXCLUDE. This tells QRAM.SYS not to map memory into some area of addresses. Typically you use this because those addresses are already in use, perhaps by a network adapter's ROM that OPTIMIZE didn't notice. If after OPTIMIZE installs QRAM.SYS you have some trouble—from the PC not working to the network connection not operating—you might look to Manifest to see if some memory conflict was the source of that trouble. In Manifest you might see that a ROM was at addresses E000 to E8FF. In some cases Manifest might even miss this fact, and you'd have to turn to Section III of this book, Quarterdeck's technical support staff, or the manuals for your various hardware add-ons (such as the network adapter) and programs to see what addresses they used. When you deduce that addresses E000 to E8FF should be off limits to QRAM use, you add the EXCLUDE parameter to the QRAM.SYS line, like this

```
DEVICE=C:\QRAM\QRAM.SYS EXCLUDE=E000-E8FF
```

See Chapter 8 for details on QRAM.SYS parameters. There's a lot to learn there, and a lot to be gained in QRAM subtlety and memory freedom. Many of the QRAM.SYS parameters are identical to those of QEMM386.SYS, although QEMM386.SYS has more because of the extra abilities it can bring to 386 and 486 systems.

QEXT.SYS (QRAM only)

QEXT is an extended memory manager for QRAM users. (QEMM is both an extended and an expanded memory manager.) QEXT.SYS can and should replace the DOS 5 or Windows HIMEM.SYS extended memory manager.

You need it only on 286 PCs, and then only when you want to load 63K of DESQview into the HMA area of extended memory or to handle any requests by programs for XMS-style extended memory.

To use QEXT.SYS, put the following line in CONFIG.SYS that loads it:

```
DEVICE=QEXT.SYS
```

Beyond that, there are many parameters that tell QEXT.SYS just how much extended memory to allocate and in what ways. Chapter 12 has details on these parameters.

LOADHI (QEMM and QRAM)

LOADHI is probably the most obvious part of QEMM or QRAM. It doesn't operate all on its own. LOADHI needs to have QEMM386.SYS or QRAM.SYS loaded first and working. LOADHI loads software into upper memory, relocating it from conventional memory. That frees conventional memory for your standard DOS programs.

There are two parts to LOADHI: LOADHI.SYS loads drivers into upper memory, and LOADHI.COM loads TSRs and DOS resources into upper memory. LOADHI.SYS works from a line in CONFIG.SYS, LOADHI.COM from a line in AUTOEXEC.BAT or from the DOS prompt.

To load a driver into upper memory, put a line such as

```
DEVICE=C:\QEMM\LOADHI.SYS C:\DOS\DRIVER.SYS
```

into CONFIG.SYS. (Enter QRAM instead of QEMM if you're using QRAM). The short version of this, without the paths, is just

```
DEVICE=LOADHI.SYS DRIVER.SYS
```

which replaces the standard DOS device loading line of

```
DEVICE=DRIVER.SYS
```

To load a TSR or DOS resource (if you use one of the QEMM or QRAM DOS resource programs such as BUFFERS.COM, FILES.COM, FCBS.COM, or LAST-DRIV.COM) into upper memory, put a line such as

```
C:\QEMM\LOADHI C:\TSR
```

into AUTOEXEC.BAT. (You could also use such a line from the DOS prompt.) The short version would be

```
LOADHI TSR
```

which replaces the standard DOS program for loading a TSR of

```
TSR
```

If you want to see what drivers and TSRs have been loaded into upper memory, just type

```
LOADHI
```

at the DOS prompt.

There are parameters for LOADHI.SYS and LOADHI.COM that let you dictate the loading order for TSRs and drivers, and the size of the areas they'll occupy in upper memory. See Chapter 9 for the details on these parameters.

DOS Resource Utilities—BUFFERS, FILES, FCBS, LASTDRIV (QEMM and QRAM)

DOS has resources—areas of memory it organizes to keep records of such information as where recently opened files are on disk, what is in those files, which disk drive letters are legal, and so on. It has default amounts of memory it sets aside for such resources, and it can set aside more when told to by commands in CONFIG.SYS, AUTOEXEC.BAT, or from the DOS prompt.

These resources use up conventional memory. QEMM and QRAM come with utility programs that can replace these resources. BUFFERS.COM replaces BUFFERS, FILES.COM replaces FILES, FCBS.COM replaces FCBS, and LASTDRIV.COM replaces LASTDRIVE. In each case the QEMM or QRAM replacement can be loaded into upper memory, thus saving conventional memory that would otherwise have the original DOS resources in it.

To use these QEMM or QRAM resource programs, you must take three steps:

1. Cut the DOS resources configuration back to the minimum (don't just leave the DOS command out altogether or you'll end up with the default level, which may be more than the minimum).

2. Put the QEMM or QRAM resources command into AUTOEXEC.BAT

3. Put a LOADHI statement in front of each QEMM or QRAM resource line in AUTOEXEC.BAT.

For example, you might make change the CONFIG.SYS DOS statements from

```
BUFFERS=20
FILES=30
LASTDRIVE=M
```

to

```
BUFFERS=1
FILES=1
LASTDRIVE=D
```

and then put into AUTOEXEC.BAT

```
LOADHI BUFFERS=20
LOADHI FILES=30
LOADHI LASTDRIV M
```

Chapter 10 has details on parameters for these resources.

VIDRAM (QEMM and QRAM)

PC displays have text modes and graphics modes. In text modes they only put characters on the screen, typically in boxes organized as grids of 80 columns and 25 lines. In graphics modes they build images and text out of dots, without organizing those dots into strict boxcs into grids. Text mode uses far less video memory because it doesn't have to remember what is at every dot on the screen (which could be hundreds of thousands of dots) but just which character or numeral is at each grid box (which would be only 2000 boxes).

If you have an EGA or VGA graphics adapter, there is memory on the adapter for graphics modes. This can be as much as 512K of RAM. If you run those adapters in a text mode, however, most of that memory lies unused.

VIDRAM can grab that memory. Because the memory is at addresses just above 640K, it can actually be added to conventional memory, making as much as 736K of conventional memory. That's wonderful for programs that run only in text mode and that need as much conventional memory as possible. You can use this alongside other QEMM or QRAM programs, such as LOADHI.

So if you have a program that runs only in text mode—such as traditional DOS databases and accounting programs—you may be a candidate for VIDRAM. Check your program's documentation to see if it runs in text mode. If it does, then either type this line at the DOS prompt, before you run your program, or put it in the AUTOEXEC.BAT file:

```
VIDRAM ON
```

You should now have more conventional memory, which you can check with Manifest or, when using QEMM on a 386 or 486, with QEMM.COM.

Chapter 11 has details on parameters for VIDRAM.

EMS2EXT.SYS, EMS.SYS, and EMS.COM (QEMM and QRAM)

EMS2EXT.SYS and the EMS.SYS and EMS.COM programs are often lumped together. In fact, even here they're sort of lumped together. That can be misleading because they do quite different work. However, they do involve expanded memory, and they do have some interaction. They are rarely used except by experienced and knowledgeable programmers or system experts.

EMS2EXT.SYS

EMS2EXT.SYS is for older programs that need an old form of extended memory. XMS is today's specification for extended memory use. Drivers adhere to it, boards work with it, programs depend on it. QEMM supports XMS. But older programs created before XMS became the standard want extended memory. Some use extended memory because it's faster than extended. They don't know XMS. Instead they work with the DOS INT 15 interface. For these program, such as VDISK, you can use EMS2EXT to convert expanded memory into extended memory that behaves the old-fashioned way. Just put a line like this

```
DEVICE=C:\QEMM\EMS2EXT.SYS MEMORY=nnn
```

in CONFIG.SYS. You put some number of K of memory you want to convert to Extended memory, such as 128 or 512, in place of the "nnn". Chapter 13 has details on parameters.

EMS.SYS and EMS.COM

EMS.SYS and EMS.COM control expanded memory handles—the names programs and the expanded memory manager (QEMM or QRAM) use to refer to specific pieces of expanded memory.

Type

```
EMS
```

while at the DOS prompt in the QEMM or QRAM directory to see a report on the amount of expanded memory in your PC. Other commands such as

```
EMS CREATE
```

create, rename, and otherwise manipulate handles. If you want to perform such actions from CONFIG.SYS instead of as a command in AUTOEXEC.BAT or from the DOS prompt, just enter a line such as the following in CONFIG.SYS:

```
DEVICE=EMS.SYS
```

Chapter 13 has details on parameters.

CHAPTER FOUR

How Memory Works

This chapter explains how memory works, defining lots of terms along the way. To master QEMM's powers you need to understand these ideas and terms.

Why Computers Have Memory

Memory is absolutely vital to computing. After all, computers manipulate information. To do this a computer must have something that manipulates—called a processor—and something to manipulate—called data.

The processor must know how to add, subtract, move, compare, and otherwise handle data. Today's typical processor is a microprocessor chip—circuits on a single fingernail-sized slip of silicon crystal. These microprocessors, sometimes known as CPUs (central processing units), can perform millions of additions or comparisons every second.

Where does the computer keep data before, during, and after manipulation? In memory. How do we make memory? By creating a device that can store information, send information to the processor, and receive information from the processor. When the processor gets information from memory we call it reading from memory. When the processor sends information to memory we call it writing to memory.

Disks and Chips—Cost, Capacity, Speed, and Volatility

Real memory devices differ in cost, capacity, performance, and permanence. Some store a lot of information at a low cost; some store less information at a higher cost. The faster the memory—at giving data to and receiving data from the processor—the more it costs. Also, some memory loses its data as soon as you turn off the power; other memory holds on to data for years, even without a power supply. So engineers building computers typically include several kinds of memory to balance cost, capacity, performance, and permanence.

Slow, inexpensive memory is called mass storage. A typical mass storage device is the disk drive. This holds data as magnetic or optical blips on a flat, rotating surface. Disk drives read and write information from that rotating surface the way audio LPs or compact disks do. Tape drives are another mass storage device. They read and write information from a long, wound-up tape, the way audio cassette tapes do. Because a piece of information exposed on the surface of a disk can be found faster than a piece of information buried inside a wound-up tape, disk drives are faster than tape drives. They are also more expensive per stored megabyte. Their ability to quickly locate a piece of information from anywhere on the disk is generally called random access.

Disk drives can be either hard disk drives or floppy disk drives. Because hard disks are sealed into protective boxes and rotate faster than floppy disks, they can hold many times more information. A hard drive can also read and write that information much faster than a floppy drive. However, a hard disk drive typically works only with the disks initially implanted in it. A floppy disk drive can read and write on any number of floppies that you plug in and then remove from the drive. That makes floppies superior for transferring information.

Fast, expensive memory in a computer is often just called memory. (Remember that computers also need the slower, less expensive memory called mass storage, such as disk drives.) The typical example is a memory chip, a tiny electronic circuit on a fingernail-sized piece of silicon crystal. These are made with the same technology as the microprocessors mentioned earlier in this chapter. Such a memory chip reads and writes information as tiny, stored electrical charges. Like a disk drive it offers random access. A big difference is that chips are thousands of times faster than disk drives. They're also much more expensive per stored megabyte. Memory chips, however, are the only form of memory that can keep up with the speed of today's processors.

The typical memory chip is volatile; that is, it loses its information as soon as it loses its supply of power. Disk drives and tape drives, in contrast, hold on to their information for years.

Most computer designers, therefore, include in their computers

hard disk mass storage—for vast, fast, non-volatile memory
floppy disk mass storage—for data transfer and archiving
chip memory—for immediate reading and writing by the microprocessor

The three memory devices work in concert.

RAMs and ROMs

The memory chips described above are called RAM (random access memory) chips. That name isn't really appropriate. It's true, the chips do allow random access to their data. But then so do the other kind of memory chips: ROMs (read only memory). The difference really comes in reading and writing, as the ROM name indicates. A processor can read information from a RAM chip, or write new information to it. When a processor writes to a RAM, the information it sends replaces some information that's already in the RAM. Because microprocessors can read data from and write it to RAM chips, they use RAM as a sort of scratch pad for data manipulation.

But RAM is volatile; that is, RAM chips lose their data as soon as they lose their power supply. The ROM memory chip is not volatile. Instead of depending on electrical charges that stay only while power is applied, ROM chips hold on to their data forever. The data is implanted at the chip factory. However, as the name says, microprocessors can only read information from these chips. Because ROM memory is permanent, microprocessors can't write new data to the ROMs. Therefore, ROMs are good only for information that stays the same. Data to manipulate doesn't qualify; it changes as the microprocessor adds and compares things.

ROMs, BIOS, and Adapters

What does fit well in ROMs is program information, especially program information that the computer always needs. Programs such as word processors and spreadsheets are sequences of instructions to the microprocessor. These typically are held on disk, then loaded into memory where the microprocessor can quickly refer to them. But such programs come and go; each computer owner may use a different word processor or spreadsheet.

Some programs are used by every computer owner, however. These are operating system programs, the basic software that animates the computer. When you first turn on the computer, for example, the microprocessor gets power and immediately asks "What do I do?" It is designed to look to a certain place in memory for the answer. Most computers put a ROM memory chip at that place in memory with Power On Self Test (POST) operating system instructions to test the chips, the screen, and the disk drives, and then read more operating system instructions from the disk. Computers also use ROMs for fundamental instructions that get used again and again, such as "read data from the disk drive," "send this image to the screen," "check to see if a key has been pressed on the keyboard," and so on. By permanently storing these BIOS (basic input/output system) instructions in a ROM, the computer relieves the individual programs. They can call on the BIOS to handle such chores instead of including all the instructions themselves (which would be redundant and awkward).

Some erasable ROM chips are called EPROMS. They can be cleared by intense ultraviolet light. Another type, the EAROM or Electrically Alterable ROM, can be erased and then rewritten by a special power circuit. This "Flash" memory is becoming a popular form of ROM because you can update your system's "Firmware" (software on chips) without taking your machine in for a service call.

A special kind of RAM called a CMOS (complementary metal-oxide semiconductor) RAM eats up little power and so can easily keep its information permanently, or at least for years, if backed up by a tiny battery. A little CMOS RAM is put into most PCs to hold information that remains fairly constant—such as the setup configuration—but that can change occasionally. The Manifest program described in Chapter 5 can tell you if your PC has CMOS RAM and what the information is within it. It's a good idea to copy the information down somewhere in case you need to feed it back in when the battery dies.

People are always adding peripherals to their computers. New disk drives, optical scanners, new displays, and so on feed peoples' needs for improved computing. Most new devices need to add their own fundamental program instructions, as mentioned above, to the computer's operating system software. Most do this in two parts: a ROM full of instructions on an adapter board that plugs into the PC and a driver program that loads into the PC's RAM memory chips during operation. Those two parts crop up again and again when using QEMM, as you'll see throughout this book.

Chip Speed—DRAMs and SRAMs

RAM chips come in two main types: SRAMs (static RAMs) and DRAMs (dynamic RAMs). Most, perhaps all, of the memory in your computer is DRAMs. DRAMs are less expensive and hold four times as much data. When you're computing you won't notice any difference between the two. Your programs will never know which is in your computer, except perhaps for a speed difference, as explained below.

DRAMs have some disadvantages. The first is their speed. Memory chips need a certain amount of time to accept new information that is written to them or to divulge information that is to be read from them. This speed is called the access time. Typically it is measured in nanoseconds (ns), billionths of a second. DRAMs range from access times of 200 ns down to about 70 ns.

The faster the chip, the faster your computer can process information. But the faster chips also cost more.

Speed has become more important as microprocessors have become faster. Once most computer designs didn't worry too much about memory speed because the memory was always faster than the microprocessor. But as microprocessor clocks (the main pulse that drives their operation) leapt from 1 MHz (megahertz, or a million beats a second) to 2, 8, and then 16 MHz, they came up beside and then passed by memory speed. A 386 or 486 chip running at 25, 33, or even 50 MHz would ideally work with memory chips that had access times of as little as 20 ns. DRAMs that fast are not to be found.

If you're so inclined, you can figure what memory speed a processor needs with this equation

```
chip speed (in nanoseconds) = 1000 / clock speed (in MHz)
```

As a classic example, an 8-MHz AT would need chips with 125-ns access times.

This equation shows how the advent of the faster 386 chips created a need for new memory designs. Even a relatively slow 386 runs at 16 MHz. This requires 62.5-ns chips. The 125-ns and 100-ns chips are relatively cheap. Even 80-ns chips can be had, but 60-ns chips can be far more expensive. Unless the systems were built with more expensive memory chips, they would slow down waiting for memory. Faster chips also eat up more power, which makes a system run hotter. That means yet more expense to keep the system cool.

Using faster chips than necessary doesn't hurt the system but does increase its costs for no performance reason. The system can run only as fast as the slowest component—processor or memory.

If a fast microprocessor is hobbled by slow memory chips, it must add wait states when it wants to read or write information. Hardware can be put into the system to force wait states, so the processor treads water waiting for memory. That's like telling a very fast thinker to take a mandatory half-hour break every hour; it slows everything down. You'll see some computer ads mention zero wait state operation, which means either they've used memory fast enough to keep up with the microprocessor, or they've used some other clever design techniques to accommodate memory and processor speeds.

DRAMs pack so much memory into a small space by using a minimum number of tiny capacitors, batteries really, that hold an electrical charge. A charge at a particular spot places a 1 there, no charge places a 0, and all information is built from the pattern of those basic binary bits of information. Because the charges are so small, they tend to fade away. DRAMs need to be "refreshed" every few milliseconds. The computer checks its own memory and pumps back up each 1 before it dissipates. While this refresh operation is running, the memory isn't available to be read from or written to. The result: a longer access time.

Special kinds of DRAM chips, called such things as paged-mode access chips, avoid some of the refresh delay. They perform tricks such as refreshing part of the chip while leaving the rest open to reading and writing. This cuts down on the number of wait times but still leaves some. Another such scheme is interleaved RAM, in which successive requests for memory access go to different memory chips instead of to different parts of the same chip. A two-way or four-way interleave can also cut wait states.

Another special DRAM is used for video display work. PCs often store the information that's going to the video screen in a section of memory, called a buffer. Unfortunately, video moves very fast, so information must be read at a very high speed to send it on time to the screen. The microprocessor can't be writing new information to that video buffer at the same time the video display is reading it. That means there's little time for the microprocessor to change it. However, a more expensive kind of DRAM, called VRAM, helps. VRAM is dual-ported, with separate doors for reading and writing. It can accept new information from the microprocessor at the same time that it sends information to the video display.

SRAMs don't need a refresh cycle. They are only one-fourth as dense with data as DRAMs because they use a more stable circuit that doesn't lose its charge. So SRAMs, while more expensive than DRAMs, can be found with access times of 60, 40, and even 20 ns. However, because they're so much more expensive, few PCs are designed with SRAMs for their memory. Instead, they are designed with SRAM in caches.

But before we get into that, we need to step aside briefly to consider capacity and packaging of chips. (This stuff is all interrelated, and there's no perfect, linear way to walk through it).

Capacity—Bits, Bytes, K, and MB

Remember that memory holds both programs (the instructions telling what to do) and data (the stuff programs work on).

Memory is measured in kilobytes (K), megabytes (MB), and bytes.

1MB = 1024K, or approximately 1 million bytes
(1,048,576 bytes to be precise)
1K = 1024 bytes
1 byte = 8 bits

One bit (Binary digIT) is a single 1 or 0 of information. That's the binary way: building single bits of information into programs, documents, images, and any other sort of information.

The 8-bit byte came about because 8 bits in a row offer 256 different possible patterns, from 00000000 through 01010101 to 11111111. And that's just the minimum number of patterns necessary to represent all the basic letters (uppercase and lowercase), numerals, punctuation marks, and foreign characters. So a computer working with 8 bits of information as its smallest unit can handle text and number information. A byte equals a character (or number or whatever). The byte's pattern is translated into that character by the ASCII (American Standard Code for Information Interchange) code.

More complex information, such as graphics or programs, follows other codes for translation from byte patterns to final information.

A program, for example, is built of instruction codes that tell the microprocessor what to do. A code might take up a single byte, or it might occupy successive bytes. What it means depends on the computer language and the microprocessor chosen.

A byte isn't enough to do much, then. It could hold a single character or possibly a single instruction. Better have more to get any real computing done.

How about 1000 bytes? That's a better number, though still relatively small. It might hold only 1000 characters, or half a page of text. And 1000 instructions would mean a pretty small program, not able to do much. If program and data were sharing that 1000 bytes, each would be even smaller.

Besides, 1000 may be a nice even number to you and me, but it isn't to the computer. Computer designers think in binary, base-2, terms and are more comfortable with multiples of 2 than multiples of 10, at least for counting memory. That's the natural way to design the hardware circuits. So instead of dealing with 1000 bytes, you'll almost always deal with 1024 bytes (2 times 2 ten times). That's called a kilobyte for short, sort of following the metric practice.

If a kilobyte isn't enough to do serious work, how about 16, 32, or 64K? (Notice again the multiples of 2.) In fact, the first IBM PC was equipped with 16K. It's enough to do some things, but computers are expected to do much more now. Programs are larger, data is more encompassing and more complicated. For example, to work on a 100-page report you need at least 256K just to hold the report. A single graphic image added to that report could boost memory needs to 512K. And if your word processing program were up to today's standards of sophistication, it might ask for 640K for itself, or even 1024K, a full 1MB. Want to run more than one program at a time, and have the data in memory too? You're talking more memory. That's why today's PCs are often equipped with 2, 4, or even 8MB of memory.

Chip Packages—DIPS and SIMMs

As long as we're into memory chips and their capacities, you might also like to know about their physical appearance: the packages they're put in.

The memory chip itself is about as thin as a fingernail and covers about as much area as an aspirin. To make it useful, to give it wires that can connect to other circuits, it is put inside a package.

The typical package is the DIP, dual in-line package. This is a small plastic or ceramic rectangle, about an inch long and a half-inch wide. Protruding from each long side of this rectangle are legs that plug into sockets on a circuit board. A typical DIP holds 256 kilobits (Kbits) or 1 megabit (Mbit) of memory—not bytes but bits. That means it takes eight of each (or nine when one more is added for parity, as explained below) to make up 256K or 1MB. (Remember there are eight bits to the byte.)

Parity tracks whether there are an even number or odd number of 1-bits in each byte. A ninth bit can be used for each byte, with that ninth bit holding a 1 if there are an odd number of 1-bits in the other eight. The computer can then monitor the parity bits and the oddness or evenness of the stored information. If there is ever a discrepancy—the parity bit saying one thing and the other eight bits another—the computer knows that some part of that memory byte has failed. Memory hardware isn't perfect, after all. It can lose some of the electrical charge that represents information. When there is such a parity error, the computer can try to repair it by copying information again from disk, or it can simply tell you there has been an error so you'll know your program may not work or may not produce correct results. PCs test their memory when you first turn the power on, and report any such parity errors.

A more recent package design is the SIMM (single in-line memory module). This harnesses eight or nine memory chips into a single set on a tiny circuit board. This board snaps into a SIMM holder on a circuit board.

PCs typically start with a bank, or set, of memory chips on their main circuit board, the motherboard. To add memory you can often plug more DIPS, or snap more SIMMs, into sockets or holders on the board. If there aren't any more openings, you can plug a memory board into one of the PC's slots (special holders for additional circuit boards) and then plug or snap memory DIPS and SIMMs into that.

Caches—Making Slower Memory Act Faster

Computer designers try to maximize performance and minimize cost. They're always looking for ways to use the slower, less expensive forms of memory and still have a PC that's as fast as possible. The cache is the key to this. It is used in many ways in PCs and often several kinds of caches are packed into a single PC.

The cache is based on two facts. First, the typical PC programs request the same memory information over and over, before turning to other memory information. Second, the typical PC program needs information in sequence, looking for data 1, then data 2, then data 3, and so on. That's much more common than looking for data 1, data 23, data 4, data 16, and so on. (This is true partly because microprocessors spend three-fourths of their time getting their instructions from memory, and instructions are sequential.)

So the designers built the main memory into the system and then added a smaller area of much faster memory. This small area, or cache, automatically gets a copy of the most frequently requested information from the main memory. Then the microprocessor is told to look first in the cache when it wants something from memory. For typical programs, and if the cache has a good algorithm, or recipe, for knowing what information is most frequently requested, the microprocessor finds the information in the cache—it will have a hit. If that hit rate is 90 to 95% or more, then the computer is almost running as if all of its memory were the fast cached sort instead of the slower main memory sort. Yet the designers didn't have to pay the price that making all memory fast would cost.

In RAM this is done by adding a small piece of SRAM to a main memory of DRAM. For example, 2MB of DRAM could be sped up dramatically by a 32K SRAM cache. Some systems let you add more SRAM to make a cache as large as 256K. The 486 processor has 8K of cache right on the chip. How much cache you need depends on your PC.

Caches can also be used to speed up disk performance. Again, a small amount of the faster memory speeds a larger amount of the slower memory. The most frequently used information from disk is copied to a small area of RAM. (Often this is just DRAM. SRAM isn't necessary. DRAM is already thousands of times faster than disk, so the additional improvement of working with SRAM isn't worth the expense.) Then when a program wants information from disk, it first turns to the cache. If the information is in the cache, if a hit happens often enough, the disk appears to be many times faster than it was previously.

Addresses—Memory Locations

Memory is organized. Each byte in memory has an address so the microprocessor can know where it is putting information and where to find information.

The addresses are binary values, naturally, because the computer operates on the binary system. That is, they are patterns such as 10000000 or 01100110. But because these are hard to read when they reach 8 or 16 bits at a time, they are often rendered as hexadecimal numbers instead. As explained in Appendix F, hexadecimal, or base 16, uses the numerals from 0 to 9, and then the letters from A through F. These represent the decimal values 0 through 15, and similar binary values, as shown below:

Hexadecimal	Binary	Decimal
0	0000	0
1	0001	1
2	0010	2
3	0011	3
4	0100	4
5	0101	5
6	0110	6
7	0111	7
8	1000	8
9	1001	9
A	1010	10
B	1011	11
C	1100	12
D	1101	13
E	1110	14
F	1111	15

As you can see, each set of four binary values can be replaced by a single hexadecimal value. That's easier to remember and read, so memory addresses are nearly always given in hex values. Sometimes they are followed by a small "h" to indicate hexadecimal, as in

```
0000h
A000h
CFFFh
```

and so on. For more on hex, see Appendix F.

Address Lines and Address Space

A microprocessor signals what memory address it wants to send information to or read information from with its address line. It takes one line to signal either of two addresses, two lines can signal any of four addresses, three lines any of eight addresses, and so on. So a processor with 16 lines can signal any of 64K of addresses. That's called a 16-bit address—able to reach 64K of address space.

Before the IBM PC, 64K is just what personal computers were limited to: a maximum address space of 64K. That's all they could signal so that's all the memory they could use. It wouldn't have mattered if you had plugged a gazillion megabytes of memory into one of those systems—it would have only used the first 64K because that's all it could address.

The IBM PC's microprocessor, the 8088 chip from Intel, had 20 address lines, so it could signal 1024K, a full megabyte of memory. But to keep some compatibility with previous chips, it did this by adding a 16-bit address to a four-bit segment address, making the total of 20. Most PC programs worked within 64K of memory but could venture outside that to anywhere in the 1024K. The PC saw the 1024K as made up of 16 segments of 64K each. PC programs still show signs of that early orientation.

The IBM AT used the 80286 processor chip, often just called the 286. This had 24 address lines and so could reach 16MB of memory. The more recent 386 and 486 chips have 32 address lines, and so could reach as much as 4GB (gigabytes, or a thousand megabytes) of memory, as shown in the following table:

Processor	Address lines	Address space
8088	20	1MB
80286	24	16MB
80386	32	4096MB (4GB)
i486	32	4096MB (4GB)

(The 386SX and 486SX are less expensive versions of the 386 and 486 chips. They stick to the pattern above but run a little slower because they must reuse some of the address lines.)

Address Space and Processor Modes—Real, Protected, and Virtual-86

To keep compatibility in the Intel line of microprocessors (and all the competing microprocessors that try to be compatible with Intel's), processor modes appeared. These are mindsets for the processor chips. The 8088/8086 runs in real mode, which can address 1024K, or 1MB, of memory. The 80286 offers real mode too, in which it can reach only 1MB of memory. That way it can run all those 8088/8086programs without any trouble. Because the 80286 runs faster than the 8088/8086, people bought 80286 computers to replace their 8088/8086s.

But the 80286 also offers protected mode operation. There it can reach 16MB of memory, as well as run some more sophisticated instructions. The 80286 can switch easily from running in real mode to running in protected mode, although it doesn't switch back too easily.

The 386 can run in real mode, reaching 1MB of memory and handling 8088/8086 programs. The 386 can also run in protected mode, acting like the 286. But in protected mode the 386 can reach 4096MB. It is faster than the 8088/8086 or 286, and so can run real mode and protected mode programs faster than either. Again, people bought 386 PCs to replace 8088 and 286 PCs.

But the 386 has yet another mode: virtual-86 (V-86) mode. In this mode it can set up any number of real modes within all of its memory. Each operates like an 8088/8086 system in real mode, though much faster. This lets a 386 PC multitask 8088/8086 programs, running more than one at a time. Each can use 1MB of memory. The 386 can switch from real to protected to V-86 mode and back much more smoothly than the 80286 can.

Chips Aren't Addresses, Addresses Aren't Chips

After the discussions above of chips and addresses, you may have realized something: For a computer to use an area of memory, it must have both chips and addresses for that area. Just one or the other isn't enough. Plug in all the chips you like, and without address lines to reach them the microprocessor won't even know they exist. Have a 486 processor that can reach gigabytes of memory addresses but supply it with only a few memory chips, and it will have only a few usable memory locations.

Memory Maps

Memory addresses naturally lead to memory maps—diagrams that show what memory a PC has and how it is used. Figure 4-1 is a typical example.

Memory maps show the lowest addresses at the bottom, the highest at the top. They are often labeled with hexadecimal addresses, for tradition's sake and because that's the simplest way to break up the base 2 addressing. Along the sides of the map are the addresses, and within the map are labels for the programs and data contained in that memory.

Manifest, the analysis utility with QEMM, builds memory maps of its own to show you what's in memory. These are often more detailed than the overall map in Figure 4-1. Figure 4-2 shows a Manifest map, with the details of the actual information found within a small section of memory.

Most computers have a system ROM that uses the addresses from F000 to FFFF and a video ROM at C000. IBM PS/2s can have as much as 128K of system ROM, and so often use addresses E000 to FFFF.

Figure 4-1.
A typical map of PC memory

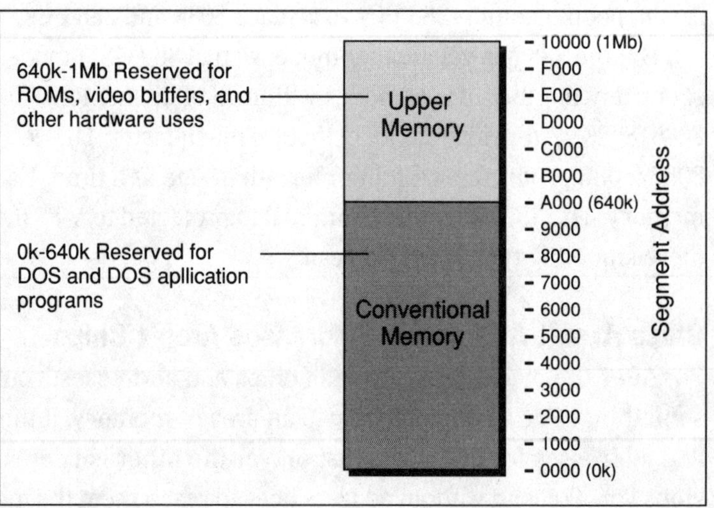

Figure 4-2.
An example of a MANIFEST map of memory

Memory Remapping

The 386 processor has special circuits for converting logical addresses into physical addresses; That is, it can take the address that some program wants to write to or read from, look it up in a table, and then reroute the request to some other address. The program thinks in logical addresses, and the 386 changes those to the current physical addresses on the memory chips. The result is something like automatically forwarded mail or phone calls. The program makes a call, and the central system knows where to actually route the message.

This means the 386 doesn't have to stick to a single address permanently. Using the right software it can reroute, or remap, addresses from one place to another. That makes it very flexible for running programs or holding data. An 8088/8086 that has a ROM at a certain address, for instance, always has the ROM at that address. A 386 doesn't have to. If you want to use that address for some other kind of memory, such as RAM, you can adjust the remapping table so that the ROM appears to be somewhere else. This is vital to QEMM's ability to move programs about in memory.

Definition of DOS

DOS, short for disk operating system, is the fundamental software that runs on nearly all PCs. It is sometimes given a variety of names: MS-DOS (for Microsoft DOS), PC-DOS (IBM's name for it), and other similar monikers.

DOS consists of a kernel, made up of several basic central programs, and scores of related but independent utility programs. The kernel remains nearly identical from one computer to another. The utilities change a bit more, but not much.

Programs that run on the PC actually pay more attention to DOS than to the PC's hardware. DOS is the layer between them and the hardware. Programs send DOS requests, it passes those requests on to the hardware, the hardware responds to DOS, and DOS passes the responses to the programs.

This middle-man use of DOS makes programming easier. Each person developing a word processor, spreadsheet, or other program, needs to learn only how to work with DOS and its request structure. That person doesn't have to learn each different PC's hardware and write a different version of the program for each type of PC. Standardizing on DOS, and making it compatible from one PC to another, allowed for a standard software market. That was the foundation necessary for the tens of thousands of programs now available for PCs.

DOS—Real Mode Means 1MB

DOS runs in an 8088, 8086, 286, 386, or 486 processor's real mode. It does not run in protected mode. That means it is limited to the 1MB of memory that real mode can address. (The newer OS/2 operating system can run in protected mode, and so can directly reach 16MB of memory.)

That 1MB seemed like a lot to the original PC designers. They were used to personal computers that had only 64K of memory; 1MB is 16 times as much.

DOS—384K of Upper Memory Reserved for System

Within that 1MB that real mode permits, the designers knew there would need to be room for programs, data, and the ROMs with basic instructions for devices. They decided to give 384K to the ROMs and to related system work, such as the video buffer memory. The video buffer holds the image that appears on the computer screen. The microprocessor puts bits in the right positions in the buffer memory, and then the video controller puts it out on the screen. The video buffer memory chips are typically on a video adapter board plugged into a slot, but their addresses are within the 384K of memory.

It seemed reasonable to reserve 384K of that for adapter ROMs and video buffers. Would a 756K or even a 1MB barrier have been more comfortable? Not much and not for long. More software to run and larger programs have been the rule since the beginning of computing. And certainly there needed to be some room for ROMs and adapters.

This 384K is at the top of the 1MB, as shown in Figure 4-3. It is the addresses A000H to FFFFH. It is called many names, including reserved memory (reserved for ROMs and such), upper memory, and high memory. That last is sometimes confusing because there is a high memory area just above the 1MB mark, as explained later in this chapter. So if you want to use high, call it high-DOS memory to avoid confusion.

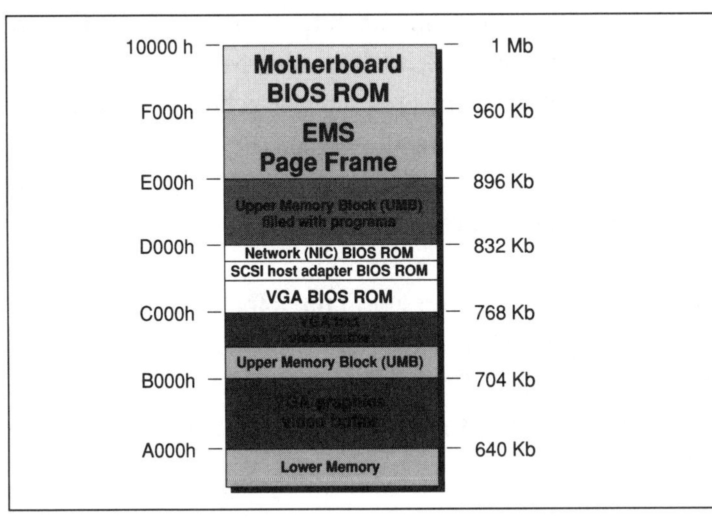

Figure 4-3. Example map of Reserved, High, or Upper memory

PCs sometimes don't have any RAM chips for the upper memory addresses. Sometimes all they have is some ROMs using some of those addresses and the video buffer RAM on the video adapter board.

The basic ROMs, the ones that hold the BIOS as explained earlier, are pretty standard from PC to PC, although there are some variations. There are also a variety of video buffer sizes and a wide range of ROMs and RAM to be found on other plug-in boards such as network interface cards and disk controllers.

The result is that while there are some basics in most PCs, there is also variety in what addresses of upper memory will be used. QEMM and its OPTIMIZE utility work with these variations, as you'll see.

DOS—640K of Conventional Memory for Programs

The top 384K of the 1MB that DOS can reach is called upper memory, or reserved memory. The rest, the lower 640K, is called conventional memory. (Some refer to the entire 1MB as conventional memory and consider reserved memory as a different part within conventional memory.)

Conventional memory is the main site for programs and data. Programs load from disk into conventional memory and then operate from there. Data loads into conventional memory and then is operated on there.

When the PC was young, 640K was a big ranch for those programs to ride on. Later, as programs grew more powerful, it felt smaller. Now there are many programs that have a hard time fitting all the program instructions they want into just 640K of memory, not to mention fitting all the data they need into such a space. But DOS is strict. It only allows 640K of conventional memory; that is, unless you bend some rules (that's a foreshadowing of what QEMM does, as explained later in this chapter).

In fact, before programs and data even get to dip a toe into conventional memory, some of that memory is spirited away and locked up. It is occupied by DOS itself, by memory-resident TSR programs, by device drivers, and by network programs. This is sometimes referred to as RAM-cram or "running into the 640K barrier."

DOS Kernel Takes From the 640K

As if 640K weren't limit enough, you don't even get all that for your programs and their data. DOS takes up part of conventional memory: from 18 to 90K, depending on the version of DOS you use. From DOS 1 to DOS 4 more and more was eaten up by the basic DOS demands, the central part of DOS called the kernel. Even more could disappear if you were wanton with DOS configuration, offering it lots of memory for its resources (explained later).

DOS 5 cut back on memory consumption. It has a smaller kernel and some memory management utilities. These utilities don't measure up to QEMM's or QRAM's, but sometimes they can work with QEMM or QRAM (see Chapter 15). Also, DOS 5 is generally faster, smoother, and equipped with other utilities that users of any other DOS versions should move up to. (Get my drift? Everyone should move to DOS 5, unless they're adventurous to try one of the DOS competitors, such as DR-DOS 6, that possibly offer more features.)

Get DOS 5 and use it with QEMM or QRAM.

DOS Resources Take From the 640K

DOS uses memory to store information it needs as it works. For example, when a program asks for information from disk, DOS pulls that information in one sector at a time. (Sectors are the basic unit of information on disk.) But if the program doesn't need all of the sector; DOS stores the excess in a buffer, a small area of memory. It keeps one buffer in its kernel, so it always has at least one. That's all any program truly needs. Then it loads more buffers, if told to, to store more requested data. Keeping data in buffers is like a simple form of disk caching. It speeds performance. Manifest (see Chapter 5) shows you where these other buffers are in memory. Other resources are called FILES and FCBs. Chapters 10 and 15 explain these in more detail.

TSRs Take From the 640K

But wait! DOS isn't alone in eating up conventional memory. There are also memory-resident programs, known in "acronymese" as TSRs (short for terminate and stay resident, which is what these programs do).

Standard programs load into conventional memory, run, and then are dumped from conventional memory when they're through. TSRs load into memory and stay there. They may run immediately, or they may wait. Often they don't even appear on the computer screen. They just wait in computer memory to do their jobs. They may wait for some hotkey combination on the keyboard. When you press that hotkey combination, the TSR appears on screen. You then can use it and when done press some other hotkey to make it disappear again. Some TSRs aren't watching the keyboard. Instead they're watching the PC's clock or some other activity, ready to do whatever it is they're programmed for when the right cue comes their way.

Each TSR in conventional memory means less left for your standard programs and data. A small TSR may take only 5 to 10K, but large TSRs can eat up 50 to 100K. Just a few of these, along with DOS, will leave significantly less conventional memory for your word processor, spreadsheet, or other program. (As explained in Chapter 10, some of DOS's own utilities are TSRs.)

Device Drivers Take From the 640K

More bad news: DOS and TSRs aren't the only things that use conventional memory. Small programs, called device drivers, add to DOS and help it understand a particular model disk drive, memory board, modem, or other device that is added to the PC. They typically have names that end in .SYS. Unfortunately, they also subtract from the conventional memory that a program or data can expect.

Drivers load in from disk and stay in conventional memory until you turn off your PC or reboot (press the Ctrl-Alt-Del keys simultaneously).

Network Drivers and Shells Take From the 640K

When you connect your PC to a local area network, you typically see several pieces of software grabbing some conventional memory, including both a redirector (a program that knows to send network requests to the network operating system instead of just to DOS) and a network shell (a program that gives you commands to control the basic network abilities, such as printing and sending messages). These cut into that 640K you want for application programs. See Chapter 19 for details on how QEMM and QRAM ease this network burden.

CONFIG.SYS and AUTOEXEC.BAT

When a PC starts, it first runs some self-tests, then it loads the basic DOS kernel into memory (including the COMMAND.COM program), then it sucks in the configuration commands in the CONFIG.SYS file on disk, and then it runs the AUTOEXEC.BAT files and any programs in it.

CONFIG.SYS is a text file with statements that tell DOS how to set itself up. The setup can use a little or a lot of memory, depending on how many of DOS's options are exercised—such as those for its resources.

You may add your own commands to CONFIG.SYS and AUTOEXEC.BAT to make your PC behave certain ways when you start it. QEMM and QRAM load themselves as device drivers, with a line in CONFIG.SYS. Some of QEMM's or QRAM's commands then are available if you add statements to AUTOEXEC.BAT.

When you run QEMM's installation routines along with the OPTIMIZE utility, these QEMM-starting statements automatically appear in CONFIG.SYS and AUTOEXEC.BAT.

CONFIG.SYS and AUTOEXEC.BAT are the levers you use to move your PC's memory use.

To change CONFIG.SYS or AUTOEXEC.BAT, you can use a word processor (that will save files as pure ASCII text), the DOS EDLIN program, or some DOS commands, as shown below.

First, find CONFIG.SYS or AUTOEXEC.BAT using the DOS dir command. Then copy both files to make sure you don't lose their old versions (type copy config.sys config.old and copy autoexec.bat autoexec.old). Then enter the type command—type config.sys or type autoexec.bat—to see what's in those files. Figures 4-4 and 4-5 show how MANIFEST can view these files.

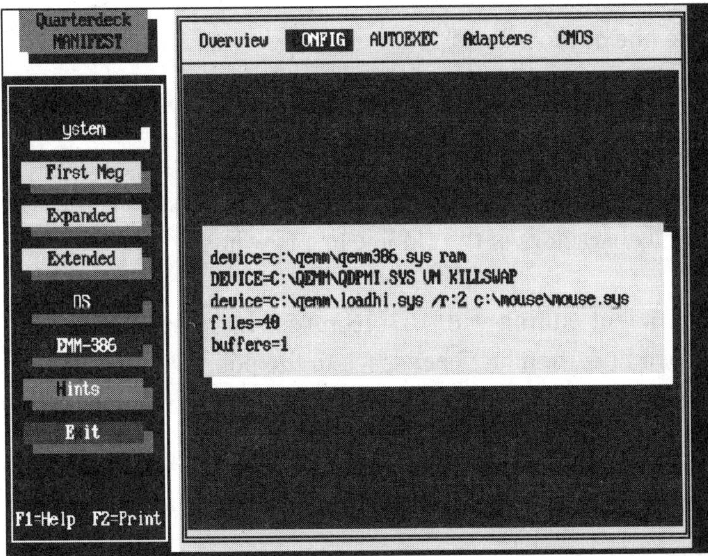

Figure 4-4. Example of CONFIG.SYS viewed in MANIFEST

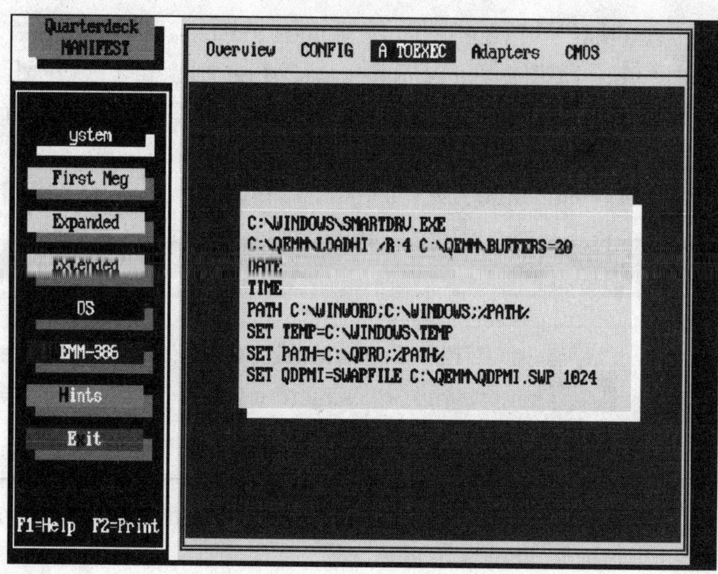

Figure 4-5. Example of AUTOEXEC.BAT viewed in MANIFEST

If you use EDLIN to edit the files, type edlin, a space, and the name of the file you want to edit (such as config.sys) at the DOS prompt, and then press Enter. You'll see an asterisk prompt. Now you type the number of the line you want to edit, and then an EDLIN command, such as one of these:

d...........delete one or more lines
e...........end editing, save the changed file to disk
i...........insert new lines
l...........list or display one or more lines
q...........quit editing, without saving the changed file to disk
F3........copy all characters of the old line to a new line

For efficient editing with EDLIN, press F3 to see the old version of a line, then just backspace to the point where you want to make changes and type the changes or use the LeftArrow and overtype.

To change CONFIG.SYS or AUTOEXEC.BAT with DOS commands, copy both files to back them up (as mentioned above), then type

```
copy con config.sys
```

and press Enter (to make a new version of CONFIG.SYS, for example). Type the first line of the new file, and press Enter. Type the second line, and press Enter. Continue for the rest of the lines. You can backspace within a line to make a correction, but you cannot back up to a previous line without starting over. When you've typed all the lines, press Ctrl-Z (the Ctrl key and the Z key at the same time). Your new CONFIG.SYS file is saved on disk. You can check this by typing type config.sys.

After you've changed CONFIG.SYS or AUTOEXEC.BAT, you must reboot (turn the power off and then on, or press Ctrl-Alt-Del) to have the changes take effect.

Memory Management—Getting More and Making the Most of It

So now you know the necessity and the limits of memory. Memory is vital to anything a computer does, and yet the PC's memory is limited to 1MB. Even that 1MB is compromised by the exclusion of 384K for system use and the bites taken out of the 640K that remain for the DOS kernel, the DOS resources, TSRs, drivers, and network software.

What can you do? Two things: Get more memory and make the most of the memory you've got. You'll need both memory chips and memory addresses. This section describes the various approaches to both—the ways you can manage memory. QEMM and QRAM help you do both.

The first method is simply to use smaller and fewer programs. Using the most up-to-date version of a program also helps; for example, using DOS 5 instead of DOS 4 saves tens of kilobytes. But this denial system is limited and limiting. You soon run into real limits on how small a program can be, and it limits the power of those programs, and their speed, because it emphasizes small size over power.

The next method is to add memory chips. This works for some programs but still leaves those limits on memory addresses.

The other management methods spring from utility programs such as QEMM that can juggle memory chips, memory addresses, and programs to make more out of what you have and let you add more to the PC. The following sections describe these memory management techniques in general and the video, upper, expanded, extended, and HMA memory they use.

Adding memory

It helps to have enough memory chips. You'll want at least 640K for any work, 1MB for some memory management, 2MB for DESQview, and 4MB or more for Windows.

How do you add memory to your PC? By plugging in new chips, SIMMs, or boards.

Start by adding chips to the motherboard. Unless you're going to disable some of these for multitasking (as explained later in this chapter), fill it to 640K or 1MB—as much as it can take.

Next, for a 386 or 486, see if the system has a special slot for plugging in a high-speed memory board. If it does, plug in such a board and fill it with memory chips. For an 8088 or 8086, add an EMS 4.0 expanded memory board (explained in the next section). Fill that with at least 1MB and preferably 2MB or more of chips. For an 80286 that will be used for multitasking, add an EMS 4.0 expanded memory board and put chips on it. For an 80286 that won't be multitasking, you can add an extended memory board (explained later in this section).

When you get chips, buy all of the same brand and speed, to avoid troubles.

Don't buy chips of different brands and speeds, even if they all meet your specifications. Subtle differences could make trouble for some of your programs.

When you plug in the chips, orient their notches or dots properly (look to the chip's documentation). Avoid static electricity damage to the chips by not touching their metal legs and by grounding yourself (touch a pipe, for instance) before picking up the chip or SIMM. Get SIMMs if you can—they're easier to install. If you think you have a faulty chip or SIMM (perhaps you see a "Parity error" message when starting your PC), have your machine serviced.

Multitasking, task switching, and backfilling

Multitasking means running more than one program at a time. In fact, most computers do this by first loading both programs into memory and then switching back and forth between two or more programs at extremely high speeds, giving a little processor time to this one, then to that one, and then back to this one. (This is called "time slicing".) The process is done so quickly that the user doesn't know that both aren't actually churning away doing their work simultaneously.

DOS is not made for multitasking. It doesn't have a way to divide the processor time among programs. Nor is it good about sharing its memory with more than one program at a time. But if you add special control programs such as Microsoft Windows or Quarterdeck's DESQview to DOS, multitasking becomes possible. Other operating systems, such as DR-DOS and OS/2 also offer multitasking.

The advantage of multitasking is that you can get more done in less time. Not only do you avoid the lost time of shutting down one program and starting another every time you change what you're focusing on, you also gain the advantages of directly exchanging information between programs. For example, instead of having to leave your spreadsheet to open a word processor to make a quick note, then leaving the word processor to open the spreadsheet again (the single-tasking process), you could have spreadsheet and word processor working side by side, switching quickly to the word processor to make a note, going back to the spreadsheet to calculate something, and then copying a figure from the spreadsheet to the word processor (the multitasking process). The other advantage of multitasking is running long-duration tasks in the background.

In multitasking typically one program has a higher priority for processing time—generally the one that is displayed to the user. This is the foreground application. Any other programs that are running are called the background applications. Multitasking systems have commands to let you change this order by bringing a background application to the foreground and sending the current foreground application to the background.

For example, you could work on a foreground word processor, while in the background your spreadsheet cranked away on some difficult calculations.

Some PCs that claim multitasking really only offer task switching. The difference is that task switching allows various programs to be in memory at once, but they can't run all at once. Only the foreground program actually operates; those in the background are suspended until they are brought to the foreground.

Task switching does make it easier to move from program to program, saving some time. And it does typically allow for moving information among programs. But it certainly doesn't allow background processing, so it is not as powerful a technique as full multitasking.

If your motherboard doesn't have a full 640K of memory, or if you can disable some of that memory (as is possible on many PCs), then you can backfill conventional memory addresses. This means mapping expanded memory into those conventional memory addresses. Backfilled memory is better for multitasking than standard conventional memory because it can more easily be remapped from chips holding one program to chips holding another. At the same time, backfilled memory is just as capable of handling traditional conventional memory roles. If you have a 386 or 486 system, there's no need to backfill because all memory addresses can be remapped.

Expanded memory

In the quest for more useful memory, even with a 1MB limit on memory addresses, some engineers wondered, How can we have more memory when we can't have more memory addresses? Someone bright thought, How about if they share addresses? And expanded memory was born.

But that could be confusing, other people said. The only way you'll get away with such a crazy sharing scheme is if you set down some serious rules about how they'll share—who gets what when. Again, that made sense, so experts from Lotus (the biggest maker of spreadsheets whose users wanted to load larger files into memory), Intel (one of biggest makers of memory boards who wanted to sell more memory boards by making them more useful), and Microsoft (makers of DOS who wanted in on anything that would so fundamentally extend how DOS works) got together. They created the LIM EMS (Expanded Memory Specification) rules.

The first LIM version was called 3.2. It permitted up to 8MB of expanded memory that could hold data—just what the spreadsheet owners ordered. Then AST and Quarterdeck defined the Extended EMS (EEMS) standard, which allowed a 64K swapping page instead of 16K, and supported swapping program code in addition to data. Recognizing the superior technology, the LIM group updated their specification. The second version of LIM was called 4.0. It permitted up to 32MB of expanded memory, alongside the 1MB of real mode memory. Better yet, it let you both store data in and run programs from that expanded memory.

Here's how expanded memory works: You plug an EMS memory board into your PC. It has a few hundred kilobytes to 8MB or even 32MB of memory chips on it. It also has special mapping hardware to let the PC flex the addresses for those memory chips. An Expanded Memory Manager program (an EMM) runs in the PC and sets aside 64K of reserved upper memory addresses as a page frame. Inside that frame it recognizes four pages of 16K memory addresses each.

Then the EMM waits for programs that were written to understand expanded memory. When one runs and asks for access to expanded memory, the EMM gives it access to anywhere from one to four pages in the page frame. The EMM takes the details of the program's request to map that page to a page of real EMS memory from the EMS memory board. The program has to wait a little longer than it would to see what was in conventional memory, but it gets the information all the same. When it needs some other information, or another program wants some other information, the EMM and the memory board's mapping registers change their direction again, letting one of the pages in the frame refer to some other part of the megabytes of expanded memory.

The effect is like viewing the world through a small window in a wall. The view outside is the large area of expanded memory, the wall is real mode's 1MB of memory, the small window is the page frame, you tied to a chair is the application program tied to conventional memory, and you released from the chair, able to look through the window from any angle, is the PC equipped with LIM EMS hardware and an EMM. When in the chair you could see only what was on the wall and just outside the window. Once free you could still see only what was on the wall apart from the window, but through the window you could see in many different directions just by changing your vantage point. Programs can change what memory they see the same way, by changing the way the page refers to expanded memory. (Of course the analogy fails because the programs can write information to memory, not just "read" it the way you do the view through the window.)

Figure 4-6 is a diagram of expanded memory.

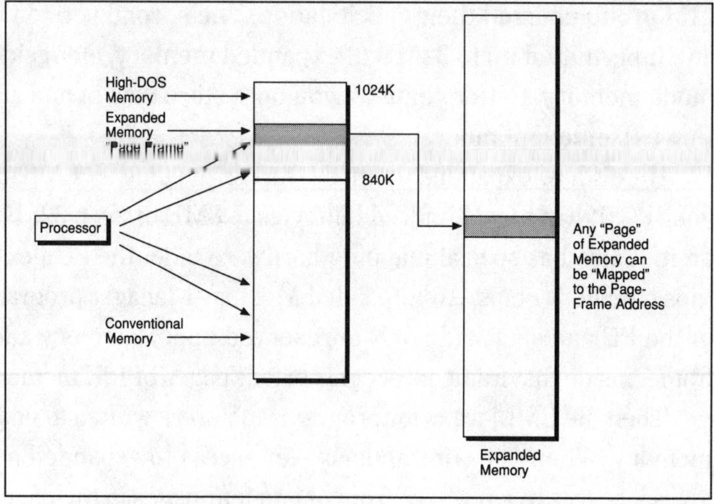

Figure 4-6. Expanded memory diagram.

LIM 4.0 gives you a larger sky to see than LIM 3.2, and it lets you put the window in more places—all the way down to the 256K mark in memory. That makes LIM 4.0 more flexible and able to handle programs as they operate, not just data. In fact, some users like this flexibility so much they disable their memory chips down to the 256K address and backfill all memory addresses above that with memory chips from the expanded memory board.

It is the LIM 4.0 mapping hardware that lets QRAM load TSRs and DDs high on an 8088, 8086, or 80286 PC. Be sure to get a board that is fully EMS 4.0 compatible with a driver that is also fully EMS 4.0 compatible.

Unfortunately, expanded memory doesn't really help increase conventional memory, the most useful memory in a PC. Only programs written to use expanded memory can use it at all, and even they can't use it as flexibly as any program can use conventional memory.

Extended memory

Although DOS can only reach its real mode limit of 1MB of memory, the processors in 286, 386, and 486 PCs can reach a lot more. Those processors can address 16MB (the 286) and 4GB (the 386 and 486) of memory. They do that in protected mode.

If there were some way to move a PC from DOS into protected mode, you would get at a lot more memory. This memory, beyond the 1MB mark, is called extended memory.

A 286, 386, or 486 PC can have both expanded memory and extended memory.

Although DOS cannot use extended memory, some DOS programs can. For example, a variety of disk cache programs can use extended memory for their data—the most recently used information from the disk. They do this while remaining in real mode, however.

Some programs, called DOS extenders, can be built into applications. A word processor or spreadsheet with a DOS extender built in can automatically bump the processor into protected mode and then later back into real mode. While in protected mode that application program can use extended memory. Lotus 1-2-3 Release 3 and Paradox 386 are famous examples of such applications. Microsoft Windows version 3 also includes a DPMI DOS Extender. Phar Lap and Rational Systems are two of the best-known DOS extender makers.

You don't need to worry about DOS extenders because they are built into programs; they do their work without you even knowing (although you are aware of having all that delicious room for program and data, of course).

To make sure programs that use extended memory don't bump into each other, Microsoft, Lotus, AST, and Intel came up with the XMS standard (for eXtended Memory Specification). Programs that follow its rules won't bother one another while using extended memory. XMS doesn't let programs automatically run in extended memory, but it sets the rules for them to cooperate if they do use extended memory, through DOS extenders or other means. (Then there's always the OS/2 operating system, which runs automatically in protected mode.)

Unfortunately, extended memory doesn't do a thing to help with RAM-cram. It doesn't add to conventional memory, the memory necessary for most programs to run programs.

Grabbing video buffer RAM

One of the most straightforward ways to get more conventional memory is to steal some. As you can see from Figure 4-7, the memory addresses just above the 640K mark are still within the standard DOS range. Normally these are part of reserved memory as addresses used for video buffers.

Figure 4-7. Pushing Conventional memory into the Video RAM area

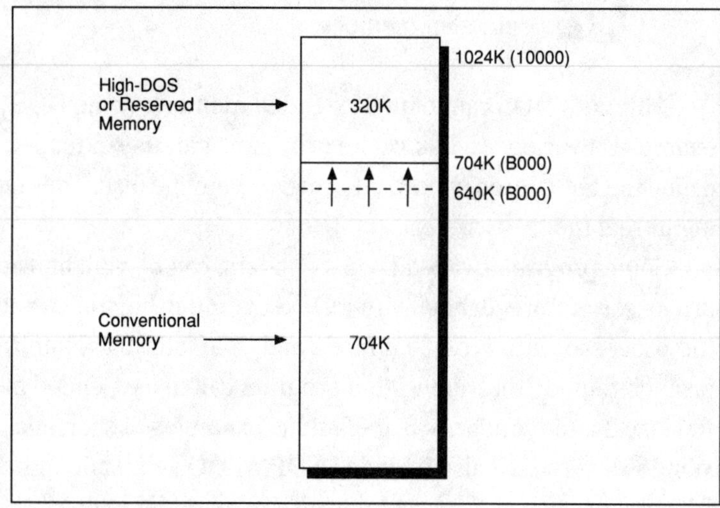

But suppose you don't use all those video buffer addresses. What if you have a color graphics VGA video system, which needs 128K of addresses, but you only run it in monochrome text mode, which needs only 4K of addresses. That leaves 124K of unused addresses. The right utility can take these and add them to the bottom 640K of memory, making a total of 764K (minus whatever DOS is using for itself). QEMM's VIDRAM utility does just that.

This theft means you can't use graphics, naturally, because the video memory necessary for graphics is busy acting as conventional memory. It means that if you run a program that has both text and graphics modes, and you switch to the graphics mode, you could even crash your PC (disrupting any current programs and requiring that you turn the power off and lose all information in memory). VIDRAM can detect such a switch and ask if it is what you really want, so you normally are not in much danger, but you are running a less stable system than before the theft. See Chapter 11 for details on VIDRAM.

Loading high

384K of memory addresses is reserved for ROMs, the video buffer, and other system uses. This is upper or high DOS memory. But typically, as shown in the memory maps of Figure 4-8, fewer than half of those addresses are used. In fact many PCs have more than 200K of upper memory addresses that aren't used.

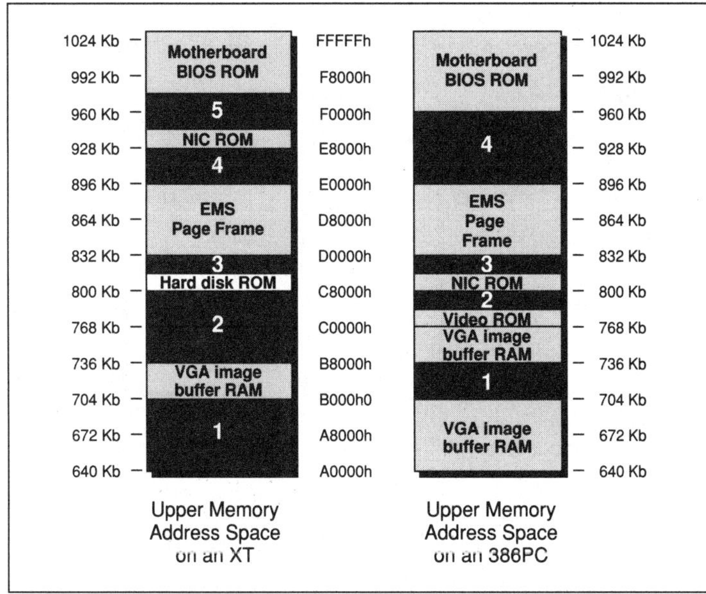

Figure 4-8. Example of unused Upper memory

The right memory management utility can create UMBs (upper memory blocks) by mapping RAM from extended memory into upper memory addresses. Then that utility can load many TSRs and device drivers into those UMBs. It can place them in upper memory instead of in conventional memory, conserving conventional memory for programs and data. This is called loading high.

QEMM and QRAM are both equipped with a program called LOADHI that puts TSRs and device drivers up there, out of the way. It is explained in detail in Chapter 9. DOS 5 also has a load high feature, as explained in Chapter 15, but it is not as capable as LOADHI from QEMM or QRAM.

Figure 4-9 shows an example of loading high. Not all TSRs or DDs work when loaded high, by the way. But for those that do, including some that are part of DOS, the trick is to fit as many as possible into the upper memory addresses. You can do this yourself using Manifest (see Chapter 5) to analyze memory to see the size of the open areas in upper memory. Or you can do it automatically by letting QEMM's OPTIMIZE utility inspect and count the open areas. Then if you want you can second-guess OPTIMIZE and try to load even more into high DOS memory.

Figure 4-9. Example of Loading High to take advantage of unused Upper memory

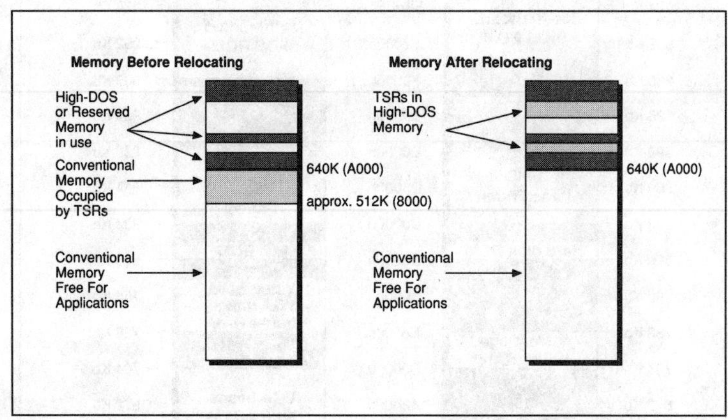

But having the addresses to load to isn't enough. You need memory chips at those addresses. Most PCs come with at least 1MB of memory these days, and older models can be beefed up to that level. But they generally make 640K conventional and put the rest up above the 1024K mark where it is extended memory—384K of extended memory. Upper and reserved memory addresses do not have chips.

Loading into the High Memory Area

The 8088, 8086, 80286, 386, and 486 processors address memory in 64K segments, as mentioned previously. They can work with any segment of 64K that starts on any 16-byte division in the first megabyte of memory.

But what if that 16-byte division is only 16 bytes shy of the 1024K, 1MB line (as shown in Figure 4-10)? Then the 64K segment wraps around to the bottom of memory, through the 0K line, as shown.

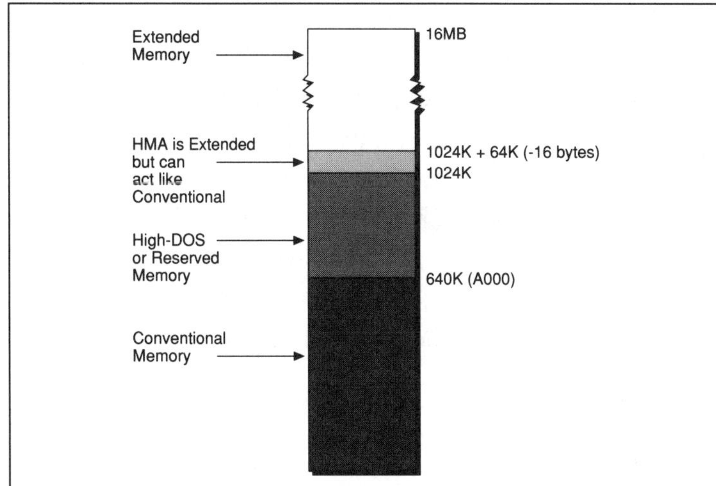

Figure 4-10. How addressing "wraps around" from the 1024K mark to 0K

Well, that's what is supposed to happen. But someone (Quarterdeck says it was their someone, Microsoft says it was theirs) discovered a bug in the chips. By manipulating the A20 address line—found only on the 286, 386, and 486 chips, not the 8088 or 8086—you can stop the wrap-around. The PC can address 64K, minus 16 bytes that is, of memory beyond 1024K.

The 8086 and 8088 processor chips have 20 address lines, as mentioned earlier in this chapter. These are the wires that carry signals to tell which address in memory to read or write from. These 20 lines are enough to specify addresses for 1MB of memory. They are numbered A0 through A19.

The 286, 386, and 486 processors have more address lines. The first one after the original 20 is called A20 (remember that the numbering started with A0). A PC with an A20 address line can use extended memory—they have the signals to get at more than 1MB of memory. The software that controls the state of this A20 line, and consequently controls whether a read or write request is going to conventional or extended memory—is called an A20 handler. A driver program such as HIMEM.SYS has an A20 handler built in. HIMEM.SYS lets you specify how this handler works with its machine switch.

This is very useful memory. It isn't in the reserved memory area but is above 1024K. It acts like conventional memory because it is available in real mode. And it isn't occupied because most programs didn't even know it was there.

This is called the HMA (high memory area) and is quite useful, as explained in the memory management section below. QEMM and DESQview make good use of it. Although applications can't use the HMA directly because it's separate from the rest of conventional memory, some utilities can load into it.

QEMM lets you choose from several programs that can be loaded into, and run from, the HMA. DOS 5 can load part of itself into the HMA. DESQview is the master of HMA loading, able to use nearly 63K of the HMA for its own program instructions. It uses the QEXT.SYS driver to do so, as explained in Chapter 12. In each case these programs load into the HMA instead of into conventional memory, conserving conventional memory.

Shadow RAM and top memory

ROM is generally slower than RAM. RAM is read 16 bits at a time (on 286s or 386SXs) or 32 bits at a time (on 386s and 486s) while ROMs are read 8 bits at a time on most machines and at 16 bits at a time on some machines.

But who wants slow ROMs? The instructions in those ROMs get used over and over, so slow ROMs can slow down the computer's entire performance.

To speed up the ROMs, some PCs automatically copy the contents of the basic ROMs, such as the BIOS and video ROMs, into RAM memory. They remap addresses so the RAM copies are at the former ROM addresses. Then when programs want ROM instructions, they go to the ROM address and are fooled into using the instructions from the RAM copies, which are much faster. This helps system performance and is called Shadow RAM. Manifest in its QEMM memory screen can tell you if you have Shadow RAM (see Figure 4-11 and Chapter 5).

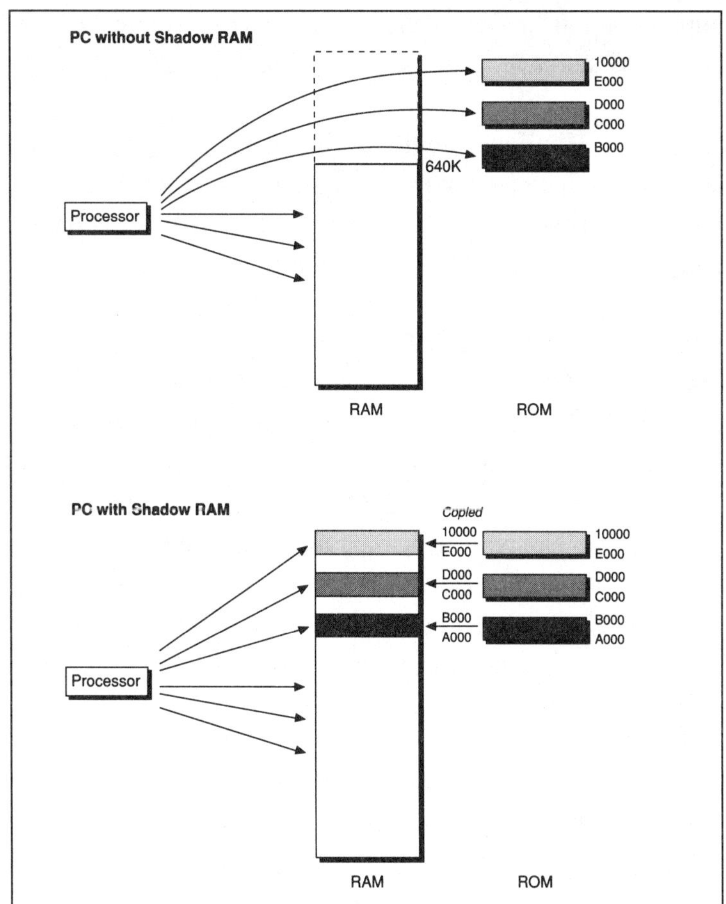

Figure 4-11. A diagram of Shadow RAM

The Chips & Technologies company makes chips that are at the heart of many PCs, chips that work alongside the microprocessor and memory. There are other chip companies that offer similar features, however. Such alternate chips may use less than the full 384K of remapped RAM that C&T chips use. You can use Manifest to see how much Shadow RAM is in your PC.

Manifest can't automatically find the Shadow-RAM-creating chips from companies other than Chips & Technologies. Those other chips sometimes use a different approach than C&T's chips. To deduce that some Shadow RAM feature is present, compare the total and available memory measurements in Manifest (see Chapter 5).

You can use Manifest's ability to time memory speed to find Shadow RAM. If on the FirstMeg screen for Timings you see that the ROM addresses are responding as quickly as RAM conventional memory, then the ROMs are being shadowed.

You don't have to depend on a Shadow RAM feature to improve ROM performance. QEMM can shadow ROMs itself by copying ROM contents into RAM, mapping the RAM into the ROM spaces, and then write-protecting that RAM so its information can't be changed. Put the ROM option on the QEMM386.SYS line of CONFIG.SYS (see Chapter 6). Then test with Manifest's First Meg screen for Timings to see it at work. You can choose to copy only some of the ROMS—a partial shadow. You can do it to one small area of ROM or to several areas of ROM. The PS/2, for instance, has 128K of RAM for shadowing system and video ROM from E000 to FFFF. A ROM on a network card should not be shadowed. If you knew its address as XXXX-YYYY, then you could add the ROM=XXXX-YYYY option to QEMM to not shadow that ROM.

However, Shadow RAM confuses load-high schemes because some of the extended memory is already taken, and the ROMs can't be so easily remapped to better locations. As explained in Chapter 6, you sometimes need to disable Shadow RAM.

Disable Shadow RAM and use QEMM's ROM option instead to save memory or to shadow a ROM that the system doesn't remap.

Stealth and remapping ROMs

Part of the upper memory area is occupied by vital ROMs, as mentioned earlier. But it sure would be nice to have those areas available for loading TSRs and DDs high. What can you do? How about sharing addresses, as was done in creating expanded memory.

QEMM version 6.0 introduced the STEALTH feature that remaps the ROMs to RAM and puts RAM into upper memory where it can be used for loading high.

When any ROM routine is called for, STEALTH immediately reverses the mapping so the ROM routines can be used. Then when the ROM is through, it is removed again, and the data or programs loaded into the RAM at those upper addresses show through. This makes more upper memory space available, at the price of some extended memory where the ROMs must be copied.

VCPI

QEMM and other programs sometimes make the most flexible remapping of memory by putting the PC's processor into virtual-86 mode. This mode, as explained earlier in this chapter, can run a number of simultaneous programs, each able to use 1MB of memory (with the standard 640K barrier, naturally).

But what happens if more than one program tries to remap memory using virtual-86 mode and each remaps memory differently? To make such programs cooperate, they all need to follow the VCPI (Virtual Control Program Interface) specification.

There are two parts to VCPI: server and clients. Clients ask the server for memory and processor mode changes. The first VCPI-supporting program loaded into a system will become the VCPI server. Others loaded after it will make any memory-mapping requests to it and so won't making conflicting mappings.

When QEMM-386 is installed, it is the server, and DOS extended applications are the clients. Without QEMM, the DOS extender part of DOS extended programs becomes the server. DESQview can use QEMM and run more than one extended or standard DOS real mode program at a time. On 286 systems you can run more than one DOS extended application if the DOS extender uses XMS services. (QEMM can't be the server on 286s because QEMM doesn't run on 286s.)

DPMI

The DPMI (DOS Protected Mode Interface) standard was a competitor to VCPI, but is becoming something of a successor. It lets DOS applications access protected mode features of the 386 and 486 processors. Quarterdeck, Borland, IBM, Intel, Locus, Lotus, Microsoft, Phar Lap, Phoenix, Rational Systems, and others collaborated on DPMI.

Programs that implement DPMI functions are called DPMI hosts. QEMM can do this when you add the companion program QDPMI, described in Appendix G. Protected-mode applications that request DPMI functions are DPMI clients. DPMI clients can run in Windows, DOS, DR DOS, DESQview 386, and other environments, if a DPMI host is present.

Simulating expanded memory

The 386 and 486 PCs have built-in memory-mapping circuits, so they don't need the mapping hardware of a LIM EMS board. In fact, with the right memory management program, you can emulate expanded memory from extended memory. That is, you can temporarily convert some extended memory so it acts like expanded memory. (Such an emulator is sometimes called a LIMulator.) QEMM can do this. That way you don't need to buy an expanded memory board for a PC just because you have a program that likes expanded memory more than extended memory. Most programs today prefer extended, but some of the older ones only tolerate expanded.

Emulated expanded memory can't do everything true expanded memory can. It is often not as fast as true expanded memory and so is not useful for some multitasking work.

Windows and DESQview

Windows and DESQview are programs that manage multiple programs running in memory at once. Windows likes extended memory best and has its own utilities to dynamically convert extended memory to expanded as needed. Chapters 16 and17 explain this in more detail.

DESQview combined with QEMM is called DESQview-386. This gives even more memory management powers than QEMM alone. See Chapter 16 for more detail.

CHAPTER FIVE

Manifest

How can you manage your PC's memory if you don't know how much memory there is and what's in it? You can't. That's why Quarterdeck packs a copy of Manifest with each copy of QEMM and QRAM.

Manifest analyzes and reports on your PC's memory, detailing where it is and what it's doing. In fact, Manifest also tells you about other parts of your PC, not just the memory. It tells you what kind of processor is in the system and what disk drives are available. It even tells you the date the BIOS in your system was created.

Manifest can report wrong information or miss some facts when it's run on an incompatible PC. This is rare, but it does happen, for example, when a driver or TSR interferes with it or an Expanded Memory Manager doesn't report information properly.

You even can use Manifest to learn about memory, to work through its various screens, and when referring to Chapter 4 or the Glossary, to understand the terms there.

Experiment with Manifest. See what it can tell you about your PC. That's the best way to learn about memory and the flexibility QEMM or QRAM can give you.

This chapter explains how to use Manifest, from just viewing its fundamental summaries of PC memory to its detailed options for looking at every little bit in your PC.

Manifest is vital to any manual configuration of QEMM, including fine-tuning the results of OPTIMIZE. Manifest even suggests how you can best manage memory.

 Manifest 1.1 supports DOS 5.0.

Manifest works as a standard DOS program or as a TSR. That is, it can run by itself, telling you about your PC's internals, or it can run in memory alongside some other program, so you can see what that other program is doing to memory and interrupts.

 Manifest can print its information so you have a page showing what is in your PC or what is happening to it.

 Manifest can run in a DESQview window and analyze that window.

Installation

Installing Manifest is easy, whether your copy of Manifest is by itself or bundled with QEMM or QRAM.

If you have a copy of Manifest by itself on disk, do the following. Turn on your PC, wait for the DOS prompt (probably C>) to appear, and then put the Manifest disk into floppy drive A on your PC. Now type

```
a:install
```

and press Enter.

 If you have an LCD or gas-plasma display (both are typical on portable PCs) you should type the command a:install /m to get a more readable display.

The INSTALL program starts and asks you which drive and directory you want to put Manifest into. Tell it by either leaving the default choice or typing the drive and directory you want. INSTALL creates the appropriate directory, copies the Manifest files to it, and quits.

Manifest is now ready to use.

If you have Manifest bundled with some other Quarterdeck program, such as QEMM or QRAM, it is installed along with them. (To install QEMM or QRAM, look to Chapter 1 and to Appendices A and B of this book.) You find Manifest in the \QEMM or \QRAM directory. To check for it, change to the directory by entering the commands

```
c:
cd qemm
```

and then typing

```
dir mft.exe
```

You'll see DOS confirm that the MFT.EXE file is in the directory (unless it's not there and you need to run the installation again).

Running Manifest

After installing Manifest, you are ready to run it. First you must change to the directory that has the MFT.EXE file. That's the Manifest program. That directory also includes related files, such as MFT.HLP, that you'll also find in that directory.

From here there are three ways to run Manifest:

- as a standard DOS program with lots of organized screen displays
- as a TSR with those displays
- as a command-line option to see the raw facts without the screens

Running as a DOS program with screens

Change to the directory with Manifest by typing

```
cd \qemm
```

if Manifest is in the QEMM directory. Then type

```
mft
```

and press Enter. You see a transitory screen mentioning Manifest's version number and your Manifest's serial number. Then the System Overview screen appears, as in Figure 5-1.

Figure 5-1. MANIFEST System Overview screen

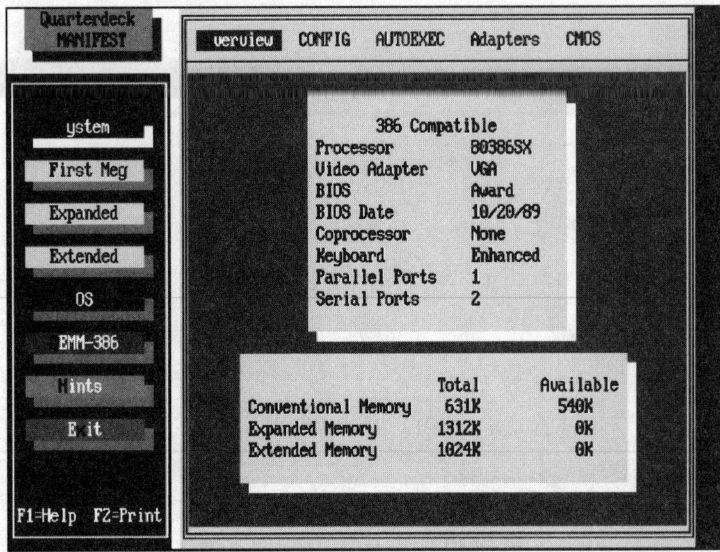

From here you can shuttle to all the other Manifest screens as well. The rest of the chapter explains those screens and what they tell you about your PC.

When you're done with Manifest, press the Esc key twice to return to DOS.

Running as a TSR with screens

As explained in Chapter 4, TSR (terminate and stay resident) programs stay in memory and pop up whenever you need them. This keeps them closer at hand than a program you must load from disk and run, but it eats up memory that other programs might want.

Manifest can run as a TSR. You can run it alongside some other program to see what that program is doing to memory (as well as what interrupts it uses and what files it keeps open). Troubleshooters constantly use Manifest as a TSR.

To run Manifest as a TSR, start from the DOS prompt in the Manifest directory, and type

```
mft /t
```

You see the Manifest opening screen, and then the DOS prompt reappears. Manifest is now in memory. (It takes up about 121K—too much to let you run some other programs, unfortunately.)

Press F1 at any time to get Help information on using Manifest.

Typically at this point you run whatever other program you want to analyze. From the DOS prompt you type the command for that program, for example,

```
123
```

and then press Enter. That program starts. At any point while using that program, you can press the ***hotkey*** combination for Manifest. The default is LeftShift-Ctrl (press the left-side Shift key and the Ctrl key at the same time).

Manifest's System Overview screen appears, as in Figure 5-1. From here you can use any of the Manifest screens to analyze your PC, as explained in the rest of this chapter.

You also can run Manifest as a TSR by leaving it resident. That is, you start it as a normal DOS program and then choose to leave it in memory when you quit. To do this, start it as a normal DOS program (type mft and press Enter at the DOS prompt), and choose the Exit category by pressing Esc or X. Then press R (or use the RightArrow key) to choose the Stay Resident topic, as in Figure 5-2. Finally, hold down the key combination you want to use to pop up Manifest later. The default is LeftShift-Ctrl, as mentioned above. You may also press RightShift-Ctrl or LeftShift-RightShift-Alt. Whichever you press, Manifest disappears (it's in memory, though) and the DOS prompt reappears. Now Manifest is a TSR waiting for your chosen key combination to make it reappear.

To change the hotkey combination that pops up Manifest, run Manifest and then choose the Exit category and the Stay Resident topic.

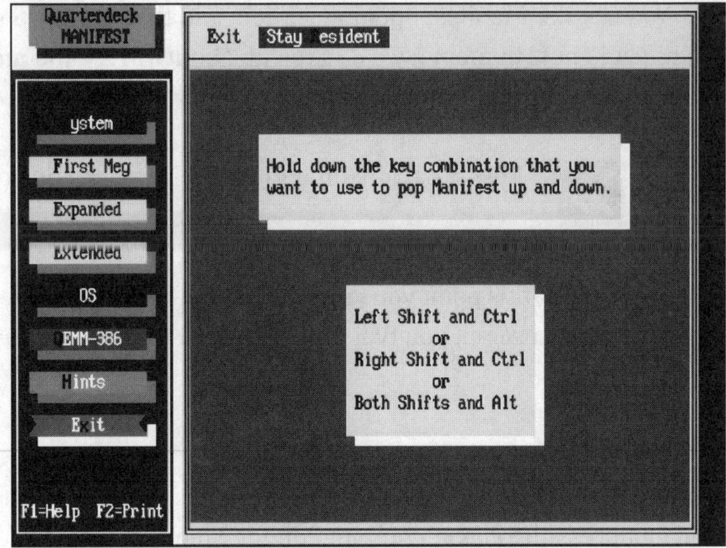

Figure 5-2. MANIFEST Stay Resident topic screen

You can remove Manifest from memory (to stop it being a TSR) if you don't load any other TSR after you load Manifest. Run Manifest, choose the Exit category, and from there press Esc or Exit to get back to DOS.

Running as a command-line option (without screens)

If you want to see the information Manifest provides as reports, without all the screen organization described in the rest of this chapter, you can run Manifest with command-line options. For example, instead of typing mft, you type

```
mft system overview
```

or just

```
mft s o
```

to see the System Overview screen information. Manifest doesn't remain in memory, and you don't have to quit it to work with other programs. Instead you just get the details you want, as in Figure 5-3.

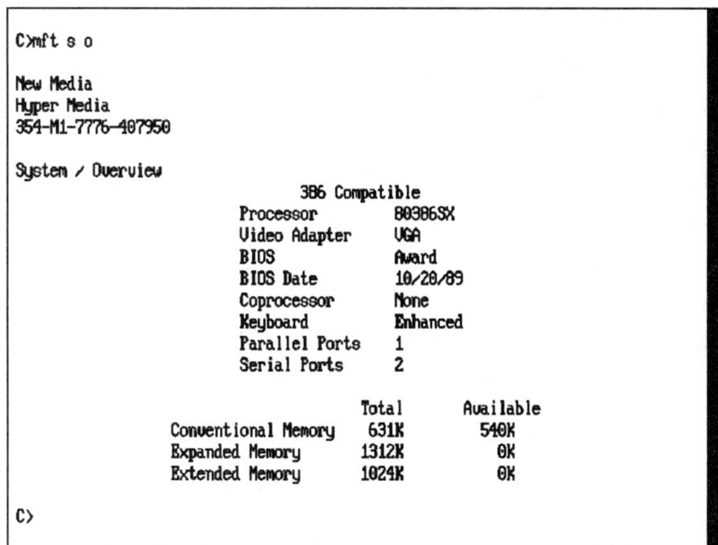

Figure 5-3. Example of getting a quick report from MANIFEST

Here are the options:

```
s o    System Overview
s c    System CONFIG.SYS
s u    System AUTOEXEC.BAT
s a    System Adapters
s m    System CMOS
f o    First Meg Overview
f r    First Meg Programs
f i    First Meg Interrupts
f b    First Meg BIOS Data
f m    First Meg Timings
p o    Expanded Memory Overview
p a    Expanded Memory Pages
p n    Expanded Memory Handles
p m    Expanded Memory Timings
p b    Expanded Memory Benchmark
t o    Extended Memory Overview
t m    Extended Memory XMS Analysis
d o    DOS Overview
```

```
d r    DOS Drivers
d f    DOS Files
d e    DOS Environment
q o    QEMM-386 Overview
q y    QEMM-386 Type
q a    QEMM-386 Accessed
q n    QEMM-386 Analysis
q m    QEMM-386 Memory
v o    DESQview Overview
v m    DESQview Memory Status
h o    Hints Overview
h e    Hints Detail
x e    Exit Manifest
x r    Exit Manifest and Leave It  Resident (TSR)
```

You can also use wildcards to see more than one report. Just as in DOS, the asterisk character (*) stands for "all possible letters here." So if you type

```
mft s *
```

you're asking for the reports for all the topics in the System category. The command

```
mft * *
```

asks for all reports from all categories and topics.

Multiple reports scroll off the screen, so you may want to send them directly to a printer or disk file.

Command-line switches

Besides the options that produce reports, there are command-line switches that affect how Manifest runs. You type these when starting Manifest. You enter them on the DOS command line after a forward slash. For example, the command

```
mft /m
```

displays Manifest's displays in two-color (monochrome). The other switches are

`/l` ...... to display in 43-line EGA mode or 50-line VGA mode
`/n` ...... to opt for "no snow" with a CGA adapter (no synch)
`/a` ...... to show the alternate screen format first
`/p` ...... to pause after each screen
`/t` ...... to run as a TSR
`/BD` ..... to tell Manifest that CONFIG.SYS and AUTOEXEC.BAT are in the root directory of drive D.
`/?` ..... to see this list of switches

Scrolling reports won't work with the 43-line or 50-line display command-line switches mentioned below. The special display is ignored and the reports appear in normal display.

Categories and Topics—How Manifest Is Organized

There are lots of things to know about your PC's insides, from processors and adapters to all the kinds of memory. They can't all be shown on one page or screen, so Manifest breaks them up into categories. These are listed as a menu on the left side of the System Overview screen, as shown in Figure 5-1. You move from one category to another by pressing the UpArrow and DownArrow keys (to move the highlighting on screen) or by pressing the emphasized letter of the category's name. For example, you'd press F to see the First Meg category.

Within each category are smaller divisions of information called topics. These appear across the top of the screen (again, see Figure 5-1 for an example.)

The first topic of each category is a summary of that category's information.

You move from one topic to another by pressing the LeftArrow and RightArrow keys (to move the highlighting on screen) or by pressing the emphasized letter of the topic's name. For example, you press A to see the Adapters in the System Overview category.

This chapter explains those categories and topics in order. The categories are

- System
- First Meg
- Expanded
- Extended
- DOS
- QEMM-386
- DESQview
- Hints
- Exit

System covers the hardware in the PC and the CONFIG.SYS and AUTOEXEC.BAT files. These are the fundamentals you need to understand what your PC will do and to supply to tech support experts when you have troubles.

Manifest screens tell you about the PC's status as of the moment you popped up that screen. If you want to see if the status has changed while you've been watching that screen—such as a change in interrupt or memory use—press the Space Bar. This updates the information.

First Meg covers the first megabyte of memory. This includes the conventional memory that QEMM tries to conserve and the upper memory that QEMM uses as a place to put drivers and TSRs. (See Chapter 4 for explanations of these terms.) Here's where you learn how much memory your programs and adapters are using and the addresses of that memory. If you're trying to fine-tune QEMM's use of upper memory, you need First Meg to find unused memory areas. Here you also find lists of the interrupts programs use, a way to identify conflicts between programs.

Expanded covers expanded memory, telling you how much there is and how it is used. It even times the memory so you can see how fast your system can work.

Extended covers extended memory: how much and what sort of XMS Extended Memory Manager driver is operating.

DOS covers the DOS uses of memory, including the kernel, drivers, buffers, and so on.

QEMM-386 appears as a category only if you have QEMM running on your PC. It tells how QEMM has set up memory, as well as how upper memory is being used.

DESQview appears as a category only if you have DESQview running on your PC. It tells you about the DESQview window Manifest is running in and on the memory that DESQview controls.

Hints gives tips on managing memory.

Exit is the place to quit Manifest or to leave it in memory as a TSR.

Some topics can't pack all their information into a single screen. When you see one of these, press the PgUp and PgDn keys, or the Home and End keys, to move to other parts of the information.

Some topics can display information in two different formats. Press F3 to switch back and forth between formats.

You can use a mouse with Manifest. Have a Microsoft-compatible mouse and mouse driver installed, and then just point the mouse cursor (a diamond) at the category, topic, or command you want. Then click the left mouse button.

If Manifest should be displaying in color but is not, some program you ran has changed the standard video mode.

Printing information

Press F2 at any time to print what Manifest is showing. In fact, you can

- print to paper
- print to a new disk file
- print to append to an existing disk file

Press F2 at any time to print what Manifest is showing.

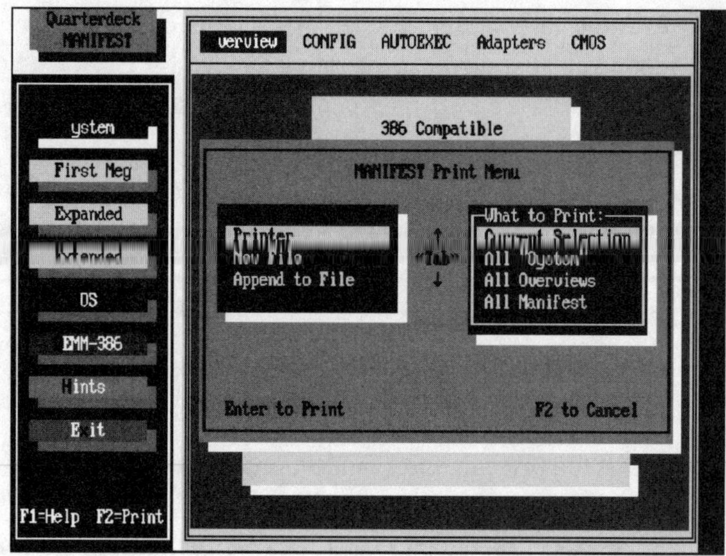

Figure 5-4. MANIFEST's Print menu

When you press F2 you see the Print menu, as in Figure 5-4. Here you choose Where to print and What to print. Switch back and forth between Where and What by pressing the Tab key.

When you choose Where, you press the UpArrow and DownArrow keys to move among the choices of

Printer
New File
Append to File

If you choose New File or Append to File, you must select a filename, as shown in Figure 5-5. Type the name, including the path (directory and drive) you want to use.

Press the Tab key to move from the Where menu to the What menu. Then press the UpArrow and DownArrow keys to move among the choices of

Current Selection
All "System"
All Overviews
All Manifest

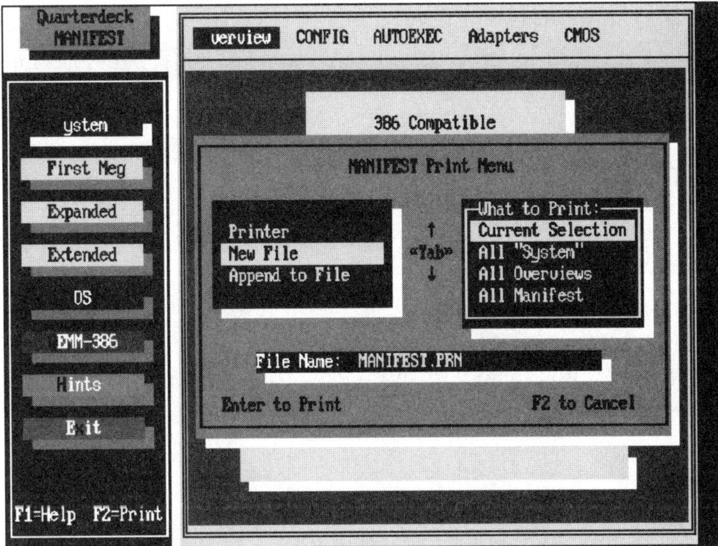

Figure 5-5. Choosing a filename for a saved report

Leave the highlighting on the one you want.

After selecting Where and What, press Enter to print. If you decide not to print, press F2 again, or press Esc, to cancel the printing.

Manifest assumes you're printing to the standard LPT1 printer port. If that's not what you want, you should save to a disk file, then pull that file into a word processor that allows you to print to other ports.

System category

System information tells about what hardware is in your PC and what commands are in your two most important DOS files: AUTOEXEC.BAT and CONFIG.SYS.

The hardware information includes processors, memory, video adapters, and other peripheral adapters. It also includes details on the BIOS ROM chips that are the foundation software for your PC.

Manifest uses a variety of methods to ferret out what is in your PC. Sometimes these methods come up with different answers, because PCs don't agree on all ways of holding and presenting their information. If you see a contradiction in two of Manifest's answers, it could be an unimportant example of this divergence from standards.

When Manifest is run inside DESQview, it reports on memory and ports the way DESQview sets them, not the way they are initially in the PC.

System Overview topic

The System Overview topic shows you the hardware information in Figure 5-6. The first line tells you the system type. The other lines tell you

Processor ....the main processor chip in the PC
Video Adapter.......the video adapter type in the PC
BIOS ....the maker of the BIOS software
BIOS Date ....the version of the BIOS software
Coprocessor...........any math coprocessor in the PC
Keyboard................standard 84-key or enhanced 101-key
Parallel Ports ....the number of such ports
Serial Ports ....the number of such ports
Memory ....explained below

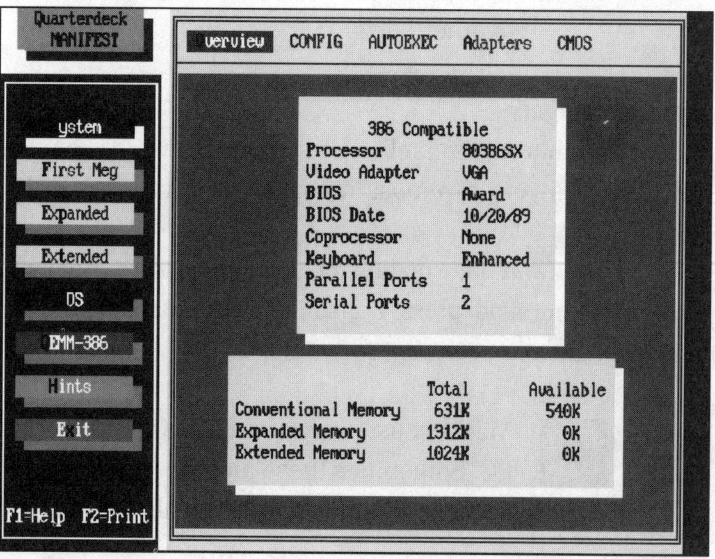

Figure 5-6. Hardware information in the System Overview

Possible mistakes include the following:

- Keyboard may say standard when it is really enhanced, perhaps because a TSR loaded before Manifest doesn't support enhanced keyboards or because the system has a standard keyboard BIOS ROM.

- Video Adapter may say that some sophisticated adapter is only the standard adapter, such as EGA or VGA, that it comes closest to.

- BIOS may not report correctly because not all BIOS chips follow a standard pattern of telling what they are.

- Coprocessor is determined directly, by trying program instructions, not from the coprocessor status reported in the CMOS memory or the BIOS Data area. (A 486DX or 486DX2 has a built-in coprocessor. A 486SX or Cyrix CX486DLC does not.)

Conventional, expanded, and extended memory are the various kinds of memory, as explained in Chapter 4. Conventional memory is that from 0K to 1024K. Expanded memory is the EMS 3.2, EEMS, or EMS 4.0 memory. Extended memory is the XMS memory.

Total memory is what the PC starts with. Available memory is how much is ready for use. Total and available memory amounts won't always be the same because some of the total memory may be used by programs or drivers.

Possible confusions and mistakes include the following:

- Expanded memory won't be counted unless Manifest finds a properly installed Expanded Memory Manager driver.

- Extended memory that is converted into expanded memory is counted twice—as total extended and total expanded.

- Some 286 and 386 PCs use 384K of memory as Shadow RAM (see Chapter 4 for details). Some use it as top memory (in Compaq computers). Shadow and top memory are typically not counted in the Manifest totals.

- If you're running DESQview, the conventional and expanded memory available are just for the window running Manifest, not what is available in the system.

System CONFIG.SYS topic

Your CONFIG.SYS file contains instructions to DOS on how to set up the PC and its memory. (See Chapter 4 for details on CONFIG.SYS.) QEMM must insert itself as one of these instructions. Any technical expert figuring out what is happening in your PC will want to know what is in the CONFIG.SYS file. This topic shows the file on screen, as in Figure 5-7.

Figure 5-7. System CONFIG topic screen

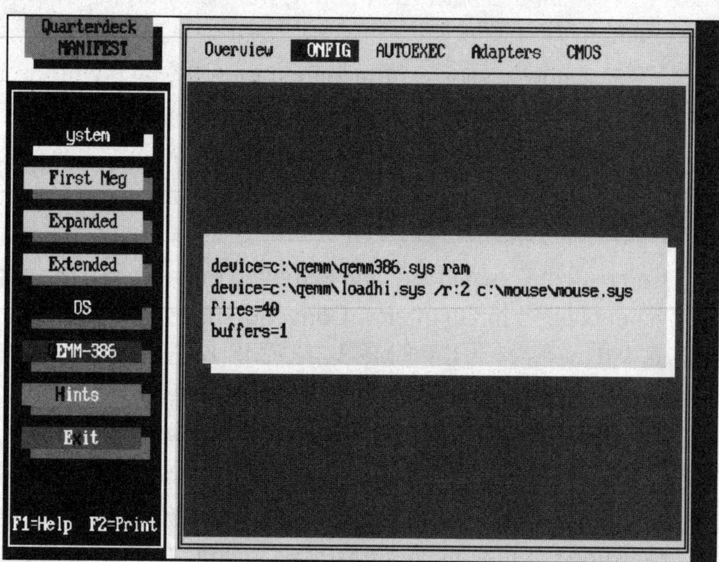

If a CONFIG.SYS line is too long to show on screen, it wraps to the next line. Manifest shows this with an ellipsis (...) at the head of the additional lines.

Note that on PCs using DOS 2.0 to 3.3, Manifest uses the COMPSEC= environment variable to figure out the boot drive that will hold the CONFIG.SYS file. If this variable is wrong—for example, if you boot from a floppy disk and then change that floppy—you'll be looking at the wrong CONFIG.SYS file on screen. You can use the /B command-line switch mentioned previously to cure this problem.

System AUTOEXEC.BAT topic

Your AUTOEXEC.BAT file is a batch file of commands that your PC executes when it first starts. Batch files load important initial programs into memory, and sometimes lead to other batch files. (See Chapter 4 for details on AUTO-EXEC.BAT.) QEMM's LOADHI program, for instance, often inserts itself into AUTOEXEC.BAT. Any technical expert figuring out what is happening in your PC will want to know what is in the AUTOEXEC.BAT file. This topic shows the file on screen, as in Figure 5-8.

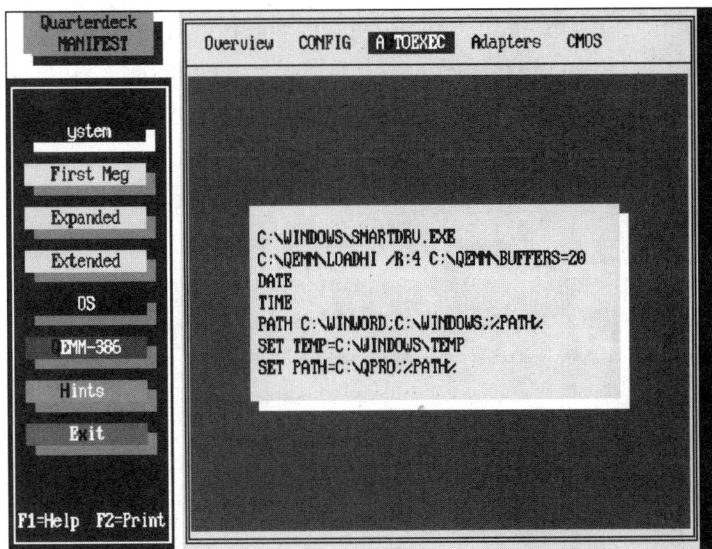

Figure 5-8. System AUTOEXEC topic screen

If an AUTOEXEC.BAT line is too long to show on screen, it wraps to the next line. Manifest shows this with an ellipsis (...) at the head of the additional lines.

Note that on PCs using DOS 2.0 to 3.3, Manifest uses the COMPSEC= environment variable to figure out the boot drive that will hold the CONFIG.SYS file. If this variable is wrong—for example, if you boot from a floppy disk and then change that floppy—you'll be looking at the wrong CONFIG.SYS file on screen. You can use the /B command-line switch mentioned at the beginning of this chapter to cure this problem.

System Adapters topic

This topic often covers several screens, because it tells you the type and memory use of the various peripheral adapters in your PC. These are the hardware and software packages that add to your PC, such as video display and disk drive adapters.

Figure 5-9 shows a typical video display adapter screen, with details on the type (VGA, color display) of the adapter. Here you'll also find the vital information on what memory addresses the adapter is using for its ROM (C000-C7FF) and its RAM (A000-AFFF when in graphics mode, B800-BFFF in text mode). This is vital for two reasons: You need to know what's used when you tell LOADHI where to put drivers and TSRs in upper memory; and you need to know what memory VIDRAM can steal from upper memory to add to conventional memory. (In this case the area from A000-AFFF could be used as long as you only used programs in text mode).

Figure 5-9. Typical Video Display Adapter screen

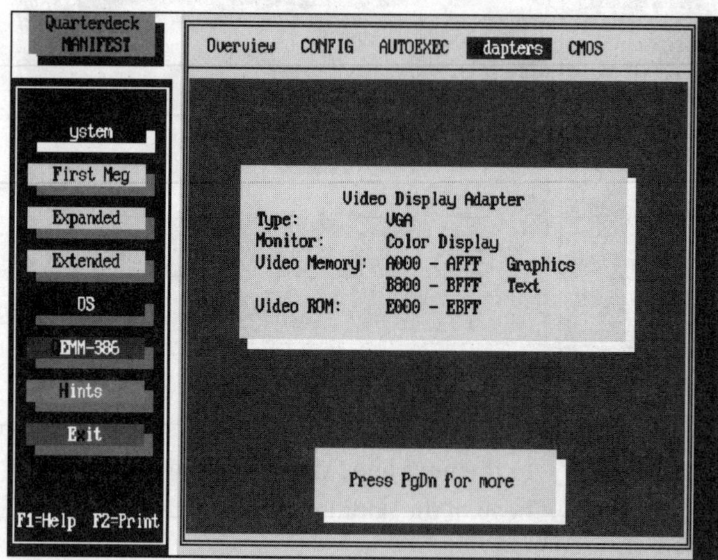

You can also use this screen if you have two video adapters in your PC and want to know if both are working. To see the other adapters in this topic, press the PgDn key.

In our example you'd first see Figure 5-10 (with details on the type and capacity of the disk drive adapters—"diskette" means floppy disk, "cyls" means cylinders, "sects," sectors).

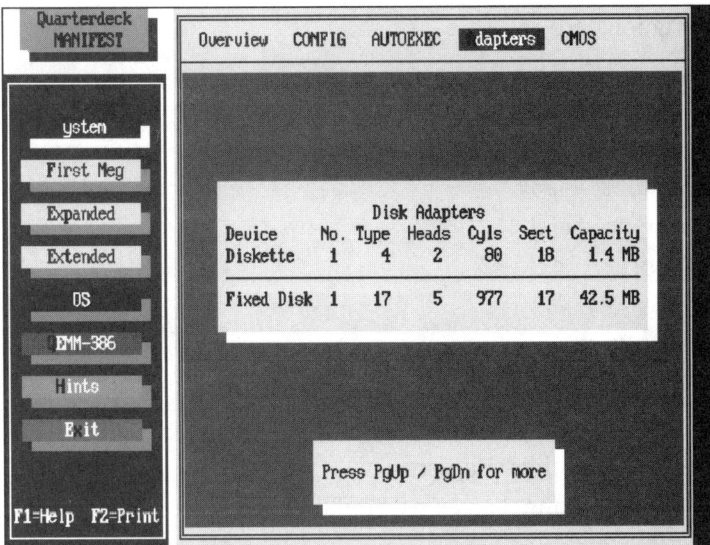

Figure 5-10. Example additional adapters screen

The reported capacity of disk drives is the physical capacity, not the partitions. Use of a disk utility program may corrupt the disk adapter information.

Next comes the information on ports. Figure 5-11 shows the details on serial and parallel adapters, the ports the PC uses to reach printers, modems, and so on. The port signals are active (*) or inactive (-).

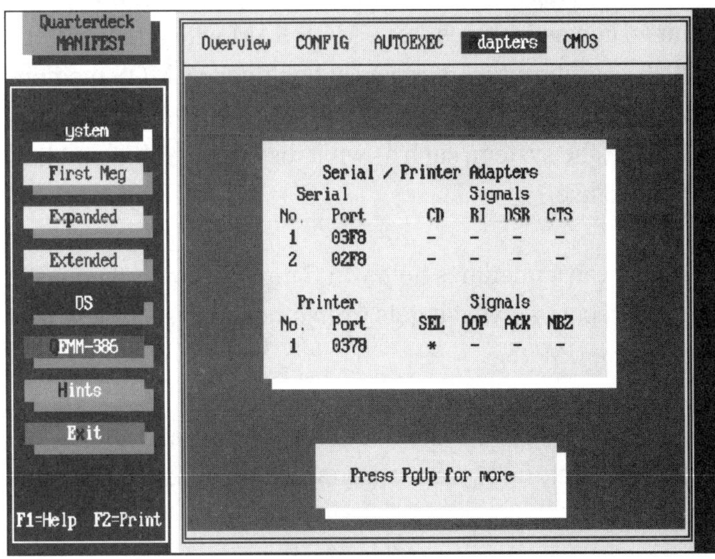

Figure 5-11. Serial and parallel adapter port details screen

The signal abbreviations are

```
CD ......Carrier Detect
RI ......Ring Indicator
DSR .....Data Set Ready
CTS .....Clear To Send
SEL .....Select
OOP .....Out of Paper
ACK  ....Acknowledge
NBZ .....Not Busy
```

Press PgUp to get back to other adapters.

On PS/2 or other Micro Channel systems, you'll see a screen of information about MCA adapters. This includes details from the MCA.ADL file on the slot number, device type number, identifying name, and area of memory used by each MCA adapter.

System CMOS topic

ROM memory chips only remember what was put into them at the factory. RAM chips can keep new information that is written to them by the computer. But RAM chips lose their information when their power supply is turned off. However, a special type of RAM chip called CMOS RAM needs very little power and so can hold information for a long time if attached to a tiny battery. Many PCs include a small amount—such as 64 bytes—of CMOS RAM with a tiny battery. (PCs with 8088 and 8086 microprocessors typically don't have CMOS memory and so won't show this topic.) They use this CMOS RAM to hold valuable configuration information about the system, such as what disk drives it has and how much memory it is set up to use.

This report can sometimes help you figure out contradictions in Manifest's reports—what it gets from other analyses and what it gets from the CMOS.

As you can see in Figure 5-12, the System CMOS topic screen shows you what is in your PC's CMOS. (Naturally, your screen will look different from this example, since you have a different PC than I.) This first format shows the information by topic. Press F3 and you can see it by memory address in the CMOS List, as in Figure 5-13. This is by address offset, meaning of the byte, and setting of the byte.

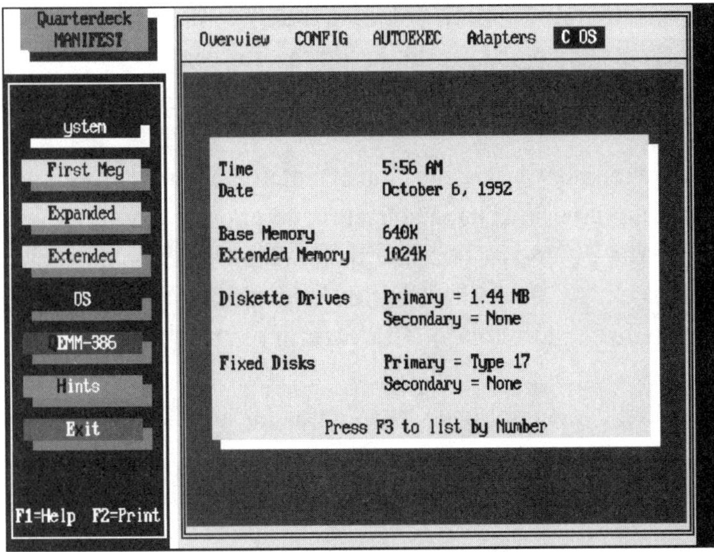

Figure 5-12. System CMOS topic screen, by topic

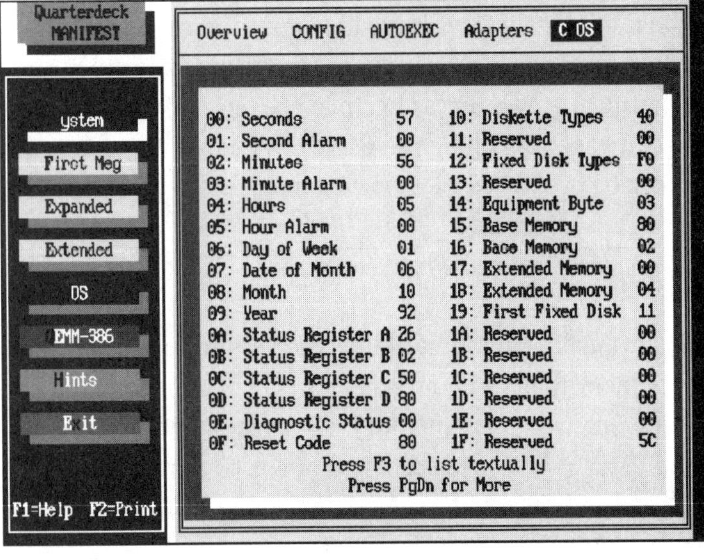

Figure 5-13. System CMOS topic screen, by list

It's a good idea to copy this information down somewhere, because when the battery fails (which could take years if it is new) or some oddball program attacks CMOS, the CMOS setup will be lost. Setting up again from a saved report is easier than setting up from nothing. PC Magazine published a pair of programs, CMOSGET.COM and CMOSPUT.COM, that do this for you. They are available on CompuServe. Also, many tool programs, such as PC Tools and Norton Utilities, do this for you.

First Meg category

The first megabyte of memory is the most important. It includes conventional memory (where most programs and DOS itself run) and upper memory (where the ROMs that support the PC and its peripherals reside, where the expanded memory page frame typically sits, and where QEMM puts drivers and TSRs from conventional memory to make more room). This category gives the lowdown on doings in the first meg of memory.

Remember that your PC may not have RAM chips for all of the addresses in the first meg. Some of these addresses may not have any chips at all, and some may have RAM or ROM from adapter boards, which cannot be used by typical programs.

First Meg Overview topic

This is a map of the first megabyte, arranged by hex address of area, size of area in K, and description of area use, as you can see in the example in Figure 5-14. It starts at 0 and goes up to 1024K. Press PgDn to see more of the map, right up to the 1024K limit and past, to include the 64K HMA (which is technically extended memory but can be used as conventional memory, as explained in Chapter 4). Figure 5-15 shows this upper area.

This first meg map is vital to loading high, as explained in Chapters 5, 7, and 15.

DESQview makes the First Meg screen show its memory area as all memory that a window can use, even that beyond the normal end of conventional memory. Also, all mappable areas outside of DESQview are hidden from programs running in DESQview and show in First Meg as "Unused."

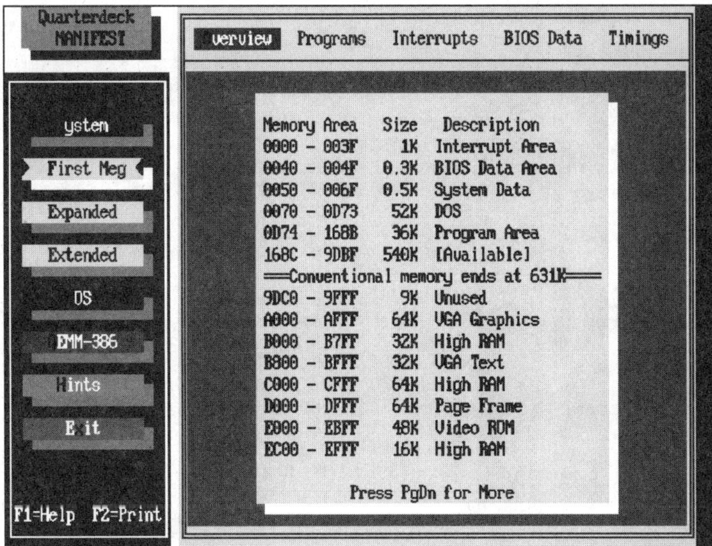

Figure 5-14. First Meg Overview screen

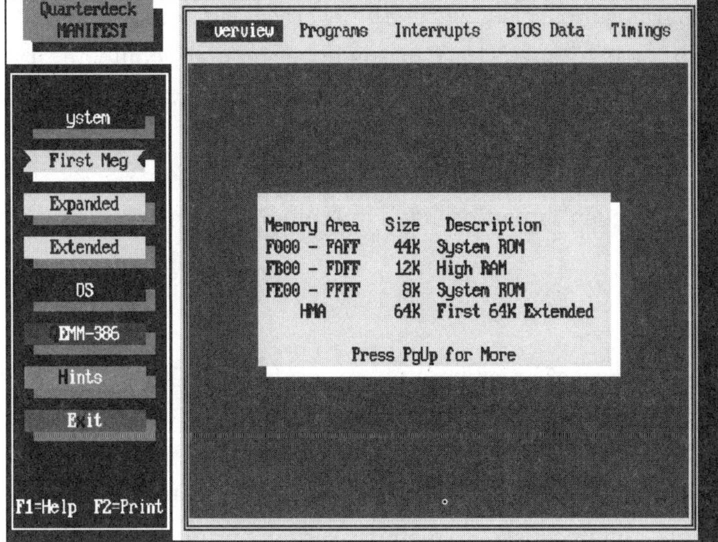

Figure 5-15. Extension portion of First Meg Overview

First Meg Programs topic

This topic gives you more detail on the programs running in memory, which may have just shown as Program in the map of the First Meg Overview topic. Figure 5-16 shows an example. (If Manifest can't find the name of the program in that area, it just calls it by the address of the area.)

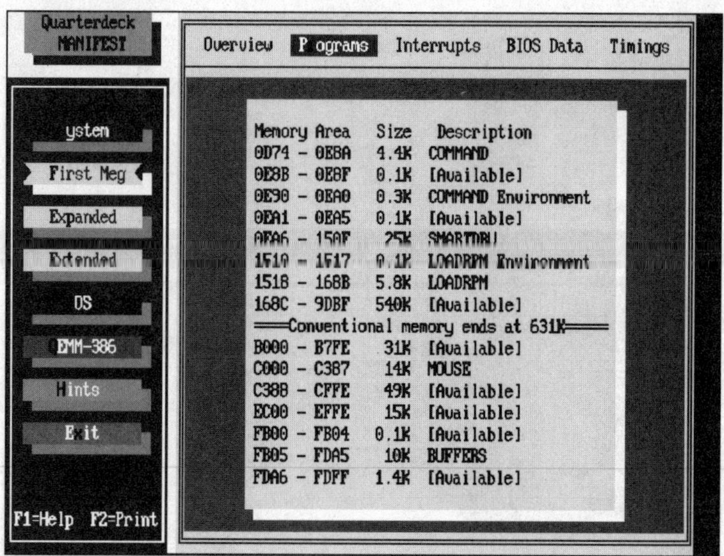

Figure 5-16.
First Meg Programs screen

The First Meg Programs topic also tells you what areas of memory are available for use, as you can see in Figure 5-16. Those in upper memory could be candidates from programs to relocate from conventional memory by loading high (see Chapters 5, 7, and 15).

Manifest doesn't mention itself in memory unless you leave it resident.

First Meg Interrupts topic

Interrupts are the PC's way of breaking off from one task to take on another, and then knowing how and where to return to the first task. The "where" is kept in memory interrupt vectors. If more than one program tries to use the same interrupt, a conflict could arise, leaving the wrong return information. This screen helps you identify such troubles, often caused by memory-resident programs (TSRs).

Interrupts can be listed two ways: by owners and by interrupt number. Figure 5-17 shows the owners list, which includes the programs, drivers, and ROMS with interrupt services and the interrupt numbers they handle. Press F3 to see the interrupt number list, which includes the numbers and the names of the programs or drivers using them. Interrupts from C0 to FF aren't given program identities because they are rarely used.

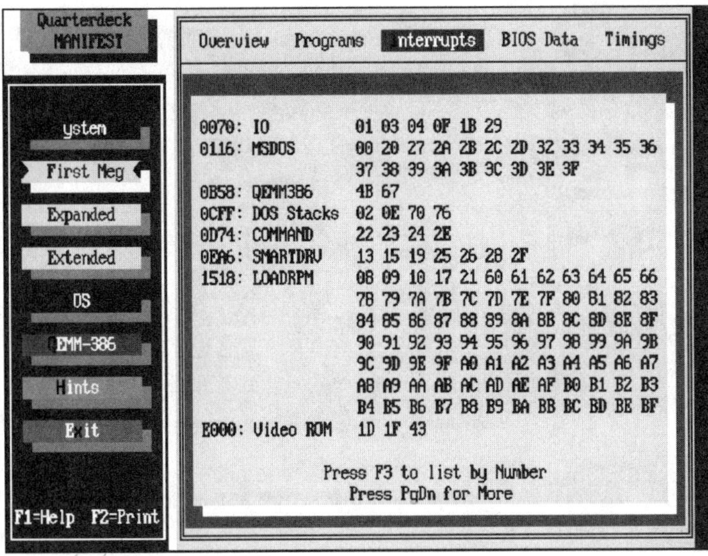

Figure 5-17.
Owner list for First Meg interrupts

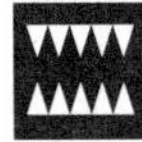

The lists show only the most recent user of the interrupt. Other programs also may be using any of the interrupts. (This is known as "cascading.")

On a color display, programs and drivers are cyan, DOS and ROMS white.

Press PgDn to see more of either list. (The interrupt number list goes on for 16 screens—you can leap to any one of these by pressing Alt-X, where X is the first digit of the hex interrupt number.)

First Meg BIOS Data topic

The BIOS ROM holds fundamental instructions for the PC. These instructions must grab some RAM area to hold changing information for their work—their scratchpad area. This BIOS Data area, typically 172 bytes, is displayed in the First Meg BIOS Data screen, as in Figure 5-18. Here you'll see the addresses, the data description, and the values currently stored. The values will change as DOS and BIOS work (although you won't see these changes unless you press the Space Bar to update the display).

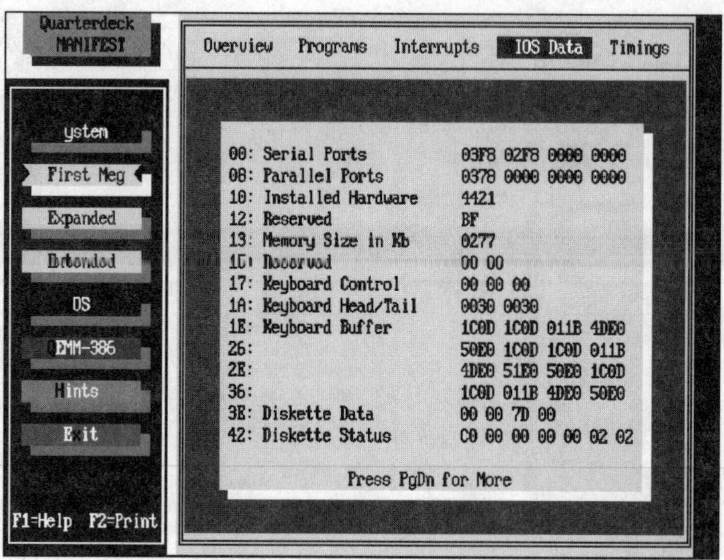

Figure 5-18.
First Meg BIOS Data screen

Some PCs have an extended BIOS segment to hold more data. Typically this is at 0E and replaces a fourth parallel port, limiting such PCs to 639K of conventional memory. QEMM relocates this data automatically.

First Meg Timings topic

Not all RAM runs at the same speed. ROMs are typically the slowest because they work 8 bits at a time, where PC RAM runs at 8 bits, AT at 16 bits (twice as fast), and 386 at 32 bits (four times as fast), followed by adapter RAM. The First Meg Timings topic tests the speed of your RAM and reports it as shown in Figure 5-19. The memory area tested, its speed in kilobytes accessed per second, and how that compares to a typical XT's speed are shown in the table.

Memory speed can vary by 10% or so from one measurement to the next. Don't worry about such changes

You can use these speed measurements to see how fast your PC is in general, to see how much a cache is helping memory speed (the cache will be listed and named as such), to inspect the performance boost of Shadow RAM, and to consider QEMM's ability with the ROM switch to move ROM information to RAM (see Chapter 6).

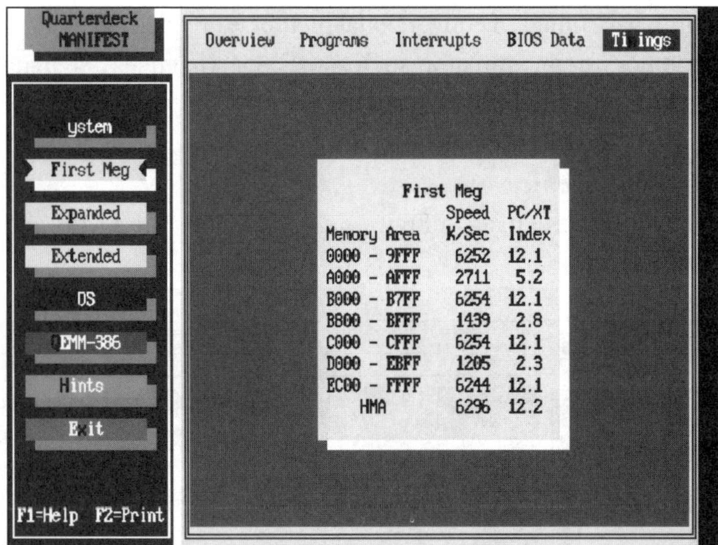

Figure 5-19.
First Meg Timings

If your ROM memory is listed at RAM speed, it is probably already mapped into RAM by the system.

Expanded Memory category

This category tells you how much expanded memory is in your PC and how it is being used. Expanded memory is vital to some programs, such as many spreadsheets. It is also the foundation material for DESQview's multitasking.

Expanded memory needs both special hardware and software. On 8088, 8086, and 80286-based PCs, expanded memory comes as an EMS or EEMS expanded memory board and an Expanded Memory Manager (EMM) driver program to support it. On PS/2 Model 50 or 60 systems with the 286 Memory Expansion Option or IBM 80286 Expanded Memory Adapter/A or compatible systems, only an EMM program is necessary. On 386 and 486-based PCs, only an EMM is necessary because the processor has the circuits to handle expanded memory mapping.

The PC works with expanded memory through a page frame area in memory. It maps pages of the expanded memory to the addresses of the page frame, attaching "handles" to the pages so it can recall them when needed. (See Chapter 4 for more details on expanded memory.)

Many LIMulator programs that convert extended memory into expanded memory make EMS memory that is too slow for anything more than storing data.

If you want multitasking, backfilling of conventional memory, or video filling, you need real expanded memory or an emulator, such as QEMM, that uses 386 mapping abilities to make fast expanded memory.

Expanded Memory Overview topic

The Expanded Overview screen, as in Figure 5-20, describes the EMM and the expanded memory in your PC.

Figure 5-20. Expanded Memory Overview

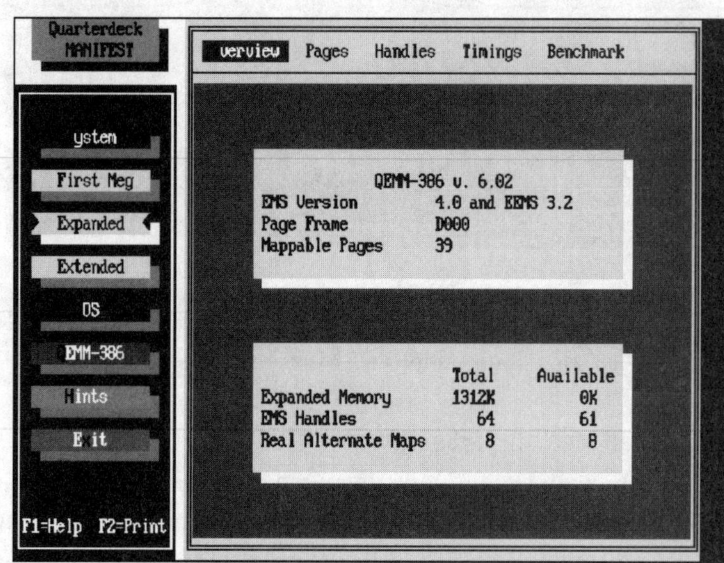

On top you'll see the EMM information:

EMS Version ....which specification the EMM follows (or no name if it can't be figured—such as the Intel Aboveboard's EMM)

Page Frame..............the address of the frame

Mappable Pages ....the number of 16K pages you can page—more means better multitasking (DESQview running will limit this to 4)

On the bottom of the screen you'll see the total and available (not yet used) expanded memory in your PC:

Expanded Memory.......the actual memory (with EMS 4.0, conventional memory that is mappable is counted twice, as conventional and expanded)

EMS Handles.................the handles the EMM can carry—more means more flexibility in giving expanded memory to programs (EMS 3.2 can't report available handles—those unused)

Real Alternate Maps......the number of alternate maps available—real means from hardware, not the software simulated maps that don't work as quickly (QEMM offers eight by default)

Naturally this screen only reports if your PC has both expanded memory and a working EMM.

If Manifest crashes when you try for the Expanded Memory topic, there could be a bug in the EMM or in a TSR that uses EMS calls.

Expanded Memory Pages topic

This topic shows a map of the expanded memory uses of the first megabyte of memory, as in Figure 5-21. Again, it only shows if you have expanded memory and an EMM.

The table at the top right of the screen summarizes the mappable pages of expanded memory, with their addresses, sizes, and logical page numbers (the page frame always gets numbers 0 through 3).

The table on the left details which 16K pages of the first megabyte are mappable (+), unmappable (U), or in the page frame (F). Mappable memory includes backfilled conventional memory addresses. Unmappable memory includes areas converted by QEMM into high memory for loading high and areas below the backfill boundary of your PC (typically 256K). Page frame memory is the area for mapping converted by programs that support EMS 3.2. Those that support EMS 4.0 can use any of the mappable areas.

PS/2 Model 50 and 60 systems can disable all motherboard memory, which is great for multitasking but means that memory just sits idle.

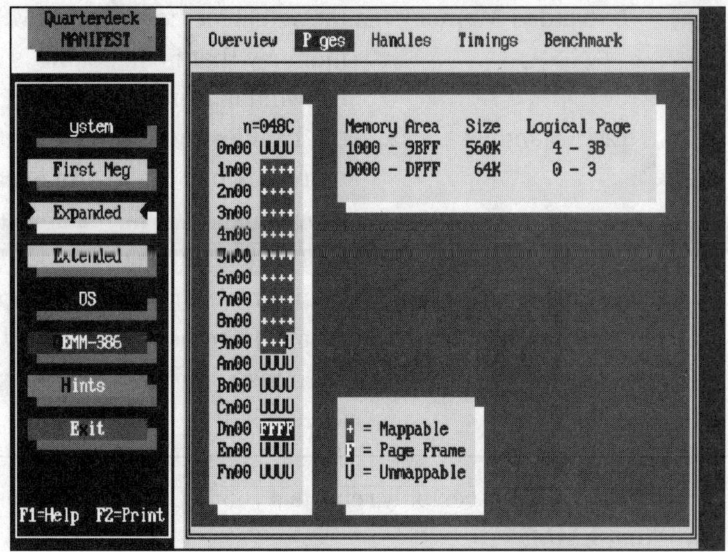

Figure 5-21. Expanded Memory Pages screen

If you install some device in an area of mappable memory, that device may not work; when it wants to run it might not find its driver.

For best DESQview multitasking, have as much memory as possible mappable, which means as much EMS 4.0 support—in hardware and software—as possible. You can get full 4.0 support on any 386 or 486 system with QEMM.

Expanded Memory Handles topic

This topic simply lists the current EMS handles by number (from 0 to 255 in EMS 4.0), amount of memory allocated to it, and any program that has named a handle. This is useful when you need to know which programs are using expanded memory and how much they use. Figure 5-22 is an example.

DESQview lets you limit how much expanded memory a program can grab—so you can use this topic to find out if a program is using too much and then adjust it in DESQview.

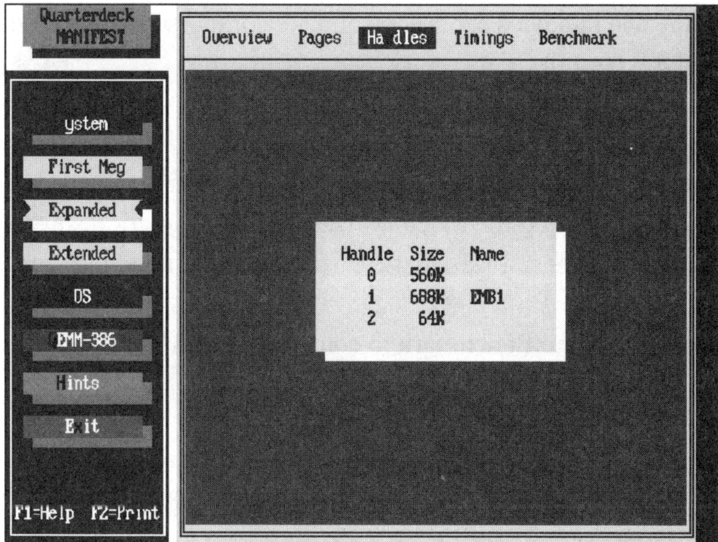

Figure 5-22. Expanded Memory Handles screen

Expanded Memory Timings topic

This topic, as in the example of Figure 5-23, tests the speed of your expanded memory. You could use this to see if its worth moving your ROM instructions into expanded memory, using QEMM's ROM option. (Compare the speeds here to the ROM speeds from the First Meg Timings topic.) Remember that speed may vary up to 10% from one test to the next.

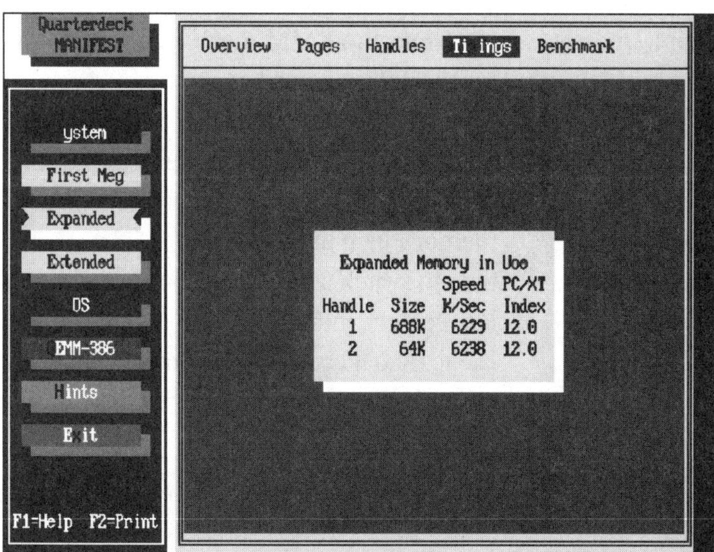

Figure 5-23. Expanded Memory Timings screen

The speeds are shown in kilobytes per second and are compared to the speed of memory in a typical XT (as 1.0).

Expanded Memory Benchmark topic

This topic also tests speed of your expanded memory, along with the Expanded Timings topic. But instead of testing the memory itself, the Benchmark tests the expanded memory manager—the software that controls your expanded memory.

You could use the Benchmark to compare two EMMs, to figure out which one is faster to use.

The Benchmark lists the maximum, minimum, and average times in microseconds to perform some typical tasks. Shorter times mean faster work.

Not only does this test need expanded memory and an EMM to run, but also it uses 64K of expanded memory itself. A blank row means your EMM doesn't support a particular task or that your EMM is out of handles for that task.

The Benchmark numbers will keep changing as more tests are made—eventually they'll settle down.

The tests are:

Timer Interrupt Latency........how long the EMM disables interrupts—below 500 is allowed

Map Single Page.....................time to map a single page of expanded memory—a critical measurement because this is perhaps the most common expanded memory instruction.

Real Alternate Map Set ....time to switch a map—critical for multitasking, such as in DESQview—this plus timer latency should be below 500 for smooth background 9600 bps communications

Save All—nn pages................time to save all EMS pages

Map Multiple—nn pages ....time to map all pages

Restore All—nn pages ....time to restore all pages

Save Page Frame....................time to save state of page frame
Restore Page Frame...............time to restore the state of the page frame
Open Handle—4 pages..........time to open an EMS handle with 4 pages
Close Handle—4 pages..........time to close EMS handle with 4 pages
Open Handle—31 pages........time to open EMS handle with 31 pages
Close Handle—31 pages........time to close EMS handle with 31 pages

When comparing EMM performances, make sure you're comparing the same nn number of pages saved, mapped, or so on.

Using both Add Save All and Restore All gives you a feel for how quickly the EMM could multitask without real alternate maps.

Using both Save Page Frame and Restore Page Frame gives you a feel for how quickly the EMM could map the page frame for a TSR or device driver's work—faster means better performance from disk caches in expanded memory.

Extended Memory category

This category tells you how much extended memory is in your PC and some of the details of the driver that controls it.

Extended Overview topic

As you can see in Figure 5-24, this topic simply shows a map of extended memory use. It tells you the

Memory Area (by beginning and ending address)
Size (in KB)
Status (used from the bottom up, from the top down, or still available for use)

Some programs—such as VDISK and QEXT—start their extended memory use at the 1024K bottom and count higher. Others—such as QEMM and DOS extenders—start their extended memory use at the top and count down.

Figure 5-24. Extended Memory Overview screen

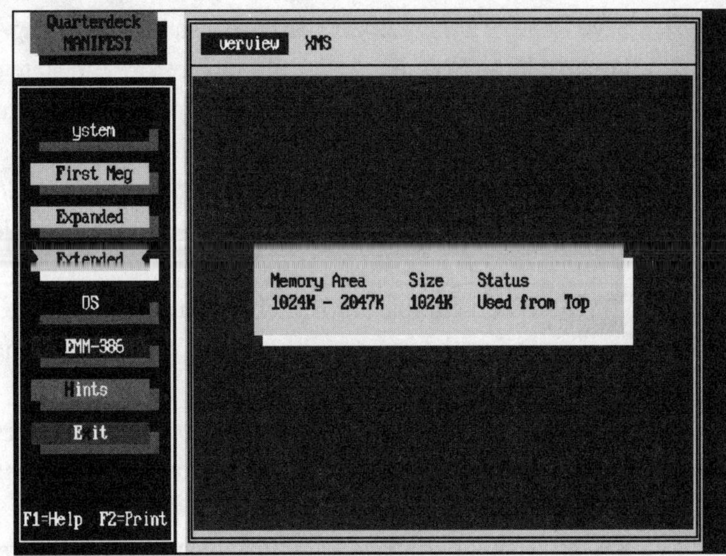

Some programs—such as AST's FASTDISK.SYS—are hard to detect in extended memory and so won't appear on Manifest maps and can conflict with other programs.

Extended XMS topic

This topic tells you about the XMS (Extended Memory Specification) driver program that was loaded from CONFIG.SYS to control extended memory. This could be QEMM, QEXT, or HIMEM.SYS.

QEXT didn't support XMS until QEXT version 2.26.

As you can see in the example of Figure 5-25, the XMS driver and its work are explained by

XMS Version.................the number of the specification
Driver Revision.............the number of the particular program
High Memory Area.......the status of the HMA, the first 64K of extended memory above 1024K that can be used as conventional memory (see Chapter 4 for details)

A20 ....the status of the A20 address line, which must be enabled to use the HMA and extended memory (see Chapter 4 for details)

Handles Available..........each block of extended memory used has an assigned handle

Memory Block Type.....Upper (UMBs) refers to pieces of extended memory mapped into the upper memory area from 640K to 1024K, areas that can be used by QEMM for loading high TSRs and drivers

Extended (EMBs) ....refers to extended memory not mapped into upper memory locations or used as HMA

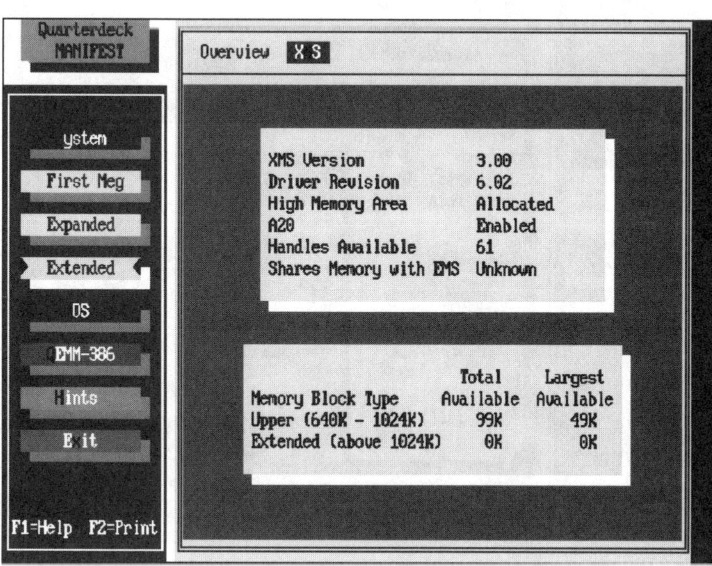

Figure 5-25. Extended Memory XMS screen

You may need to restrict the grasp of some programs that request all available extended memory, which will exhaust both extended and (if you're using QEMM) expanded memory that any other programs might want.

Windows 286 Version 2 can request the HMA, as can DESQview, so running these two programs may cause a warning message about this. Don't worry about the message; avoid it by configuring either program not to take the HMA.

DOS category

DOS uses memory. It puts its own kernel, drivers, and temporary data into memory. How much memory it uses and where in memory it puts these items is partially under your control, largely through the statements you put in the CONFIG.SYS and AUTOEXEC.BAT files. To know what DOS is doing, and to adjust its behavior you can use this category of Manifest.

DOS Overview topic

Naturally this topic summarizes what Manifest can tell you about DOS's use of memory. As in the example of Figure 5-26, you'll see two tables on screen.

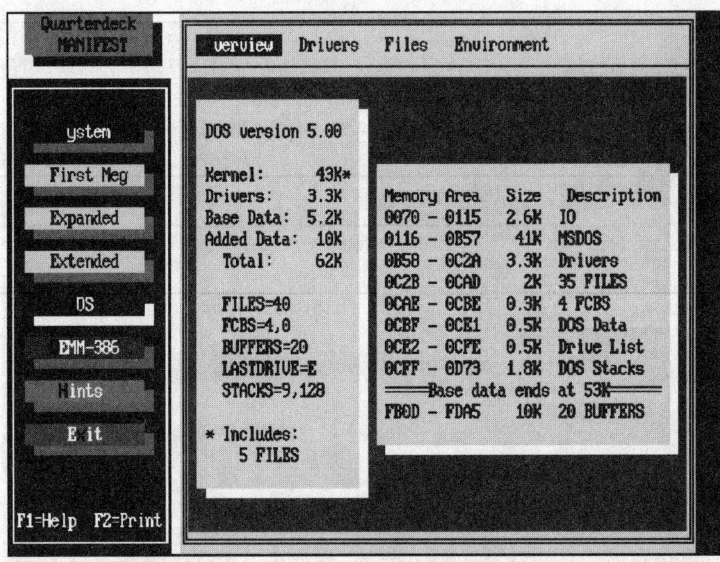

Figure 5-26. DOS Overview screen

On the left is a description of the DOS version you're using, along with the amount of memory taken by each of its purposes. This is followed by a list of the DOS statements—from CONFIG.SYS or the default values—that dictate these memory uses.

These are the listings:

DOS version..........the number of the DOS you're using (as explained in Chapter 4, the different generations of DOS use different amounts of memory)

Kernel....................how much memory the central core of DOS uses (for PC-DOS this is IBMBIO and IBMDOS for PC-DOS, IO.SYS and MSDOS.SYS for MS-DOS), plus those items listed in the "INCLUDES" section, below

Drivers..................The amount of memory used by the programs that extend DOS, the ones loaded with DEVICE statements in CONFIG.SYS

Base Data..............The amount of memory used by the DOS resources—those loaded in CONFIG.SYS statements such as FILES= and the defaults—use

Added Data.............how much memory the DOS SHARE program and QEMM or QRAM's BUFFERS and FILES programs use

Total.......................how much memory all the above DOS purposes take

FILES=...................a maximum number for the files that can be open simultaneously—each additional file means another 53 bytes

FCBs=....................file control blocks, each takes 53 bytes (only work in DOS 3.0 and later) and are important if you have a network server system

BUFFERS=............how many disk buffers to speed disk performance, each takes 528 bytes

LASTDRIVE=........the last permitted letter for a disk drive, each after E takes 81 bytes

STACKS= ....the amount of memory for handling hardware interrupts, more stacks eat more memory (only work in DOS 3.1 and later)

Includes.................any use of memory included with the kernel measurement above (some versions of DOS include some BUFFERS and FILES area in the kernel)

The table on the right lists the actual areas used by DOS. This memory map lists

Memory Area (by beginning and ending address)

Size (of the area, in K)

Description (what part of DOS, what DOS program, is using the area)

Remember that you can often cut DOS's use of conventional memory by loading parts of DOS high, as explained in Chapters 9 and 15.

DOS Drivers topic

This topic tells you all about your PC's drivers—those little programs that help DOS understand and control various hardware added to the system. There are mouse drivers, network drivers, and memory drivers. There are also some standard drivers built into the DOS kernel, such as the drivers for the serial and parallel ports.

All drivers are part of the device driver chain. This chain is shown from its first driver—typically the NUL device—to last, as in the example of Figure 5-27.

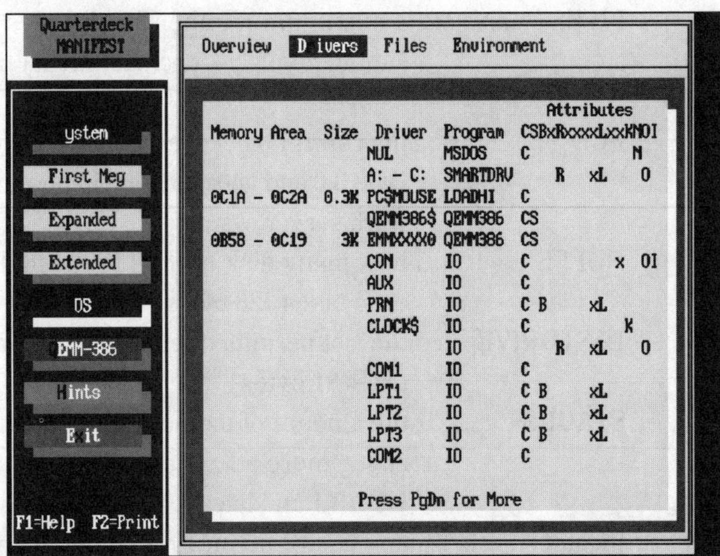

Figure 5-27.
DOS Drivers screen

For each driver you'll see listings for

Driver (the name of the driver)
Program (the name of the driver program)
Attributes (16 bits of information that tell about the driver's abilities)

Here are the meanings of those bits (X bits means nothing):

C...........a character or block device
S...........supports the standard DOS I/O control calls
B...........supports output until a device is busy
R...........supports removable media such as floppy or CD-ROM drives
L...........supports logical drives
K...........a clock device
N..........a NUL device
O..........the standard output device
I............the standard input device

For drivers specified in CONFIG.SYS you'll also see this information:

Memory Area (beginning and ending address)
Size (the amount of memory taken)

You don't see this information for the standard drivers, those that are part of the DOS kernel.

Some drivers are loaded by memory-resident programs. These won't have memory addresses in the driver chain list here, but you can find more about them by looking to the First Meg analysis by Manifest.

Some drivers remove themselves from the chain, and so won't appear in this list.

Drivers loaded into high memory by QEMM's LOADHI.SYS driver won't show their addresses here—the address will only be for LOADHI.SYS itself. See the First Meg analysis for more details on memory use by the particular driver.

DOS Files topic

This topic digs deeper into the FILES and FCBs, those DOS resources that use memory (see Chapter 10 for details). As you can see in Figure 5-28, it not only displays the number of FILES and FCBs specified (which set the maximum possible), but lists the actual files open (with their names, filename extensions, and the names of the programs opening the files). Note that the standard AUX, CON, and PRN devices are always open as standard files.

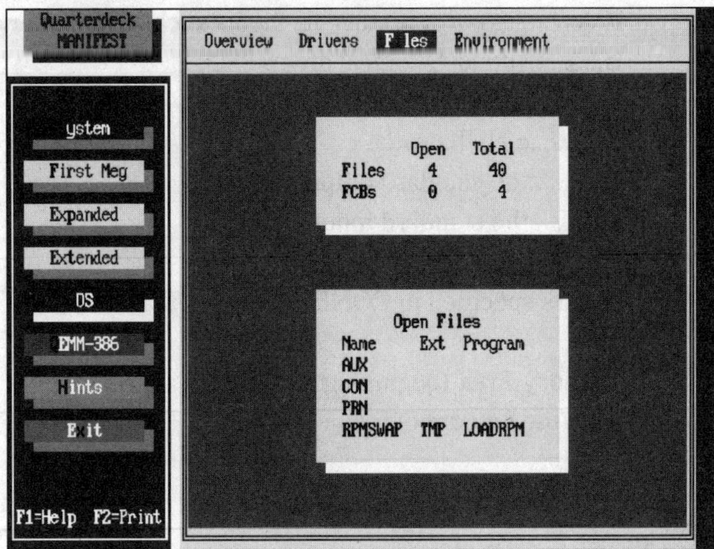

Figure 5-28.
DOS Files screen

This is useful when you want to minimize the necessary FILES setting to save memory and when you face conflicts by programs using FCBs.

Manifest on a networked PC shows the files opened only on that PC, not those opened on other parts of the network. For a node that means the files open on that node. For a server, that means the files opened by the server on the server and by any node on the server.

An “Unknown” label on an open file probably means a bug has left a file marked open when it is actually not in use. This file won’t be usable until the PC is rebooted.

FCBs can be reused in some circumstances, thus confusing the programs that use them.

DOS Environment topic

This topic tells you what is in the DOS environment, that area of memory DOS uses to store its own variable names and the values for those names. These variables perform such services as

- tell DOS where the vital COMMAND.COM program is
- tell DOS the PATH to follow when looking for files
- set up the DOS prompt you see on screen

DESQview lets you set up different environments in different windows using batch files. Manifest will report on the environment of the window it is in.

At the bottom of the screen, as in the example of Figure 5-29, you'll see the actual statements that make up the environment. At the top you'll see the memory this occupies, both how much room DOS started with for the environment, and how much of that is still available for more variables and values. (You can increase the total set aside for the environment with a DOS command.)

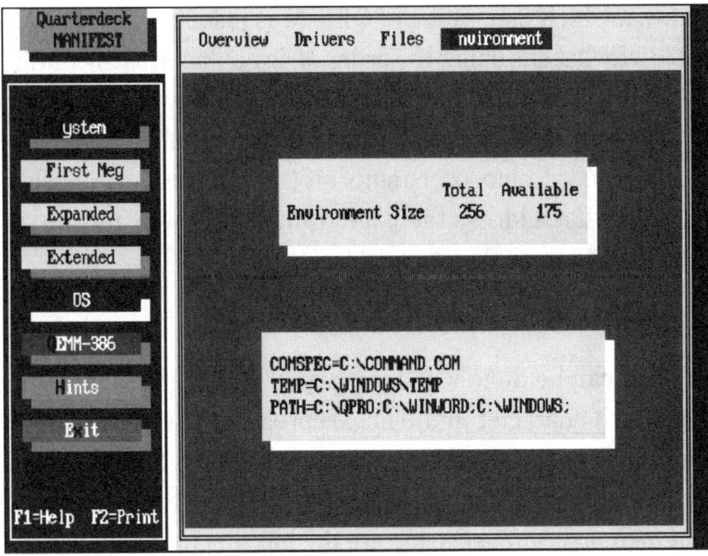

Figure 5-29. DOS Environment screen

Making a larger environment takes up more memory, not only because the environment occupies some hundreds of bytes, but also because every program in memory is given its own copy of the environment, multiplying a large environment's impact.

QEMM-386 category

If you have QEMM-386 installed in your 386 or 486 PC, you can see this category in Manifest. It details what QEMM does to

- convert extended memory into expanded memory
- map extended memory into upper memory addresses
- load TSRs and drivers into upper memory

This category also suggests ways to better use QEMM.

QEMM-386 Overview topic

This topic summarizes what QEMM is doing for your PC's memory. As you can see in Figure 5-30, you'll learn about

QEMM version ......which generation of QEMM is installed
QEMM status ....what it is doing (by order of any options installed with it by you or by OPTIMIZE); whether it is making expanded memory, upper memory
Mode ....on, off, auto/on, or auto/off (see Chapter 7 for details.)
Page Frame ....what address the page frame is at (none means no page frame, not no address)

QEMM-386 Type topic

QEMM's view of what can be done with memory is shown here, as in the example of Figure 5-31. Each character in the map represents that state of a 4K chunk of memory, the smallest unit QEMM can work with. On the left side of the map is a column of addresses, each referring to the beginning of a 64K segment of the first megabyte of memory. Across the top are the hexadecimal address values for the sixteen 4K parts of that 64K segment.

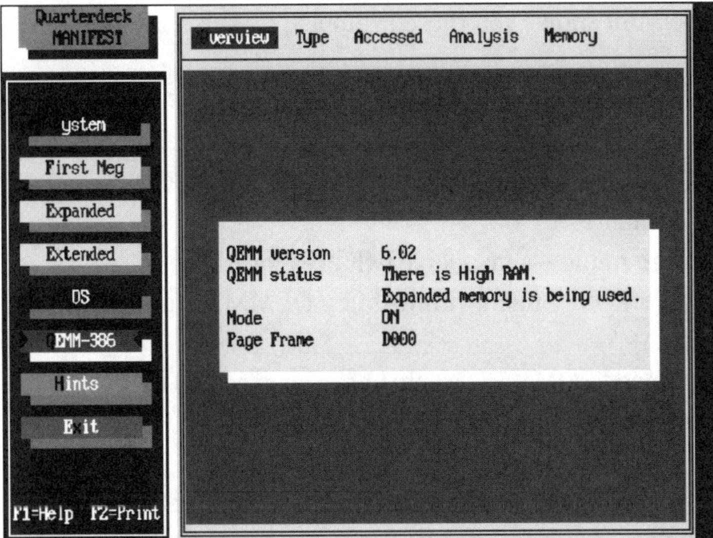

Figure 5-30. QEMM-386 Overview screen

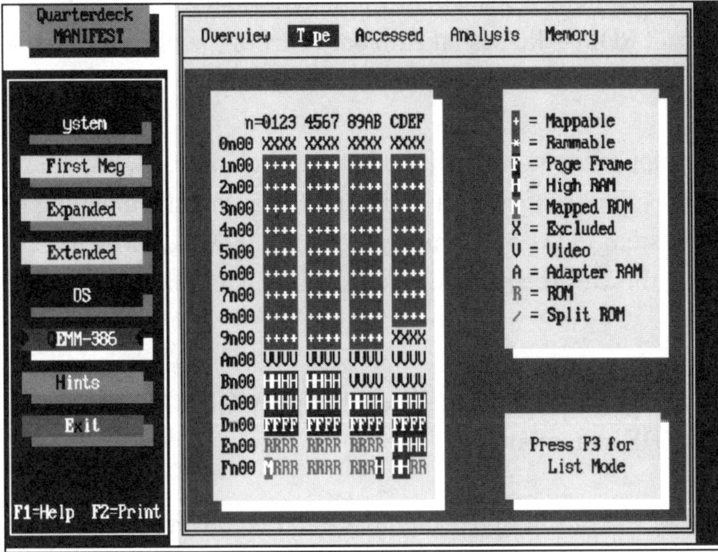

Figure 5-31. QEMM-386 Type screen

The legend on the right shows you these symbols:

+ ......means mappable—areas of at least 16K, aligned on 16K boundaries, that can be mapped with EMS calls
* ......means RAMable—mappable by QEMM but not as EMS because it is smaller than 16K
F......means page frame—a mappable 64K area for EMS
H.....means high RAM—filled with RAM by QEMM, so useful for loading high
M.....means mapped ROM—ROMs that have been copied to RAM to run faster and then mapped to their original addresses
X......means excluded—areas the EXCLUDE option keeps from QEMM's use to avoid conflicts with devices that need that memory
V......means video—areas for the video buffer
A......means adapter RAM—areas for adapter cards other than video
R......means ROM—ROMs not remapped by QEMM's ROM switch
/.......means split ROM—ROMs take up only part of the 4K area, so the QEMM ROM switch can't remap this

Mapped ROM can appear even without the ROM switch on the QEMM line in CONFIG.SYS, both as the 4K of system ROM and the automatic mapping of the video ROM and system ROM on Compaq Deskpro 386s. (QEMM has to because the otherwise the Deskpro would remap for itself and not do as good a job of it.)

0000 to 0FFF is automatically excluded by QEMM, without an EXCLUDE statement.

Any + or * areas in upper memory can be converted into H by adding the RAM switch to the QEMM line in CONFIG.SYS (see Chapter 6).

You can also see the QEMM map of memory possibilities in a different format, as a simple list of memory areas from 0 to 1024K. Press the F3 key and you'll see this list, as in Figure 5-32, detailing

Memory Area ....beginning and ending addresses of the areas
Size ....size in K
Status ....status of the area, as from the symbol list above

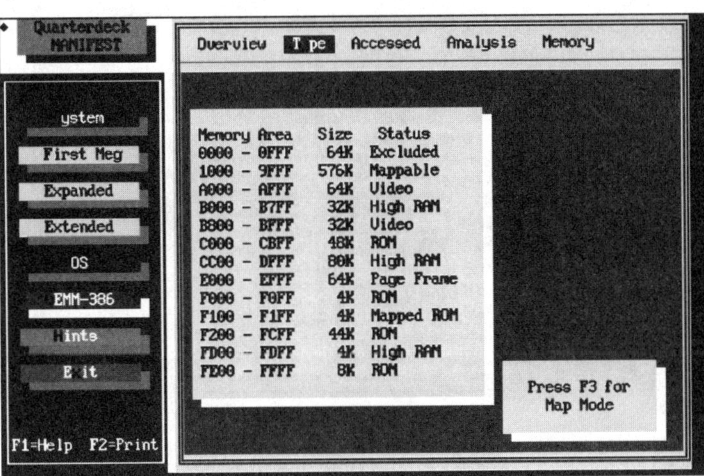

Figure 5-32. QEMM-386 Type screen in list format

QEMM-386 Accessed topic

Here you see how memory has been used. QEMM monitors the first megabyte of memory and can show you whether each 4K chunk has been

A (Accessed) ....read from by some program
W (Written) ....written to by some program
U (Unaccessed) ....neither read or written by any program since the PC was booted

Figure 5-33 shows an example.

This map is extremely useful because you can deduce from it how large programs are—how much memory they access—and what areas of memory are lying unused. Unused areas above 640K could conceivably be converted into UMBs for loading high.

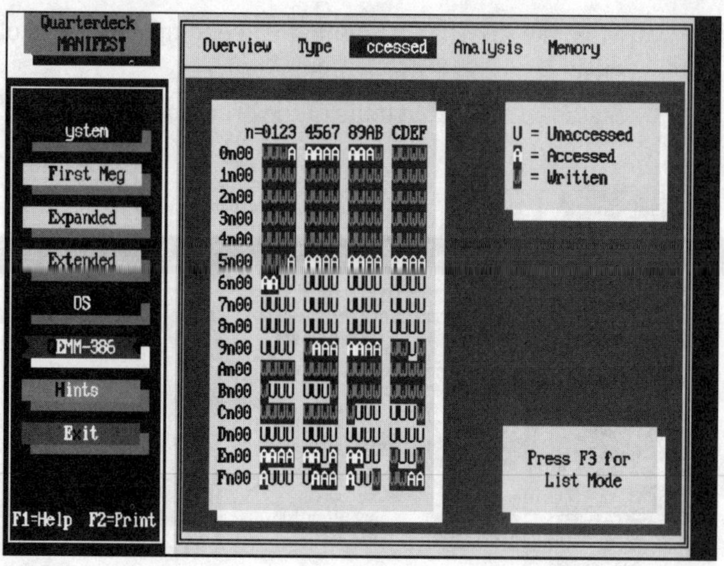

Figure 5-33. QEMM-386 Accessed screen

Don't trust the A, W, and U status of areas that are mappable memory (see the QEMM-386 Type map above). Mapping makes memory look unaccessed even when it has been read from or written to.

You can also see the access history of memory as a memory list by pressing F3, as in Figure 5-34.

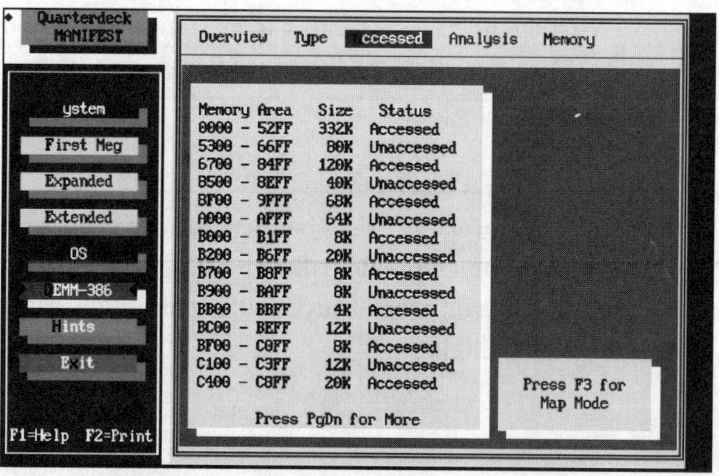

Figure 5-34. QEMM-386 Accessed screen in list format

QEMM-386 Analysis topic

Here you find QEMM's ideas about what memory you should and should not put to use. This comes from Manifest watching what your programs do and what memory they access. Therefore, before you use this map, you must run those programs to give Manifest some experience. Follow this analysis procedure, and don't run any memory utilities other than Manifest while you do:

1. Make sure the QEMM line in CONFIG.SYS has the ON switch and the MAPS=0 switch, and no others.
2. Save CONFIG.SYS and reboot the PC.
3. Run your programs and use all their abilities.
4. Start DESQview and then immediately quit from it—without running any programs in it. (Do this only if you want to use DESQview.)
5. Use all your computer hardware, from video displays to disk drives, printer, and network interfaces. Be sure to format floppy disks in each floppy drive.
6. Run Manifest.
7. Move to the QEMM-386 category and the Analysis topic.
8. Put the EXCLUDE and INCLUDE suggestions from the map into the QEMM line in CONFIG.SYS, and take out the ON switch and the MAPS=0 switch.
9. Reboot the PC.
10. For best results, repeat the process until the alternate analysis list (press F3) shows simply "0000-FFFF 1024K OK."

The map, as in the example of Figure 5-35, shows the first megabyte of memory in your PC. Along the left side are the 64K segment addresses, in hexadecimal. Along the top are the additional hex addresses for each 4K chunk within those segments.

Within this map the symbols mean

O (OK) .... memory you can use
X (Exclude) ...... memory you should exclude from QEMM's use (this is memory that QEMM didn't exclude already because it was mistakenly believed OK to use)

I (Include) ....memory you should use the INCLUDE switch to let QEMM put to work

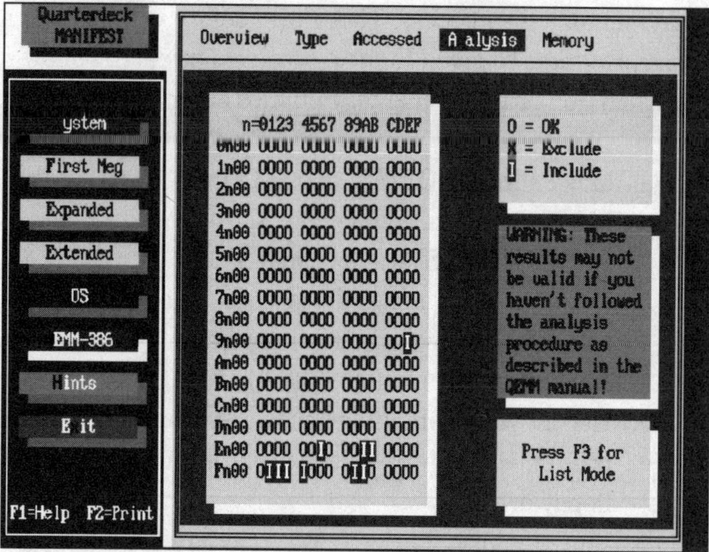

Figure 5-35. QEMM-386 Analysis screen

You can also press F3 to see the map as a list of memory areas. Figure 5-36 is an example.

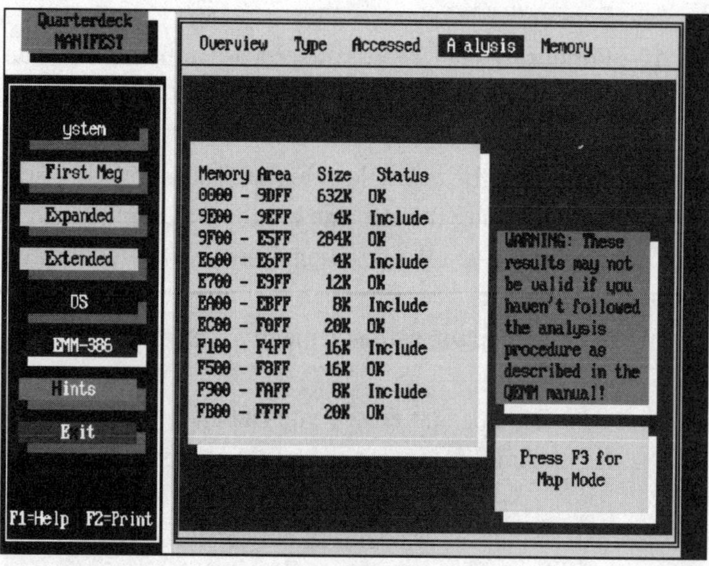

Figure 5-36. QEMM-386 Analysis screen in list format

QEMM-386 Memory topic

The Accessed topic tells you what memory has been used, the Analysis topic tells you what QEMM thinks you should do with memory, and now the Memory topic tells you what QEMM has done to configure memory.

In the top table, as in the example of Figure 5-37, you see the amounts of conventional, extended, top, or Shadow RAM and expanded and high RAM in your PC. You also see how QEMM changed these amounts from the initial state, through the amounts unavailable to QEMM (because a driver loaded before QEMM got it or its Shadow RAM, which QEMM can't use) and the amounts converted by QEMM, to the final leaving state.

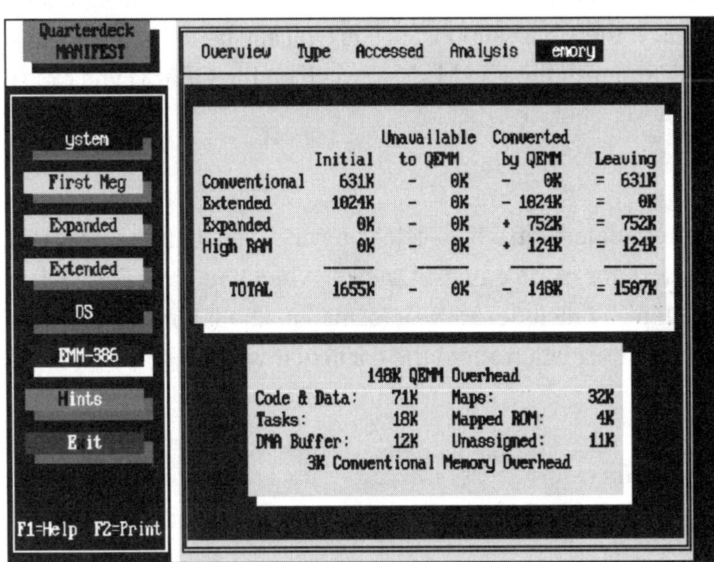

Figure 5-37. QEMM-386 Memory screen

If any of these numbers seems wrong, you could have a wrong entry in the CMOS setup information or even a loose or defective memory chip.

In the bottom table of Figure 5-37, you see how much memory QEMM used for itself to perform the conversions listed in the top table. QEMM needs memory for its code and data, maps, tasks, DMA buffer, mapped ROM, and even a bit of conventional memory overhead. (A little QEMM stays in conventional memory.) Unassigned memory is memory left over after QEMM's work, and memory that isn't at least the 16K needed to become more EMS memory. You can fine-tune QEMM's switches to use up some of the unassigned memory or to free more until a full 16K is available so it can become expanded memory.

Top memory is something you find in some Compaq PCs; Shadow RAM is found on PCs with Chips & Technologies chip sets. See Chapter 4 for more details.

If a program needs extended memory and supports the EMS, XMS, or VCPI specifications, then QEMM can allocate memory to them even when no extended memory is officially left. If they don't support it, it is typically better to leave some extended memory for them with the EXTMEM= switch on the QEMM line rather than by loading their drivers before QEMM.

DESQview category

DESQview lets you multitask on a PC—lets you run more than one program at a time. (See Chapter 16 for more on DESQview.) When you have DESQview running on your PC, Manifest includes some information about it in a DESQview category. Manifest gives information about the particular window in which Manifest is running.

DESQview Overview topic

The summary of DESQview information in the Overview topic includes:

DESQview version......................the version number of the program you're using
DESQview window number.......the number of the window Manifest is running within
Window memory size................the memory size of the window
Window max height...................the maximum height of the window
Window max width.....................the maximum width of the window
Window height...........................the current height of the window

Window width ....the current width of the window
Window row ....the current row position on screen of the window
Window column ....the current column position on screen of the window

You can change the memory size of the window by using DESQview's Change a Program feature.

You can move the window Manifest is in, press the Space Bar to see the new current row and column positions, then fix those positions by using DESQview's Change a Program feature.

With DESQview 1.xx, only the version and memory size appears.

DESQview can load a lot of itself into high memory. Manifest's DESQview Memory Status screen can tell you if there is more upper memory than DESQview can use. Run Manifest as the only window in DESQview, then subtract the largest available conventional memory from the total available conventional memory. That's how much high memory can be used for loading TSRs or drivers without cutting into the conventional memory for DESQview windows.

DESQview needs real alternate maps, as diagnosed in Manifest's Expanded Memory category, to handle multitasking of high-speed communications programs. Without them it can lose characters when running in background—so you should at least open the communications program first. It also needs such maps to virtualize graphics and have protection. DESQview uses one for itself and one for each window opened.

QEMM can give you 32K more expanded memory if you set MAPS=0 in the QEMM CONFIG.SYS line. This doesn't work for DESQview, however. DESQview needs at least one map for itself, plus one map for each window.

DESQview Memory Status topic

The Memory Status topic for DESQview tells you about the memory DESQview can use. (You can see the same information in DESQview itself, in the Memory Status program.) This lets you decide what the largest program you can run is and how much expanded memory is available. Total memory is the amount of expanded memory you have when DESQview starts (and it may not all be contiguous). Total available memory is the amount still available for use. Largest available memory is the largest contiguous block available for use. Common memory is the memory DESQview uses for itself and its own utility programs. This is specified in DESQview's setup and is measure in bytes, not kilobytes. Conventional memory is the conventional and high (upper) memory in which DESQview can run programs, not including memory used by DESQview or taken before DESQview started. Expanded memory is memory managed by an Expanded Memory Manager.

If "0K" appears in the Largest Expanded Memory Available area, then there is no backfilled memory because it is all used or the system, EMM, or EMS board doesn't permit backfilling.

If the Common Memory Available section of the screen displays less than 1500, you may not be able to open more windows. Increasing common memory means decreasing conventional memory, however, so increase common memory only when necessary. If you have trouble opening a large window because there isn't enough memory, upgrade to at least DESQview 2.2, because that and later versions tell you how much more memory is necessary to get the window open.

Hints category

Perhaps you haven't made optimum use of memory. Manifest is watching and kindly lets you know if it thinks memory management could stand some improvement.

As in the example of Figure 5-38, the Hints category tells you in its Overview what you can do to get more from memory. Then its Details screen of Figure 5-39 explains how to do it. A separate Detail screen appears for each suggested improvement. Each screen tells you why you would do something, why you might choose not to make the change, and how to make the change. Most of the hows involve making changes to DOS statements in CONFIG.SYS and AUTOEXEC.BAT, but some are more involved.

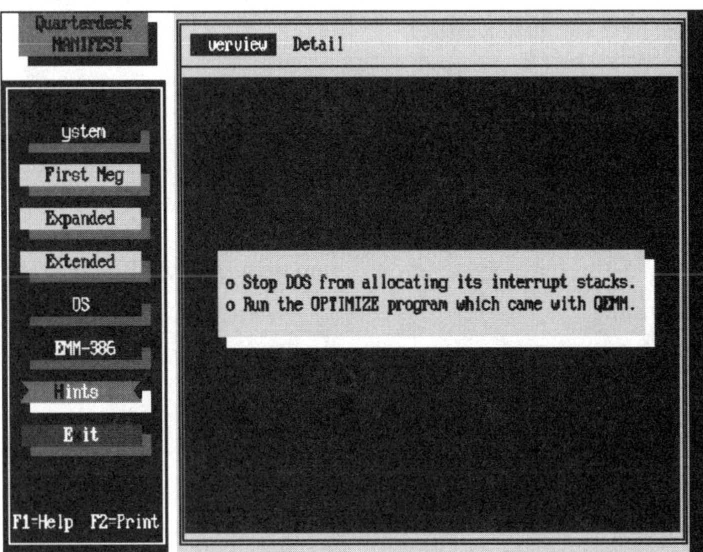

Figure 5-38. Hints example screen

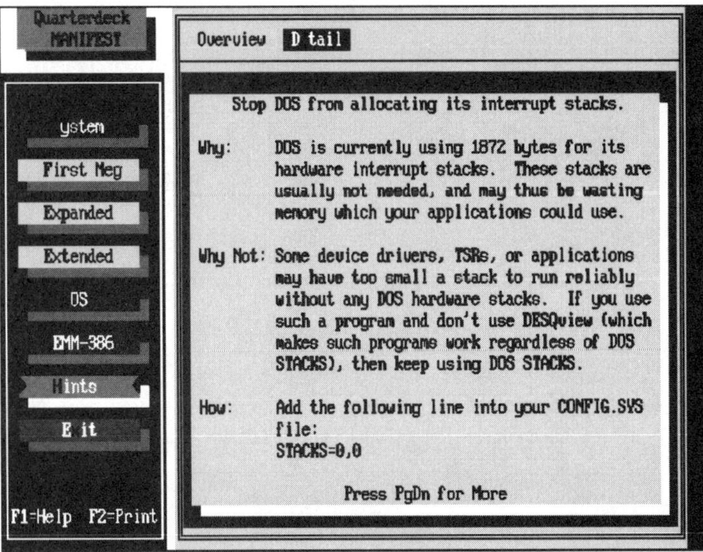

Figure 5-39. Hint Details example screen

Note that these figures are examples—your own PC will almost certainly present a different situation and therefore different hints.

Exit category

This is simply the place to get out of Manifest. If you choose the Exit topic, you can press Esc to leave Manifest and return to the DOS prompt. If you choose the Stay Resident topic, you can press either

LeftShift-Ctrl
RightShift-Ctrl
LeftShift-RightShift-Ctrl

to quit Manifest and leave it in memory waiting to pop up again when you press that same key combination.

If you want to return to using Manifest, press the UpArrow or DownArrow key to select some other Manifest category.

CHAPTER SIX

QEMM386.SYS

QEMM386.SYS is a driver—a program that loads into memory to extend DOS's abilities on PCs with a 386, 386SX, 486, 486SX, or compatible chip. It is the heart of QEMM.

QEMM386.SYS loads into your PC for operation if CONFIG.SYS includes a line such as

```
DEVICE=QEMM386.SYS
```

OPTIMIZE automatically installs this line along with the necessary parameters to make good use of memory in your PC. However, there are plenty of parameters you can use to change (that is, improve) this configuration.

The QEMM386.SYS device line in CONFIG.SYS should be the first line in CONFIG.SYS, with only a few exceptions (which are noted in Section III).

Two of the newest features in QEMM386.SYS for optimizing the use of memory—STEALTH and SQUEEZE—are available as parameters you can call on and are used by OPTIMIZE when necessary.

STEALTH uses QEMM's mapping ability to force ROMs in upper memory to share their addresses with RAM. That is, it maps RAM to the ROM addresses and then monitors program requests for RAM or ROM. If the request is for RAM, then QEMM maps the RAM to those addresses and lets them use the RAM. If the request is for ROM, then QEMM maps the ROM to those addresses and lets them use the ROM. This can add as much as 211K more to the usable upper memory of some PCs.

SQUEEZE lets loading TSRs or drivers temporarily use more memory than they'll finally need. That is, they can borrow some other memory, as long as they relinquish that memory when installation is complete. This helps you load more TSRs and drivers into upper memory, because some that would fit in their final configuration are too big in their installation state.

This chapter tells you how to use parameters and gives you the "grammar rules" necessary for putting them into your PC. For this discussion, the parameters are divided into three types: frequently used parameters (look in this section first), those used for fine-tuning (when you want to adjust precisely the amounts and speeds of memory use), and problem-fixing parameters (which, as the name suggests, are for solving conflicts between QEMM386.SYS and various hardware or software combinations).

How to Use Parameters

The parameters you can use to tell QEMM386.SYS just how to do its work come as codes on its command line. As noted above, you put QEMM386.SYS to work with a device line in CONFIG.SYS, DEVICE=QEMM386.SYS, or with a more elaborate path name to tell DOS just where to find it, such as

```
DEVICE=C:\QEMM\QEMM386.SYS
```

You can add a parameter at the end of this line, after typing a slash, as in

```
DEVICE=C:\QEMM\QEMM386.SYS /parameter
```

Some parameters also have numeric values or address specifications associated with them, like these hypothetical examples:

```
DEVICE=C:\QEMM\QEMM386.SYS /parameter=128
DEVICE=C:\QEMM\QEMM386.SYS /parameter=A000-AFFF
```

Most parameters also have an abbreviation; for example, if "P" were the abbreviation for "parameter," you could enter either

```
DEVICE=C:\QEMM\QEMM386.SYS /parameter=128
```

or

```
DEVICE=C:\QEMM\QEMM386.SYS /P=128
```

You may specify more than one parameter on a line, separating them by a space. In fact, you can use the same parameter several times on one line—to exclude several, noncontiguous areas, for example. Parameters are processed from left to right in the order they appear on the line.

Do not put spaces within parameters.

Frequently Used Parameters

- `RAM`

  Use this parameter to fill areas from 640K to 1024K that are mappable (also known as usable)—that is, those that don't have adapter RAM or ROM in them and aren't in the page frame. LOADHI can use these. So can DESQview's XDV. RAM also forces QEMM on and cannot be overrided. If you specify RAM=XXXX-YYYY then you fill areas from address XXXX to address YYYY with memory, and into any other mappable areas as well.

- `ROM`

  Map all ROM code and data into RAM (because generally it's faster). If you specify ROM=XXXX, then you map ROM code beginning at address XXXX into RAM. If you just specify the starting address this way, QEMM tries to determine the ending address of the ROM to map. An EGA ROM might map with ROM=c000. ROM forces QEMM on and cannot be overrided. If you specify ROM=XXXX-YYYY, then you map ROM code and data from address XXXX to YYYY into RAM.

  When you use the ST:M or ST:F parameters (which are explained later), you can use ROM only on 16K regions, aligned on 16K boundaries (although this doesn't apply to ROM regions affected by XST or, in the case of ST:F, ROM regions outside of the page frame). For example, ROM=D000-D6FF only maps D000-D3FF into faster RAM when ST:M or ST:F are specified. ROM=D000-D7FF maps the entire region into faster RAM, even if ROM does not occupy the entire region.

- `INCLUDE=XXXX-YYYY`
  or
  `I=XXXX-YYYY`

  The range of addresses from XXXX to YYYY are mappable. XXXX should be a multiple of 4K. Normally QEMM detects all usable areas. This parameter can help do that and generally is found after using the Analysis procedure and the report of QEMM.COM (see Chapter 7). For example, INCLUDE=B800-BFFF includes an unused video area from a VGA adapter with a monochrome monitor. INCLUDE and EXCLUDE are done sequentially, so you can exclude a large area and then include a smaller area from within it.

- `EXCLUDE=XXXX-YYYY`
  or
  `X=XXXX-YYYY`

  The range of addresses from XXXX to YYYY (within the first megabyte) are unmappable. You exclude memory from being filled if it has some other use, such as being the addresses of some adapter's ROM. QEMM automatically excludes memory that it detects as having a ROM or adapter RAM. XXXX must be a multiple of 4K. You can use exclude several times to exclude several ranges.

  Leave at least 64K free above 640K (in the range from A000 to FFFF) because QEMM needs that much for a page frame. If it can't find it, then the address 576K (9000) will be the page frame location. This reduces conventional memory by 64K. (See the FRAME parameter.)

  QEMM with the ST:X parameter relocates a ROM, even when that ROM is excluded, but EXCLUDE does stop any mapping of RAM to that area. Programs can still reach the ROM at the original location, with QEMM redirecting their calls. EXCLUDE can prevent the ROM parameter from mapping a ROM into faster RAM. If that happens when the ST:M or ST:F STEALTH parameters are in use, any EXCLUDE in a region prevents that entire 16K region, to its 16K boundaries, from being mapped into RAM. However, this limit doesn't apply to ROMs affected by the XST parameter. Nor, when ST:F is in effect, does it affect ROM regions outside of the page frame.

Because parameters are processed from left to right, you could exclude some area, then include some smaller area within it.

- `STEALTHROM:X`

  or

  `ST:X`

  This parameter enables STEALTH. Replace X with the letter of the memory management method you want to use: M for mapping, F for frame. Frame mode will at most provide 64K of ROM space as EMS page frame RAM, while mapping mode frees up the maximum unexcluded ROM. Not all systems can use mapping mode, however.

Fine-Tuning Parameters

- `HELP`

  This parameter describes all QEMM parameters.

- `?`

  Use this parameter to obtain a list of all parameters and their abbreviations.

- `ADAPTERRAM=XXXX-YYYY`

  or

  `ARAM=XXXX-YYYY`

  There is adapter RAM in addresses from XXXX to YYYY, such as from a network adapter or 3270 adapter. QEMM automatically tries to find these but misses some. You help it with this parameter. RAM in an adapter helps performance—it lets the PC reach some memory on the adapter as though this memory were part of standard PC memory, instead of working through slower interrupts and I/O instructions. ADAPTERRAM is like EXCLUDE, but the memory is shown on a type display (such as from QEMM.COM) as adapter RAM, not excluded.

- `ADAPTERROM=XXXX-YYYY`

  or

  `AROM=XXXX-YYYY`

  There is adapter ROM in addresses from XXXX toYYYY, such as from a network adapter, 3270 adapter, or video adapter. QEMM automatically tries to find such ROM but sometimes misses it. You help with this parameter. It works like exclude but gives a specific reason (which can help you remember why you excluded this area).

- AUTO
  or
  AU
  Use this parameter to turn on QEMM when it's needed—allowing it to put the PC into virtual-86 mode and manage expanded memory when a program requests expanded memory. This generally is the best setting to choose, rather than ON or OFF. Remember that QEMM is automatically on after a ROM or RAM parameter.

- COMPAQEGAROM
  or
  CERT
  This parameter relocates Compaq's video ROM. Compaq systems automatically copy the slow EGA or VGA ROM from address C000 to fast memory at E000. QEMM reverses that so there's more high memory on Compaq systems, and also it automatically maps RAM into the addresses of the ROM at C000 to increase ROM speed. QEMM looks for Compaqs, and when it finds one (QEMM386.SYS does this) it uses COMPAQEGAROM as a default. To stop that you must use NOCOMPAQFEATURES on the QEMM386.SYS command line.

- COMPAQHALFROM
  or
  CHR
  Use this parameter to split Compaq's system ROM in half. Most Compaq 386 systems have a ROM with two halves, with addresses from F000-F7FF and F800-FFFF. The halves have redundant information. QEMM386.SYS splits them off and uses one of the redundant areas for high memory. The COMPAQHALFROM parameter is set as a default. To shut it off, use NOCOMPAQFEATURES on the QEMM386.SYS command line.

- COMPAQROMMEMORY

  or

  CRM

  Include this parameter in the command line to use Compaq ROM. Compaq Deskpro 386 systems have 128K of high memory addresses to speed up system ROM and EGA ROM. QEMM386.SYS can speed up the system ROM using the ROM parameter and make the high memory addresses for loading high. When QEMM detects a Compaq 386, it uses COMPAQROMMEMORY as a default. To turn it off, use NOCOMPAQFEATURES.

- DOS4

  or

  D4

  This parameter alters EMS page order for DOS 4. QEMM386.SYS will deviate from EMS 4.0 specification to handle bugs from the early versions of PC-DOS 4.00 or 4.01 and MS-DOS 4.0. (They didn't follow the EMS 4.00 specification closely enough.)

If you're using DOS versions PC-DOS 4.00 or 4.01 and MS-DOS 4.00, don't use the /X parameter to BUFFERS, VDISK, and FASTOPEN.

- EMBMEM=XXXXX

  or

  EMB=XXXXX

  Set XXXXX as the maximum amount of extended XMS memory that XMS-supporting programs will see available. XXXXX is the amount in kilobytes, with the default being 12288K (12MB). This parameter can prevent Windows 3.0 from controlling all extended memory so programs that use the VCPI to allocate memory, or the EMS, can find memory available while running in Windows 3.0 in standard mode.

- `EXTMEM=XXXXX`
  or
  `EXT=XXXXX`
  QEMM386.SYS should not use XXXXX amount of extended memory. XXXXX is from 1 to 31744 and means that many kilobytes of memory. This lets you use RAM disks and disk caches, such as VDISK, which allocate extended memory through the older INT 15 interface. If EXTMEM is left out, QEMM uses all extended memory. EXTMEM and MEMORY parameters have opposite meanings. EXTMEM leaves a certain amount of memory; MEMORY uses as much as a certain amount of memory. Memory left after EXTMEM can't be used by programs that allocate extended memory through the XMS or VCPI specifications.

- `FASTINT10:N`
  or
  `F10:N`
  This parameter tells QEMM not to replace certain BIOS video functions with QEMM routines (even though this is commonly done to add speed). This can prevent some video card compatibility problems that appear when STEALTHROM is used.

- `FORCEEMS`
  or
  `FREMS`
  This parameter allows EMS calls even though there is no page frame. Use only if you use FRAMELENGTH with a value less than four. This parameter lets the program have some access to expanded memory even without a full page frame.

Some programs can't work with a partial or missing page frame.

- `FSTC`
  This parameter enables accurate access analysis within excluded ROM areas when using Stealth (ST:M or ST:F).

- FRAME=XXXX

  or

  FR=XXXX

  Set the page frame location to address XXXX. (XXXX is a segment address or NONE.) This is the beginning address of the 64K segment for mapping expanded memory by the EMS spec. Typical are C000, C400, C800, CC00, D000, D400, D800, DC00, or E000. Sometimes A000 is used if there are no other good areas and there's a monochrome or CGA video adapter card. Above E000 can be used if the system has ROM holes, that is, if QEMM has split the ROM on a Compaq system, or if STEALTH is used. For EMS to work, 64K must be available. If FRAME is left out, XXXX is chosen by QEMM after it looks at your PC's hardware. Don't set FRAME except when QEMM's automatic choice fails because of a hardware conflict—one that QEMM must have missed. (Another reason to set FRAME is to hand-optimize by overlaying the upper ROM with the FRAME.) If there are no good addresses, QEMM can still fill memory, sort it, fill high RAM, multitask, and map ROMS, but it can't manage expanded memory. For those uses, specify FRAME=NONE. But don't use FRAME=NONE with ST:M or ST:F—it stops them from working.

The highest page frame possible is EC00 with ST:F—this often leaves a sizeable area of high memory available.

- FRAMELENGTH=X

  or

  FL=X

  Set the size of the page frame to X, which is the number of pages from 0 to 4. A 0 for X means no page frame, the same thing as FRAME=NONE. A 4 for X means a standard EMS page frame (four pages of 16K each). In other words, FRAMELENGTH lets you free one or more pages for other uses. You can use it with the FORCEEMS parameter if there are programs that can use partial page frames or no page frame. You may need to do this if there isn't enough space in upper memory for a standard page frame.

- `HMAMIN=XX`

  Set the minimum amount of the HMA that a program can request and still get the HMA within the range of 0 to 63K. Only one program can use the HMA at a time, and several may request it, so setting a minimum amount keeps it from being used inefficiently. XX should be from 1 to 63.

- `INCLUDE386`

  or

  `I386`

  Use this version of INCLUDE for MCA.ADL files. It works identically to INCLUDE. It is useful if you have MCA.ADL files that will be read by QEMM-50/60, QRAM, or QEMM-386. It is a QEMM-386 specific switch that won't be recognized as a parameter by QEMM-50/60 or QRAM.

- `MAPS=XXX`

  or

  `MA=XXX`

  This parameter sets the number of alternate register sets to XXX, from 0 to 255. Each map uses 4K extended memory. Having more alternate maps improves multitasking—have at least one for each program to run simultaneously. The default is 8. If you are not multitasking, you can set MAPS=0 and save 32K.

- `MEMORY=XXXXX`

  or

  `MEM=XXXXX`

  or

  `ME=XXXXX`

  Use XXXXX kilobytes of 386 extended memory for QEMM and for expanded, XMS, and VCPI memory. XXXXX is from 128 to 32128. If you leave MEMORY out, QEMM takes all available extended memory.

- `NOEMS`

  This parameter tells QEMM not to act as an expanded memory manager. You can use this if you want QEMM for its other features but want to load a different Expanded Memory Manager.

- NOPAUSEONERROR

  or

  NOPE

  Use this parameter to tell QEMM not to pause when there's an error. QEMM normally stops at command-line errors to show the message "Press to unload QEMM or any other key to continue with QEMM." Only use this parameter if you already know about the error and know it won't bother your system.

- NOVIDEORAM

  or

  NVR

  This parameter excludes video addresses from use as high RAM for loading high. (Video addresses are from 640K to 736K.) QEMM normally fills unused video memory and attaches it to conventional memory—called "video filling." If you don't want conventional memory increased, use the parameter. If you want the area treated as high RAM, use NOVIDEOFILL, and RAM. If you don't want high RAM there, use NOVIDEORAM, which stops any area below C000 not set aside as high RAM from becoming high RAM. You rarely need this parameter.

- NOWINDOWS3

  or

  NW3

  Use this parameter to disable the features that support running Windows 3.0 in protected mode. Windows 3 still runs in real mode with this parameter. Also, using this option reduces QEMM's use of conventional memory by about 1K.

- OFF

  or

  OF

  This parameter turns QEMM off.

- ON

  This parameter turns QEMM on.

- PAUSE

  This parameter causes QEMM to pause while parsing commands. This lets you press to stop QEMM386.SYS from installing. You might need this if you're experimenting with parameters and choose one that doesn't work. You'll need to interrupt QEMM386.SYS on so you can change CONFIG.SYS and eliminate the troublesome parameter.

- SORT:Y

  Use this parameter to sort memory by speed. QEMM tests all conventional and extended memory speeds and uses the fastest memory first. This parameter can improve system speed, but it doesn't work with Windows 3 in enhanced mode.

- SUSPENDRESUME

  or

  SUS

  This parameter tells QEMM the PC has a suspend/resume feature (which is commonly found on systems).

- SUSPENDRESUME=XX

  or

  SUS=XX

  This tells QEMM the PC has the suspend/resume feature (common on). XX is the interrupt number the uses; 2, 72, 73, and 77 are common choices. This parameter is only necessary if QEMM doesn't recognize the suspend/resume feature on a PC.

- VIDRAMEGA

  or

  VREGA

  This parameter excludes video addresses from mapping. This has the same effect as EXCLUDE=A000-BFFF. Use it when you extend conventional memory using and want to use memory already available on video adapter board. You preserve expanded memory that would have been mapped into the video memory addresses. The disadvantage is that the video memory is typically much slower than the expanded memory.

- `VIDRAMEMS`
  or
  `VREMS`
  Use this parameter to map EMS memory into video areas when VIDRAM is on. Conventional memory and RAM are not extended into the video areas. Then VIDRAM can map fast EMS memory into the video area. This is the same as I=A000-AFFF .

Don't use VIDRAMEMS with DESQview versions earlier than 2.26.

VIDRAMEMS can cause problems with programs that make great use of expanded memory.

- `WATCHDOG=[0,1,2]`
  or
  `WD=[0,1,2]`
  This parameter sets the type of watchdog timer. DESQview's Change a Program Protection level (0-3) setting lets level one represent protection against programs that lock interrupts for too long. Watching for locked interrupts depends on the hardware. There are two kinds of hardware that QEMM386.SYS supports: one for PS/2s and another for Compaq Deskpro 386 systems. By default QEMM386.SYS tries to figure out which to use. WD=0 means no watchdog timer; WD=1 means PS/2; WD=2 means Compaq.

Problem-Fixing Parameters

- `COMPAQ386S`
  or
  `C386S`
  Tells QEMM the PC is a Compaq 386S. QEMM identifies the 386S if you

use Compaq Setup program version 6.02 or greater. If you use an earlier version, this parameter lets QEMM know how to optimize for the 386S.

- DISKBUF=XX

  or

  DB=XX

  This tells QEMM the disk buffer for handling bus-mastering disk drives is XX kilobytes of memory. Bus-mastering hard disks have a special way of accessing memory, a way for which QEMM's DMA buffering doesn't work. This parameter sets a separate SCSI buffer for fixed-disk access. Larger buffers means better disk performance but loses conventional memory.

- DISKBUFFRAME=XX

  or

  DBF=XX

  Use this parameter to buffer INT 13 interrupts that directly access the EMS page frame (these are disk reads and writes). This is good for programs that write directly into the page frame using BIOS-level calls, such as some EMS-using disk caches. You often get better performance if you reconfigure the cache so it uses XMS extended memory. Then you don't need DISKBUF-FRAME. The XX value is the number of kilobytes of conventional RAM for buffering. This can be any value; 2 and 10 are common. A larger XX value means better performance but also more conventional memory used. QEMM prompts you for most programs that need this parameter.

- DMA=XXX

  or

  DM=XXX

  This sets the size of the DMA buffer to XXX, which can be any value from 12 to 128K, with 64K the default on PS/2 and XT systems, 12K the default on others.

- DONTUSEXMS

  or

  DUX

  This tells QEMM not to make XMS calls to an XMS driver loaded before QEMM.

- FORCESTEALTHCOPY:Y

  or

  FSTC:Y

  Use this parameter to save video ROM, disk ROM, and system ROM in QEMM's own address space. QEMM does this by copying tables in the video ROM, disk ROM, and system ROM into QEMM's own data areas when the STEALTHROM parameter is relocating those ROMs. The default is that QEMM does not copy tables out of regions that are affected by the EXCLUDE parameter, even if those regions contain relocated ROMs. This parameter makes QEMM copy these tables even out of regions excluded. It is used for troubleshooting.

- FRAMEBUF:X

  or

  FB:X

  This enables or disables breaking up DOS-2-style disk reads into and writes from the expanded memory page frame. DOS 2 does such reads and writes with file handles instead of FCBs. The default enables this when the STEALTH mapping or frame method are used. Otherwise the default is disabled. Replacing X with Y enables always; replacing with X with N disables always.

- GETSIZE

  or

  GS

  This is an OPTIMIZE internal parameter.

- `HANDLES=XXX`

  or

  `HA=XXX`

  Use this parameter to set the number of EMS handles to XXX, which is a value from 16 to 255. Each application using expanded memory needs at least one handle, some need more. The default is 64. Larger values use more extended memory—each takes about 28 bytes.

- `IGNOREA20`

  or

  `IA`

  This parameter tells QEMM not to trap the 8042 keyboard controller. By default QEMM traps the 8042 ports to detect programs that try to manipulate the A20 line, to reach extended memory. That manipulation can cause keyboard problems. IA disables support of HIMEM.SYS but can solve keyboard problems. QEMM supports XMS, so you don't generally need HIMEM.SYS if you have QEMM.

- `IOTRAP=XX`

  This changes the way of monitoring I/O port addresses. Older systems had the I/O port addresses repeated after a certain interval in the I/O port address space. Newer systems assign I/O ports without that duplication. QEMM can work either way. XX is 1 or 64, where 64 means using the older way.

- `LABEL`

  or

  `LB`

  This is an OPTIMIZE internal parameter.

- `LOCKDMA`

  or

  `LD`

  This parameter changes interrupt enable behavior to let interrupts stay disabled during DMA transfers. Normally QEMM tries to keep interrupts enabled as much as possible. This parameter is for the 10-Net network program, which requires interrupts to remain disabled during DMA transfer setup.

- `NOCOMPAQFEATURES`
  or
  `NCT`
  Use this parameter to disable EGAROM, HALFROM, and ROMMEMORY use on a Compaq computer. If QEMM thinks it is on a Compaq system, it turns on all three COMPAQ parameters: COMPAQEGAROM, COMPAQHALFROM, and COMPAQROMMEMORY. You can turn them all off with this parameter and then turn them on one at a time if you want.

- `NOFILL`
  or
  `NO`
  This parameter tells QEMM not to fill conventional memory (below 640K). This is useful only if the PC has less than 640K of conventional memory, because then QEMM automatically fills up to 640K from extended memory. Use NOFILL when you don't want QEMM forced to turn on and stay on, which would happen with filling. NOFILL also prevents video filling, so you do not need to use the parameter.

- `NOHMA`
  This tells QEMM not to put anything into the HMA and to act as if it is already in use. Use NOHMA if there is an XMS driver loaded before QEMM that is already using or allocating the HMA. You can also use NOXMS.

- `NOROM`
  or
  `NR`
  This parameter tells QEMM not to map the page of the system ROM. QEMM normally maps one 4K page of system ROM to detect reboots. QEMM386.SYS can detect reboots without this, most of the time. You may specify NOROM and save the 4K.

- NOROMHOLES

  or

  NRH

  When this parameter is included in the command line, QEMM does not look for holes in the system ROM. Holes are unused addresses in ROM. Many system ROMs between F000 and FFFF have lots of unused addresses. QEMM386.SYS automatically finds these and includes them for its use. The detection could be wrong, however, especially for areas that look unused for awhile but then come into use later. If you have problems that look like system functions that worked for awhile but now don't, you can use this parameter in troubleshooting and then check areas specified by the QEMM.COM Analysis report.

- NOSHADOWRAM

  or

  NOSH

  This parameter tells QEMM not to use Shadow RAM. Shadow RAM is the 384K of reserved memory in low memory with an I/O port-selectable method of getting at that memory. QEMM automatically sees if a PC does this. If QEMM fails when starting, it may be that the detection failed and you need the NOSH parameter.

- NOSORT

  or

  NS

  Use this parameter when you don't want to sort memory by speed—which is the default in QEMM versions 6 and later.

- NOTOKENRING

  or

  NTR

  This parameter tells QEMM no to use the alternate method of detecting a token ring adapter. Most token ring adapter boards don't follow the typical way adapters are recognized as installed. QEMM tries a different means to find token ring adapters and their use of memory in order to exclude them. This method could interfere with other adapters. If so, you could use this parameter and exclude the area used by the token ring adapter.

Don't use QEMM's ROM parameter when your PC is already shadowing ROM. This just duplicates RAM copying, thus wasting some RAM. At most, use the ROM parameter on those ROM addresses that aren't already shadowed.

Although most PCs cannot, some can use Shadow RAM as extended memory. If yours can, do so. Then use QEMM to copy ROM to RAM. It's more efficient than shadowing the entire reserved memory area. If your PC cannot use Shadow RAM as extended memory, then let the Shadow RAM do the copying; otherwise you lose that RAM entirely.

No PC has 384K of ROM to shadow, but Shadow RAM often is 384K of RAM. With QEMM's NOSH parameter you can get back the unused RAM and add it to the memory pool. Some programs don't work correctly, however, if Shadow RAM is used as expanded or high memory. (That's what QEMM can do with it.) Some Shadow-RAM-style memory is different enough from C&T to prevent QEMM from using it. For any of these circumstances, use NOSH. When QEMM takes Shadow RAM, it uses all that's not at ROM addresses within its mapping area. Shadow RAM that is at excluded addresses is not used. Shadow RAM is used in 16K chunks on 16K boundaries. If any portion of it is not being mapped by QEMM, none of it will be used in that 16K area. Excluding a single 4K area stops QEMM from using the entire 16K of Shadow RAM.

- `NOTOPMEMORY`
  or
  `NT`
  Use this parameter to tell QEMM not to look for top memory. Some PCs put 384K of memory just below the top of standard AT 16MB address

space—384K below to be precise. QEMM386.SYS automatically looks for memory there and makes it available for use. A conflict could occur, however, if something is using that area or the hardware of the computer doesn't want software looking to those addresses. Try NT if your PC hangs when starting, especially if it is a Compaq PC.

- `NOVDS`

  This parameter disables support of the Virtual DMA Services specification. This specification defines the interaction between a 386 memory manager and a bus master device.

- `NOVIDEOFILL`

  or

  `NV`

  Use this parameter to tell QEMM not to fill video memory, the memory from A000 to B7FF, with conventional memory. It is useful mainly on monochrome and CGA PCs on which QEMM adds memory from 640K to the bottom of video adapter card (B000 for monochrome or B800 for CGA) and adjusts memory size of DOS according to that.

- `NOXBDA`

  or

  `NX`

  This parameter tells QEMM not to move the extended BIOS data area. When machines have that area, QEMM moves it from the 639K address into another place. Otherwise XBDA would get in the way of and video filling on monochrome and CGA systems. If a program running on a PS/2 Model 80 or other PC with XBDA has trouble, it may be assuming the XBDA is at 639K.

- `NOXMS`

  This tells QEMM not to manage extended memory.

- `OLDV`
  or
  `ODV`
  Use this parameter when you want to support DESQview versions 1.3 to 2.00. QEMM uses 4K to 8K more conventional memory than it does for newer DESQviews.

- `REGION:N`
  or
  `R:N`
  This is an internal OPTIMIZE parameter. Because QEMM with ST:X can load a portion of itself into high RAM, it responds to an R:N parameter on the command linc. Sctting thc rcgion number to R:0 forces QEMM to stay in low memory, otherwise QEMM loads high into the specified region.

- `SHADOWROM=XXX`
  or
  `SH=XXX`
  Forces using a specific ShadowRAM type.

- `TASKS=XX`
  or
  `TA=XX`
  This parameter sets the interrupt nesting level by setting the number of internal data structures for handling interrupts out of protected mode to XX, with 16 as the default.

- `UNMAPFREEPAGES=Y/N`
  or
  `UFP=Y/N`
  Controls whether freed expanded memory pages are returned to the extended pool.

- UNUSUAL8042

  or

  U8

  The 8042 keyboard controller chip is not standard. Use this parameter if turning QEMM on or running DESQview disables the keyboard.

- UNUSUALEXT

  or

  UX

  The system needs a way to determine the amount of extended memory. If QEMM hangs at boot time, this could help, but it can make QEMM.COM's memory report on extended memory inaccurate.

- VIRTUALHDIRQ:N

  or

  VHI:N

  This parameter tells QEMM not to disable advanced disk features for disk caches when using STEALTH parameters M and F.

- VCPISHARE:Y

  or

  VS:Y

  This parameter allows VCPI clients to share the first page table. This could cause incompatibilities with DOS-extended software.

- VXDDIR=directory name

  In this parameter, directory name is the location of the WINHIRAM.VXD and WINSTLTH.VXD files that give high RAM (upper memory) and STEALTH features for Windows 3 in enhanced mode. This is for users of diskless network stations or any system where the .VXD files are in a directory other than the one from which QEMM-386 is loaded.

- WINSHRINKUMBS=Y/N

  or

  WSU=Y/N

  Controls whether Stealth shrinks upper memory blocks when Windows Enhanced mode starts up. The default is WSU=Y.

- EXCLUDESTEALTH=XXXX

  or

  XST=XXXX

  XXXX is the starting address of ROM that is not relocated by the STEALTH ST:X parameters. You provide the starting address of the ROM, not the full range. (On PS/2s the video ROM at E000 and the system ROM at F000 are separate ROMs. Even though they also are contiguous, they should be specified separately with this parameter.) To use the XST parameter on more than one ROM region, use a separate XST parameter for each ROM.

XST sometimes gives trouble to a system that was fine before using XST.

- EXCLUDESTEALTHINT=XX

  or

  XSTI=XX

  This parameter tells QEMM not to grab the software interrupt XX (in hex) when STEALTH parameters are working. Use this if you have a program that won't start if it detects that a particular interrupt is not pointing to the system BIOS or to 0000:0000. XSTI crashes a system if the specified interrupt is ever called and eventually executes at BIOS level, as QEMM has given up managing the interrupt. You rarely need this parameter.

Fine-Tuning STEALTH

You can use the ST:X and XST:XXXX parameters to get even more from memory than OPTIMIZE can manage.

ST:X is the STEALTH parameter for QEMM. Quarterdeck's experts knew that ROMs take up a considerable amount of the memory addresses in upper memory (640K to 1024K), so they designed a way to have the benefit of those

ROMS and still leave the addresses open for RAM use as well. That lets QEMM map memory into those addresses, and then load TSRs and drivers into them.

ST:X can get at all of the ROM addresses in upper memory. It does this even when, as is the typical case, those addresses aren't contiguous. But using ST:X or XST:XXXX to relocate ROMs isn't enough. You also need to use QEMM's other parameters to make sure RAM is mapped into those addresses.

QEMM parameters are processed sequentially from left to right. If two parameters contradict each other, the last one in line wins.

You can use the ROM parameter to map a ROM into fast RAM, and then use the STEALTH parameter to relocate that ROM again so the addresses are open for RAM. But if there is yet another ROM parameter on the same line, its position determines how STEALTH affects the ROM's address.

The parameter

```
ROM X=FC00-FFFF
```

tells QEMM to map the ROMs into faster RAM, excluding (designated by the X) the FC00-FFFF address, or to use it for anything else. This is sometimes done because the area FC00-FFFF has the floppy-drive control instructions, and when these are sped up they may not work properly.

Now if you add STEALTH with

```
ROM X=FC00-FFFF ST:M
```

the ST:M parameter relocated all ROMs, excluding the ROM not overlaid with high RAM at FC00-FFFF.

But if STEALTH were added before EXCLUDE, as in

```
ROM ST:M X=FC00-FFFF
```

then the ROM will already have been relocated by STEALTH. EXCLUDE still makes the area FC00-FFFF off limits for any uses. (Remember that with STEALTH, programs can still find ROM instructions at their original addresses, when they call for ROM help, but otherwise they find RAM there.)

There are other parameters that affect ROMs and so must be placed before or after STEALTH, depending on how you want them to act:

```
INCLUDE=XXXX-YYYY
INCLUDE386=XXXX-YYYY
ADAPTERROM=XXXX-YYYY
ADAPTERRAM=XXXX-YYYY
RAM=XXXX-YYYY
```

RAM without a range won't be affected by its line order, because it puts RAM everywhere that isn't stopped by other parameters. You must place any ROM address range parameter before STEALTH or it is ignored.

QEMM tries to put the page frame in the best place, but it doesn't always succeed. You can use the FRAME parameter to put the page frame where you want it. One reason to do this is to combine two divided areas of upper memory into one larger area that might fit more TSRs and drivers. (Use the Analysis feature in Manifest or QEMM.COM to see how memory looks with the page frame location.)

Some programs have trouble with a moved page frame. If you run into that problem, but temporarily need more memory to load some TSRs or drivers high, OPTIMIZE's SQUEEZE ability may be enough.

If you have problems using STEALTH with the ST:M or ST:F parameters, try moving the page frame. Put it at the beginning addresses of the ROMs on the system—only ROMs that QEMM relocates, naturally, or with adapter RAM. With SF:F you might try EC00. Don't use F000 even with the ST:X parameter, because STEALTH itself needs the last 64 bytes of the F000 region.

If you use FRAME=NONE, QEMM ignores ST:M and ST:F parameters, because they need a page frame.

If you have trouble while running STEALTH and using a Super VGA mode (resolution above 640x480) try EXCLUDE=C000-C0FF or EXCLUDE=C000-C1FF.

CHAPTER SEVEN

QEMM.COM

QEMM.COM does two things: turns QEMM on or off and tells you what's going on in the first megabyte of your PC's memory.

Turning QEMM On or Off

When you load QEMM386.SYS into memory by a line in CONFIG.SYS, QEMM is on. But you may want to turn it off later without completely changing your CONFIG.SYS (and without rebooting to pull it out of memory). To do so, you change to the directory with the QEMM.COM program (the directory you installed QEMM to initially), type

```
QEMM OFF
```

and press Enter. QEMM stops, and so expanded memory is no longer available to programs (QEMM was the expanded memory manager) and the processor will be operating in real mode (QEMM had put it into virtual-86 mode—see Chapter 4 for details).

But what if some program needs expanded memory? You could then turn QEMM on again by typing

```
QEMM ON
```

and pressing Enter. Expanded memory would be available again (which you would notice as the program called for and received use of it), and the processor would hop out of real mode into virtual-86 mode (which you probably wouldn't notice).

If you don't want to have to remember to turn QEMM on and off just to get expanded memory when it is needed, you can type

```
QEMM AUTO
```

and press Enter. QEMM is now in automatic mode and will turn on when a program needs expanded memory. (AU is an acceptable abbreviation for AUTO, incidentally.)

QEMM is always on if it has filled conventional or video memory, remapped RAM or ROMs, or is managing expanded memory.

Reporting On Memory

QEMM.COM can show you five reports on how memory is used.

- Summary .....QEMM's mode, expanded memory available, page frame address
- Types...........what types of memory are in the first megabyte
- Accessed ......what areas of memory have been accessed since QEMM was installed or reset (discussed later in this chapter)
- Analysis........checks Types and Accessed to suggest what parameters could make better use of memory
- Memory ....details of all memory in the PC before and after QEMM management—conventional, high RAM, extended, and expanded

Summary Report

To see the summary, just type

```
QEMM
```

with no parameters, and then press Enter. You'll see a display like that of Figure 7-1.

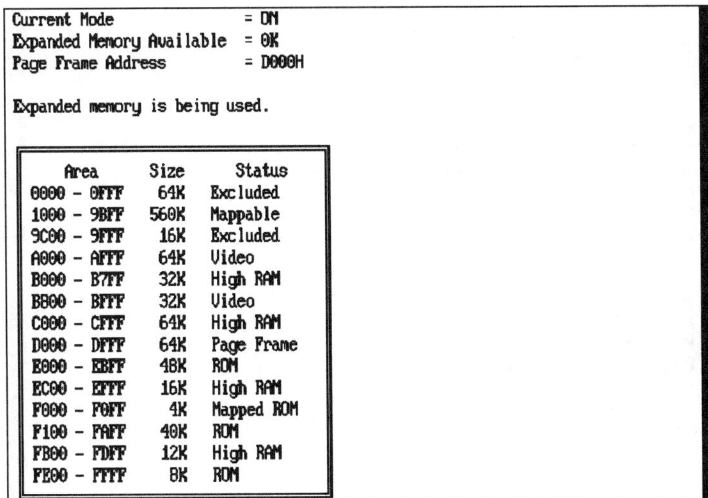

```
Current Mode              = ON
Expanded Memory Available = 0K
Page Frame Address        = D000H

Expanded memory is being used.
```

Area	Size	Status
0000 - 0FFF	64K	Excluded
1000 - 9BFF	560K	Mappable
9C00 - 9FFF	16K	Excluded
A000 - AFFF	64K	Video
B000 - B7FF	32K	High RAM
B800 - BFFF	32K	Video
C000 - CFFF	64K	High RAM
D000 - DFFF	64K	Page Frame
E000 - EBFF	48K	ROM
EC00 - EFFF	16K	High RAM
F000 - F0FF	4K	Mapped ROM
F100 - FAFF	40K	ROM
FB00 - FDFF	12K	High RAM
FE00 - FFFF	8K	ROM

Figure 7-1. QEMM.COM status report example

The basic terms at the top are straightforward:

Mode..........Is QEMM on, off, auto/on (on automatic, and on at this point), or auto/off (on automatic, and off at this point)?

Expanded Memory Available..........How much is available, how much is or is not being used?

Page Frame Address..........Where is it (in hex addressing)?

QEMM is always on if it has mapped RAMs or ROMs, filled memory, or is managing expanded memory that is in use.

After that top summary you see a quick list of the areas of memory by area (address), size (in kilobytes), and status (what it is or can be used for). This is the Type report.

Type Report

QEMM's view of what can be done with memory is shown here, as in the example of Figure 7-2. You get this by typing

```
QEMM TYPE
```

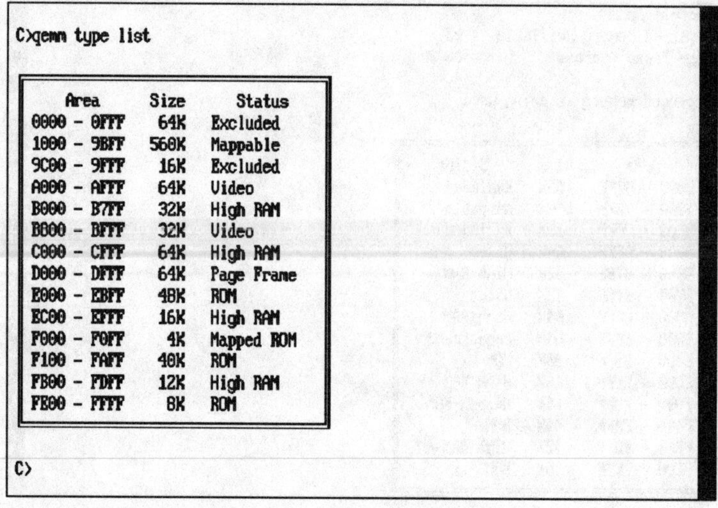

```
C>qemm type list

     Area        Size     Status
0000 - 0FFF       64K   Excluded
1000 - 9BFF      560K   Mappable
9C00 - 9FFF       16K   Excluded
A000 - AFFF       64K   Video
B000 - B7FF       32K   High RAM
B800 - BFFF       32K   Video
C000 - CFFF       64K   High RAM
D000 - DFFF       64K   Page Frame
E000 - EBFF       48K   ROM
EC00 - EFFF       16K   High RAM
F000 - F0FF        4K   Mapped ROM
F100 - FAFF       40K   ROM
FB00 - FDFF       12K   High RAM
FE00 - FFFF        8K   ROM

C>
```

Figure 7-2. QEMM.COM Type report, List format example

This is a simple list of memory areas from 0 to 1024K, showing:

Memory Area ....the beginning and ending addresses of the areas
Size ....the size in kilobytes
Status ....the status of the area, as from the symbol list above

You can also see this as a map, by typing

```
QEMM TYPE MAP
```

as in Figure 7-3. Each character in the map represents that state of a 4K chunk of memory, the smallest unit QEMM can work with. On the left side of the map is a column of addresses, each referring to the beginning of a 64K segment of the first megabyte of memory. Across the top are the hexadecimal address values for all 16 of the 4K parts of that 64K segment.

The legend on the right shows you these symbols:

+ ....means mappable—areas of at least 16K, aligned on 16K boundaries, that can be mapped with EMS calls
* ....means rammable—mappable by QEMM but not as EMS because it is smaller than 16K

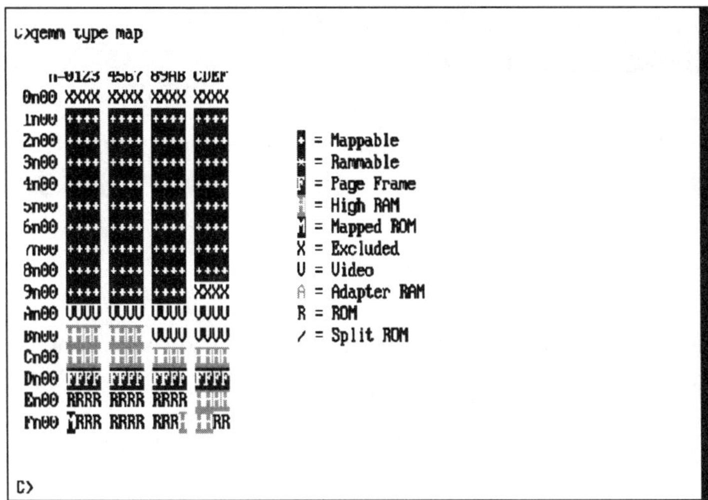

Figure 7-3. QEMM.COM Type report, Map format example

F...........means page frame—a mappable 64K area for EMS

H..........means high RAM—filled with RAM by QEMM, so useful for loading high

M ....means mapped ROM—ROMs that have been copied to RAM to run faster and then mapped to their original addresses

X..........means excluded—areas the EXCLUDE parameter keeps from QEMM's use to avoid conflicts with devices that need that memory

V...........means video—areas for the video buffer

A ....means adapter RAM—areas for adapter cards other than video

R..........means ROM—ROMs not remapped by QEMM's ROM parameter

/ ....means split ROM—ROMs only take up part of the 4K area, so the QEMM ROM parameter can't remap this

Mapped ROM can appear even without the ROM parameter on the QEMM line in CONFIG.SYS, both as the 4K of system ROM and the automatic mapping of the video ROM and system ROM on a Compaq Deskpro 386. (QEMM must do this because otherwise the Deskpro would remap for itself and not do as good a job of it).

0000 to 0FFF is automatically excluded by QEMM, without an EXCLUDE statement.

Any + or * areas in upper memory can be converted into H by adding the RAM parameter to the QEMM line in CONFIG.SYS (see Chapter 6).

Accessed Report

In Figure 7-4 you see how memory has been used. You get this view by typing

```
QEMM ACCESSED
```

Figure 7-4. QEMM.COM Accessed report, List format example

Area	Size	Status
0000 - 61FF	392K	Accessed
6200 - 93FF	200K	Unaccessed
9400 - 9DFF	40K	Accessed
9E00 - 9EFF	4K	Unaccessed
9F00 - B0FF	72K	Accessed
B100 - B6FF	24K	Unaccessed
B700 - C8FF	72K	Accessed
C900 - CEFF	24K	Unaccessed
CF00 - CFFF	4K	Accessed
D000 - DFFF	64K	Unaccessed
E000 - E5FF	24K	Accessed
E600 - E6FF	4K	Unaccessed
E700 - E9FF	12K	Accessed
EA00 - EBFF	8K	Unaccessed
EC00 - ECFF	4K	Accessed
ED00 - EEFF	8K	Unaccessed
EF00 - F0FF	8K	Accessed
F100 - F4FF	16K	Unaccessed
F500 - F8FF	16K	Accessed
F900 - FAFF	8K	Unaccessed
FB00 - FFFF	20K	Accessed

QEMM monitors the first megabyte of memory and can show you whether each 4K chunk has been touched or not. Note that this list can be so long that it does not fit on a single computer screen and scrolls off the top. (You could use DOS commands to pause it or to redirect it to a disk file where you could view it all.)

Type

```
QEMM ACCESSED MAP
```

and you can see this same report as a map, as in Figure 7-5, showing what areas have been:

A (Accessed) ....read from by some program
W (Written) ....written to by some program
U (Unaccessed) ....neither read or written by any program since the PC was booted

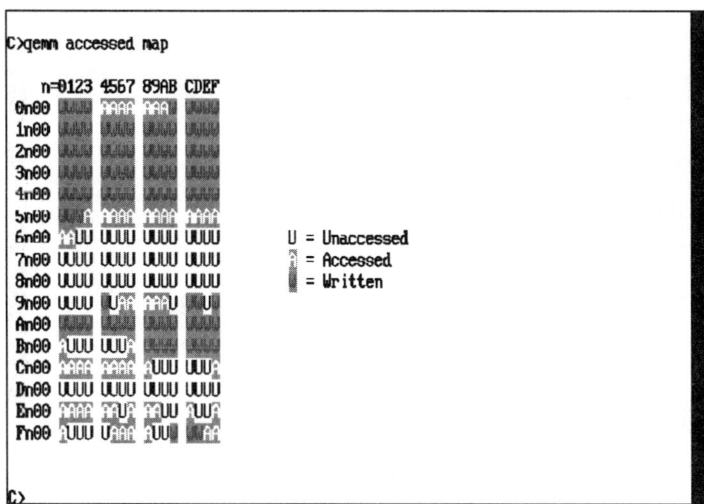

Figure 7-5. QEMM.COM Accessed report, Map format example

This map is useful because you can deduce from it how large programs are—that is, how much memory they access—and what areas of memory are lying fallow. Unused areas above 640K could conceivably be converted into UMBs for loading high.

Don't trust the A, W, U status of areas that are mappable memory (see the QEMM-386 Type report discussed above. Mapping makes memory look unaccessed even when it has been read from or written to.

Analysis Report

In Figure 7-6 you find QEMM's ideas about what memory you should and should not put to use. You get this by typing

```
QEMM ANALYSIS
```

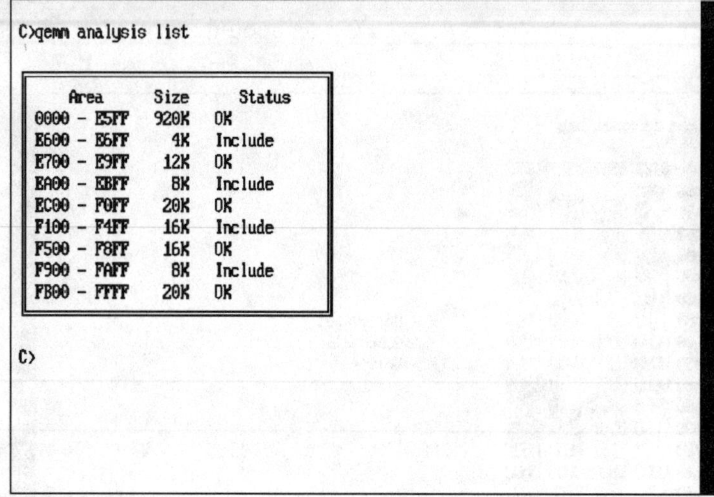

C>qemm analysis list

Area	Size	Status
0000 – E5FF	920K	OK
E600 – E6FF	4K	Include
E700 – E9FF	12K	OK
EA00 – EBFF	8K	Include
EC00 – F0FF	20K	OK
F100 – F4FF	16K	Include
F500 – F8FF	16K	OK
F900 – FAFF	8K	Include
FB00 – FFFF	20K	OK

C>

Figure 7-6. QEMM.COM Analysis report, List format example

You can also see this information as a map, as in Figure 7-7, by typing

```
QEMM ANALYSIS MAP
```

Figure 7-7. QEMM.COM Analysis report, MAP format example

```
C>qemm analysis map

     n=0123 4567 89AB CDEF
  0n00 0000 0000 0000 0000
  1n00 0000 0000 0000 0000
  2n00 0000 0000 0000 0000
  3n00 0000 0000 0000 0000
  4n00 0000 0000 0000 0000
  5n00 0000 0000 0000 0000
  6n00 0000 0000 0000 0000         0 = OK
  7n00 0000 0000 0000 0000         X = Exclude
  8n00 0000 0000 0000 0000         I = Include
  9n00 0000 0000 0000 0000
  An00 0000 0000 0000 0000
  Bn00 0000 0000 0000 0000
  Cn00 0000 0000 0000 0000
  Dn00 0000 0000 0000 0000
  En00 0000 00I0 00II 0000
  Fn00 0III I000 0II0 0000

C>
```

This comes from QEMM watching what your programs do, what memory they access. Therefore, before you use this list, you must run those programs to give QEMM some experience. Follow the following analysis procedure, and don't run any other memory utilities other than QEMM while you do the following:

1. Make sure the QEMM line in CONFIG.SYS has the ON parameter and the MAPS=0 parameter and no others.
2. Save CONFIG.SYS and reboot the PC.
3. Run your programs and use all their abilities.
4. Start DESQview and then immediately quit from it—without running any programs in it. (Do this only if you want to use DESQview.)
5. Use all your computer hardware, from video displays to disk drives, printer, and network interfaces. You must format a floppy in each floppy drive.
6. Get QEMM.COM's report.
7. Put the EXCLUDE and INCLUDE suggestions from the map into the QEMM line in CONFIG.SYS, and take out the ON parameter and the MAPS=0 parameter.
8. Reboot the PC.
9. For best results, repeat the process until the alternate (press F3) Analysis list shows simply "0000-FFFF 1024K OK."
10. If you are using Stealth (ST:F or ST:M) add X=F000-FFFF FSTC to the QEMM command line to get the most accurate analysis. Once you find the smallest exclusion that works, remove the FSTC parameter.

The map—as in the example of Figure 7-7—shows the first megabyte of memory in your PC. Along the left side are the 64K segment addresses, in hexadecimal. Along the top are the additional hex addresses for all 4K chunks within those segments.

Within this map the symbols mean

O (OK) ....memory you can use

X(Exclude) ....memory you should exclude from QEMM's use (this is memory that QEMM didn't exclude already because it was mistakenly believed OK to use)

I (Include) ....memory that requires the INCLUDE parameter for QEMM to put to work

Memory Report

The Accessed topic tells you what memory has been used, the Analysis topic tells you what QEMM thinks you should do with memory, and the Memory topic tells you what QEMM has done to configure memory.

Figure 7-8. QEMM.COM Memory report example

```
C>qemm memory

                    Unavailable  Converted
             Initial  to QEMM    by QEMM     Leaving
Conventional:  631K  -    0K   -     0K    =  631K
Extended:     1024K  -    0K   -  1024K    =    0K
Expanded:        0K  -    0K   +   752K    =  752K
High RAM:        0K  -    0K   +   124K    =  124K
              ------   ------    ------      ------
   TOTAL:     1655K  -    0K   -   148K    = 1507K

                 148K QEMM Overhead
     Code & Data:    71K    Maps:          32K
     Tasks:          18K    Mapped ROM:     4K
     DMA Buffer:     12K    Unassigned:    11K
             3K Conventional Memory Overhead

C>
```

In the top table, as in the example of Figure 7-8, you can see the amounts of conventional, extended, top or Shadow, expanded, and high RAM in your PC. You get this report by typing

```
QEMM MEMORY
```

And you'll see how QEMM changed these amounts, from the initial state, through the amounts unavailable to QEMM (because a driver loaded before QEMM got it or its Shadow RAM, which QEMM can't use) and that converted by QEMM, to the final leaving state.

If any of these numbers seem wrong, you could have a wrong entry in the CMOS setup information or even a loose or defective memory chip.

In the bottom table of Figure 7-8, you can see how much memory QEMM used for itself to perform the conversions listed in the top table. QEMM needs memory for its code and data, maps, tasks, DMA buffer, mapped ROM, and even a bit of conventional memory overhead. (A little QEMM stays in conventional memory.) Unassigned memory is memory left over after QEMM's work, but it is less than16K and so cannot become more EMS memory. You can fine-tune QEMM's parameters to use up some of the unassigned memory or to free more until a full 16K is available to become expanded memory.

Top memory is something you find in some Compaq PCs; Shadow RAM is found on PCs with Chips & Technologies chip sets. See Chapter 4 for more details.

If a program needs extended memory and that program supports the EMS, XMS, or VCPI specifications, then QEMM allocates them memory even when no extended memory is officially left. If they don't support it, it is typically better to leave some extended memory for them with the EXTMEM= parameter on the QEMM line rather than by loading their drivers before QEMM.

Parameters

You use QEMM.COM's parameters by typing them after QEMM on the command line, like this:

```
QEMM parameter
```

You don't need to precede them with a slash, the way you do in some other QEMM programs. If you are asking for a particular report from QEMM.COM, put the parameter after the report name, such as

```
QEMM TYPE parameter
```

The parameters are as follows:

?..lists parameters
HELP ....describes parameters

MAP ....shows reports in map format (instead of as a list)
NOPAUSEONERROR ..
or
NOPE ....no stop to show the error message "Press to unload QEMM or any other key to continue with QEMM" when bumping into a QEMM error
PAUSE.............................pause and don't execute this QEMM.COM command until a key is pressed
RESET ....QEMM watches all memory to see if it is accessed or not; this parameter resets its records so that all memory is listed again as unaccessed until this point

Use RESET when analyzing how a particular program accesses memory.

CHAPTER EIGHT

QRAM.SYS

QRAM.SYS is a device driver—a program that loads into memory to extend DOS's abilities. QRAM.SYS can do two things: create high RAM (setting up for the LOADHI program) and allow use of video RAM for conventional memory (setting up for the program and moving the XBDA from its 639K address).

QRAM can map memory to addresses in the 640K to 1024K area, but it cannot do this for just any PC. It needs special hardware and software. The software is an Expanded Memory Manager (EMM) program. The hardware can be either expanded memory hardware (such as an expanded memory board) or a PC built on a Chips & Technologies chipset (the basic chips beside the processor) with the Shadow RAM feature to make high RAM and some extended memory. In summary you need:

1. An EMS board with expanded memory and an EMM
2. A C&T chipset with the Shadow RAM feature and some extended memory

EMS boards and C&T chipsets with Shadow RAM offer some circuits for remapping memory addresses. See Chapter 4 for more details on this technology.

Quarterdeck offers a free testing program called QTEST that can tell you what QRAM can offer to your PC.

You need expanded memory or extended memory because some memory chips must be remapped to those upper memory addresses. Just having addresses without chips doesn't do any good. (Chapter 4 explains this.)

Many PCs that ship with 1MB of memory make 640K of that conventional memory and 384K extended memory. C&T chipsets, called AT/386, NEAT, LEAP, or SCAT, automatically turn the 384K into Shadow RAM, giving it upper memory addresses from 640 to 1024K.

After QRAM maps memory to addresses in upper memory, the LOADHI and DOS Resource programs that come with QRAM can put drivers, resources, and TSR programs into that memory. This saves conventional memory where those drivers, resources, and TSRs would otherwise be loaded.

Because QRAM works with an EMM, you should always keep in mind that any adjustments or configuration changes can be made with QRAM parameters or with parameters of the EMM.

QRAM.SYS loads into your PC for operation by a line in CONFIG.SYS such as

```
DEVICE=QRAM.SYS
```

OPTIMIZE automatically installs this line along with the necessary parameters to make good use of memory in your PC. However, there are plenty of parameters you can use to change (that is, improve) this configuration.

QRAM.SYS Parameters

The parameters you can use to tell QRAM.SYS just how to do its work come as codes on its command line. As noted above, you put QRAM.SYS to work with a line in CONFIG.SYS, such as DEVICE=QRAM.SYS, or with a more elaborate path name to tell DOS just where to find it, such as

```
DEVICE=C:\QRAM\QRAM.SYS
```

You can add a parameter at the end of this line, after typing a slash, as in

```
DEVICE=C:\QRAM\QRAM.SYS /parameter
```

Some parameters have numeric values or address specifications associated with them, like these hypothetical examples:

```
DEVICE=C:\QRAM\QRAM.SYS/parameter=128
DEVICE=C:\QRAM\QRAM.SYS/parameter=A000-AFFF
```

Most parameters also have an abbreviation; for example, if “p” were the abbreviation for “parameter,” you could enter either

```
DEVICE=C:\QRAM\QRAM.SYS /PARAMETER=128
```
or
```
DEVICE=C:\QRAM\QRAM.SYS /P=128
```

You can specify more than one parameter on a line, separating them by a space. In fact, you may use the same parameter several times on a line—to exclude several, noncontiguous areas, for example. Parameters are processed from left to right in the order they appear on the line.

The parameters are briefly summarized in the following sections.

- `?`
  Use this parameter to list all parameters.

- `EXCLUDE`
  or
  `X`
  This parameter tells QEMM not to fill any area of high memory.

- `EXCLUDE=XXXX-YYYY`
  or
  `X=XXXX-YYYY`
  This tells QRAM not to fill the area of memory from address XXXX to address YYYY. You exclude memory from being filled if it has some other use, such as being the address of some adapter’s ROM. (You may also exclude memory with the parameters of most EMMs.)

Because parameters are processed from left to right, you could exclude some area and then include some smaller area within it.

- FORCEEMS
  or
  FEMS
  Use this parameter to have QRAM honor EMS memory requests. This is only necessary if you use the FRAMELENGTH parameter with a value less than four. FORCEEMS is necessary then to give programs some access to expanded memory, even though there is not a full page frame in existence. (Some programs, however, won't use expanded memory unless they have a full page frame to work with.)

- FRAMELENGTH=X
  or
  FL=X
  This parameter says the page frame is made of 0 to 4 pages, with 0 meaning no page frame and 4 the EMS standard (4 pages of 16K each). This frees one or more pages for use as high RAM. Only use this if you have programs that can get by with fewer than four page frame pages—you may need to also use FORCEEMS as described above.

- GETSIZE
  or
  GS
  This tells QRAM how much high RAM it needs. (OPTIMIZE uses this when it works.)

- HELP
  Use this parameter to obtain a description of all QRAM parameters.

- HIDE=XXXX-YYYY
  or
  H=XXXX-YYYY
  This parameter tells QRAM not to use memory in addresses from XXXX

to YYYY, even if it is mappable. (You can get the same effect with most EMMs' exclusion parameters.)

- `INCLUDE=XXXX-YYYY`
  or
  `I`
  With this parameter QRAM uses the memory from address XXXX to address YYYY.

- `LABEL`
  or
  `LB`
  This is an internal OPTIMIZE paramcter.

- `NOFILL`
  or
  `NO`
  This tells QRAM not to fill conventional memory or video memory below 640K . Normally when a PC has less than 640K conventional memory, QRAM fills it by mapping extended or expanded memory into those addresses.

- `NOPAUSEONERROR`
  or
  `NOPE`
  Use this parameter to tell QRAM not to pause and show the error message "QRAM: Press to unload QRAM, or any other key to continue with QRAM" even if encountering an error. That's useful if you've already seen and dealt with the error.

- `NOSH6ADOWRAM`
  or
  `NOSH`
  When you enter this parameter, QRAM does not use Shadow RAM. (Normally QRAM automatically detects Shadow RAM and uses it to make

high RAM.) Shadow RAM can sometimes cause QRAM trouble, and you can use this parameter to see if that is the problem.

- `NOTOKENRING`
  or
  `NTR`
  This parameter tells QRAM not to try to detect a token ring adapter for networks. (Normally token ring adapters are not found in the same way that other adapters are, and not wanting to miss one and use memory addresses it shouldn't, QRAM automatically uses special tests to find it. These tests can make trouble for other adapters, however.) You may need to look up the token ring adapter's address, however, and use an EXCLUDE statement to make sure it isn't in conflict with QRAM.

- `NOVIDEOFILL`
  or
  `NV`
  With this parameter QRAM does not fill memory addresses from A000 to B7FF with memory. This matters only on PCs with monochrome or CGA adapters. On a monochrome PC, QRAM normally increases conventional memory from 640K to 704K. On a CGA PC it increases it from 640K to 736K. However, these increases can sometimes cause problems.

- `NOVIDEORAM`
  or
  `NVR`
  Use this parameter to tell QRAM not to make high RAM in mappable memory in addresses from A000 to B7FF. This is rarely used because its work can be done by VIDRAMEMS (see VIDRAMEMS for details).

- `NOXBDA`
  or
  `NX`
  This parameter tells QRAM not to move the extended BIOS data area, the XBDA. Normally QRAM automatically moves it from its place at 639K

into some other space so that conventional memory can be extended above 640K. Some programs need to find it at 639K, however.

- `PAUSE`

  This parameter pauses the display when sending messages—so you can press the key to stop QRAM installation. This is useful when experimenting with parameters.

- `RAM`

  Use this parameter to fill areas from 640K to 1024K that the EMM says are mappable, or usable.

- `RAM=XXXX-YYYY`

  Use this parameter to fill areas from address XXXX to address YYYY with memory, and to any other mappable areas as well.

- `REGION=NN`

  or

  `R=NN`

  This parameter loads QRAM itself into upper memory region NN. Normally QRAM loads most of itself high, but this parameter lets you specify which region. REGION=0 means loading into conventional memory.

- `VIDRAMEGA`

  or

  `VREGA`

  This tells QRAM not to map the video area, the memory addresses from A000 to BFFF (or on monochrome systems from B000 to B7FF). This is necessary if the VIDRAM utility (see Chapter 11) is to use this video memory as additional conventional memory. (Video memory used this way is slower than EMS memory.) It has the same effect as HIDE=A000-BFFF.

Video memory is typically much slower than expanded memory.

- VIDRAMEMS

  or

  VREMS

  This makes the video memory, from addresses A000 to BUFF, mappable. When the VIDRAM utility (see Chapter 11) extends conventional memory, it does so with EMS memory, which is faster than the video memory chips. This has the same effect as VIDEORAM INCLUDE=A000-B7FF.

Sometimes you need to use VIDRAMEMS when you want to extend conventional memory with VIDRAM, because a big speed difference between video memory and conventional memory can crash some programs or peripherals.

Don't use VIDRAMEMS with versions of DESQview before 2.26.

VIDRAMEMS works only with an EMS card that can map A000-B7FF and an EMM that has included those addresses.

Multitasking On An 8088/8086

Here are some guidelines for setting up an 8088, 8086, or 80286 PC for multitasking.

Configure memory as conventional memory and then EMS 4.0 (or EEMS) expanded memory. (On a 286 PC, configure 64K as extended memory, which many expanded memory boards can do, though some demand that you do this in larger chunks than 64K.) Disable motherboard memory as far down as possible. Configure the memory on an expanded memory board to backfill or map to the addresses of that disabled motherboard memory.

Use QRAM to map unused areas of high memory (640K to 1024K) if your expanded memory board allows. Then use LOADHI to load TSRs, device drivers, and resources into these unused areas.

Put QRAM.SYS into the CONFIG.SYS file after your Expanded Memory Manager. Use LOADHI.SYS in CONFIG.SYS to load device drivers into high memory. Use LOADHI.COM in AUTOEXEC.BAT to load TSRs into high memory.

It is important to put QRAM.SYS in CONFIG.SYS immediately after the line for the Expanded Memory Manager.

CHAPTER NINE

LOADHI

Probably the single most important feature of QEMM and QRAM is the LOADHI program. This lets you load drivers, DOS resources (such as BUFFERS and FCBs), and TSRs (memory-resident programs) into upper memory (also known as high memory), at addresses from 640K to 1024K. By loading them there, instead of in conventional memory from 0K to 640K, they free conventional memory. That's a boon because conventional memory is the only place many programs can run. Freeing it means more programs can run, and those that do have more memory to improve their performance. If you have enough room in upper memory, it can also mean the freedom to load more TSRs, resources, and drivers than before, permitting more powerful use of your PC. If you run DESQview, it can mean more memory for each DESQview window.

The exchange isn't completely free, however. Before loading drivers and TSRs into upper memory, there must be some memory at those addresses. In most PCs this means a memory manager—such as QRAM or QEMM—must fill those addresses with extended or expanded memory. It must map memory to those addresses. (This is called making UMBs—upper memory blocks. Not all PCs can do it—you need a 386 or 486 processor, an expanded memory board, or a special Chips & Technologies chipset, as explained in Chapter 4.) Naturally that means you have less extended or expanded memory to use for other things. However, extended and expanded memory are less precious than conventional memory. You can have only 640K of conventional memory; you can have as much as 32MB of expanded memory, and from 16 to thousands of megabytes of extended memory. The trade is almost always worthwhile. Figures 9-1 and 9-2 show typical diagrams of before and after loading high.

Figure 9-1. Typical memory map before loading high

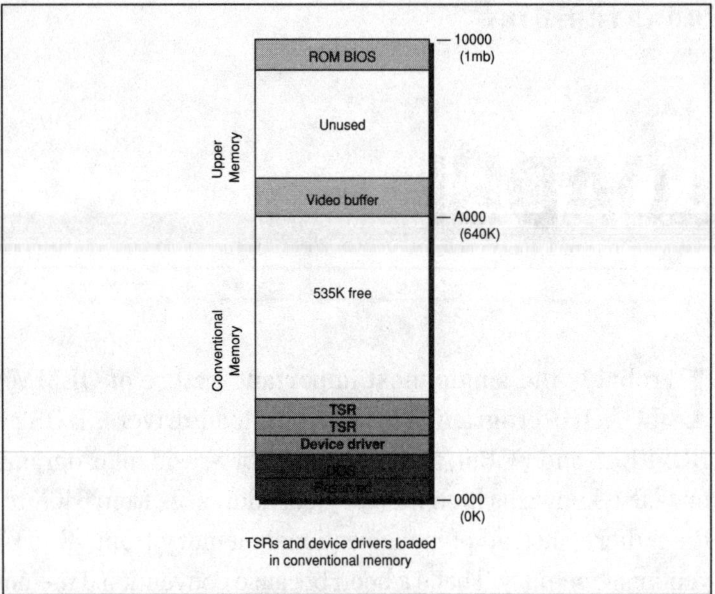

Figure 9-2. Typical memory map after loading high

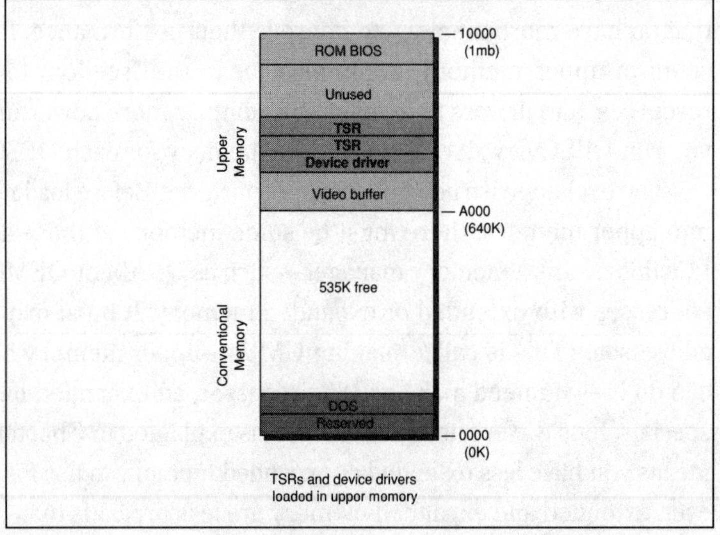

As you can see, the upper memory addresses you can use are not going to be contiguous. It won't be one big stretch of free memory. Instead it will be a series of memory regions, broken up by addresses used for BIOS ROM, video adapter memory, and other such uses. When LOADHI wants to put something into one of these regions, it creates a new block in that area to fit the program or driver.

If you run OPTIMIZE and your PC can benefit from LOADHI, it should automatically put the proper QEMM or QRAM statements to create UMBs and then to load drivers and TSRs into them efficiently. For QEMM this means you need the RAM parameter on the QEMM.SYS line in CONFIG.SYS.

If LOADHI cannot put something into upper memory, it loads it into conventional memory—it won't just leave it out of the configuration.

LOADHI is actually two programs: LOADHI.SYS and LOADHI.COM. Both load software into upper memory. LOADHI.SYS loads device drivers. It is a DEVICE statement in CONFIG.SYS. LOADHI.COM loads programs such as TSRs and DOS resources. It is a statement in AUTOEXEC.BAT or can be used directly from the DOS prompt.

Both LOADHI.SYS and LOADHI.COM have the same set of parameters, chosen as parameter codes on their command lines.

LOADHI.COM reports on what's loaded high

Because you can use LOADHI.COM from the DOS prompt, it is always available to tell you what has been loaded high. Just type

```
LOADHI
```

and press Enter, and you see such a report. (Without any parameters it doesn't change loading, it just tells you what is loading.) Figure 9-3 shows an example. This report tells you the region of usable upper memory (the contiguous area of upper memory), the block used in that region to load some program (by beginning and ending addresses), the size of the block (in kilobytes), the status of the block (either Used or Available), and the name of the program using it.

LOADHI.SYS Loads Drivers High

LOADHI.SYS loads device drivers into upper memory. You use it as a line in CONFIG.SYS. It can put as many as 32 device driver definitions into upper memory. Most device drivers can load high. A few cannot work from upper memory; and some can work only with the appropriate LOADHI parameters (as explained later). QEMM.SYS cannot load high.

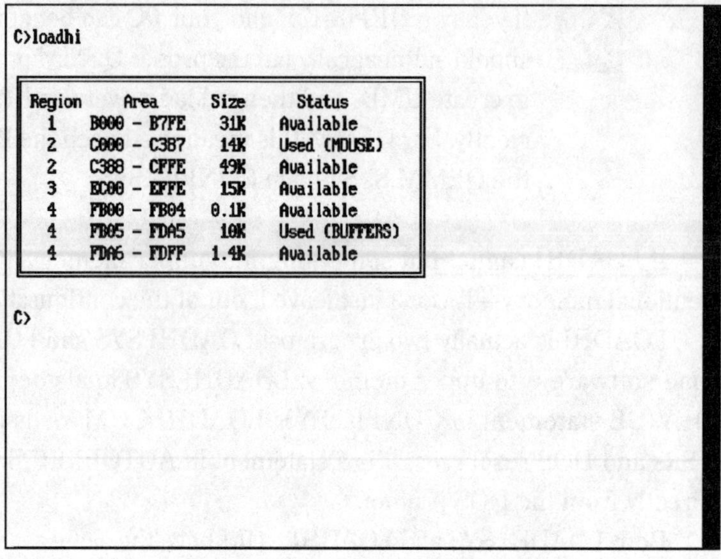

C>loadhi
Region Area Size Status
1 B000 - B7FE 31K Available
2 C000 - C3B7 14K Used (MOUSE)
2 C3B8 - CFFE 49K Available
3 EC00 - EFFE 15K Available
4 FB00 - FB04 0.1K Available
4 FB05 - FDA5 10K Used (BUFFERS)
4 FDA6 - FDFF 1.4K Available
C>

Figure 9-3. Example LOADHI.COM report on memory

To use LOADHI.SYS, just make it part of any device loading line in CONFIG.SYS. For example, the line

```
DEVICE=DRIVER.SYS
```

in CONFIG.SYS becomes

```
DEVICE=LOADHI.SYS DRIVER.SYS
```

In most cases you want to include the paths for these files so the PC knows where they are on disk. Thus you might enter a line such as

```
DEVICE=C:\QEMM\LOADHI.SYS C:\DOS\DRIVER.SYS
```

You do this for each DEVICE= device driver that needs to be loaded.

If you need to add any option parameters to LOADHI.SYS, or if the DRIVER.SYS file has some, you make them part of the line. See the following parameters section for examples.

LOADHI.COM Loads TSRs and Resources High

The LOADHI.COM program loads other TSR programs and DOS resources (if you use QEMM or QRAM's resource utilities) into upper memory.

To have LOADHI.COM load a TSR into upper memory, you simply add LOADHI to the command line for that TSR. For example, if your TSR was called TSR.COM, you normally load it into conventional memory with the command

```
TSR
```

This can be at the DOS prompt or more typically is a line in the AUTOEXEC.BAT file or some other batch file. To load it into upper memory, you make this line

```
LOADHI TSR
```

If you need to tell DOS where LOADHI.COM or TSR.COM are, you add path information, such as

```
C:\QEMM\LOADHI C:\TSR
```

If you want to add parameters to LOADHI.COM or TSR.COM, you put these on the same line, as in

```
C:\QEMM\LOADHI /loadhiparameter C:\TSR /tsrparameter
```

(substituting the actual parameter abbreviations for "loadhiparameter" and "tsr-parameter").

To save the most memory, work through your AUTOEXEC.BAT and other batch files and see if you can load all the various TSRs high.

LOADHI.COM can also load DOS resources high. These include BUFFERS, FILES, FCBs, and LASTDRIVE resources. Normally these data structures are in conventional memory, but if you use the QEMM or QRAM resource programs in place of the DOS commands, and you also use LOADHI, you can put the data structures into upper memory (see Chapter 10 for details). Generally the approach is to

1. Set the DOS resource statements to minimums in CONFIG.SYS.
2. Put the QEMM or QRAM resource programs to work in AUTOEXEC.BAT, with the parameters to give you enough of each resource.
3. Add LOADHI to the beginning of each resource line to make sure the resource program loads into upper memory. Then any data structure it creates for the resource will be in upper memory after the program itself finishes its work.

For example, you could create BUFFERs to improve disk performance with the AUTOEXEC.BAT line

```
C:\QEMM\LOADHI C:\QEMM\BUFFERS=30
LOADHI.SYS and LOADHI.COM parameters
```

LOADHI can do its work well without any special considerations, most of the time. OPTIMIZE puts LOADHI on the case in the most efficient way, most of the time.

But for those times when you want more control, when you need to help LOADHI, there are command-line options. These parameters are codes you put after the LOADHI command to tell it just how to use memory. A program might not load into upper memory without the right parameter. Several programs may not all fit into upper memory at once, without the right parameters. You can use more than one parameter just by putting them all on the same LOADHI command line.

Parameters follow LOADHI as a slash, a code word (or its abbreviation), and sometimes a colon followed by a value, like this:

```
LOADHI /parameter:value
```

For two parameters, this would be

```
LOADHI /parameter1:value /parameter2:value
```

Because LOADHI must also be followed by the name of the program, driver, or resource it is loading high (a driver by LOADHI.SYS, a program by

LOADHI.COM) the full line, with paths, might be

```
DEVICE=C:\QEMM\LOADHI.SYS/parameter:value
C:\DRIVER.SYS/driverparameters
```

for CONFIG.SYS, or

```
C:\QEMM\LOADHI /parameter:value
C:\program /programparameters
```

for AUTOEXEC.BAT or the DOS command line.

The parameters for LOADHI.SYS and LOADHI.COM are briefly described in the following sections.

- ?
  Use this parameter to see a list all LOADHI.SYS and LOADHI.COM parameters.

- HELP
  This parameter gives you a display of the Help screen.

- PAUSE
  This parameter causes LOADHI to pause while analyzing parameters.

- NOPAUSEONERROR
  or
  NOPE
  This parameter tells LOADHI not to pause to show an error message when there is an error (so you don't have to view error messages you know about and have already dealt with or accepted).

- @:FILENAME
  With this parameter you can search a response file called FILENAME for the parameters for loading this program. If no filename is specified, an environment variable called LOADHIDATA is searched for the name

of the response file. LOADHIDATA comes from running OPTIMIZE with the /RESPONSE parameter. The default filename is LOADHI.RF.

The response file is a series of lines like these

```
programname   LOADHI parameters
programname   LOADHI parameters
```

with the program names from the LOADHI command line and the one or more parameters as the codes and values you want to use. If there is no line for a program that was referred to the response file, that program will just load into conventional memory.

- `BESTFIT`

  or

  `B`

  This parameter causes LOADHI to use smallest block of memory that fits.

- `HAPPIEST`

  or

  `H`

  This parameter causes LOADHI to use the smallest block of memory that fits and doesn't cause an error.

- `REGION:N`

  or

  `R:N`

  Use this parameter to load into region number N.

- `LARGEST`

  or

  `L`

  Use this parameter to load into the largest block.

- `LARGEST:N`

  or

  `L:N`

  With this parameter LOADHI loads into the Nth largest block.

- `SMALLEST`

  or

  `S`

  Use this parameter to load into the smallest block.

- `SMALLEST:N`

  or

  `S:N`

  With this parameter LOADHI loads into the Nth smallest block.

- `EXCLUDEREGION:N`

  or

  `XR:N`

  This parameter tells LOADHI not to use region number N to load this program.

- `EXCLUDELARGEST`

  or

  `XL`

  This parameter tells LOADHI not to use the largest block to load this program.

- `EXCLUDELARGEST:N`

  or

  `XL:N`

  With this parameter in the command line, LOADHI does not use the Nth largest block to load this program.

- `EXCLUDESMALLEST`

  or

  `XS`

  This parameter tells LOADHI not to use the smallest block to load this program.

- `EXCLUDESMALLEST:N`

  or

  `XS:N`

  Use this parameter to tell LOADHI not to use the Nth smallest block to load this program.

- `GETSIZE`

  or

  `GS`

  This parameter causes LOADHI to find the precise amount of memory this program needs in bytes to load and initialize (the first value it tells you) and to stay in memory (the second value), then load the program into conventional memory.

  GETSIZE is used for experimenting, because its result is to load a program or driver into conventional memory.

- `GETSIZE:F`

  or

  `GS:F`

  This parameter works the same as GETSIZE above, but it includes the filename (F) where the two found amounts of memory (initial and final) are to be saved on disk (as either a new file or appended to an existing file).

  OPTIMIZE uses the GETSIZE parameter to create its own file listing the amounts of memory various programs and drivers need to load high.

- `LINKTOP`

  or

  `LINK`

  This parameter connects free memory in upper addresses to the DOS memory chain, which can then be of some use to DOS programs. Don't use this with any other parameter or with any program name to load high. Use it just before loading an application that might use the chained memory. See UNLINKTOP.

- `UNLINKTOP`

  or

  `UNLINK`

  Use this parameter to disconnect free memory in upper memory from the conventional memory DOS chain. See LINKTOP.

- `LO`

  With this parameter LOADHI uses conventional memory instead of upper memory (high RAM) to load the program. (This parameter sometimes is used temporarily when editing CONFIG.SYS and AUTOEXEC.BAT files—sort of like putting a REM comment in an AUTOEXEC.BAT line—it keeps the information in the file but temporarily disables it.)

- `NOLO`

  or

  `NL`

  This parameter tells LOADHI that, if this program won't fit into upper memory, it should not be loaded (not into conventional memory, that is).

- `RESIDENTSIZE=NNNN`

  or

  `RES=NNNN`

  This parameter tells LOADHI the final size (NNNN) of the program to let LOADHi verify there is enough memory to load the program. Use this with SQF or SQT parameters. (OPTIMIZE uses RESIDENTSIZE in its work.)

- RESPONSE:F

  or

  R:F

  Use this parameter to tell LOADHI to look in a response file for the parameters for this program. The file is either named (by whatever substitutes for F) or is the default LOADHI.RF. With no specified name, LOADHI.COM looks for the environment variable LOADHIDATA that OPTIMIZE makes to find the name of the response file.

- SIZE:NNNN

  This parameter allocates from a block that will best fit NNNN bytes of program. (You typically choose NNNN from a GETSIZE report or by some other analysis of just what minimum memory a program or driver needs to initialize.)

- SIZE:NNNNK

  This parameter has the same effect as SIZE:NNNN but measures the block in kilobytes instead of in bytes.

- SQUEEZEF

  or

  SQF

  Use this parameter to make temporary use of the page frame area of upper memory so the device or program has room to initialize (though not to overlap the page frame when finally resident in upper memory). This is a SQUEEZE parameter that OPTIMIZE makes. This parameter is ignored if QEMM's STEALTH is in effect as ST:M or ST:F, because STEALTH uses the page frame area.

- SQUEEZET

  or

  SQT

  This parameter allows LOADHI to make temporary use of an area of upper memory so the device or program has room to initialize (though not to overlap the area when finally resident). OPTIMIZE uses SQT while it works with its SQUEEZE parameter.

- `TERMINATERESIDENT`
  or
  `TSR`
  This parameter terminates a TSR, leaving only a stub of about 100 bytes resident. Use it to avoid an error message of the DOS 4 INSTALL command that suggests a TSR hasn't loaded when it actually has loaded into upper memory.

DOS 5 and Loading High

Version 5 of DOS was the first version with its own ability to load some programs and TSRs high—into upper memory. It does this through the DEVICEHIGH and LOADHIGH commands, but does not allow specifying regions or Squeezing. These commands work much like LOADHI.SYS and LOADHI.COM and appear in LOADHI.COM reports.

CHAPTER TEN

DOS Resource Utilities—BUFFERS.COM, FILES.COM, FCBS.COM, LASTDRIV.COM

DOS has a number of features that use memory. Some of these are *resources*—data structures that help improve system performance. There are default settings for these resources in DOS (although the defaults differ somewhat with the various versions of DOS, and some early versions of DOS don't even provide all of these resources). CONFIG.SYS statements can increase the allocations from the default levels.

The resources use memory, and unfortunately some of the resources cannot be loaded high, so they eat up previous conventional memory. But QEMM and QRAM are equipped with some utility programs that take the place of the DOS resources: BUFFERS.COM, FILES.COM, LASTDRIV.COM, and FCBS.COM.

All four of these programs let you specify how much resource to create or to add, using lines in the AUTOEXEC.BAT file such as

```
BUFFERS=10
```

to create 10 buffers, or

```
BUFFERS=+10
```

to create 10 buffers more than existed before.

If used without parameters, the commands tell you how much and what memory is currently allocated to that resource. All can be loaded into upper memory with the LOADHI program of QEMM or QRAM, as in

```
LOADHI BUFFERS=10
```

Because these resources run in AUTOEXEC.BAT as programs instead of in CONFIG.SYS as drivers, you get more conventional memory. The standard DOS CONFIG.SYS settings for resources are decreased and the corresponding resources in AUTOEXEC.BAT are increased.

OPTIMIZE automatically configures your PC for best use of DOS resources (although you can fine-tune this if you know enough about DOS and QEMM or QRAM).

BUFFERS.COM

Buffers are small areas of memory that hold recently used information from disk. If a program can find disk information it needs in memory chips, a lot of time is saved. So having buffers effectively speeds apparent disk performance and overall computer performance.

But buffers are areas of memory, so devoting memory to them subtracts from the memory that other software can use.

DOS has a default minimum number of buffers, ranging from 2 to 15 depending on the version of DOS you use. Each takes 528 bytes of memory, or 0.5K (enough to buffer one sector of the disk). With the statement

```
BUFFERS=
```

in CONFIG.SYS, you can increase the number of buffers to improve performance. However, DOS makes these buffers in conventional memory.

If instead you create buffers using QEMM or QRAM's BUFFERS.COM program in AUTOEXEC.BAT, you can use the LOADHI command to put those buffers into upper memory.

When using a disk cache, you may not want any more than the minimum number of buffers, because the cache will probably do a better job of speeding disk performance.

DOS 4 doesn't benefit from BUFFERS.COM because it uses a different buffer structure. DOS versions 2, 3, and 5 work well with BUFFERS.COM.

DOS 5 can load much of itself into HMA with the DOS=HIGH statement in CONFIG.SYS. This also puts BUFFERS into the HMA, as explained in more detail in Chapter 15.

Some networks, such as Artisoft's LANtastic, do not function properly with BUFFERS.COM loaded high.

To use BUFFERS.COM to get 30 buffers, for example, change the line in CONFIG.SYS to a minimum BUFFERS setting, such as

```
BUFFERS=1
```

and then put a linc in AUTOEXEC.BAT such as

```
LOADHI BUFFERS=30
```
or
```
LOADHI BUFFERS=+29
```

Don't leave out the CONFIG.SYS minimum setting or you'll end up with the default buffers, which could be significantly more in conventional memory.

Make this the first statement in AUTOEXEC.BAT, and all following statements can use the faster disk performance. (Include the path if necessary so DOS knows where to find the QEMM or QRAM BUFFERS.COM program.)

Finally, to check on the number of buffers, type

```
BUFFERS
```

and press Enter from the DOS prompt. You are told how many buffers there are. You can add to this at any time with a statement such as

```
BUFFERS+somenumber
```

FILES.COM

Files are the basic unit of computer information stored on disk. A file could be a document, a program, or an image. DOS opens files before using them, and closes them again when done. It uses a resource called FILES to keep track of which disk files are open. The number in the FILES= statement sets the maximum number of files that can be open at once. Each additional open file means 53 more bytes of memory used. The default setting is smaller than most users need, so most CONFIG.SYS files have a line such as

```
FILES=20
```

to increase the default setting.

Because DESQview encourages multitasking, it often needs 20 or more files open at once.

QEMM and QRAM replace DOS FILES with the FILES.COM program, which lets the FILES resource be loaded high into upper memory. It is typically run in AUTOEXEC.BAT with a line such as

```
FILES=20
```

or

```
FILES+19
```

To load it high, the full line in AUTOEXEC.BAT would be

```
LOADHI FILES=20
```

At the same time you'll want to cut the CONFIG.SYS FILES setting to a minimum, such as FILES=10.

To test how many files your system has, enter the command

```
FILES
```

and press Enter. You see a report on how many files you can open at once.

LASTDRIV.COM

DOS can support more than one disk drive at a time. It assigns a drive letter to each disk drive. Also, the SUBST program that appears in recent versions of DOS lets you create logical disk drives—new disk drive letters that refer back to other physical disk drives. Keeping track of physical and logical disk drive letters takes some memory—about 80 bytes each.

The DOS LASTDRIV resource sets the last usable disk drive letter, and so sets the amount of memory devoted to disk drive letters. QEMM and QRAM's LASTDRIV.COM program lets you load this resource into upper memory.

To use LASTDRIV.COM, change any LASTDRIVE= statement in CONFIG.SYS to represent only the actual disk volumes you have. Use the

```
LASTDRIV
```

command at the DOS prompt and press Enter to see which disk drives are assigned currently. Then put that minimum in CONFIG.SYS, such as LASTDRIVE=C for a simple system with a floppy drive A and a hard drive C.

Then add a line such as

```
LOADHI LASTDRIV H
```

into AUTOEXEC.BAT. You can also use a numeric addition, as you did in the LASTDRIVE=C statement in CONFIG.SYS above. Thus you would enter

```
LOADHI LASTDRIV +5
```

into AUTOEXEC.BAT to get to drive H.

Each time you use the LASTDRIV command you create a full new drive resource table and cannot recover the memory from the previous table.

FCBS.COM

FCBs (file control blocks) are anachronisms. That is, although they were used in version 1 of DOS to keep track of files, later versions of DOS (2 through

5) use file handles. However, because some programs written for DOS 1 depended on FCBs, later versions (except DOS 2, unfortunately) keep the resource to support those programs.

FCBS.COM is only useful if you have an FCBS statement in CONFIG.SYS, are using the SHARE command from DOS, and don't have DOS 2.

The DOS FCB statement in CONFIG.SYS has two parameters. The first tells how many FCBs you have and the second how many of those should be protected when DOS closes an FCB. Each FCB needs 53 bytes.

FCBS.COM lets you load this resource high instead of having it in conventional memory. To do this

1. Look for the FCBS statement in CONFIG.SYS. Note the parameters with it.
2. Delete that FCBS statement from CONFIG.SYS.
3. Add a line to AUTOEXEC.BAT that says

   ```
   LOADHI FCBS=X,Y
   ```

   where X and Y are the parameters you saw in the CONFIG.SYS statement.
4. Reboot the PC.

Now you can check on the FCBs allocated by typing

```
FCBS
```

in the QEMM (or QRAM) directory. You see a report on how many FCBs are allocated. Remember that you can change this value at any time with a statement from the DOS prompt such as

```
LOADHI FCBS +2,2
```

which would add two more FCBs.

Like LASTDRIV.COM, the FCBS resource uses a new block of memory each time you reallocate FCBs, and the old table is not recovered until your reboot the PC. So you'll lose memory if you willy-nilly change FCBs.

CHAPTER ELEVEN

VIDRAM

QEMM's (and QRAM's) VIDRAM utility can give you as much as 96K more conventional memory, completely usable by most programs. In fact, this is the only way you can actually break the 640K barrier, reaching as much as 736K of standard, conventional memory. The only catch is that you are restricted in the display modes you can use. For some programs that's a terminal catch; for others it doesn't matter a whit.

You can use VIDRAM whether or not you're loading high, STEALTHing, or using other such QEMM (and QRAM) features. In fact, you can use it without even loading the QEMM driver in CONFIG.SYS.

This chapter explains how to use VIDRAM.

Quick VIDRAM

If you're running a program that produces only a text-mode display, you have an EGA or VGA display adapter, and you have at least a full 640K in your PC, then change to the directory that has the QEMM files and type

```
VIDRAM ON
```

You have 64K to 96K more conventional memory available from that point on.

Technology background—how VIDRAM works

The display screen of your PC is connected to the PC's video adapter. Sometimes this is some chips built into the motherboard (the main circuit board). Usually it is a separate circuit board plugged into one of the PC's slots.

The video adapter, under control from the microprocessor, puts images on the display. The video adapter needs memory to work. This memory comes in two forms:

- ROM instructions telling the computer how to put information on the display
- RAM to hold the actual image that will be sent to the display

The ROM is given address space in upper memory. As explained in Chapter 9, QEMM can work with and around the ROM addresses to load TSRs and drivers into upper memory.

The RAM chips the video adapter uses are typically on the video adapter board itself. It is given addresses in upper memory. The amount and location depends on the video adapter, as you can see in Figure 11-1.

Figure 11-1. Diagram of video memory that VIDRAM can use

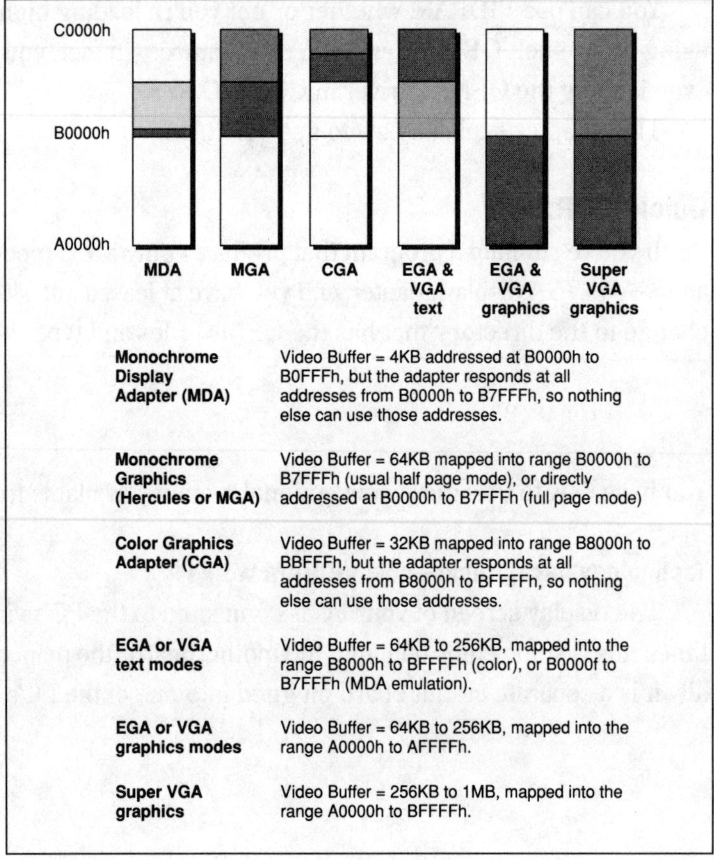

C0000h
B0000h
A0000h
MDA
MGA
CGA
EGA & VGA text
EGA & VGA graphics
Super VGA graphics
Monochrome Display Adapter (MDA)
Video Buffer = 4KB addressed at B0000h to B0FFFh, but the adapter responds at all addresses from B0000h to B7FFFh, so nothing else can use those addresses.
Monochrome Graphics (Hercules or MGA)
Video Buffer = 64KB mapped into range B0000h to B7FFFh (usual half page mode), or directly addressed at B0000h to B7FFFh (full page mode)
Color Graphics Adapter (CGA)
Video Buffer = 32KB mapped into range B8000h to BBFFFh, but the adapter responds at all addresses from B8000h to BFFFFh, so nothing else can use those addresses.
EGA or VGA text modes
Video Buffer = 64KB to 256KB, mapped into the range B8000h to BFFFFh (color), or B0000f to B7FFFh (MDA emulation).
EGA or VGA graphics modes
Video Buffer = 64KB to 256KB, mapped into the range A0000h to AFFFFh.
Super VGA graphics
Video Buffer = 256KB to 1MB, mapped into the range A0000h to BFFFFh.

Video adapters often offer more than one mode of operation. This lets them provide only the resolution (number of dots on the screen) and colors that you actually need for a particular task. It also lets them be compatible with previous generations of video adapters.

The simplest mode is monochrome text, which needs only 4K of memory. It stores 80 columns of 25 characters each, a total of 2000 characters. Each character needs two bytes, one for the character and another for that character's attributes (such as blinking, bright, underlined), for a total of 4K of information to set up the display.

Graphics modes demand more memory. VGA, for example, at 320 dots across the screen by 200 dots top to bottom means 64K dots on screen. If each dot can be any of 256 colors, then each dot needs a byte. (The 8 bits of the byte can represent 256 different patterns and therefore stand for 256 different colors.) That means 64K bytes are for the display memory—the video buffer.

EGA and VGA adapters can use lots of upper memory addresses for their graphic mode video buffers. But if you run an EGA or VGA adapter in the monochrome text mode, those memory addresses lie unused. Only 4K are needed for the buffer.

Unused memory! Just what QEMM and QRAM love to hear. In this case they offer you the utility program VIDRAM to take advantage of that unused memory. VIDRAM captures any contiguous memory addresses just above the 640K mark and attaches them to conventional memory. As long as you operate that EGA or VGA in text mode, this memory is available to your DOS programs. (A few DOS programs can't use it because they are unable to understand memory beyond the 640K mark.)

Part of the VIDRAM program is a TSR. It loads into memory and stays there. It doesn't need the help of a memory manager such as QEMM, and it works on 8088, 8086, 286, 386, and 486 PCs. It can work with a memory manager, however, as explained later on in this chapter.

VIDRAM takes memory on the EGA or VGA adapter that isn't used and gives it to DOS programs. It can do this only if those programs work in text mode, not if they use any graphics. However, attempting to run a graphics program or graphic part of a program won't automatically crash your PC with VIDRAM. The VIDRAM program is smart enough to intercept and stop requests to go graphic.

VIDRAM can give you 96K more memory if you have an EGA or VGA color display, 64K if you have an EGA or VGA monochrome display or a pair of displays.

Using VIDRAM

You can run VIDRAM each time you need it, or run it through the AUTOEXEC.BAT file to always be available.

To run VIDRAM when you're about to use a text-mode program, just change to the directory with the VIDRAM program (the QEMM or QRAM directory), type

```
VIDRAM ON
```

and press Enter. VIDRAM loads into memory, captures the video memory and attaches it to conventional memory, and tells you what it has done. It continues to provide that memory until you turn off VIDRAM or the PC.

If you always want VIDRAM running, just add the lines

```
CD QEMM
VIDRAM ON
```

to your AUTOEXEC.BAT file (assuming QEMM is the name of the directory where you installed the QEMM files, including VIDRAM). Then reboot your PC.

Learning VIDRAM status

If you don't know if VIDRAM is already running or not, just change to the directory with the VIDRAM program, type

```
VIDRAM
```

and press Enter. You see a quick report telling you if VIDRAM is active or not and how much DOS memory is available.

VIDRAM parameters

You can adjust VIDRAM's behavior with certain parameters. You implement these parameters with switches, code letters you put after the VIDRAM command. (The ON parameter has its own parameters, as you'll see.) The following sections briefly describe the VIDRAM parameters.

- `NOCGA`

  This stops any CGA, EGA, or VGA graphic use of memory and makes VIDRAM resident, but it doesn't extend conventional memory.

- `NOEGA`

  This parameter stops any EGA or VGA graphic use of memory and makes VIDRAM resident, but it doesn't extend conventional memory.

  Use the NOEGA parameter to avoid memory conflicts when some video RAM is mapped with EMS memory by a program other than VIDRAM and a graphics program also tries to use that memory.

- `RESIDENT`

  or

  `RES`

  This parameter puts VIDRAM into memory but doesn't enable it.

- `OFF`

  or

  `OF`

  Use this parameter to turn VIDRAM off so you can use graphics.

- `ON`

  Use this parameter to turn VIDRAM on, adding to conventional memory and stopping any graphic use of memory.

- `ON OVERRIDE`
  or
  `ON OV`
  or
  `ON OR`
  This parameter tries to turn VIDRAM on even when VIDRAM's own intelligence doesn't think it should, perhaps because there are two video adapters or when a memory manager is using part of the video RAM. (It isn't always successful in forcing VIDRAM on.)

- `ON EGA`
  This turns VIDRAM on and makes it use video RAM memory instead of EMS memory when video RAM is mappable. This is the default when video RAM is not mappable.

- `ON EMS`
  This parameter turns VIDRAM on and makes it use EMS memory, which is the default if video RAM area is mappable (the memory manager needs to have made A000-B7FF mappable).

When you use VIDRAM with EMS memory mapped in the video area by QEMM or QRAM, use VIDRAM EMS or VIDRAM EGA.

- `Loading VIDRAM high`
  Part of VIDRAM is a TSR, but only a very small part. This is the part that intercepts requests to change to graphics mode. Still, if you want to conserve every possible byte of conventional memory, you can load that part into upper memory by entering the LOADHI command

```
LOADHI VIDRAM RESIDENT
```

and then pressing Enter. This won't be enough to turn VIDRAM on, however, because the part that isn't resident is the part that converts video memory to conventional. You still must enter the command

```
VIDRAM ON
```

and press Enter to see more conventional memory.

CHAPTER TWELVE

QEXT.SYS

QEXT.SYS is a program that comes with QRAM. It manages extended memory in two ways:

- It lets DESQview load part of itself in HMA so there's more conventional memory for each DESQview window.
- It handles any program's extended memory requests as long as they follow XMS rules.

QEXT.SYS gives you everything that the DOS 5 or Windows extended memory manager—HIMEM.SYS—offers, plus that ability to load DESQview into HMA.

You load QEXT.SYS as a device driver, with a line in CONFIG.SYS such as

```
DEVICE=QEXT.SYS
QEXT.SYS parameters
```

QEXT also offers lots of parameters if you need or want to fine-tune it for your PC. You choose these by adding words and values to the CONFIG.SYS line above. (Put a space between "QEXT.SYS" and any parameter word, put all the parameter words on the one line, and don't put any spaces between parameter words and their = signs or values.) The parameters are described briefly in the following sections.

- ?

  This parameter gives you a list of all QEXT.SYS command-line parameters.

- BLOCKSIZE=XXXXX

  This tells QEXT the number of bytes—2 to 65535—transferred at a time to and from EMBs (extended memory blocks, those above 1024K). Because EMB transfers use the BIOS extended memory support routines, they can lock out any interrupts. That could cause damage if an important interrupt comes during a large block transfer.

- EXTMEM=XXXXX

  or

  EXT=XXXXX

  Use this parameter to tell QEXT not to manage 1K to 15360K of extended memory (in case you want that memory for a disk cache or other use that must operate outside QEXT control, through the old BIOS management). The default is for QEXT to manage all extended memory.

  Don't use EXTMEM unless you know there's a program that needs old-fashioned extended memory. Any memory you EXTMEM out cannot be used by XMS programs.

- HANDLES=XXX

  or

  HA=XXX

  This parameter tells QEXT to make 16 to 255 EMB handles available. The default is 32. Each application using EMBs needs at least one handle, some take more, but each handle takes up about 20 bytes of extended memory.

- HELP

  This parameter displays and describes all QEXT parameters.

- `HMAMIN=XX`

  This tells QEXT not to let any program request and receive any less than 0 to 63K of the HMA. Only one program can use HMA, and if you don't set some minimum limit such as this, a program that uses only a small amount of it may beat out some other program that would use more, and therefore make more efficient use of memory.

- `MEMORY=XXXXX`

  or

  `MEM=XXXXX`

  or

  `ME=XXXXX`

  This parameter tells QEXT to make 128 to 32128K of extended memory available as EMBs. (The default is to make all extended memory available as EMBs.)

- `NOPAUSEONERROR`

  or

  `NOPE`

  With this parameter QEXT does not pause to display an error message when there's any parameter error. This is useful if you are aware of an error that isn't really hurting anything, so you don't want to keep seeing the message.

- `NOXMS`

  This tells QEXT not to manage extended memory by XMS rules, only to handle DESQview's use of the HMA.

- `PAUSE`

  Use this parameter to tell QEXT to pause when starting so you can press Esc to stop QEXT from loading. This is useful when testing parameters.

- UNUSUAL8042
  or
  U8
  This parameter tells QEXT that the keyboard controller isn' t standard. It is useful if some program such as DESQview disables the keyboard.

- VDISKVERSION=X.XX
  This tells QEXT what version of the VDISK program you're using (VDISK uses extended memory). It is necessary only when you're using a different VDISK than the one that came with your DOS.

CHAPTER THIRTEEN

EMS2EXT.SYS, EMS.SYS, and EMS.COM

EMS2EXT and EMS are utility programs that come with both QRAM and QEMM. They both control expanded memory dynamically, changing its allocation on demand, and can be used by themselves or together.

EMS2EXT

EMS2EXT can convert expanded memory into extended memory. The extended memory it makes is only good for programs that want extended memory the old-fashioned way, through the INT 15 interface. That is, these programs don't actually look to see if the memory is physically present at addresses above 1024K. They don't follow the XMS standard. Instead they work with logical addressing through the BIOS, requesting extended memory from it and not worrying where the BIOS gets the memory. VDISK.SYS, the RAM disk that comes with DOS, works this way. The extended memory manager that DESQview uses to load part of itself into HMA does not work this way and so cannot use the extended memory created by EMS2EXT.

Remember that programs supporting XMS don't need EMS2EXT.

EMS2EXT can sense whether memory is slow or fast and can allocate slow or fast memory as its converted extended memory.

To use EMS2EXT you need to load it through a device statement in the CONFIG.SYS file, such as

```
DEVICE=C:\QEMM\EMS2EXT.SYS MEMORY=NNN speed
```

Follow these rules when entering this line:

1. It must come after the line that loads your Expanded Memory Manager.
2. NNN refers to the number of kilobytes of expanded memory to change to extended.
3. The speed parameter tells EMS2EXT to use faster or slower memory, so you put either FAST or SLOW here.

You can devote expanded memory converted to extended memory to a program for just the time that program is running. Make EMS2EXT resident, but don't specify how much memory it will convert. It won't begin with any converted memory, but will have an expanded memory handle named EMS2EXT. Then you can use the EMS program (described below) to devote some expanded memory to that handle via its "CREATE" option. Use the EMS commands to allocate and then free expanded memory into a batch file that starts the program (the one wanting extended memory), and the conversion will last only as long as the program.

EMS

EMS is actually two programs: EMS.SYS and EMS.COM. Both specialize in controlling expanded memory handles.

A block of expanded memory may be any number of EMS pages. Each block of expanded memory that is used has a handle, which will always have a number and may also have a name. The EMM uses the handle to refer to the block of expanded memory. Programs that want to use expanded memory ask for blocks of it, by the handle numbers and names, from the EMM. You can use the EMS programs to get at the same blocks.

Take care with EMS.SYS and EMS.COM because they let you control the EMS handles that may already be allocated to programs, and you don't want to confuse the relationship between programs and their expanded memory.

EMS.SYS and EMS.COM can be used to report on expanded memory use or to control that use in detail. Type

```
EMS
```

at the DOS prompt and you'll get an expanded memory report that includes

- the total expanded memory
- the expanded memory available
- thc pagc framc address

You can add parameters to EMS on the command line. These parameters are briefly described in the following sections.

- `?`
  Use this parameter to see a list of all the EMS parameters.

- `DIR`
  This parameter gives you a list of the current expanded memory allocations by handle, pages, name, and amount.

- `CREATE`
  or
  `CR`
  Use this parameter to allocate expanded memory. You specify the name and the amount of memory. The name is from 1 to 8 characters—enclose it in quotation marks if you want a blank in the name. The amount is in pages, at 16K per page, or in kilobytes that the EMM will round up to the nearest page amount.

There are two formats for the CREATE parameter:

CREATEFAST
or
CFAST

(tells EMS to allocate from fast memory).

CREATESLOW
or
CSLOW

(tells EMS to allocate from slow memory).

You can use Manifest to see if there is significantly faster and slower memory in your PC. You might want to use EMS to allocate the fast or slow memory before you load some driver or TSR that would then use only the other speed of memory that was available. Then you could turn the EMS allocation off again to free the fast or slow memory for your other uses.

- FREE
  Use this parameter to deallocate a named or numbered handle and so free the expanded memory.

- HELP
  This parameter lists all help information on the EMS programs.

- LOAD
  Use this parameter to restore the contents of pages from a file. You specify the handle name (or number) and the filename. (See SAVE.)

- NOPAUSEONERROR
  or
  NOPE
  This parameter tells EMS not to pause when there's an error.

- PAUSE

  This parameter causes EMS to pause until you tell it to continue.

- RENAME

  or

  REN

  This parameter assigns a new name to a handle (you follow RENAME with the old handle number of name and then the new name).

- RESIZE

  or

  RES

  Use this parameter to increase or decrease the number of pages assigned to a handle. (You specify the name and the amount, as with CREATE.)

- SAVE

  This parameter saves the contents of the pages specified by the handle you name (or give the number of). You must also specify the filename to save the contents to. This parameter and LOAD are useful if you want to recover a particular setup and could lose it during computing, such as during program development.

You should be an expert to truly use EMS.SYS and EMS.COM.

EMS.SYS and EMS.COM have the same command-line parameters. They differ in that EMS.SYS loads from a CONFIG.SYS line and EMS.COM works from AUTOEXEC.BAT or from the DOS prompt. That means EMS.SYS can work sooner than EMS.COM, because it can occur sooner during the boot process.

CHAPTER FOURTEEN

OPTIMIZE

OPTIMIZE is a program that automatically tries to set up the best possible QEMM (or QRAM) use of your PC's memory. It installs along with QEMM (or QRAM) and then analyzes your PC's memory along with the drivers and programs you load into memory (by looking at CONFIG.SYS and AUTOEXEC.BAT). It tests to see how much memory each TSR or driver needs. Then it calculates the most efficient way to load those into upper memory to give you the most conventional memory possible. It puts the proper commands into CONFIG.SYS and AUTOEXEC.BAT (saving the old versions, in case you want to reverse course at some point) and reboots the PC with the improved memory management in place. If you did all of this manually, it could require thousands or even millions of AUTOEXEC.BAT and CONFIG.SYS changes and PC reboots.

For most people, OPTIMIZE does a fine job automatically, not needing any extra help from QEMM or QRAM parameters. However, you can often gain an extra 48K of high RAM by using ST:F and FR:EC00.

If you want to dig into OPTIMIZE to get more out of your PC, or to help it avoid some problem that its automatic but limited intelligence can't outwit, you can use the OPTIMIZE parameters. You can change OPTIMIZE decisions or add to them.

OPTIMIZE runs automatically when you first install QEMM or QRAM (since version 6.0 of QEMM, at least. But you should use it again whenever you add or remove hardware with ROM or RAM, or software that can be loaded high.

Don't change OPTIMIZE decisions unless you have a pretty good idea how memory works and what you're changing—one command may depend on another, and you could corrupt the memory management system with even a simple change of a single parameter or value.

To Run OPTIMIZE

To run OPTIMIZE at any time (after you've installed it a la Chapter 1), change to the QEMM (or QRAM) directory, then type

```
OPTIMIZE
```

and press Enter. OPTIMIZE begins running, presenting you with instructions on screen for what to do as it works.

If you have a monochrome, LCD, or gas plasma display (the typical kinds on many laptop or notebook computers) you should add the /MONO parameter when you run OPTIMIZE. See the description of this in the parameters list later on in this chapter.

You may accept the default setup just by pressing Enter repeatedly. As OPTIMIZE works, your PC reboots, perhaps more than once. When finished, OPTIMIZE reports on its work, telling you about the TSRs and drivers it managed to load into high memory. You can see more details by looking at the Region Layout parameter just before OPTIMIZE finishes, or by using Manifest after OPTIMIZE is done. Manifest is explained in Chapter 5 (use the First Meg Overview and the Programs displays.)

The parameters appear during the final phase of OPTIMIZE's work. You can choose from three features: Region Layout, Modify Data, and What-If.

Region Layout lets you see the results of the OPTIMIZE decisions. It displays where the TSRs and drivers are loaded. It also lets you know what parameters are used when loading them.

Modify Data lets you see why OPTIMIZE made its decisions and what it was able to learn about your PC during its analysis.

What-If lets you experiment with changing the order of program loading in CONFIG.SYS and AUTOEXEC.BAT. This doesn't actually make the changes, but it shows you how they would change memory use. (It does not guarantee that the changed order will let all programs operate, however. Some may need to be loaded before others to be operational, even if they have enough memory.)

If you're just going to accept OPTIMIZE's defaults, you don't need to press Enter so many times. Instead you can use the /QUICK parameter by typing

```
OPTIMIZE /QUICK
```

when you run OPTIMIZE. This sends it through its work without stopping to ask you questions. It finishes by telling you how much memory you've saved.

OPTIMIZE puts new commands in your CONFIG.SYS and AUTOEXEC.BAT files as it sees fit to load programs into high memory, if possible, and thus conserve conventional memory. OPTIMIZE saves the previous versions as CONFIG.QDK and AUTOEXEC.QDK, so you can go back to them if you want to later. Trap: Sometimes OPTIMIZE can't finish on its own because some program in your AUTOEXEC.BAT file doesn't return to the DOS prompt. You may have to quit by pressing Esc to let OPTIMIZE continue.

OPTIMIZE works to put any TSRs or drivers from CONFIG.SYS and AUTOEXEC.BAT into high memory most efficiently. If you have a line in AUTOEXEC.BAT that jumps to another batch file, and TSRs are in that batch file, OPTIMIZE won't find them and so won't put them into high memory. To let it find them, you must place a CALL command in front of the batch file line. Then OPTIMIZE can automatically find the batch file and try to put its TSRs into high memory as well. DOS didn't include the CALL command until version 3.3, but used "COMMAND.COM /C Batchfile" instead. Here is an example:

AUTOEXEC.BAT file

```
TIME
DATE
MOUSE.COM
CLS
EXAMPLE.BAT
EXAMPLE.BAT file
```

```
CD\U
TSR2.COM
MAINPROG.EXE
CD
```

Such batch files are typical when loading a particular set of TSRs for some particular use, such as loading a spell-checker and the driver for a label printer with a word processor. In that case OPTIMIZE would try to load MOUSE.COM into high memory but would not find nor try to load TSR1.COM or TSR2.COM into high memory. However, if you changed AUTOEXEC.BAT to this

AUTOEXEC.BAT (new version)

```
TIME
DATE
MOUSE.COM
CALL EXAMPLE.BAT
CLS
```

then OPTIMIZE would go out to the EXAMPLE.BAT file, find the mention of TSR1.COM and TSR2.COM, and then try to load them into high memory.

OPTIMIZE does not include conditionally executed programs in its analysis. “IF EXIST...”, “IF ERRORLEVEL”, “IF %VAR%=XX” should be removed before running OPTIMIZE.

Parameters

You use OPTIMIZE parameters by typing them on the command line after OPTIMIZE, like this:

```
OPTIMIZE /parameter
```

Some of the parameters listed below are really only useful for OPTIMIZE itself—there isn’t much reason for you to use them. Some don’t work on 8088, 8086, or 286 machines—they need 386s or 486s. These are marked.

- ?

  This parameter lists all OPTIMIZE parameters.

- AUTOEXCLUDES

  An internal OPTIMIZE parameter (on 386 and 486 systems only).

- BOOT:D

  or

  B:D

  This parameter tells OPTIMIZE that CONFIG.SYS and AUTOEXEC.BAT are on drive D. This is necessary when you boot from a floppy or when your PC changes the COMSPEC DOS variable that points to CONFIG.SYS and AUTOEXEC.BAT. You don't need this parameter if CONFIG.SYS and AUTOEXEC.BAT are in the root file of the hard disk you booted from.

Networked PCs sometimes have COMSPEC changes, so you should look to see if the boot parameter is necessary.

- COMMANDFILE:filename

  or

  CMD:filename

  This lets you list commands and programs for OPTIMIZE to skip when it works through AUTOEXEC.BAT and CONFIG.SYS. Filename is the command file on which this list appears. Use this when you don't want particular programs or DOS resources loaded into high memory. In COMMANDFILE put one program or command name on each line, without filename extensions or any path (drive, directory, subdirectory) information. You may add comments to a commandfile by putting the # character at the beginning of the comment line. An example command file is on the QRAM disk, called 4DOS.CMD. The 4DOS program is a command shell that replaces COMMAND.COM. This command file is useful for anyone who uses 4DOS, because it includes the 4DOS commands you don't want OPTIMIZE to put in high memory.

If you have a line such as LOADHI TSR.COM in AUTOEXEC.BAT and TSR.COM appears in the command file, OPTIMIZE does not try to load TSR.COM high, but the LOADHI command already placed there does try.

The file named OPTIMIZE.EXC automatically processes as a command file by OPTIMIZE even when you don't use it with the CMD parameter.

- `DIRECTORY`
  or
  `DIR`
  This is an internal OPTIMIZE command.
- `EMM:F`
  If you have renamed your expanded memory manager driver program, then OPTIMIZE needs to be told that new name. You do that with this parameter. F is the new name.
- `FILE`
  or
  `F`
  This is an internal OPTIMIZE command.
- `FINISHED`
  or
  `DONE`
  This is an internal OPTIMIZE command.
- `HELP`
  Use this parameter to get a description of all the OPTIMIZE parameters.

- `LARGE`
  or
  `LA`
  With this parameter OPTIMIZE uses 43- or 50-line displays, if the video adapter permits.

- `LOADHIONLY`
  or
  `L`
  This parameter tells OPTIMIZE to analyze or change only the command lines that already have a LOADHI on them.

- `LOADLOW`
  or
  `LOW`
  This removes all LOADHI statements and REGION parameters—forcing all programs to load into conventional memory.

- `MONO`
  or
  `M`
  Use this parameter to make the video look best for a monochrome display, such as the LCD on a typical laptop PC.

- `NOPAUSEONERROR`
  or
  `NOPE`
  This parameter tells OPTIMIZE not to pause to give an error message if there's an error in an OPTIMIZE command line.

- `NOSQF`
  or
  `NF`
  This tells OPTIMIZE not to allow LOADHI SQUEEZE to load a program by temporarily using the page frame memory addresses.

- `NOSQT`

  or

  `NT`

  This tells OPTIMIZE not to allow LOADHI SQUEEZE to load a program by temporarily using mapped memory (only on 386 and 486 machines).

- `NOSYNC`

  or

  `N`

  With this parameter OPTIMIZE does not use synchronization to improve a CGA display (to remove any "snow" effects). Don't bother with this parameter unless you have a CGA display—synchronization won't be used with other displays.

- `PATH`

  or

  `P`

  This adds the subdirectory path of the QEMM (or QRAM) files to the environment variable PATH. That lets you take QEMM (or QRAM) path information out of command lines, such as those in AUTOEXEC.BAT. You may need to do this if you use lots of parameters, because the lines cannot be more than 128 characters long (the DOS COMMAND.COM program that handles lines can't take any more than that).

- `PAUSE`

  With this parameter OPTIMIZE pauses and waits for input while it works.

- `QUICK`

  or

  `Q`

  This lets OPTIMIZE use all the defaults when it runs.

- `RESPONSE`
  or
  `RF`
  This parameter allows OPTIMIZE to create a response file called LOADHI.RF. This file contains information on your PC's use of high memory—the details of each driver and TSR that should be loaded into upper memory. (You can use a name other than LOADHI.RF by following the parameter with a colon and a filename.)

  RESPONSE lets you simplify your AUTOEXEC.BAT, CONFIG.SYS, and other batch files, because you don't need to enter all the various LOADHI parameters in those files. This is good for individual PCs, or for PCs on a network that use public batch files. Public batch files can be used by many PCs on a network, each with different parameter requirements because of different memory and program setups. If each PC has its own response file, then all you need do is put the response parameter in the public batch file, and each PC reacts differently, according to its own situation. The public batch file can be common to all; each private response file can be different.

- `SEGMENT`
  or
  `SEG`
  This is an internal OPTIMIZE command.

- `STEALTH`
  or
  `ST`
  This runs a STEALTH analysis before doing other OPTIMIZE work—trying all of the ST:X possibilities to find which is best (only on 386 and 486 systems).

If you choose to run OPTIMIZE with STEALTH, your PC reboots several times to discover which STEALTH method is best.

- `STPASSDONE`

  This is an internal OPTIMIZE command (only for 386 and 486 systems).

Some reports about OPTIMIZE in QEMM versions 5.1 and before complained that it wasn't conservative enough, grabbing memory that it shouldn't. The version with QEMM 6 is reported to be better behaved.

SECTION III

Experience:
Special Fixes and Solutions for Best QEMM and QRAM Use

CHAPTER FIFTEEN

With DOS

QEMM and QRAM can't operate without DOS. They depend on it. While at the same time, they add memory management abilities to it.

Until recently, DOS did little with extended, expanded, high, or other forms of memory beyond the conventional 640K. DOS was necessary, but it could also be a burden, using up precious conventional memory with its own kernel, with resources such as FILES and BUFFERS, and with its driver and TSR utilities.

Then came DOS 5, which introduced memory management abilities to DOS.

DOS 5

DOS 5 appeared in mid-1991, years after version 4.0 (which many never be used because of its larger-than-ever use of memory and some initial bugs) and version 3.3. It has many improvements over both previous versions, including more powers and less use of memory.

Memory management was one of the most important new features. It didn't eliminate the 640K barrier, but it did let you move TSRs, device drivers, and even much of its own software pieces out of conventional memory to make more of that 640K usable. For example, at a fairly minimum setting, DOS 5 uses 60K of RAM where DOS 4 used 64K and DOS 3.3 used 54K. DOS had been getting bigger with each release. Now it was shrinking again.

DOS 5 on 286, 386, and 486 systems with at least 64K of extended memory can load most of DOS into the 64K region known as the HMA. That saves about 45K of conventional memory.

The processor can get at this without switching to protected mode. All you need to do to get DOS out of the way is to load the HIMEM.SYS device driver with this line in CONFIG.SYS:

```
DEVICE=HIMEM.SYS
```

and then add this statement to CONFIG.SYS:

```
DOS=HIGH
```

DOS loads most of its kernel and parts of COMMAND.COM in the HMA. If there's room, DOS also loads the BUFFERS disk buffers into the HMA. There's room for about 48 buffers up there, along with DOS. This leaves 620K free conventional memory on a 640K system.

On 386 and 486 systems, you can do more with DOS 5 memory management. The EMM386.EXE driver lets you take unused regions of memory between 640K and 1024K (1MB), which normally are reserved for video buffer and adapter ROMs. You can backfill this with extended memory and use that to load TSRs and device drivers. Then the DOS 5 LOADHIGH command can load some TSRs and drivers into high memory, freeing conventional memory.

You can then use the LOADHIGH and DEVICEHIGH commands to load programs into upper memory. LOADHIGH loads a TSR into upper memory. DEVICEHIGH works like a DEVICE line in CONFIG.SYS to load a device driver, but instead of loading it into conventional memory it loads it into upper memory. EMM386.EXE typically opens 30K to 130K more memory that you can fill with TSRs and device drivers.

EMM386.EXE also lets you use extended memory on 386 and 486 systems as expanded memory through emulation. For applications that can only use expanded memory, you can use some extended memory to make them happy.

DOSKEY enhances the command line editing and recall in DOS 5. It is a small TSR you can put in upper memory with LOADHIGH on a 386 or 486.

The DOS 5 EMM386.SYS driver manages expanded memory. Together with HIMEM.SYS it approximates the basic functions of QEMM386.SYS. QEMM-386 does a better job, however, and even takes up less space for itself than do those two drivers.

QEMM does more than DOS 5, saving more memory and also configuring itself automatically through OPTIMIZE. DOS 5 savings must be configured manually. But you can save even more memory by using DOS 5 and QEMM together.

For best performance, use DOS 5 and QEMM together. (Upgrade from whatever other version of DOS you're using to DOS 5.)

Here's what QEMM has that DOS 5 doesn't:

1. **Automatic setup.** OPTIMIZE automatically configures memory management, from estimating how much memory a TSR or driver needs to trying all the thousands of possibilities for loading them into the various regions of high memory.
2. **Analysis.** Manifest, QEMM.COM, and LOADHI.COM can tell you just what is in memory, what types of memory are available, and many other details that DOS cannot.
3. **Efficiency.** For efficient use of high memory, QEMM gets more memory (96K on PCs, 40K more on PS/2s) in its default than DOS 5 does, and yet more (75K to 115K when mapping, 20K to 64K when framing) when using STEALTH. Using SQUEEZE to load TSRs that need more memory during initialization can yield even more memory.
4. **Control.** DOS 5's EMM386 doesn't let you dictate which regions to use for custom fitting, while QEMM's Region parameter can specify just where TSRs or drivers should go.
5. **More conventional memory.** This is gained both through better use of high memory and through VIDRAM's ability to extend conventional up through unused graphics video memory, getting as much as 96K more conventional memory.
6. **Dynamic allocation.** QEMM provides EMS and XMS from the same common pool without having to be reconfigure and reboot the PC between changes.
7. **Performance improvements.** Mapping ROM into faster RAM speeds computing.
8. **Compatibility.** QEMM supports Windows 3.x in standard mode, has special files to ensure support of MCA adapters that can trouble DOS's EMM386, supports Shadow RAM and top memory. (Compaq DOS 5 supports top memory, but Microsoft and IBM do not, and even Compaq's DOS doesn't reclaim as much top memory as QEMM.)

DOS 5's new memory management abilities won't do much for an 8088 or 8086 PC. For that you need QRAM and an expanded memory board.

DEBUG and MEM Versus Manifest

DOS has several tools for telling you about memory.

The DEBUG command has been part of DOS for years. It is actually a utility program that can display or change what's in memory. To use it you type

```
DEBUG
```

when in the DOS directory. DEBUG then shows its own prompt, the hyphen, as shown in Figure 15-1.

Figure 15-1.
DEBUG at work

```
C>cd dos

C>debug
-d fe00:0
FE00:0000  41 77 61 72 64 20 53 6F-66 74 77 61 72 65 49 42   Award SoftwareIB
FE00:0010  4D 20 43 4F 4D 50 41 54-49 42 4C 45 20 33 38 36   M COMPATIBLE 386
FE00:0020  20 42 49 4F 53 20 43 4F-50 59 52 49 47 48 54 20    BIOS COPYRIGHT
FE00:0030  41 77 61 72 64 20 53 6F-66 74 77 61 72 65 20 49   Award Software I
FE00:0040  6E 63 2E 0A 53 65 72 69-61 6C 20 23 3A 20 01 2D   nc..Serial #: .-
FE00:0050  41 77 F6 00 11 01 01 6F-66 74 77 E9 B4 1F 20 43   Aw.....oftw... C
FE00:0060  57 33 38 36 53 58 20 4D-6F 64 75 6C 61 72 20 42   W386SX Modular B
FE00:0070  49 4F 53 20 47 43 2D 32-31 20 56 33 2E 31 31 20   IOS GC-21 V3.11
-
```

Now you can type individual DEBUG commands. After typing a command, press Enter to see the results. For instance, the D command "dumps" a display of what's in 128 bytes of memory, 16 bytes per line, with the hex address of the first byte, the values, and the corresponding ASCII characters (or periods if there aren't ASCII equivalents). Add an address after the D (with an optional space in between) to investigate a particular part of memory. For example,

```
D FE00:0
```

shows the part of memory that typically holds the copyright information for the system BIOS ROM. (Figure 15-1 shows an example.)

Beginning with DOS 5, DEBUG can handle expanded memory. The XA command allocates expanded memory pages and returns handles for them. XD deallocates logical pages for a handle. XM maps a logical page to a physical page. XS displays the status of expanded memory, as in Figure 15-2.

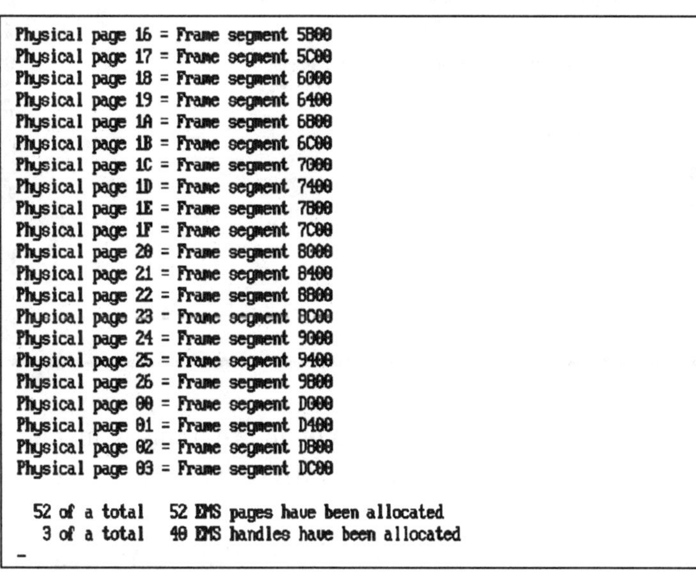

```
Physical page 16 = Frame segment 5800
Physical page 17 = Frame segment 5C00
Physical page 18 = Frame segment 6000
Physical page 19 = Frame segment 6400
Physical page 1A = Frame segment 6800
Physical page 1B = Frame segment 6C00
Physical page 1C = Frame segment 7000
Physical page 1D = Frame segment 7400
Physical page 1E = Frame segment 7800
Physical page 1F = Frame segment 7C00
Physical page 20 = Frame segment 8000
Physical page 21 = Frame segment 8400
Physical page 22 = Frame segment 8800
Physical page 23 = Frame segment 8C00
Physical page 24 = Frame segment 9000
Physical page 25 = Frame segment 9400
Physical page 26 = Frame segment 9800
Physical page 00 = Frame segment D000
Physical page 01 = Frame segment D400
Physical page 02 = Frame segment D800
Physical page 03 = Frame segment DC00

  52 of a total   52 EMS pages have been allocated
   3 of a total   40 EMS handles have been allocated
-
```

Figure 15-2. **DEBUG's XS command showing the status of expanded memory in DOS 5**

Type Q to leave DEBUG and return to DOS.

Type ? for a list of DEBUG commands.

MEM is another DOS memory-inspection command. It first appeared in DOS 4 but was improved with DOS 5. As shown in Figure 15-3, it can give an overview of how much and what types of memory are in the PC.

MEM has parameters—options to give you different views of memory. You leave a space after MEM, type a slash, and then type one of the following parameters:

PROGRAM ....Lists all programs and drivers in memory by address and size

DEBUG.............Adds details on system drivers to the program parameter list

Figure 15-3.
MEM's fundamental view of memory

```
C>mem

    646144 bytes total conventional memory
    646144 bytes available to MS-DOS
    551584 largest executable program size

   1343488 bytes total EMS memory
         0 bytes free EMS memory

   1048576 bytes total contiguous extended memory
         0 bytes available contiguous extended memory
         0 bytes available XMS memory
           High Memory Area in use

C>
```

CLASSIFY ....Lists the names and sizes of all programs in memory (including UMBs and the HMA with DOS 5)

Figure 15-4 shows the DOS MEM command with its CLASSIFY parameter (cut off because it occupied more than one screen).

Figure 15-4
The CLASSIFY parameter at work

```
  Name              Size in Decimal         Size in Hex
 ____________     __________________       ____________
  MSDOS             51632     ( 50.4K)        C9B0
  QEMM386            3088     (  3.0K)         C10
  QDPMI              1984     (  1.9K)         7C0
  LOADHI              256     (  0.3K)         100
  COMMAND            4704     (  4.6K)        1260
  SMARTDRV          26256     ( 25.6K)        6690
  LOADRPM            6080     (  5.9K)        17C0
  FREE                 64     (  0.1K)          40
  FREE                 64     (  0.1K)          40
  FREE             551744     (538.8K)       86B40

Total  FREE :      551872     (538.9K)

Total bytes available to programs :                     551872   (538.9K)
Largest executable program size :                       551584   (538.7K)

   1343488 bytes total EMS memory
         0 bytes free EMS memory

   1048576 bytes total contiguous extended me^C
C>
```

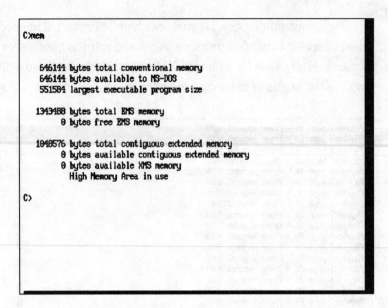

As detailed in Chapter 5, QEMM's Manifest does far more than either of these tools, offering you more detailed analysis of the uses of each 4K piece of memory, of the DOS resources in memory, and even of the speeds of the memory chips.

HIMEM.SYS Versus QEMM

DOS 5.0 comes with an extended memory manager called HIMEM.SYS. This program works only with 286, 386, and 486 PCs, naturally, because extended memory doesn't exist on 8088 and 8086 PCs. The XMS (eXtended Memory Specification) details how extended memory can be used. HIMEM.SYS follows the XMS standard. HIMEM.SYS manages the allocation of XMS memory to programs and device drivers.

QEMM does everything HIMEM.SYS can do, and more. If you use QEMM, you can and should take HIMEM.SYS out of the CONFIG.SYS file.

One of the most important areas of XMS memory is the HMA (high memory area). In DOS 5 HIMEM.SYS can make the HMA work as an extension of conventional memory. In other words, you can have more conventional memory. Using just DOS 5 and HIMEM.SYS you can have as much as 620K of conventional memory for applications.

To install HIMEM.SYS you include this line in CONFIG.SYS:

```
DEVICE=HIMEM.SYS
```

and have the HIMEM.SYS file in your root directory on disk. If HIMEM.SYS is in another directory, such as in a DOS directory, you could use

```
DEVICE=C:\DOS\HIMEM.SYS
```

When you start HIMEM.SYS you can set its parameters by adding switches to its line in CONFIG.SYS. Most of the time you don't need these parameters. HIMEM.SYS handles extended memory for programs and device drivers without any special tuning.

HIMEM.SYS Parameters

- /HMAMIN

  This parameter specifies the minimum memory a device driver or TSR must use before HIMEM.SYS lets it use the HMA. The default is 0K, and the highest you can set this is 63K. This prevents a program that needs very little memory from occupying all of the HMA. The classic example is having two programs that could use the HMA, one that needs 10K and one that needs 50K. If the 10K one grabs the HMA, you must find 50K elsewhere for the second program, or not run that program. But if you set HMAMIN to 20K, then the first program can't hog the HMA. Then the 50K program fits in HMA, and all you need find elsewhere is 10K for the first program. (You're more likely to find a 10K unused block in high memory than a 50K block.)

  The parameter would work this way:

  ```
  DEVICE=HIMEM.SYS /HMAMIN=20
  ```

- /NUMHANDLES

  This parameter sets the maximum number of extended-memory block handles that can be used at once. Each program that wants to use extended memory can use one or several handles. If too many programs want to use extended memory, you can run out of handles. The default setting is 32, but you may set any number from 1 to 128. Each handle uses only 6 bytes of memory, so even a high setting doesn't cost much. To set the number of handles to 64, use a line like this in CONFIG.SYS:

  ```
  DEVICE=HIMEM.SYS /NUMHANDLES=64
  ```

- /INT15=XXXXK

  Before the XMS standard for extended memory appeared and then was widely adopted, many programs used DOS's INT15 interrupt for the same purpose. This interrupt was a signal to the system to hold other processing momentarily so that a program could make some special request for memory.

This parameter allocates extended memory for programs such as QEMM that use the interrupt 15 interface to get at extended memory. (Other such programs are Paradox, Oracle, and Turbo EMS.) You may need to set the amount both with this parameter and in the parameters of the program that will use the extended memory. In CONFIG.SYS this line would allocate 1024KB through the interrupt 15 interface:

```
DEVICE=HIMEM.SYS /INT15=1024
```

The INT15 parameter will probably fade away as XMS grows more popular.

- `/MACHINE:XXXX`
  This switch specifies which A20 handler to use. (The A20 line is explained in more detail in Chapter 4 on memory. The address line lets a PC reach the first 64K of extended memory.) Some PCs have a system BIOS that requires special handling to get reliable extended memory. HIMEM.SYS is designed to handle a variety of these systems. Set the /MACHINE parameter from the following table to properly inform HIMEM.SYS of what sort of A20 handling will be necessary:

BIOS number	Name	Machine or BIOS
1	AT	IBM AT
2	PS2	IBM PS/2
3	PT1CASCADE	Phoenix Cascade BIOS
4	HPVECTRA	HP "Classic" Vectra (A and A+)
5	ATT6300PLUS	AT&T 6300 Plus
6	ACER 1100	Acer 1100
7	TOSHIBA	Toshiba 1600 and 1200XE
8	WYSE	Wyse 12.5 MHz 286 m/c
9	TULIP	Tulip SX
10	ZENITH	Zenith ZBIOS
11	AT1	IBM PC/AT
12	AT2	IBM PC/AT (alternative delay)
13	PHILIPS	Philips
14	FASTHP	HP Vectra

With the parameter you may use the BIOS number or the BIOS name. For example, to use the Philips A20 handling method, you can use this line in CONFIG.SYS:

```
DEVICE=HIMEM.SYS /MACHINE:13
```

or this:

```
DEVICE=HIMEM.SYS /MACHINE:PHILIPS
```

- /A20CONTROL

  This parameter tells the system whether the A20CONTROL is on or off. When it is on, HIMEM.SYS controls the A20 address line, even if another program was controlling A20 when HIMEM.SYS was loaded. When off, HIMEM.SYS controls A20 only if no other program was controlling it when HIMEM.SYS was loaded. Generally don't set this parameter to on, because having two programs enabled to control A20 can cause conflicts. To set it off, use this line in CONFIG.SYS:

```
DEVICE=HIMEM.SYS /A20CONTROL:OFF
```

When you first start or reboot your PC after setting HIMEM.SYS in the CONFIG.SYS file, you'll see a message about the control of A20.

- /SHADOWRAM

  Many PCs are set to copy the ROM BIOS chips to RAM during startup. As explained in Chapter 4, this can improve PC performance because the BIOS instructions can run faster from the RAM chips than from ROM. Typically the area copied to is part of the UMBs (again, see Chapter 4). To save that area for device drivers and TSR programs instead of for Shadow RAM, but to lose that RAM BIOS performance improvement, use a line like this in CONFIG.SYS:

```
DEVICE=HIMEM.SYS /SHADOWRAM:OFF
```

The default is SHADOWRAM:ON.

- /CPUCLOCK
  If your PC runs slower after installing HIMEM.SYS, you can use this parameter to fight the sloth. Add a line such as

```
DEVICE=HIMEM.SYS /CPUCLOCK:ON
```

Loading DOS Into the HMA

If you're running DOS 5, once HIMEM.SYS (or QEMM386.SYS) is loaded on a PC with an HMA, you can load part of the DOS 5 kernel into the HMA. You add the command

```
DOS=HIGH
```

to the CONFIG.SYS file.

If you're using DESQview, don't load DOS into the HMA. DESQview can load 63K of itself there; DOS can load only 45K of itself. Only one program at a time can use the HMA.

The parameters for the DOS command are

=HIGH ....Puts 50K of DOS into the HMA
=LOW ....Leaves all of DOS in conventional memory (the default)
=UMB...........Prepares to create UMBs, for loading drivers and TSRs high
=NOUMB....Does not make UMBs (the default)

For example, the command

```
DOS=HIGH,UMB
```

both loads DOS into the HMA and creates UMBs.

The DOS command needs at least 350K of extended memory, a 386 or 486 PC, and HIMEM.SYS (or QEMM) installed (on a line in CONFIG.SYS before the DOS line) to make UMBs.

If DOS can't load into the HMA, you'll see an error message such as "HMA not available: loading DOS low." Some other program may have been using the HMA, or the XMS driver (HIMEM.SYS or QEMM386.SYS) may not have been loaded before the DOS command.

If you use DOS=HIGH, then don't use QEMM's BUFFERS command. It will take away from the UMB pool available.

EMM386 Versus QEMM

DOS 5.0 comes with an expanded memory manager program called EMM386.EXE. This has features that overlap QEMM's. Both are 386 memory managers. Both provide upper memory for loading TSRs and device drivers, and both can convert extended memory of 386 and 486 PCs to LIM 4.0 expanded memory.

But QEMM-386 version 6.0 has more functions than are in EMM386.EXE. These include the following:

1. QEMM makes more upper memory available than does EMM386.
2. QEMM makes upper memory available without forcing you to know as much as EMM386 wants you to know. EMM386 can make significant upper memory available if loaded with the I parameter, but you need to know which areas of upper memory to use. In other words, while QEMM finds these areas for you, DOS 5.0 EMM386 demands that you know where the adapter ROM and RAM, system board ROM, video buffers, and EMS page frames are. The Manifest utility with QEMM gives a complete analysis of memory use, as well as of other system factors.
3. QEMM can remap memory so slow ROMs are relocated to addresses with fast RAM. This improves PC performance.
4. QEMM is compatible with Windows 3.0 standard mode. EMM386 is not.
5. QEMM 6.0 has STEALTH, which lets you make more upper memory in areas that have ROM.

Although it looks like a program (with that .EXE extension), EMM386 loads as a driver in CONFIG.SYS, with a line such as

```
DEVICE=C:\DOS\EMM386.EXE
```

Naturally EMM386 has its parameters:

RAM..................Creates UMBs from extended memory and simulates expanded memory from extended—with the default amount of 256K

MEMORY ....Simulates expanded memory from extended without creating UMBs

NOEMS............Creates UMBS without simulating expanded memory (which saves 64K more for UMBs because there will be no page frame)

If you specify both NOEMS and RAM, NOEMS takes precedence.

EMM386 also can work from the DOS prompt if you've already installed it as a driver from CONFIG.SYS. Without parameters it will tell you the status of expanded memory support, or you can use the parameters to turn expanded memory support on or off (and to turn Weitek math coprocessor support on or off). Its command-line parameters are

ON............Turns expanded memory support on (this is the default)

OFF..........Turns expanded memory support off

AUTO.......Sets expanded memory to automatically turn on when a program requests it

W=ON......Turns Weitek support on

W=OFF.....Turns Weitek support off (this is the default)

Just as with QEMM, expanded memory support cannot be disabled if UMBs have been created or if any programs are using expanded memory.

That's all there is to EMM386.EXE. QEMM does everything EMM386.EXE does, and more. As you can see from Chapters 6 and 7, QEMM386.SYS and QEMM.COM offer an entire world of control, with scores of parameters for specific uses and situations. QEMM has features you won't find in EMM386.EXE. For one thing, it relocates some data structures such as DOS resources, set up by CONFIG.SYS statements, to high memory. It also lets you swap slow ROMs for fast RAM. To do that it runs a timing test on every byte of memory in the PC. ROM is several times slower than RAM on 386 systems, so it's easily noticed by such tests. This sloth can hurt performance. QEMM then copies the information in the ROM addresses to faster RAM by remapping the addresses with the 386 page tables. One of the best reasons for using this feature is that some EGA and VGA display adapters have a ROM with instructions, which is a very slow ROM. Another reason, though not as significant, is that sometimes the RAM below 640K is slower than the RAM above. QEMM can remap so that fast RAM is in the lower addresses. This speeds up all conventional memory uses, including DOS itself and DOS programs.

If you have the DOS=UMB statement in CONFIG.SYS when running DOS 5, then you can use DOS LOADHIGH and DEVICEHIGH commands with QEMM386. If you don't have that DOS=UMB statement, you must use QEMM's LOADHI instead.

EMM386 runs DOS in the virtual-86 mode of the 386 or 486 processor. Some programs aren't compatible with that mode. Some of those will tell you; some will just crash.

AUTO puts the processor in real mode until an application requests expanded memory. Then EMM386 automatically parameters to virtual-86 mode for as long as that expanded memory request lasts. When the expanded memory is released—such as when the requesting program quits (terminates, in technical terms)—EMM386 returns the processor to real mode. The AUTO parameter is useful if only a few programs need expanded memory, because programs generally run a little slower in virtual-86 mode (there is some overhead processing to keep memory managed). Remember too that the processor can't return to real mode if EMM386 is providing upper memory management, with UMBs that have loaded high programs and drivers.

As a default, EMM386 sets up a 64K page frame in the D segment of upper memory. That subtracts 64K from the UMBs that could be used for loading high. If you like, on most systems—not on PS/2 and other Micro Channel systems—you may use the /E parameter to put the page frame at the E segment. If this won't work, EMM386 will let you know. Moving the page frame makes for a less-fragmented UMB area.

» EMM386 assumes the page frame should be at D000. This is unused on most PCs.

» Remember you can get an extra 64K of memory when using EMM386 if you add the NOEMS parameter. This eliminates the page frame and so eliminates use of expanded memory, but saves 64K of upper memory.

» EMM386.SYS comes with Windows 3.0 and DOS 4.01 (and later versions of each). EMM386.EXE comes with DOS 5.0.

LOADHIGH and DEVICEHIGH Versus LOADHI

DOS 5 took a tip from QEMM, as well as other products such as DR-DOS, and learned to load drivers and TSRs into upper memory. This "loading high" conserves conventional memory by moving programs out to upper memory. DOS does it with the DEVICEHIGH and LOADHIGH commands. QEMM does it with the LOADHI.SYS and LOADHI.COM commands.

DEVICEHIGH and LOADHIGH can move just about any driver or TSR. All they need is UMBs large enough in upper memory. This includes many drivers and TSRs that are part of DOS itself. (Sometimes they're disguised as one another, such as the ANSI.SYS and MOUSE.SYS, which are TSRs but look like drivers.) To run the MEM command, type

```
MEM /C | MORE
```

and you'll see a list of the TSRs and drivers normally in memory and how large they are. Figure 15-5 shows an example.

Figure 15-5. Example of using the MEM command to see what drivers and TSRs to load high with DOS LOADHIGH commands

```
QEMM386          3088      ( 3.0K)      C10
QDPMI            1904      ( 1.9K)      7C0
LOADHI            256      ( 0.3K)      100
COMMAND          4704      ( 4.6K)     1260
SMARTDRV        26256      (25.6K)     6690
LOADRPM          6080      ( 5.9K)     17C0
FREE               64      ( 0.1K)       40
FREE               64      ( 0.1K)       40
FREE           551744      (538.8K)   86B40

Total FREE :   551872      (538.9K)

Total bytes available to programs :              551872   (538.9K)
Largest executable program size :                551584   (538.7K)

    1343488 bytes total EMS memory
          0 bytes free EMS memory
-- More --

    1048576 bytes total contiguous extended memory
          0 bytes available contiguous extended memory
          0 bytes available XMS memory
            High Memory Area in use
```

Use DEVICEHIGH to load device drivers (drivers) into upper memory. In place of the line

```
DEVICE=DRIVER
```

which you would already have in CONFIG.SYS to load such a driver into conventional memory, put a line such as this

```
DEVICEHIGH=DRIVER
```

for each driver you want to load high. (Have the complete, correct path in the line.) Use the MEM command noted above to see if there is room for the driver, then use the DEVICEHIGH line. Reboot the PC and use MEM again. You should see a report that includes the driver's location. Some drivers won't load high. DEVICEHIGH won't tell you when this happens. You'll have to use MEM to find out. And if a driver takes more memory after it has loaded, your computer could crash or lock up (that is, freeze so you can't make it do anything without turning off the power). You can avoid this if you know how much memory the driver will use. Just add the size parameter, as in

```
DEVICEHIGH SIZE=XXX DRIVER
```

where XXX is the maximum number of bytes, in hexadecimal, that the driver needs.

Even so, some drivers won't load when given the room or won't work properly when loaded high. You can learn these only from experience. Then you know to leave them in conventional memory (or to replace them with more recent drivers, or competing drivers from other sources, that will load and work high). Try loading drivers one at a time, so you know if there's a troublesome one. Sometimes it is the combination or even the order of loading that makes trouble. Then you need to experiment—probably by loading the larger drivers first (to save more memory right away).

Here QEMM shines beside DOS 5, because the OPTIMIZE program automatically experiments for you, saving time and trouble.

These drivers in DOS can load and work high: DISPLAY.SYS, DRIVER.SYS, EGA.SYS, ANSI.SYS, PRINTER.SYS, RAMDRIVE.SYS, SETVER.EXE, SMARTDRV.SYS.

OPTIMIZE replaces DOS 5's DEVICEHIGH and LOADHIGH statements with QEMM LOADHI commands. However, programs loaded into high RAM using DEVICEHIGH or LOADHIGH are included in the reports produced by LOADHI.COM and Manifest, just as if they had been put there by either of the LOADHI programs (LOADHI.SYS or LOADHI.COM).

Remember that for RAMDRIVE.SYS and SMARTDRV.SYS, although the program instructions can load into upper memory, the actual RAM disk or disk cache they create can then be in conventional, extended, or expanded memory. You specify which.

Use the LOADHIGH command for those TSR programs that you would load from the AUTOEXEC.BAT file (or from the DOS prompt or any batch file). This loads memory-resident (TSR) programs into upper memory blocks just as DEVICEHIGH does for device drivers. You simply put it on the line before the program. If you would normally load a program by typing the program name and pressing Enter (or by putting it on a line of a batch file such as AUTOEXEC.BAT), you now type

```
LOADHIGH
```

followed by a space and then the program name, and press Enter (or put it on the line of a batch file). The program installs into upper memory if it can. (Make sure the path is full and correct.) You may put any parameters for the program on the same line, after the program name where you normally would put them.

You can abbreviate LOADHIGH as LH.

QEMM reports when it cannot load some driver or TSR high, but DOS 5's LOADHIGH does not—it just loads the item low without telling you.

The best scheme is to load one at a time, the largest first, and then check after each reboot to see if the program loaded where you want it (use the MEM command). If you're having trouble, change the order of loading as described for devices above. You can also remove one TSR at a time from the loading process by putting

```
REM
```

before its line in AUTOEXEC.BAT (such as REM LOADHIGH programname).

The following DOS programs are TSRs and can load high successfully with the LOADHIGH command: APPEND.EXE, DOSKEY.COM, DOSSHELL.COM, GRAPHICS.COM, KEYB.COM, MODE.COM, NLSFUNC.EXE, PRINT.EXE, SHARE.EXE.

Remember that you can use LOADHIGH only with memory-resident programs, not with regular DOS programs.

If you don't specify DOS=UMB, then DOS won't know about upper memory blocks. The DOS LH command then won't work, with or without QEMM.

If you put DOS=UMB into CONFIG.SYS (which Quarterdeck advises against), you can have conflicts. You can load high with the DOS LH command (remember LH stands for LOADHIGH) or QEMM's LOADHI command. Both Manifest and the DOS MEM command can correctly report the programs that load high.

Some TSRs won't work when loaded high. You can check their documentation to see if they are supposed to, but the only way to make sure they do is to test them: load them high and see what happens. A program "not working" doesn't necessarily show its troubles by just crashing or freezing. It may show error messages, it may act strangely (some features not working), or it may not work at all. An example is some programs with the .COM extension are written assuming they'll be loaded near the bottom of the 640K of conventional memory and so may be confused by upper memory residence.

RAMDRIVE.SYS

RAMDRIVE.SYS is the device driver used to make a RAM disk on DOS 5 PCs. A RAM disk is a section of RAM that acts like a disk drive—a very fast disk drive. You can save files to it and read files from it. Although it loses its files when you turn off the PC's power, you can first save them to a standard disk drive—floppy or hard—and so keep the files safe. And while you worked you'd have a disk drive that is faster than any floppy or hard disk could ever be.

RAMDRIVE.SYS loads from CONFIG.SYS with a line like this:

```
DEVICE=C:\DOS\RAMDRIVE.SYS
```

Then you add parameters after it:

/E.............Makes the RAM disk in extended memory (the default is conventional)

/A.............Makes the RAM disk in expanded memory (the default is conventional)

There are other parameters for setting the capacity (64K is the default) and the sector size. See a DOS manual for details. The RAMDRIVE.SYS program itself uses about 1.2K of memory, no matter how big the RAM disk it controls. You could load it more than once to make more than one RAM disk, and each would use about 1.2K of memory.

You get the most from RAM disks if you copy all of a program's files to the RAM disk before running the program, and then copy all the files back to a standard disk after the program finishes running (especially if it is a program that uses the disk drive a lot, such as for overlay files). You can also get a lot by putting entire documents into the RAM disk, such as images or long word processing documents that must be read and written to disk a lot.

Some programs, such as Windows, use TEMP variables to specify where their temporary working files should be. Specify a RAM disk for these and you'll improve performance. Some programs, such as WordPerfect and Ventura Publisher, have files such as spelling and thesaurus files that could benefit from a RAM disk.

To make your life easy when creating a RAM disk, copying files to it, and then copying files back to a standard disk when done, you should put all the necessary instructions into a batch file. See a DOS manual for details.

SMARTDRV.SYS

As explained in Chapter 4, a disk cache is a section of memory that holds the most-recently requested information from disk. This isn't a RAM disk, which acts like a disk drive. Instead it is a helper to the disk drive, letting programs grab information much faster if it has been recently used.

SMARTDRV.SYS is a disk cache program that comes with DOS 5. To install it you enter a line like this in CONFIG.SYS:

```
DEVICE=C:\DOS\SMARTDRV.SYS
```

If you add the /A parameter, the disk cache will be in expanded memory. Otherwise it will be in the default—extended memory.

Other parameters let you specify maximum and minimum sizes for the cache when it dynamically changes size responding to directions from programs such as Windows.

The SMARTDRV.SYS program instructions themselves take up 13K of memory. You can load them high with LOADHI.

If you don't have enough memory to load SMARTDRV.SYS, you can still speed disk operation with the FASTOPEN command. This comes with DOS 3.3 and later, and keeps data where recently used files are.

DOS Resources: BUFFERS, FILES, and More

DOS resources are data structures DOS creates to monitor and control the computer's behavior. These store information about where files are, what programs are running, and so on. They use memory, so you need to balance their benefits against their consumption.

QEMM (and QRAM) offer alternatives that perform the same functions as the basic resources of BUFFERS, FILES, FCBs, and LASTDRIVE but use less memory. DOS 5 can't load resources such as FILES, FCBs, and BUFFERS into upper memory.

DOS buffers are pieces of memory dedicated to holding copies of the latest information read from disk. By telling programs that request information from disk to look at the buffers first, the PC can avoid some disk accesses—when that information has already been requested and received for a previous use. The result is faster operation.

Early versions of QEMM's BUFFERS.COM don't work with DOS 5. However, QEMM versions 6 and later and QRAM versions 2 and later have a BUFFERS.COM that works with DOS 5.

At first, the more buffers you have the better this cacheing scheme works, because the more likely it is that desired information will be in one of the buffers. But each buffer set aside uses up memory. Each needs 528 bytes of memory, or about 0.5K. Losing 10K or more to buffers could be the margin between loading and not loading some important utility program. So there is an optimum number of buffers to use for maximum performance and minimum memory loss.

For most applications 10 to 20 buffers is best. Accounting and database management can call for 20 to 40. Don't use more than this unless you have DOS 4.0

or later, which lets you put buffers into expanded memory, thus conserving conventional memory for other uses. One other reason to use more disk buffers is if you have many subdirectories on disk.

In fact, surprisingly, DOS 3.0 and 4.0 actually slow down if you set up 40 to 60 buffers. This happens because more time is spent searching the buffers than would have been spent just going to disk to find the information. This effect can kick in at more than 30 buffers.

On floppy disk systems, try 10 buffers. On hard disk systems, try 20 buffers.

Whatever you start with, to find optimum performance you must experiment, adding or subtracting 1, 2, or 5 buffers at a time and watching the effects. After each change you must reboot the PC.

However, if you have a disk cache program, you don't need buffers. The disk cache does the same thing and, if it is a good one, does a better job of it (more intelligently guessing which information should be kept in the buffers and how long). A memory manager such as QEMM can set up its own disk buffers. If you're using QEMM, set the CONFIG.SYS buffers to a low number, around 2. That lets DOS read a whole sector or two sectors and keep them in memory at a time, but doesn't waste any more memory on buffers that will be redundant.

Each buffer in DOS 4.x and 5.x takes 528 bytes. (In DOS 2.x and 3.x, when using a third-party disk manager, the buffers are doubled to 1056 bytes for partitions of 33 to 64MB, quadrupled to 2112 bytes for partitions of 65 to 128MB, and octupled to 4224 bytes for partitions of 128 to 256MB. It keeps doubling for larger partitions, because the disk managers permit larger partitions by using larger sectors.)

QEMM and QRAM can move all buffers except the first kernel into upper memory for DOS versions 2.x, 3.x, and 5.x. They have a utility program called BUFFERS.COM that creates buffers that LOADHI can move into upper memory. OPTIMIZE knows this and decreases the BUFFERS= statement in CONFIG.SYS to 1 for DOS 2.x and 3.x, because DOS's default is more than that and so would eat up some conventional memory.

DOS 4.x has a different way of handling buffers. They can be put in expanded memory. That's even better, typically, than putting them into upper memory, so Quarterdeck's BUFFERS.COM doesn't load DOS 4.x buffers high.

If you specify BUFFERS with an /X parameter, the buffers load into expanded memory. Buffers put into expanded memory are allocated in multiples of 30, because expanded memory is allocated in multiples of 16K bytes—and 30 buffers takes up 15K. Choose a number between a multiple of 30 and you get a number of buffers rounded up to the next multiple.

The /X option to put DOS 4.x BUFFERS into expanded memory conflicts with many programs.

In DOS 5, buffers can't be loaded into expanded memory. But when you use DOS 5's

```
DOS=HIGH
```

statement in CONFIG.SYS, you not only load part of DOS into the HMA, you load buffers along with it. But they must all fit in the HMA, or they all load into conventional memory. This is known as brittle buffers. If buffers are loaded into more than one noncontiguous part of memory, only the last buffers loaded are used. Others waste space. In other words, load buffers into HMA with the DOS=HIGH statement, then use BUFFERS.COM to load some into upper memory, and only the upper memory buffers will work. The memory devoted in the HMA to buffers will be wasted.

The HMA can fit 48 buffers with the DOS kernel and with HIMEM.SYS control. When QEMM is in control, the DOS kernel and 51 buffers fit into the HMA.

Microsoft's Mouse Driver 8.10 can load part of itself into the HMA when DOS=HIGH is in CONFIG.SYS. It uses about 13K and so cuts the number of buffers that can fit by 25.

Compaq's DOS 3.31 is like DOS 4 in that it allows partitions larger than 32MB without third-party partitioning programs, and it does not increase buffer size.

On DOS 2.x or 3.x (not Compaq DOS 3.31) with a third-party disk partitioning program, the size of BUFFERS increases to match increased sector size. That means if you have a setting such as BUFFERS=10 or BUFFERS=20, they may suddenly be using twice or four times as much memory. You can cut back by whatever multiple the sectors increased by (see your manual or the notes above).

DOS 4.0's /X parameter for BUFFERS can disrupt your disk drive. Use a different version of DOS if possible.

The FASTOPEN resource caches information on file locations. It puts the information in special buffers in memory, either in conventional memory or in expanded memory (if you use the /X parameter). Each buffer occupies about 48 bytes. For example, if you use the command

```
FASTOPEN C:=100 /X
```

you'd use 16K of expanded memory (although it needs only 4800 bytes, expanded memory is allocated in chunks of 16K). The FASTOPEN program itself needs 1.3K.

The FCB resource was used in DOS 1. DOS 2 introduced file handling in other ways but kept FCBs for compatibility. FCBs are still used in networking, especially when the SHARE command is employed. QEMM has a utility called FCBS.COM that can load FCBs into upper memory. You use it with a LOADHI command, similar to the files command.

The FILES resource dictates the number of files that DOS can have open at once. It tracks open files with handles that take up 53 bytes per file. You need at least one for each file open. Some databases and accounting programs need 40 or more files set. The memory for FILES' handles is allocated when the computer boots. DOS uses conventional memory for these handles. QEMM has a utility called FILES.COM that can be loaded into upper memory with QEMM's LOADHI program. In fact, some of the files could be in conventional memory, with a statement in CONFIG.SYS such as

```
FILES=10
```

and the rest could be in upper memory with an AUTOEXEC.BAT statement such as

```
C:\QEMM\LOADHI C:\QEMM\FILES=40
```

The LASTDRIVE command sets the last letter you can use for a disk drive. After E, each drive you add (to Z) adds 80 bytes to conventional memory use. More drives are useful for RAM disks, network drives, and drive substitutions for subdirectories from the DOS SUBST command.

QEMM and QRAM offer a LASTDRIV.COM command that loads this resource high.

DR-DOS

DR-DOS is a competitor to Microsoft's MS-DOS (or just DOS for short). It is a compatible competitor, meaning that although it offers more features than DOS, it also manages to be enough like DOS that it follows DOS commands and can run DOS programs.

Microsoft's DOS has almost all of the DOS market, but DR-DOS does very well in reviews when compared to DOS and has some additional features. For example, DR-DOS 6 offers memory management that goes beyond what's in DOS 5. (DR-DOS had memory management before DOS had any.) But QEMM is still worth using with DR-DOS and is compatible with DR-DOS 6. (DR-DOS also works with DESQview.)

When using QEMM and OPTIMIZE with DR-DOS 6, keep these tips in mind:

- When loading DOS high (into the HMA), be sure to remove the EMM386 line from CONFIG.SYS. For best results, include these lines in the place of EMM386:

  ```
  HIDOS=ON
  DEVICE=C:\DRDOS\HIDOS.SYS /BDOS=FFFF
  ```

  The line for QEMM386 should already be in CONFIG.SYS, added by QEMM's installation process.

- If you're using DESQview as well as QEMM, try using /BDOS=AUTO instead of the /BDOS=FFFF parameter. This affects the Big DOS window in DESQview.

- If you use the /BDOS=FFFF parameter, then use DR-DOS's HIBUFFERS command to put the DOS disk buffers into HMA. If you use the /BDOS=AUTO parameter, then set BUFFERS=1 in CONFIG.SYS and use LOADHI.COM with the BUFFERS.COM command to increase the number of disk buffers.

- Don't use the DR-DOS commands HILOAD, HIDEVICE, and HINSTALL when using QEMM. They don't work with QEMM. Use QEMM's own LOADHI.COM, LOADHI.SYS, and INSTALL=LOADHI.COM.

DR-DOS comes with a powerful disk cache called SuperStor. The program that creates this is SSTORDRV.SYS. This is a device driver that automatically loads part of itself high if QEMM is in place to provide UMB management. Don't try to load the rest of SuperStor high with LOADHI.SYS. If you do, it doesn't load at all or loads low without warning (and so uses memory you thought you would have for other uses). Put SSTORDRV.SYS in the OPTIMIZE.EXC file. (See Chapter 14 for details on editing or creating this file.)

Using the SuperStor disk cache usually creates a small uncompressed drive with a minimal CONFIG.SYS file and a larger compressed drive with a secondary and chained CONFIG.SYS file. To get the most use of conventional memory, the drivers these CONFIG.SYS files load are loaded high. But OPTIMIZE doesn't recognize the DR-DOS CONFIG.SYS CHAIN command. (This command lets you work with a chain of CONFIG.SYS files.) If you have more than one CONFIG.SYS file in a chain, combine them into a single CONFIG.SYS file during OPTIMIZE work.

To use SuperStor, therefore, you need to remove the CHAIN statement from the CONFIG.SYS file on the uncompressed drive and add it to the end of the content of the second CONFIG.SYS file, the one from the compressed drive. Then copy QEMM into a QEMM directory on the uncompressed drive. You may not be able to fit all QEMM files onto the uncompressed drive, because it is typically pretty small. Therefore, just copy the files necessary. These are QEMM386.SYS (or QEMM.SYS or QRAM.SYS), OPTIMIZE.COM, LOADHI.SYS, LOADHI.COM. LOGOPT.COM, BUFFERS.COM, RSTRCFG.SYS, MCA.ADL, and WINHIRAM.VXD.

If you used DEVSWAP.COM, then you need to swap the C: and D: references in CONFIG.SYS and AUTOEXEC.BAT files and put them back after optimizing (a process you'll have to follow every time you use OPTIMIZE). In other words, you're better off in this case not using DEVSWAP.COM. If you leave it out, then you can run OPTIMIZE on the uncompressed drive after the changes discussed above.

QEMM 6's STEALTH feature doesn't work with DR-DOS unless you add the exclusion X=FFF0-FFFF.

Summary Advice for Using QEMM (or QRAM) and DOS 5

DOS 5 uses only 12K of conventional when loaded high.

When installing QEMM (or QRAM) on a system that already has DOS 5 configured and in use, just use the standard INSTALL program. It, and OPTIMIZE, can do the job. If you were to handle this manually, you'd start by editing CONFIG.SYS and AUTOEXEC.BAT to remove any DEVICEHIGH or LOADHIGH commands. That means in CONFIG.SYS you should change any DEVICEHIGH statements back to DEVICE statements. Remove any SIZE parameters from those statements. In AUTOEXEC.BAT remove any LOADHIGH or LH commands from lines that load memory-resident programs.

On 386 PCs remove from CONFIG.SYS any command that loads EMM386.EXE. Put the QEMM memory manager driver on the first line of CONFIG.SYS.

On 286 PCs put the command that loads HIMEM.SYS on the first line of CONFIG.SYS and put the QRAM driver line on the second line.

Then, on any PC, run OPTIMIZE. Follow any EXCLUDE or INCLUDE suggestions made by OPTIMIZE.

If you're using DESQview, you might want to run OPTIMIZE /STEALTH to make sure STEALTH is used for more DESQview memory.

Check the Hints in Manifest to see if there is any more memory you can squeeze out.

A DOS 5 CONFIG.SYS and AUTOEXEC.BAT might look like this:

```
DEVICE=C:\DOS\HIMEM.SYS
DOS=HIGH
FILES=40
BUFFERS=30
SHELL=C:\DOS\COMMAND.COM C:\DOS\ /P
STACKS=0,0
DEVICE=C:\MOUSE\MOUSE.SYS

@ECHO OFF
PROMPT $P$G
PATH C:\BATCH;C:\UTIL;C:\DOS
SET TEMP =C:\TEMP
DOSKEY
```

(In an 8088 or 8086 PC, leave out the HIMEM.SYS command.) The QEMM version would add QEMM386.SYS to CONFIG.SYS and the QEMM subdirectory to the path in AUTOEXEC.BAT lines. It would include LOADHI commands to put TSRs and drivers into upper memory. It might be (with HIMEM.SYS disabled with a REM instead of just removed altogether):

```
DEVICE=C:\QEMM\QEMM386.SYS RAM
REM DEVICE=C:\DOS\HIMEM.SYS
DOS=HIGH
FILES=40
BUFFERS=30
SHELL=C:\DOS\COMMAND.COM C:\DOS\ /P
STACKS=0,0
DEVICE=C:\QEMM\LOADHI.SYS /R:1 C:\MOUSE\MOUSE.SYS

@ECHO OFF
PROMPT $P$G
PATH C:\QEMM;C:\BATCH;C:\UTIL;C:\DOS
SET TEMP =C:\TEMP
C:\QEMM\LOADHI /R:3 DOSKEY
```

QEMM386.SYS loads first to manage expanded and extended memory. This lets DOS use the HMA (as HIMEM.SYS would have). The mouse driver is loaded into upper memory. Unlike DEVICEHIGH, which is a DOS 5 internal command and so doesn't need a full path, LOADHI.SYS does need a full path.

Then if you add a driver or memory-resident program, run OPTIMIZE again.

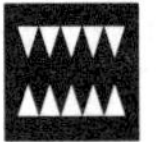

Remember that with Windows 3.0 in enhanced mode you can't use QEMM's EXT= or MEM= parameters because they prevent Windows from taking control of the HMA and so stop it from starting in enhanced mode.

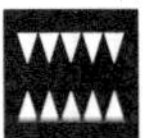

Versions of QEMM before 6.0 don't fully support DOS 5. The BUFFERS.COM program cannot be used, and the LOADHIGH, DEVICEHIGH, and UMB parameters and programs aren't fully compatible. OPTIMIZE, for instance, can't replace DOS 5 LOADHI commands with its own—you need to remove them manually. Also, PRINTER.SYS and DISPLAY.SYS can't load into high memory by QEMM 5.13 and earlier, QEMM-50/60 5.00 and earlier, or QRAM 1.01 and earlier. Manifest 1.01 or later is necessary for DOS 5.

If you want to use DOS=HIGH, and have QRAM or QEMM 50/60 with its QEXT.SYS driver, you need a QEXT version dated later than May 1991. With older versions, if you have any trouble loading RAMDRIVE.SYS or SMARTDRV.SYS, move the QEXT.SYS line so it loads before QEMM-50/60 or QRAM in CONFIG.SYS.

If you're installing DOS 5 over a system that already has QEMM-386, QEMM-50/60, or QRAM, just leave QEMM or QRAM in place and run the DOS SETUP program. This detects the memory manager and can't replace it. It changes your CONFIG.SYS file so a new line

```
DEVICE=SETVER.EXE
```

appears at the beginning, and

```
DOS=HIGH
```

appears at the end. It may also put

```
SHELL=COMMAND.COM
```

in the file. You can leave these statements. Then run OPTIMIZE. (Run it with the STEALTH parameter if you use DESQview.)

If you move the SETVER.EXE line below the QEMM or QRAM line and then run OPTIMIZE, you can load SETVER into high memory, saving about 0.4K. You may not need SETVER at all. Run it from the DOS prompt (type SETVER) to see if any programs are depending on it. If not, remove it entirely.

RAMDRIVE.SYS and SMARTDRV.SYS may not load if they come after QEXT.SYS in the CONFIG.SYS file.

CHAPTER SIXTEEN

QEMM with DESQview

Quarterdeck is famous not only for QEMM and QRAM, but also it makes DESQview. Quarterdeck's DESQview gives a PC task-switching and multitasking capabilities. It lets you open each DOS program in a window of its own. You can then switch from one program to another very quickly and easily. On a 286 system with expanded memory hardware (see Chapter 4 for explanations) or a 386 or 486 system, DESQview permits true multitasking, with programs running simultaneously, not just open side-by-side. Programs pushed to the background can still be operating, handling tasks such as working through complex calculations.

This chapter explains how QEMM helps DESQview and the details you need to adjust and look out for when using the team.

What are DESQview, DESQview-386, and DESQview/X?

DESQview is second in popularity only to Microsoft's Windows as a multitasking environment for DOS programs on PCs. Although it doesn't offer all the graphic abilities of Windows, DESQview demands far less computer. (Windows needs at least a fast 386, lots of RAM, and a big hard disk to work efficiently.)

DESQview-386 is the DESQview program and a copy of QEMM-386 in the same box. (In fact, it was because of DESQview's need to offer as much conventional memory as possible that QRAM and QEMM were invented!) It uses QEMM's control of the 386 virtual-86 mode (see Chapter 4 for details) to protect programs from one another and to virtualize their screen displays. That is, DESQview with QEMM can handle misbehaved programs—those that write directly to a screen display without following the rules—each in its own small window. Bugs in one program or failure to follow rules of programming won't bother other programs. QEMM's memory management also permits real multitasking of standard DOS programs, 286-DOS extended programs, and 386-DOS extended programs (including Windows 3.0 in real or standard mode) within a DESQview window. So you can run Windows inside a DESQview window. DESQview automatically detects QEMM-386 installed in your PC and takes advantage of it.

DESQview-386 is just DESQview with QEMM. If you get a great deal on DESQview-386, you can use it on a 286 PC, just ignoring QEMM. (Though you may then want to get QRAM.)

Quarterdeck's latest product is DESQview/X. This brings the X Windows idea down to PCs (only those with a 386SX or better microprocessor, with a future version for 286 systems). X has been popular on workstations—typically under the UNIX operating system—because it combines multitasking, graphical windows, and remote computing.

The graphical windows include a standard computing desktop with menus, windows, and icons. Unlike programs such as Microsoft's Windows, DESQview/X has scalable windows. You can change them to any size and they still show the entire program running within. It also boasts scalable fonts, using a special version of the Adobe Type Manager program. The desktop permits data transfer, macros, and customizable menus.

For multitasking, DESQview/X starts with DESQview's abilities and then adds graphics and networking, as well as the Rational Systems DOS Extenders for 32-bit operation. DESQview/X can run both DOS and Windows programs in small windows. It also can run programs remotely on other DESQview/X PCs or X workstations. That is, what you see on your PC screen can be running on some other computer. DESQview/X is the first full DOS client/server implementation of the X Windows system standard. It comes with QEMM-386 and Manifest.

How Does DESQview Work?

DESQview lets you open several different programs at once and quickly move from one to another. It moves the program no longer immediately wanted out to expanded memory or extended memory or to a hard disk acting as virtual memory. Many computer owners find such task switching vital to efficient work. DESQview permits multitasking (see Chapter 4) by controlling both processor time (also known as CPU resources) for the programs that run simultaneously and the memory those programs need.

DESQview also offers scripts (the ability to record and replay sequences of commands) as well as mark and transfer (easy movement of information from one program to another).

Each program gets its own window. Each window offers a limited amount of conventional memory for loading a program. The amount of conventional memory available for windows is restricted to whatever is left after DOS, drivers, TSRs loaded before DESQview (you can load them into their own DESQview windows instead), and DESQview use what they need.

When you start a program under DESQview on a PC with expanded memory backfilling conventional addresses, DESQview puts that program into the backfilled memory. When you start another program, DESQview checks to see if it too can fit into the backfilled conventional memory. If so, there it goes. If not, DESQview puts it into expanded memory and then changes the mapping so that expanded memory now occupies the backfilled addresses. The first program stays in its memory but is remapped to expanded memory outside of DOS's view. After awhile that first program is mapped back into the conventional addresses to run, and the second is mapped out. Any other programs started get this same treatment and join the rotation of programs getting slices of the processor's time.

You get the best multitasking on 386 or 486 PCs. Next best is a 286 that can disable its conventional memory down to at least 256K. (Only a few 286s can disable to the 000K address, which gives the same multitasking as a 386 or 486. Some disable only to 512K, restricting the room for programs.) The memory area to use reaches from the base of backfilling to the beginning of video memory and so on a typical system such as this will be 384K.

On a 286 PC, there are misbehaved programs that write their information directly to the screen instead of to the DOS BIOS or to a DESQview video buffer. (Most Hercules, CGA, EGA, and VGA text and graphic displays are misbehaved, because the BIOS route isn't fast enough for decent performance.) Such programs cannot run in the background: they overwrite, or bleed into, whatever the foreground program is showing on screen. Some can be stopped through their own configuration utilities; some can be stopped by using special loaders that come with DESQview. Some programs are "DESQview aware"—that is, they check for DESQview, and when they find it they write to its memory buffer.

You can tell if a program is writing directly to the screen by using the DESQview Change a Program menu. Set Writes text directly to the screen to N, set Virtualize text/graphics to N, blank the Starting Height, Starting Width, Starting Row, and Starting Column of the Window Position of Advanced Parameters (blank them, don't zero them), and then open the program. If the program breaks out of the small window border DESQview makes, it is writing directly to the screen. It needs to be virtualized to run in the background or in a small window.

Any programs can run under DESQview-386 (that is, DESQview with QEMM) on a 386 or 486 PC. DESQview-386 can virtualize the screen, so even so-called "direct to screen" writes are actually to an area of memory that isn't immediately used.

But DESQview distinguishes between virtualizing text and virtualizing graphics. It does so to save memory and time. Virtualizing a screen of text takes only 4000 bytes of memory (80 columns of 25 rows or 2 bytes each—for character and attributes). Using expanded memory means the smallest area is a 16K page, so it takes a single page to virtualize a text screen. Virtualizing graphics takes much more, as much as 272K for a high-resolution screen. Virtualized text appears just about as fast as nonvirtualized text. Virtualized graphics, however, use lots of processor power, slowing performance. (In the special case where the virtualized program is full-screen and foreground, DESQview stops virtualizing temporarily and writes directly to real video memory, so performance picks up again.)

VCPI-supporting, DOS-extended programs in their protected mode can have text output virtualized, but their graphic displays cannot be virtualized. Therefore, when such programs are not using full-screen displays, they are halted. DPMI-supporting programs won't have this limitation—their graphic output will be virtualized.

DESQview can virtualize a program's output only if it has enough memory. Make sure there is at least 272K free for graphics programs.

QEMM's FRAME=NONE or FRAMELENGTH=0 parameters make a page frame of 0 size and so prohibit virtualizing.

You can set the number of real alternate maps in QEMM. The default is 8. You can use the QEMM MAPS=N parameter to make as many as you need, although more than 20 is rarely useful.

If a program takes a hardware interrupt and writes directly to the screen from its hardware interrupt handler, you may need to use Manifest in TSR mode. This allows you to see the First Meg Interrupts screen, which shows you which programs are taking the interrupt. Then start DESQview with the parameter /HW:NN:V, where NN is the hexadecimal number of the software interrupt. DESQview then virtualizes screen writes that occur inside the hardware interrupt handler.

Virtualize text only when you have an application that never uses graphics. You also can do it for a program that has no need to run in the background or in a small window while graphics are displayed (such as a spreadsheet with a charting module or a word processor with a print preview feature). The program halts when in the background. Another case is the program that writes text to screen in real mode but writes graphics to screen in protected mode. Then the program can be virtualized in text mode, and can't anyway in graphics mode.

Getting Maximum Memory for DESQview

DESQview can multitask with expanded memory on a 386 or 486. It can also do so on a 286 or previous PC if at least some of the PC's memory below 640K can take an expanded memory map (backfilling) and the expanded memory board and driver can map memory there (LIM EMS 4.0). DESQview 2.26 and later can provide XMS extended memory to programs inside DESQview windows through its own QEXT.SYS driver (see Chapter 12). (You can add a memory management unit device to get some of the mapping ability of a 386. In most cases, however, you're better off just moving to a 386 or 486 PC.)

QRAM can give a computer more memory for DESQview work. On a 286 PC with real expanded memory (meeting EMS 4.0 or EEMS standards), it can offer near multitasking.

QEXT.SYS also lets DESQview put much of its own program into the HMA, or can let other programs use the HMA. If the DESQview installer detects extended memory (or expanded), it uses the XDV.COM loading program for DESQview. This puts much of DESQview into the extended or expanded memory instead of in conventional memory. You can use QEXT.SYS in place of Microsoft's HIMEM.SYS. DESQview doesn't use extended memory directly for conventional, real-mode DOS programs, but it can swap those programs to and from a RAM disk of extended memory. (Just put the driver letter of that disk into the SWAP field of the DESQview SETUP in the Logical Drives section.) This is much faster than swapping to hard disk. In fact, Quarterdeck claims that this search for DESQview freedom led to the discovery of the HMA (see Chapter 4 for details). Current versions of QEXT.SYS support the XMS standard, in much the same way as Microsoft's HIMEM.SYS does (see Chapter 4 for details on that too).

You don't need QEXT.SYS if you have QEMM-386. QEMM provides all the QEXT services, and more.

QEXT.SYS must be loaded in CONFIG.SYS in a

```
DEVICE=QEXT.SYS
```

line and must come before any drivers that use extended memory. On a 286 PC it needs real extended memory to work, not emulated extended memory (made from expanded by utilities such as QRAM's EMS2EXT.SYS). Then you load DESQview with the DV.COM loader program (see your DESQview instructions for details). If you have the XDV.COM loading program in the DESQview directory, rename that to DV.COM with this command:

```
REN XDV.COM DV.COM
```

When QEXT.SYS is working properly, the Total Conventional Memory cell in DESQview's Memory Status will show about 60K more free (than before loading QEXT).

The INSTALL program for DESQview automatically renames XDV.COM to DV.COM (for all DESQviews 2.26 and later, that is). This program puts parts of DESQview into high memory on any system with expanded memory or extended memory and the QEXT.SYS driver or with QEMM or QRAM.

If any utility loaded after QEXT.SYS doesn't support IBM's specification for VDISK-style utilities, and so overwrites QEXT, DESQview will crash.

Some programs don't get along with QEXT.SYS, unless you add the right parameters. These include AST's Superspool and FastDisk, Microsoft's RAMDRIVE.SYS (before 2.00), and some versions of VDISK.SYS (which are apparently just RAMDRIVE.SYS renamed). Often this is because the programs don't follow the standard method of detecting a VDISK.SYS device, such as QEXT, and therefore don't know QEXT is in your PC. If you have such trouble, use the latest QEXT.SYS from Quarterdeck (it's on the BBS) with the /VD parameter, which lets you know the version number of the VDISK you're using.

QEXT rarely has trouble with hardware compatibility, but it does happen. It will fail on PCs where there is extended memory and no AUTOEXEC.BAT files, and QEXT.SYS is the only driver in the CONFIG.SYS file.

If you cannot start DESQview with XDV.COM or DV.COM, but you can with DV.EXE, DESQview could be putting part of itself in an area of reserved memory that conflicts with some other device, or some other program could be battling with DESQview and QEXT.SYS for use of the HMA. Compare Manifest's

QEMM-386 Accessed screen with its QEMM-386 Type screen to discover the conflicts: Look for areas that are accessed but are listed as mappable or rammable. (Remove the RAM parameter, add the ON parameter, and then reboot the PC to use it.) Then use the QEMM EXCLUDE parameter to keep the reserved memory conflict area out of use. There is also an EXCLUDE parameter for the DV.COM and XDV.COM programs. Use it like this:

```
DV /X:A000-FFFF
```

(although naturally you wouldn't want to exclude all of reserved memory that way). This parameter can exclude any 16K or multiple of 16K area within reserved memory.

To find QEXT.SYS conflicts (or just conflicts with DESQview using that area), use this parameter setting:

```
XDV /X:FFFE
```

If problems disappear with this exclusion added, then there may be a driver or TSR in the CONFIG.SYS or AUTOEXEC.BAT file using extended memory. That driver or TSR may have its own parameters you can use to tell it to stop grabbing memory from 1024K to 1088K, the QEXT.SYS area.

With DESQview and QEMM (4.1 or later), you can run VCPI protected-mode, DOS-extended programs in DESQview windows. You don't need to reserve separate areas of extended and expanded memory for different programs, as you did previously. You can run such programs on 286 systems if all of the programs use XMS services to access extended memory. Memory cannot be converted back and forth from extended to expanded as on a 386 system. The DOS-extended programs must be assigned their extended memory; DESQview and its other programs must be assigned their expanded memory at the start.

Windows 3.0 is a special case. It is a protected-mode, DOS-extended program, but is not a VCPI client. Normally that would rule out its working in a DESQview window, alongside other programs. But DESQview 2.3 and QEMM 5.1 and later have been trimmed to let Windows 3 run in a DESQview window in Windows standard mode using protected mode.

Sometimes troubles starting DESQview with XDV.COM or DV.COM don't come from a single memory conflict; instead, many areas in memory make trouble. The problem could be that memory on a 286 was mapped into conventional addresses without disabling the motherboard memory.

Software emulation of expanded memory (making expanded memory without an expanded memory board) on a 286 doesn't make fast enough memory for multitasking. On a 386 the extended memory converted to expanded by a program such as QEMM is fast enough, because the 386 or 486 chip has hardware circuits for quick remapping.

To run a communications program from a DESQview window, you'll want expanded memory hardware with alternate page map registers in hardware (ideally one for DESQview and another for each open window). Without those, switching pages may not be fast enough for the communications program, and you could lose information received or transmitted.

If you get a "Swapping..." message when you switch away from a program, then it is not running in the background. You may need more memory for it to do so.

If you get an "Out of memory" error when loading a program for a DESQview window, you could have

- not allocated enough memory to the program (so run the Change a Program and allocate more in the Memory Size in K field)
- allocated too much, more than DESQview has available (use Change a Program to reduce Memory Size in K—and check the Memory Status program to see how much conventional memory/largest available is free—after subtracting 11K overhead for a text program or 22K for a graphics program)

- entered a value for System Memory (in K) of the Advanced Parameters menu of Change a Program (and this should be 0 for non-DESQview-specific programs, or no more than 10K for most DESQview programs—whatever number is in this field increases window overhead)

Check any application's manual to see what the minimum suggested memory size is for it—the free memory it needs, not the amount of memory chips plugged in. (You can subtract 30 to 40K from the typical requested amount, because most requests round the amount up to an even number and give some space for DOS itself and drivers.

If windows aren't as big as you'd like, then drivers and TSRs loaded before DESQview may be taking too much memory (this affects the memory free for every window, no matter now much expanded and extended memory you have). You can get rid of some of the drivers and TSRs, use QEMM or QRAM to load them high (relocate them to high memory), or you can load some of them inside DESQview. Some, such as disk caches and print spoolers, won't do their work from inside a window. Others can run just fine in a window.

You can use DESQview's DEVICE.COM utility to load TSRs or drivers into a window, even though they normally load from a line in CONFIG.SYS.

At some point, if you're loading drivers and TSRs into high memory, you won't gain any more free conventional memory. That's because parts of DESQview that load into high memory will no longer fit, and so each new driver or TSR relocated means a part of DESQview returning to conventional memory. You can fight this by searching for more unused areas in high memory using Manifest.

Another problem arises because, on systems with extended or expanded memory, less of DESQview may be located in reserved memory addresses than is ideal or possible.

On a 386 with QEMM and 286 systems with an HMA and QEXT.SYS loaded, 64K of DESQview goes into the HMA.

On systems with expanded memory, DESQview can put some of itself into unused video areas, such as the A000-AFFF segment, which is available on EGA and VGA systems that aren't using graphics. Also, the B000-B7FF area is used for monochrome text and the B800-BFFF for color text (and sometimes for Hercules graphics). If you're producing one kind of text or the other, one of those areas is not used.

You can also find more memory using the QEMM Analysis command. (See Chapter 6 for details.)

Part of the F000-F7FF area frequently can be used because it is often the address of ROM BASIC language that is not necessary. Keep a DOS boot floppy on hand when experimenting this way.

The DESQview SETUP program may be grabbing more memory than necessary. Look in the Advanced Setup Performance parameter.

The Common Memory parameter manages the windows. You need an amount proportional to the number of windows open. The default is 17K, a minimum of 14K can handle five or six windows, and few systems need more than 20K. If you have more than that specified, cut back.

The DOS Buffers for EMS parameter manages file operations into expanded memory. The default is 2K. If you're not on a network and are using QEMM, you can work with zero kilobytes, which saves about 5K. Some memory specified here can speed disk access, but anything more than 10K or 15K is probably wasted.

There are also a few other setup spots to save a few kilobytes.

On the Keyboard parameter, you can save 12K if you tell DESQview you don't want the Learn feature. This means no macros, however.

On the Video Monitor parameter, you can save from zero to 16K if you don't want text and graphics at the same time. This disables the Video Parameters menu and prevents the graphics program from being seen when in the background, and prevents virtualization of graphics.

The "What Display Adapter do you have?" question lets you answer zero for not loading a video driver, saving 2 to 9K. This means you can't save and restore graphics screens or virtualize graphics.

On the Performance parameter you can answer no (N) to "Manage Printer Contention?" to save 2K. (This defaults to N, so it may already have been done, with no more savings available.) DESQview cannot then stop two programs from printing at the same time.

The Network parameter lets you disable the network support or decrease the size of thc buffer. Only some networks need this; most DOS applications that run off the network don't. You can save about 5K plus the size of the buffer in the second field. Try cutting this out to see what you save and if any troubles arise. The default buffer is 8K.

Don't bother with DESQview on a system as small as a 286 with 1MB of memory. The best you would gain would be to multitask two small applications. A 386SX with 2MB of memory is about the practical minimum.

DESQview runs and multitasks programs on any PC in conventional memory. Unfortunately, with the DOS, TSR, and driver use of memory, there may be only 400K available. It isn't easy to find more than one application to fit into that space. Programs that need more are swapped out to expanded memory, to virtual disk (a RAM disk), or to a hard disk. Programs swapped out stop running.

DESQview can actually multitask—keep several programs running—on a system with expanded memory. It needs EMS 4.0 to emulate expanded memory on a 286 or lesser processor. Without backfilling, programs just task switch, not multitask.

You disable memory typically by moving jumpers or by adding parameters to the memory driver, or by running a computer's setup program.

DESQview by itself takes between 145K and 180K. The precise amount depends on the drivers you load with its setup and the hardware it runs on. If you follow the instructions above on minimizing the setup uses, you can get it down below even the 145K figure.

When a PC has only 640K conventional memory, all of DESQview goes into conventional.

On a PC with extended memory, DESQview puts 63K of itself into the HMA (using QEXT.SYS or QEMM and the XDV.COM loader).

On a PC with expanded memory, DESQview puts 32K of itself (more on a VGA system) in the EMS page frame with XDV.COM. It switches this code out of the way when the page frame is used for anything else.

On a PC with extended and expanded memory, DESQview can relocate about 95K of itself away from conventional memory.

On a PC with the ability to map more pages of expanded memory between 640K and 1024K, DESQview can put more of itself in high RAM. It uses the XDV.COM loader to do so. In that case it leaves as little as 1K of itself in conventional memory.

When you open a window, DESQview needs about 9K of memory as overhead, although this can be decreased somewhat by the settings in Change a Program.

When looking for the amount of memory a program needs, the only safe method is to give it more than it should need, then keep reducing the amount until it no longer works.

LOADHI's /GS parameter tries to determine the size of a program. When you run it you see two numbers: the amount of memory the program needs to load and initialize and the amount it keeps permanently. (See Chapter 9 for details.)

Configuring DESQview—Change a Program

You can optimally configure DESQview using its Change a Program screen.

You get here by accessing the DESQview menu (press Alt when in DESQview), selecting Open Window (type O or move the highlight to that parameter and press Enter, or move the mouse and press the left mouse button), and then typing CP.

On 8088, 8086, and 286 PCs, answering these questions will help you make the settings in this display:

- Does the PC have memory above 640K? (If not, you can only get task switching by adding TSRs alongside your application.)
- Does the program you want to run write directly to screen? (If so, it will not run in a small window.)

- Is the foreground program set to Share CPU=Yes? (Background programs can operate only if this is true.)
- Is the background program set to Runs in Background=Yes? (Background programs can operate only if this is true.)
- Did the program swap when you opened the second task? (Swapping comes from not enough conventional memory mappable. Swapping to the EMS page frame or to hard disk means quick switching among programs is possible, but it eliminates background processing.)

On 386 and 486 machines, answer these questions:

- Does the PC have memory above 640K? (If not, you can only get task switching by adding TSRs alongside your application.)
- If there is memory above 640K, is a memory manager such as QEMM converting extended memory to EMS 4.0 expanded memory? (If not, the PC won't have much room for additional programs for multitasking.)
- Does the program you want to run write directly to screen? (If so, it will not run in a small window unless Virtualize=Y or T is also set. Setting it to Y means both text and graphics can execute in background in a small window. Setting to T means the program can execute text only in a small window.)
- Is the foreground program set to Share CPU=Yes? (Background programs can operate only if this is true.)
- Is the background program set to Runs in Background=Yes? (Background programs can operate only if this is true.)
- Did the program swap when you opened the second task? (Swapping comes from not enough conventional memory mappable. Swapping to the EMS page frame or to hard disk means quick switching among programs is possible, but it eliminates background processing.)

Press F1 in the Change a Program display and you'll see the Advanced Parameters display, as in this Figure 16-3. Here you can see and set various memory-use parameters.

System Memory (in K) tells you how much memory the system will use. Set this to zero unless the program to run was specifically written for DESQview.

Maximum Program Size (in K) specifies the maximum memory a program can use. When this is blank, DESQview allocates the minimum memory size amount. When a number is specified, DESQview limits the program to that amount, no matter how much it requests.

Script buffer size is the memory for loading and recording DESQview macros. The default is 1000 bytes, about 1K. If you really need that 1K, you can set this to 0 and eliminate the buffer (but then not be able to use macros).

Maximum Expanded Memory (in K) is the limit of expanded memory that is given to a program. If this is blank, the program is given as much as it wants, as much as all of expanded memory. If there is a numeric limit here, the program gets only that much. Some programs that need expanded memory automatically ask for all of it, even though they may not need that much. If this happens, any other program that asks for expanded memory is out of luck.

Text Pages and Graphics Pages refer to stored images of program displays. Some programs are slow to refresh their displays on the screen, so it is quicker for task switching to keep the memory of the most recent display in memory—then when switching to that program, the display will appear instantly. The cost is in some memory set aside to hold the display image. Text Pages specifies memory allocation for saving and restoring screen information from programs that display only text. Most text-display programs need only one text page, although a few need two. Each text page uses 4 to 10K of memory. Most graphics display programs need only one graphics page, but this can eat up 16 to 256K of memory, depending on the resolution and color (the display adapter settings) of that page.

DESQVIEW-386 and Windows

As you know from reading this chapter, DESQview is a program that lets you task switch or multitask other programs. Microsoft Windows is a similar product—a program that can task switch or multitask other programs. Windows, however, does this in graphics mode, while DESQview works mainly in text mode.

There are some very popular programs written to work within Windows. What if you want to use one of these, but you don't want to give up DESQview's advantages in managing memory and programs? Easy. Run Windows inside a DESQview window. That is, you start your PC and DOS runs. You run DESQview, load Windows into a DESQview window, and then load your desired Windows program into Windows. The program is inside Windows inside DESQview running under DOS. This is a confusing but entirely useful setup.

To run Windows 3.0 or 3.1 with DESQview and QEMM, get the latest versions of DESQview and QEMM.

QEMM, DESQview, and Windows try to control and manage memory, so using them all together means a critical need for compatibility. You'll need the latest versions of QEMM and DESQview for maximum Windows support. Get at least DESQview 2.3 or later, DESQview-386 2.3 or later, and QEMM-386 5.1 or later. You can run Windows with earlier versions, but only in Windows real mode, which is not as powerful as its standard and enhanced modes. If you must use a QEMM version before 5.1, make sure you have the RAM parameter in the QEMM CONFIG.SYS line, and put these lines in the [386Enh] section of the Windows SYSTEM.INI file:

```
DUALDISPLAY=TRUE
EMMEXCLUDE=E000-EFFF
```

That keeps Windows from bothering QEMM's memory management. If you must run Windows with DESQview-386 before version 2.3, run full-screen, not virtualized. If you do virtualize, you run into mouse and video problems.

On 286 PCs running DESQview 2.3 or later, Windows 3.0 needs at least 1MB of true extended memory (not emulated). To run Windows in standard mode, you need to use the special loader program—W3-LOAD.COM—that comes on the DESQview disk. You run it from the

```
MS Windows 3 Std.
```

selection that Add a Program can add to DESQview's Open Window menu.

If the necessary configurations to run Windows in standard mode within DESQview are too difficult, and you have Windows 3.0, not 3.1, just run Windows in real mode. Many Windows programs run without trouble in Real mode. What you lose is true multitasking and some of the interprogram communications that are part of the most sophisticated applications. Larger applications, especially graphics, require Standard mode for access to large memory blocks.

CHAPTER SEVENTEEN

QEMM with Windows
and Windows Applications

Windows is a program that adds to DOS. It manages memory and processing to make any PC behave somewhat more like Apple's Macintosh computer, with pull-down menus, icons, and mouse control. (A mouse is a hand-held pointer for directing computer action.) DOS programs can run under Windows, but they don't use these special interface features. To take full advantage of Windows, programs must be rewritten to new versions.

For best compatibility, use the latest QEMM with the latest Windows. You can tell if your QEMM is version 5.10 or later by the name of the main QEMM file. Before 5.1 it was QEMM.SYS, after 5.1 it was QEMM386.SYS. (You also can look at the version number that displays when QEMM is loading.)

Windows itself was once divided into Windows/286 and Windows/386, for 286 and 386 PCs, respectively. In 1990 Microsoft introduced Windows 3.0, a large upgrade and change to Windows. This combined and improved the /286 and /386 versions. Windows 3.0 offered three operating modes: real, standard, and Enhanced-386. Real was for running on PCs with 8088 or 8086 abilities and limited memory—say just 640K of RAM. Standard was for running on PCs with faster processors, such as a 286, and 1MB or more RAM. Enhanced-386 was only for 386 and 486-based PCs and required at least 2MB of memory. Later, Windows 3.1 came along with some new features; 3.1 dropped real mode but kept the other two modes and approach to memory management. Most programs that ask for Windows these days are asking for Windows 3.x, meaning Windows 3.0 or 3.1.

If you use Windows, get at least version Windows 3.0. It has far superior memory management and performance than previous versions of Windows, and few Windows applications sold today work with earlier versions of Windows.

Some memory management is built into Windows 3.0 and 3.1. But QEMM can conserve and offer more memory than Windows can. QEMM 5.1 and later versions can support Windows 3.x in real, standard, or enhanced modes.

Don't try to use any QEMM version before 5.1 with Windows 3.x. You won't get complete support.

The best use of QEMM with Windows is to give lots of free conventional memory to DOS applications that can't use other kinds of memory, such as expanded or extended, for data storage. QEMM can increase the conventional memory for DOS applications but reduces the memory for Windows applications.

If you only use Windows applications or smaller DOS applications under Windows, or DOS applications that can use extended or expanded memory for data storage, QEMM may not be useful. In fact, Windows can run faster with a tweaked DOS 5 using HIMEM.SYS and 386EMM.EXE than with QEMM386.SYS.

You don't need QEMM to provide expanded memory for DOS applications under Windows. Windows itself does that.

Choosing A Windows Mode

Here are some rules of thumb for choosing a mode:

- Real mode is slowest. It offers compatibility with computers that don't run Windows 3.x in standard or enhanced mode. (Only Windows 3.0 offers Real mode.)

- Standard mode is generally fastest. It is the highest possible level on 286 PCs. It is best for running DOS applications in full-screen without multitasking. It is also best for DOS applications that don't need expanded memory.

- Enhanced mode requires the most hardware power. It is best for running Windows applications concurrently. For DOS applications it is best when you want to run regular DOS applications in sizable windows and want to multitask regular DOS applications. It is also the mode for running DOS applications that need expanded memory while running under Windows, and when DOS doesn't have expanded memory.

Windows 3.1 in all modes is compatible with QEMM versions 5.12 and later.

To see what version of Windows you have, use this command in the Windows directory:

```
DIR WIN*.EXE
```

If the date of creation for the files is 5/1/90, you have Windows 3.0. If it is after 5/1/90, you have Windows 3.0a or 3.1.

PageMaker 4.0 won't run in real mode.

On an 8088 or 8086, expanded memory is best. On a 286 extended memory is best—it's more useful to Windows, easier to install, and cheaper.

Real mode is for any PC or compatible with at least 640K of conventional memory. It provides you with at most 350 to 450K to launch a Windows application, depending on the drivers and TSRs you load before starting Windows and on the video you use. Higher resolutions use more conventional memory. Because the memory area isn't that large, real mode swaps parts of the Windows application out to disk. If there is some extended memory in the PC, the computer uses that as a faster swapping area. Windows 3 applications can't get at extended memory for themselves in real mode, but you can run DOS applications that use it, such as those with built-in DOS extenders. In real mode, Windows stores its own data and program code in up to 32MB of LIM EMS 4.0 memory and lets any Windows or DOS application store data and program code in LIM EMS 4.0 memory. It won't use LIM EMS 3.2 memory for itself, but lets Windows and DOS applications use that memory for data. In real mode Windows 3 is compatible with 386 expanded memory managers such as EMM386.SYS and QEMM-386.

Standard mode is for any PC or compatible with a 286, 386, or 486 processor, 640K of conventional memory, and at least 256K free extended memory. (Typically this means a 286, 386, or 486 PC with at least 1MB of memory on the motherboard.) It is the default for a 286 with enough memory and for a 386 or 486 without enough memory for enhanced mode. In standard mode, Windows uses the protected mode and the XMS extended memory manager HIMEM.SYS (or other XMS manager installed) to get at extended memory.

Standard mode is the default for Windows 3.1.

In standard mode, Windows 3 sees conventional and extended memory as one block of memory. It can use up to 16MB of conventional and extended memory for Windows applications and data. DOS applications that need extended memory can get it in standard mode, although they must adhere to the VCPI specification. Expanded memory isn't used by Windows 3 or Windows applications in standard mode, but DOS applications can use it. Standard mode doesn't officially support 386 expanded memory managers. EMM386.SYS, for instance, is automatically disabled when in standard mode. And some 386 expanded memory managers released before Windows 3 won't let Windows 3 launch in standard mode. Some updated versions, such as QEMM 5.1 and later, are compatible with it.

Windows Enhanced-386 mode runs on any PC or compatible with at least a 386 or 486 processor, 640K of conventional memory, and 1MB of free extended memory. It is the default for any such PC. In enhanced mode, Windows uses the protected mode of the processor to use virtual memory.

To force Windows to run in Enhanced-386 mode (such as on a system where standard was the default but now there is enough memory for enhanced mode), start with the command WIN /3 or WIN /E.

In enhanced mode Windows 3 can use up to 16MB of memory for Windows and DOS applications. It uses conventional and extended memory as one block. When there is less than 16MB of combined memory, enhanced mode uses virtual memory—disk space acting as memory. The maximum total of conventional, extended, and virtual memory is 16MB, although this could be less if there isn't enough free disk space to fulfill the goal. Enhanced mode lets you run DOS applications that need extended memory, but they must adhere to the DPMI standard. Some DOS-extended programs use earlier versions of the Rational Systems or Phar Lap DOS extenders and aren't compatible with DPMI, only with VCPI. Lotus 1-2-3 3.0 is in this boat, for example, although 1-2-3 3.1 is DPMI compatible. In enhanced mode Windows 3 does not use expanded memory or provide it to Windows applications. It does provide expanded memory to DOS applications, however, even if there is no expanded memory board, by converting some extended memory to expanded.

If you run in enhanced mode, you should configure any expanded -memory board memory as extended.

Paradox 3.5 can run under Windows 3.0, although it is a DOS application. If you use QEMM to load TSRs or drivers high, then Paradox must run in real mode. Trying to run it in protected mode could hang the machine.

Enhanced mode is not officially compatible with 386 expanded memory managers such as EMM386.SYS or QEMM. Windows automatically diables EMM386.SYS. If Windows cannot disable the memory manager, it won't launch (start).

When you run a DOS application under Windows, memory-resident or not, it must stick to the 640K limit of DOS. The 640K limit is often cramped even farther, perhaps 60K farther, by Windows' own code. You can use a memory manager such as QEMM to maximize the conventional memory available for such a DOS application.

You can force Windows 3.0 to run in real mode by starting with the command WIN /R.

Older Versions of Windows

Windows 3 didn't come first, as mentioned above. Previous versions could sometimes work with QEMM, but there were lots of incompatibilities. For example, Windows 2.03 couldn't work with more than one mappable area of memory larger than 48K, between 640K and 1MB. Running QEMM with it means finding and excluding all but one such area. Windows 386 and QEMM-386 are not compatible. Windows/386 provides its own memory management above 640K. The WIN86.COM program that came with Windows/386 is a subset of Windows/286 and can be run with QEMM. But you could run QEMM-386 with Windows/386 or Windows run-time programs, even on a 386 machine. The run-time version of Windows 2.1 searches the path for WIN.COM and, if it finds it, loads the full copy of Windows. When running QEMM or DESQview this could be a problem if the WIN.COM found is Windows/386. You can solve this problem by renaming the WIN.COM file WIND.COM. Another typical problem was that you needed an expanded memory manager such as QEMM to have expanded memory fast enough for the Intel Visual Edge printer enhancement board with Windows/286 2.x or run-time Windows. Another was receiving an "Incorrect 3886 system version" or "386 System Display mismatch" error message because you ran Windows/386 with QEMM. ParcPlace Systems' Smalltalk-80/386 was not compatible with Windows/386. It needed 3MB of extended memory to operate and had its own memory manager, which did not permit virtual-86 mode.

You're better off just upgrading to Windows 3.0 or 3.1.

Installing QEMM and Windows

The QEMM defaults give Windows the memory setup it needs. You don't need to install the HIMEM.SYS driver that comes with Windows nor reserve extended memory for Windows. The defaults include putting the RAM parameter in the QEMM386.SYS line of CONFIG.SYS. OPTIMIZE puts this parameter in when you install. The RAM parameter also appears without OPTIMIZE's help if you answer yes (Y) to the

```
Fill All High Memory with RAM?
```

question during QEMM installation.

Without the RAM parameter, Windows enhanced mode may fail because of confusion over filling and managing the monochrome video area B000-B7FF. If you don't want to use the RAM parameter, at least use the X=B000-B7FF excluding parameter for QEMM.

QEMM 5.1 or later needs the RAM parameter in its CONFIG.SYS line to fully support Windows 3.0, otherwise enhanced mode may fail.

Windows 3.0 and 3.0a SETUP program loads HIMEM.SYS when it finds

- a 286, 386, or 486 processor
- an HMA area (meaning at least 640K of conventional memory plus at least 64K extended memory)
- no running XMS 2.0 or later memory manager (though it will install a new HIMEM.SYS over any version 2.6 or older HIMEM.SYS), which includes QEMM

Windows 3.0 needs at least 25 file handles.

Remember that with QEMM version 5.1, the main QEMM driver was changed in name from QEMM.SYS to QEMM386.SYS. Windows SETUP has been trained to tell you that QEMM.SYS isn't compatible.

If you install QEMM before Windows 3, the Windows SETUP program changes CONFIG.SYS by inserting HIMEM.SYS before QEMM386.SYS. This steals 2.8K of conventional memory that QEMM cannot then manage. There's no need for HIMEM.SYS when you have QEMM386.SYS, so when Windows SETUP asks

```
Let you review & edit changes before modifications are
made?
```

edit out the HIMEM.SYS line from the "Proposed CONFIG.SYS file" area. Or you can remove the line later with an editor. SETUP also puts in a line for the Windows SMARTDRV.SYS disk cache after the QEMM386.SYS line in CONFIG.SYS. By default this uses lots of expanded memory. If you want that memory for other programs, you can cut the SMARTDRV.SYS setting for memory, or eliminate the disk cache altogether.

If you install QEMM and then install Windows, you can save some memory by then removing HIMEM.SYS and SMARTDRV.SYS from the CONFIG.SYS file.

If you install Windows 3 before QEMM, the Windows SETUP program already will have put HIMEM.SYS into CONFIG.SYS. QEMM puts QEMM386.SYS before HIMEM.SYS. Then, when HIMEM.SYS tries to load after QEMM, it sees QEMM386.SYS in memory and won't bother to load. You won't need it, and it won't use any memory, but this failure to load creates the following beeping error message:

```
Error: An Extended Memory manager is already installed.
```

If that bothers you, remove the HIMEM.SYS line from CONFIG.SYS. Then, as above, you may want to reduce the size of SMARTDRV.SYS or remove it altogether.

Windows SETUP reads the CONFIG.SYS file, looking for any mention of utilities that can conflict with HIMEM.SYS. QEMM.SYS is one of these. If SETUP finds QEMM.SYS mentioned, it exits and shows the error

```
Device conflict with QEMM.SYS
```

If you then remove the QEMM.SYS line and run SETUP again, the error message does not reappear.

QEMM versions 4.23 and later may be used with HIMEM.SYS if the parameter EXTMEM=64 is put on the QEMM386.SYS line.

When Windows 3 first appeared, QEMM didn't support it fully the way the newest version of HIMEM.SYS did. And you could not use both HIMEM.SYS and QEMM—only one could be in control. Microsoft then released the WIN-HIRAM.VXD, which lets other memory managers, such as QEMM, replace HIMEM.SYS. Quarterdeck released QEMM version 5.1, incorporating WIN-HIRAM.VXD.

In standard mode, QEMM can let you run some DOS applications, such as Paradox 386, that normally are considered incompatible.

QEMM is much better for programs running outside of Windows. EMM386.SYS makes you edit parameters and reboot for each program that wants different amounts of expanded and extended memory. QEMM handles extended and expanded memory as from a single "pool," changing the amounts as programs request. QEMM can load high without DOS 5, and has more precision and control than DOS 5. It can also automatically find a near-optimum setup, while DOS 5 makes you do everything by trial and error.

To keep from confusing OPTIMIZE and INSTALL for QEMM, you should remove any AUTOEXEC.BAT commands that start Windows until after QEMM is installed and configured. You may want to remove batch files and Pause commands too, perhaps just nullifying them by adding a REM and a space at the beginning of each such line. Also remove any HIMEM.SYS and EMM386.SYS lines. They don't hurt, normally, but could confuse OPTIMIZE.

If you use DOS 5, your CONFIG.SYS file probably has a DOS=UMB line (or DOS=HIGH,UMB). This tells DOS to make upper memory blocks in high memory addresses. It also tells DOS to put part of itself into the HMA (that's the high statement). With QEMM you need to remove the UMB parameter so QEMM, not DOS, can make and manage the UMBs. You should also change any DOS 5 DEVICEHIGH= statements to just DEVICE= statements. Look to the AUTOEXEC.BAT file and eliminate the LOADHIGH or LH from any lines. QEMM loads as many of these high as possible, but some versions of OPTIMIZE may be confused by the LH or LOADHIGH statements.

When installing QEMM you can normally just go with the defaults. But when you're going to use Windows as well, you should answer no to the question are the settings correct. Then answer the individual questions as follows:

- "Do you want QEMM to fill conventional memory with the fastest memory available?" Answer no. That gives you the NOSORT parameter, because the speed sorting of memory can make trouble for Windows enhanced mode.

- "Do you want to load resident programs above the video memory?" Answer yes. This puts the RAM parameter into CONFIG.SYS, which is vital to running Windows in enhanced mode. (This tells QEMM to fill unused addresses in upper memory with RAM that Windows and other applications can use.)

- "What other command line parameters do you need?" Type NOFILL. On systems without full 640K of conventional memory, QEMM converts extended memory to fill to 640K. But QEMM can't do this when Windows is in enhanced mode.

Then let INSTALL record and confirm these selections, and let INSTALL change the CONFIG.SYS file to have these changes. You'll see such parameters as RAM, NOSORT, NOFILL, and perhaps NOVIDEO and ROM after QEMM386.SYS. (NOVIDEOFILL does nothing for typical EGA or VGA systems. ROM may improve performance by copying system and video ROM into faster RAM.)

The ROM parameter should be one of the first you drop if you're having any troubles with QEMM and Windows.

There probably won't be other parameters, except perhaps a page frame address.

Reboot and run OPTIMIZE. It will find the best way it can to load your drivers and TSRs high, put the commands for that into CONFIG.SYS and

AUTOEXEC.BAT, and then reboot your PC to put them into effect. Run Windows in all available modes, run DOS applications under Windows, and look for any troubles.

If you have a driver or TSR that you know doesn't run well from high memory, take it out of CONFIG.SYS or AUTOEXEC.BAT before running OPTIMIZE. Then put it back in afterward.

If you have a PS/2 Model 50 or 60, be sure to use QEMM-50/60, not QEMM-386.

Make sure you have enough FILES and BUFFERS, probably FILES=40 and BUFFERS=30, or the equivalents to those (with BUFFERS much smaller if you have a disk cache).

If your PC uses Shadow RAM, you might want to disable it when using Windows. Add the parameter NOSHADOWRAM to QEMM. (In some PCs you can just disable Shadow RAM through the system setup program.)

In DOS 5, the EMM386.EXE driver does allow you to load drivers and TSRs high. (See Chapter 15 for details.)

The NOEMS parameter to EMM386.EXE tells it not to provide DOS applications with expanded memory. (This also prevents Windows from creating emulated expanded memory.) The RAM parameter lets you load drivers and TSRs high.

EMM386.EXE can have trouble with Windows in enhanced mode. You might see the following error message:

```
EMM386: Unable to start Enhanced mode Windows due to
invalid path specification for EMM386.
```

To get a valid path, add the /Y parameter to the command that loads EMM386.EXE, as in this example:

```
DEVICE=C:\DOS\EMM386.EXE RAM /Y=C:\DOS\EMM386.EXE
```

When you load EMM386.EXE it uses a special block of memory that Windows needs for standard mode. Try to run in standard mode and you'll get the message

```
Cannot Run Windows In Standard Mode
```

The RAM parameter tells EMM386.EXE to set aside 256K of extended memory for use as expanded memory. If applications then want more expanded memory, EMM386.EXE converts more as needed. If you don't need expanded memory, you may want to decrease to 16K the default minimum amount of converted extended memory. Put 16 after the parameter, as here:

```
DEVICE=C:\DOS\EMM386.EXE RAM 16
```

The largest UMB you can get on a typical system as about 31K. You might get as much as 95K in a block if you move the page frame. It is typically at D000h. To move it to E000h, add the parameter M9, as shown here:

```
DEVICE=C:\DOS\EMM386.EXE RAM 16 M9
```

Some PS/2 systems can't use the M9 parameter. They'll give the message

```
Warning: Parameter ROM or RAM Detected Within
Page Frame.
```

If so, remove the M9 parameter.

If you don't use a Hercules graphics card, MDA, or 256-color VGA, your PC probably doesn't use the memory between B000h to B7FFh. EMM386.EXE can grab this if you add the parameter I=B000-B7FF.

You can configure Windows 3.0 or 3.1 with statements in the SYSTEM.INI file. Most adjustments you make to that file to manage memory in concert with QEMM should be put in the file's [386Enh] section.

You can use Windows Notepad to edit the SYSTEM.INI file.

In SYSTEM.INI you can use these parameters:

`DUAL DISPLAY=YES` .... tells Windows not to use the area B000-B7FF
`EMMEXCLUDE=XXX-YYY` ...... tells Windows not to look for unused addresses in those addresses
`EMMPAGEFRAME=XXXX` .... tells Windows where the page frame should be
`NOEMMDRIVER=TRUE` .... disables the Windows EMM driver
`HIGHFLOPPYREADS=NO` ...... prevents undesired access of E000-EFFF when used with EMMEXCLUDE=E000-EFFF
`IRQ9GLOBAL=YES` .... helps solve floppy disk problems
`SYSTEMROMBREAKPOINT=NO` .. use it if there is high RAM above F000, which means you can use this as an alternative to EMMEXCLUDE=F000-FFFF
`RESERVEPAGEFRAME=NO` ..... gives more conventional memory to non-EMS-using DOS applications
`VIRTUALHDIRQ=OFF` .... use with unusual hard disks

Don't use NOEMMDRIVER=TRUE or RESERVEPAGE-FRAME=NO if any DOS program you run wants some EMS memory under Windows.

DUALDISPLAY and EMMEXCLUDE are preferable to the QEMM-386 EXCLUDE parameter. They don't prevent other programs from accessing addresses between 640K and 1024K. The largest permissible area for EMMEXCLUDE is

```
EMMEXCLUDE=A000-EFFF
```

which keeps Windows from scanning the entire A000-EFFF area for unused address spaces.

The DUALDISPLAY=YES parameter makes sure that Windows won't use the B000-B7FF area. (This is useful because many programs that use high memory use this area.)

Some systems need an additional exclusion to let QEMM run with Windows in enhanced mode. This might be an EMMEXCLUDE= statement in SYSTEM.INI or an EXCLUDE parameter for QEMM. The advantage of using EMMEXCLUDE is that programs other than Windows can still get at that memory. The disadvantage is that EMMEXCLUDE cannot specify areas as small as those QEMM can specify, which can work down to 4K at a time.

Compaq Portable 386 machines may use the X=B000-BFFF on QEMM 386 with 640x400 mode for Windows in enhanced mode.

Sometimes you need to use QEMM parameters to exclude low addresses in conventional memory where the Windows enhanced mode kernel loads. (This can also help with standard mode.) To figure out which addresses, run Manifest before running Windows, look at the First Meg Overview screen, and look for the lowest "Available" area. Windows uses less than 16K starting at that address. You could exclude 64K to be sure and then experiment with smaller exclusions, bringing the top of the EXCLUDE area down until it no longer works. EXCLUDE from 0000 to a neat multiple of 16K above the beginning of the available mark.

EMM386.SYS automatically excludes 0000-3FFF. Your clue is if EMM386.SYS doesn't give Windows any trouble but QEMM does. In that case, exclude 0000-3FFF for QEMM.

For any problem with an EMS-using application inside Windows enhanced mode, you can try changing the Windows PIF for that application so that EMS memory is locked.

If you're hoping for Windows to supply expanded memory to DOS programs under enhanced mode, then you need to make sure there's a 64K contiguous page frame for QEMM, because Windows inherits the page frame from QEMM.

When QEMM moves drivers to high memory, or when it loads them high, and then you run Windows in enhanced mode, Windows may run a bit slower than it might otherwise. It must use the WINHIRAM.VXD driver to handle loading high.

If you use QEMM 6.0 or later with STEALTH, have the

```
SYSTEMROMBREAKPOINT=FALSE
```

line in the SYSTEM.INI file. QEMM INSTALL puts this in the SYSTEM.INI automatically, so you can get it there just be installing again. (The default is =TRUE. This parameter specifies whether Windows should use ROM address space between F000 and FFFF for a break point. In enhanced mode Windows normally looks here to find a special adjust-requested privilege level (ARPL) instruction—a 63H byte value—used as a system break point. If there is something other than permanently available ROM here, you should disable with =FALSE. With FALSE Windows allocates a one-byte block of global virtual memory in low conventional memory and writes the 63H there. Because QEMM remaps the ROM, that ROM is not permanently available, and so FALSE must be used.)

Problems and Solutions For Real and Standard Modes

You will have few problems running QEMM 5.1 or later with Windows 3 in real or standard modes.

A DOS application using EMS and running in Windows standard mode may sometimes cause a "This Application Has Violated the System's Integrity" error message. After quitting the application and Windows, you may be able to avoid the error by

- excluding low memory (as mentioned above)
- excluding all high RAM above the page frame
- excluding all high RAM below the page frame
- preventing the DOS application from using EMS
- changing the Windows PIF for the DOS application so the EMS memory is locked

QEMM-386 with standard mode can use extended memory to supply the application with EMS-compliant expanded memory. The EMM386.SYS driver that comes with Windows cannot.

You might sometimes have a problem running Windows 3 in real or standard modes inside DESQview with a graphics resolution higher than standard 640x480 of VGA. You may need to adjust QEMM. If so, try first setting Windows to use standard VGA with the Windows SETUP program. If that works, but high resolution does not, the driver Windows uses for the high-resolution mode could be at fault. The fix could be to get a new driver for the higher-resolution mode and to use four graphics pages for DESQview in the Windows Change a Program menu of DESQview. also try excluding the SVGA ROM at X=C000-CFFF with QEMM.

Some users claim that the compatibility of Windows standard mode and QEMM depends on having or not having DOS interrupt stacks. Sometimes adding STACKS=0,0 to disable DOS interrupt stacks helps, sometimes removing it helps. Which method works depends on your computer.

Windows 3's standard mode behaves differently if you have DOS 5, or a previous version of DOS (such as DOS 3.3), running. With DOS 5 and its EMM386 memory manager you have some conflicts that don't occur with QEMM. QEMM lets you run Windows 3 in standard mode both outside and inside DESQview: EMM386 can't do that. QEMM handles it automatically, updating the Windows SYSTEM.INI file to set it up.

Problems and Solutions With Enhanced Mode

Enhanced mode can cause many troubles. Typical troubles are

- system won't start
- system crashes when exiting enhanced mode
- problems while running

If your system crashes or has problems while running Windows in enhanced mode, they are probably not the fault of QEMM. After all, QEMM is disabled in that case. However, they could come from changes QEMM made before it was disabled.

If you do have troubles in enhanced mode, follow this procedure:

1. Check to make sure you're using QEMM 5.1 or later.
2. Check to see if the RAM parameter is in CONFIG.SYS or that X=B000-B7FF is there.

3. Check if your computer uses different speeds of memory (use Manifest). If so, put the NOSORT parameter in CONFIG.SYS. Check to see if you have less than 640K of conventional memory, with the rest to 640K filled by QEMM. If so, have the NOFILL parameter in CONFIG.SYS. Unfortunately, QEMM must be on to use NOSORT or NOFILL, and Windows 3 enhanced mode turns QEMM off when it starts. (Real and standard modes don't turn QEMM off.) If you're not sure on either of these parameters, try them. If the system doesn't need them, they won't affect it.
4. If you have QEMM 5.10, not 5.11 or later, and are using a PS/2 or Micro Channel compatible with an extended BIOS data area, have the NOXBDA parameter in CONFIG.SYS (or upgrade to the more recent versions).
5. If your computer has Shadow RAM, add the NOSHADOWRAM parameter (NOSH). (Try this even if you don't know if there is Shadow RAM in your system.)
6. If when starting Windows you see garbage characters on the screen and hear beeping, and then see the DOS prompt again, you may be missing the WINHIRAM.VXD file in the QEMM directory. Or that file may be from an older version of QEMM; it needs to be the same as for your QEMM version.
7. Reinstall Windows from scratch using the SETUP program. Make sure you're not just using the default MS-DOS or PC-DOS System choice instead of a more specific choice you could make here.
8. Use QEMM.COM to see if the page frame is at 9000. If it is, try moving it to somewhere in the C000 to E000 range. You may need to move other things out of the way to make room.

QEMM 5.10 can have trouble with Novell's XMSNET. Get a more recent QEMM.

Have at least FILES=15 in CONFIG.SYS, instead of putting all files up high with FILES.COM. Windows may not start in enhanced mode if all files are high.

QEMM makes a page frame in between 640K and 1MB unless you add the NOEMS parameter.

If you see the UAE (unrecoverable application error), then Windows is reaching a part of memory it knows it shouldn't. Windows knows that its memory management is no longer stable. You may need to exit Windows and reboot to fix this. If that isn't enough, you could have an incompatible device driver (perhaps created for a previous version of Windows), or Windows may be fighting with a memory manager, or a TSR may be incompatible (take them out from CONFIG.SYS and AUTOEXEC.BAT, and then add them back one at a time to see which work and which don't), or you may have a page-mapping conflict (try running in standard mode to see if that fixes the trouble, and if so, add EMMEXCLUDE=A000-EFFF to the [386Enh] section of SYSTEM.INI and then go back to enhanced mode).

Some users claim that Windows enhanced mode can sometimes work better if you disable the shadowing of ROM to RAM. Other users claim that Windows enhanced mode doesn't work on systems with more than 12MB of extended memory. QEMM could be involved because only after installing QEMM is that much system memory available.

Windows in enhanced mode, QEMM, and the Ontrack disk manager DMDRVR.BIN can have troubles. Which version of DMDRVR.BIN or which disk controller leads to the trouble isn't clear. A possible solution is to change the order of loading QEMM386.SYS and DMDRVR.BIN in CONFIG.SYS.

Windows 3.0 can work with TSRs that load before Windows. Sometimes these use expanded memory, such as for disk caches, network drivers, RAM disks, or pop-up programs that swap themselves to expanded memory. Not all are compatible with Windows 3.0. Microsoft has a list of EMS calls that aren't supported by Windows 3.0.

If you get paging errors from Windows, upgrade to QEMM 5.11 or later.

If you use an XGA card with Windows, you need a Windows SYSTEM.INI file that has DISPLAY=XGAVDD.386 instead of DISPLAY=*VDDVGA. (You can also use the *VDDVGA line if you add the EXCLUDE parameter to exclude the first 4K of the 32K region, on a 32K boundary, in which the XGA ROM is located in high memory.)

Windows can have trouble with bus-mastering devices—peripherals that handle their own DMA (direct memory access). This is discussed in Chapter 20. Most bus-mastering devices are SCSI hard disk controllers. They put things into memory and assume the addresses will remain permanently. Windows 3.0 doesn't work that way because it uses virtual mode (see Chapter 4). Windows SMARTDRV.SYS driver loaded low can help solve this problem (although you shouldn't use the /B- parameter). A better way to avoid trouble is to get a driver that meets the VDS (Virtual DMA Services) specification. When not running Windows 3.0 in enhanced mode, QEMM's own DISKBUF parameter can solve the problem. (It doesn't work in enhanced mode because that mode disables QEMM.)

If Windows runs more slowly in enhanced mode than you'd like, it could be that the hard disk is too full. That makes paging difficult. Using QEMM may make this more apparent. You need at least 2MB free on the drive designated for TEMP files. A fragmented hard disk can also slow processing. You may want to set up a permanent Windows swap file, as explained in the Windows manual.

If you're running QEMM and Windows in enhanced mode on a Compaq computer and have problems, try adding the NOCOMPAQFEATURES parameter. As explained in Chapter 6, this is the same as disabling the COMPAQEGAROM, COMPAQHALFROM (CHR), and COMPAQROMMEMORY parameters. CHR is probably the most important one to disable, while the other two may be enabled if you add the parameters this way:

```
NCF CER CRM
```

However, the help you get from disabling CHR may actually come from moving QEMM's page frame. Compaq systems with COMPAQHALFROM often have a page frame at E800-F7FF. Windows enhanced mode in its default settings doesn't like a page frame that overlaps F000-FFFF. If NCF CER CRM gets you by a Windows starting problem, then check the address of the page frame. If it is in that area, you can try removing NCR CER CRM and instead putting in FRAME= to put the page frame elsewhere. That way you won't lose the 32K that CHR can get.

Another COMPAQ-oriented parameter that affects Windows is NOTOPMEMORY, or NT. Some systems need this to run Windows in enhanced mode because Windows may not like an expanded memory page frame at 9000-9FFF or any location in conventional memory. QEMM puts a page frame into conventional memory only if it can't find a good place in high memory, so to get the page framc into high memory you may need to clear a space.

Windows running in enhanced mode can fail when it reaches to its permanent swap file (an area of disk used when RAM runs out). Oddly enough, this happens when there is too much conventional memory when Windows starts. That "too much" could be 592K or as little as 576K. If Windows is failing on you, you could check for this ironic cause by using the QEMM BUFFERS.COM program to load more buffers below 640K, and so to occupy some of that memory. Try

```
BUFFERS +32
```

to use 16K more conventional memory. (It might use more than that if the disk sectors on your system are larger than normal.)

If a range of memory needed for Windows graphical display is used, you'll get an error. Standard VGA for Windows needs A000-AFFF and B800-BFFF. Some graphic adapters use A000-C7FF. By default EMM386.EXE from DOS 5 doesn't use A000-BFFF. However, on many systems you can get some use of these areas. You may need to experiment. Use the EXCLUDE parameter of EMM386.EXE to shut out parts. On VGA for example you can often use B000-B7FF.

VCPI and DOS-Extended Programs With Windows

VCPI is the Virtual Control Program Interface specification. It lets protected-mode programs work alongside one another. Windows 3.0 in Enhanced-386 mode is such a DOS-extended program. Other DOS-extended programs that adhere to VCPI can only run with Windows in its real and standard modes.

DPMI (DOS Protected Mode Interface) is a newer specification aimed at the same uses, a multitasking version of VCPI.

You cannot run Windows under PC-MOS because it too is a DOS-extended program.

If you're getting a VCPI warning that you don't need to see, you can put the

```
VCPIWARNING=FALSE
```

statement into SYSTEM.INI to dodge that warning.

Troubleshooting QEMM With Windows

To fix a QEMM-created problem, disable QEMM. Put the word REM at the beginning of the QEMM386.SYS line in CONFIG.SYS. Then reboot. If the problem is still there, it isn't a QEMM problem. If the problem disappears, it could be a QEMM problem. You can figure out what exactly QEMM is doing to make the trouble by taking away its effects, one at a time. For example, first stop loading things high, or take one at a time out of high memory.

There are three ways to stop QEMM from loading:

1. Boot from a DOS floppy without QEMM386.SYS in CONFIG.SYS.
2. Take QEMM386.SYS line out of CONFIG.SYS. (Edit it out or put REM in front of it. REM in DOS 4 or 5 nullifies the line. In DOS 3 or before you'll get an "Invalid line" error message, but QEMM still won't load and the error won't hurt anything.)
3. Reboot the computer. After hearing the first beep, press Alt. You'll see the message

   ```
   QEMM; Press any key to continue. ESC to abort.
   ```

   Press ESC and QEMM won't load.

To see if QEMM is the problem, copy your CONFIG.SYS and AUTOEXEC.BAT to back them up, then make new ones with only the basic QEMM statements and other necessary statements. (Make sure all TSRs and drivers load low and don't use the FILES.COM and BUFFERS.COM statements. Just have the QEMM386.SYS line in CONFIG.SYS for QEMM.)

For CONFIG.SYS, make the QEMM386.SYS line look like this:

```
DEVICE=C:\QEMM\QEMM386.SYS X=A000-C7FF X=F000-FFFF NO NS NT
NCF NOSH
```

Keep any other EXCLUDE=, X=, AROM=, or ARAM= parameters. Don't have any INCLUDE= or I= parameters. Don't have the RAM parameter on that line, and don't have any STEALTH parameters. (With QEMM 6.00 or later, you have STEALTH to consider. You can see if it is being used by looking for the ST:M or ST:F parameters on the QEMM386.SYS line in CONFIG.SYS. If you're having trouble with Windows, try removing the STEALTH parameters to see if it is the STEALTH feature alone making the trouble. Remove all STEALTH parameters, including ST:M, ST:F, XST=, XSTI=, DBF=, FSTC, and FRAME=.) Have at least FILES=40. Keep most drivers, but throw out any disk caches.

For AUTOEXEC.BAT, you need only PATH and PROMPT statements. Remove any LOADHI commands to make sure TSRs load low.

With these new files, reboot.

If you still have trouble, then QEMM and Windows 3 just aren't getting along. Which one is it? You must modify CONFIG.SYS to use Microsoft drivers instead of QEMM. To do this, begin by making a backup of your CONFIG.SYS and AUTOEXEC.BAT. Then find HIMEM.SYS and EMM386.SYS. Take the QEMM386.SYS line out of CONFIG.SYS, and replace it with lines for these two drivers (using the full paths to find them). For example, replace

```
DEVICE=C:\QEMM\QEMM386.SYS
```

with

```
DEVICE=C:\HIMEM.SYS
DEVICE=C:\DOS\EMM386.SYS ON 4096
```

Reboot. If you're still having trouble, then Windows is the problem, not QEMM.

Now you need to make QEMM act as much like the Microsoft HIMEM.SYS and EMM386.SYS drivers as possible. Run Manifest, and look on its First Meg Overview screen to find Page Frame. Write its starting address down. Then quit Manifest, and make backups of the CONFIG.SYS and AUTOEXEC.BAT files. Add QEMM's FRAME= parameter with the starting address of that page frame, so QEMM will put it in the same place the Microsoft drivers are putting it. Also add NX NR NRH NOVDS. Reboot and see if the problem with Windows occurs.

If you don't have problems anymore, you're in a position to put the RAM parameter in for QEMM to see if you can get some use of high RAM. Edit CONFIG.SYS to add the RAM parameter to the QEMM386.SYS line. Reboot and see if the problem comes back. If you don't have the problem anymore, then you can try to recover some of the high memory you excluded with QEMM parameters. One at a time you should remove the X= parameters, reboot, and see if problems crop up again.

If you have the problem, there is a conflict between one of the adapters and QEMM. QEMM isn't finding the adapter and is putting its own mapped memory where the adapter wants to be. You can test this by first excluding all high memory and then restoring it one piece at a time. Back up your CONFIG.SYS and AUTOEXEC.BAT files, run Manifest, use its First Meg Overview screen to see what areas of high RAM are unused, write those addresses down, then add X= parameters to the QEMM386.SYS line in CONFIG.SYS to exclude those areas. (Also, if you have a SCSI or bus-mastering hard disk controller, add the line

```
DEVICE=C:\WINDOWS\SMARTDRV.SYS 256 256
```

to CONFIG.SYS.) Reboot. If the problem is gone, then there probably was an adapter conflict. This adapter most likely needs only 16K of memory excluded for its use. To narrow to this, look at what you just added to the EXCLUDE list. Try excluding only 16K of that at a time, each time backing up your CONFIG.SYS and AUTOEXEC.BAT, then rebooting and checking for the problem. When you know which area is the troublesome one, leave that EXCLUDE in.

If you were using STEALTH and want to add that back now (after getting high RAM and its exclusions set properly), you can now add the ST:M of ST:F parameter and any other STEALTH parameters that were there back to the CONFIG.SYS line. If adding this back makes trouble, you need to work thorough STEALTH troubleshooting.

QEMM 5.11 does not support Windows standard mode, but you can use the WIN300A.PAT patch to QEMM from the Quarterdeck bulletin board (see Chapter 21) to work around this incompatibility. (You're better off getting the latest version of QEMM, however.)

If you have trouble with QEMM 6.00 and Windows 3 when using an application that wants EMS or when loading a driver or TSR that uses EMS before entering Windows, you need to upgrade to QEMM 6.01 or later.

If QEMM works with Windows but the full CONFIG.SYS and AUTOEXEC.BAT files don't, you need to take away all excess lines from those files, check to see if QEMM and Windows work, then add the lines back one at a time until you find the offender. You may then need to eliminate some device or TSR, load it into low memory instead of high, have it use conventional memory instead of XMS or EMS, or call the maker of the driver or TSR for more advice.

You may find your best multitasking comes from running a Windows program in real mode, within a DESQview window, and relying on DESQview for moving from one program to another.

Every copy of Windows comes with the HIMEM.SYS XMS extended memory manager and the EMM386.SYS EMS Expanded Memory Manager. EMM386.SYS can also convert extended memory to expanded memory for Windows 3.0 in real mode or for DOS applications in standard or enhanced modes.

The Windows SETUP program automatically copies HIMEM.SYS into your Windows directory. Then it puts a line into CONFIG.SYS to load HIMEM.SYS when you start your PC.

SETUP also copies EMM386.SYS into your Windows directory, but it does not automatically put a line into CONFIG.SYS to load EMM386.SYS. You have to do that yourself if you want Windows or a DOS application to use expanded memory.

The typical reason to install EMM386.SYS is to run Windows 3.0 in real mode to run an old Windows application that was written for Windows 2 and that needs expanded memory.

EMM386.SYS is also useful to provide DOS applications running outside of Windows 3 with expanded memory.

HIMEM.SYS won't let you load TSRs and drivers into high memory.

EMM386.SYS can provide expanded memory for Windows 3 real mode and DOS applications from real mode. It cannot provide expanded memory for DOS applications in standard mode. QEMM can replace both, can put drivers and TSRs into upper memory, can remap system and video ROM for better performance, and can provide expanded memory for standard mode. (DOS 5 added the ability to load drivers into high memory.)

Word for Windows 1.00, 1.10, and 1.10A don't install with QEMM 5.11. During setup you may just return to the DOS prompt. This happens right after the ENABLER.EXE file is copied. Removing QEMM.SYS and installing HIMEM.SYS (from Windows 3 or from DOS 5) permits installation of Word for Windows. You can then return QEMM.SYS to its place, removing HIMEM.SYS.

If you install Windows 3.0 after you install QEMM, or you don't allow QEMM to update your Windows 3 configuration upon installation, you could have problems with Windows. To avoid problems you can use the QWINFIX utility that comes with QEMM. Use it at any time to modify the Windows initialization files. Run it while logged into the Windows directory simply by changing to that directory with a DOS command such as this:

```
CD WINDOWS
```

and then typing a command with a path that will reach to and start QWINFIX:

```
c:\QEMM\QWINFIX
```

Windows 3.1 is much stabler than Windows 3.0. With STEALTH active it can give you up to 613K for each DOS window running programs. The best you can do under DESQview in similar circumstances is 592K for the first window. The secret with Windows 3.1 is loading DOS into the HMA using ST:M, putting the page frame at C000 and using 640x480 Windows video drivers so you don't have to exclude B000-B7FF. With Windows 3.1 you don't need any EMMEXCLUDE= setting. Windows automatically stuffs a lot of itself in the 224K UMB area not used by the loaded TSRs.

Windows needs about 300K of conventional memory for itself, but more if you're going to run DOS applications under Windows. You can have 536K free without loading anything high, but you can get up to 615K free if you run Windows. After you load high as many TSRs and drivers as you can, the next best thing you can do for Windows is to add memory—extended memory. The bare minimum is 2MB for the Enhanced-386 mode. Try for 4MB or more and you'll have much better performance. You could add even more and use part as a disk cache or RAM disk, too.

Windows on a PC with less than 384K of extended memory automatically run in real mode. On a 286 or 386 with at least 384K of extended memory, standard mode is the default. On a 386 with 1MB or more extended memory (2MB total memory), Enhanced-386 mode is the natural setting.

Standard and Enhanced-386 modes don't use expanded memory.

Add the Windows subdirectory to the PATH command. Put the

```
WIN
```

command at the end of the AUTOEXEC.BAT file if you want Windows to start automatically when you run your PC.

If you have an EGA graphics card and monitor, be sure the driver

```
DEVICE=C:\DOS\EGA.SYS
```

is in the CONFIG.SYS file. You could make this

```
DEVICEHIGH=C:\DOS\EGA.SYS
```

if you have DOS 5 and have created UMBs.

In Windows Program Manager, choose the Help menu, and from that choose About Program Manager. You'll see a box telling you what mode Windows is running in. If that's the mode you want, you're in good shape. If not, leave Windows and edit your CONFIG.SYS and AUTOEXEC.BAT files to change the amount of memory available. You might have to load more drivers and TSRs high, eliminate some of them, or reduce the size of disk caches and RAM disks. (You may have to buy and install more memory as well.)

Remember that virtual memory is actually hard disk memory posing as chip memory, and that may distort the amount of total memory reported in your PC under Windows.

DOS 5 installation puts a file called WINA20.386 in the root directory of your hard disk. This file is only for 386 and 486 systems. If you have an 8088, 8086, or 80286 you can delete the file to save a little disk space. WINA20.386 resolves conflicts when DOS 5 and Windows in Enhanced-386 mode both try to use the HMA—which is controlled by the A20 address line.

Set the Windows Temp file to

```
SET TEMP=D:\
```

if the RAM disk is D. DOS 5 also uses the TEMP environment variable to know where to store its temporary files. Using a RAM disk for the TEMP file speeds both Windows and DOS. With a large enough RAM disk you can put Windows program files into the speedy state—3MB should be enough for the core of Windows. Some Windows applications can take up 10 to 12MB of disk space.

Use a batch file with commands like these, where D: is the RAM disk:

```
MD D:\SYSTEM
XCOPY C:\WINDOWS\SYSTEM\ *.* D:\SYSTEM>NUL
COPY C:\WINDOWS\WIN.COM D:\ >NUL
XCOPY C:\WINDOWS\*.GRP D:\ >NUL
XCOPY C:\WINDOWS\*.INI D:\ > NUL
COPY C:\WINDOWS\PROGMAN.EXE D:\ >NUL
PATH D:\;C:\WINDOWS;C:\DOS
```

(The NUL redirection with the > sign saves you from having to read messages from the XCOPY and COPY commands.)

Manifest Under Windows 3.0

Manifest can run in Windows 3.0 as a standard DOS application. This requires a PIF file. Change the Windows default PIF by setting

```
Memory Requirements: KB Required
```

to 200, and select COM1 and COM2 so you can see what happens with the ports.

QEMM-386 disables itself when Windows 3 is running in Enhanced-386 mode.

If you load QEMM, run Windows 3 in Enhanced-386 mode, and then run Manifest within Windows, Manifest won't show its QEMM-386 information because QEMM will be disabled. In real or standard mode you can see the QEMM-386 information.

General Tips On Windows Applications and Windows Performance

To get the best performance from Windows 3.0, you need to manage memory efficiently. Although Windows has lots of memory-management abilities built in, you set the stage for these with the configuration parameters of the DOS CONFIG.SYS file. This file contains instructions to the PC about memory and file management, instructions that are implemented when the PC is first turned on.

What CONFIG.SYS should have depends on your PC: 8088 and 8086 machines are different from 286 machines (AT class), which are different from 386 and 486 machines. Here's what CONFIG.SYS should have:

- For 286 or 386/486: HIMEM.SYS, a memory manager for extended memory.

- For 8088/8086, 286, or 386/486: QEMM.SYS, the Quarterdeck memory manager for expanded memory. The original Expanded Memory Manager from Microsoft is called EMM.SYS or, on some Compaq systems, CEMM.SYS. (Note: Windows likes extended memory more than expanded memory, so use your expanded memory board's parameters to configure it as extended memory if possible.)

- For 8088/8086, 286, or 386/486: SMARTDrive, a disk-cache utility free with Windows.

- For 8088/8086, 286, or 386/486: FILES, a DOS parameter to set the maximum number of files that can be open at once, that the system can work with. This includes document and program files. The optimum setting for most systems is FILES=30. More than that uses extra memory and yet doesn't increase performance. Some programs, however, such as database and accounting packages, want a higher setting.

- For 8088/8086, 286, or 386/486: BUFFERS, a DOS parameter to set aside small pieces of memory for caching recently used information from disk, to increase the efficiency of reading information from disk. BUFFERS=20 is a good setting for many systems. Any higher can increase performance slightly but costs more used memory. If you use the SMARTDrive disk cache, there is less need for BUFFERS, so set BUFFERS=10.

- For 386/486: EMM386.SYS, an expanded memory emulator that converts extended memory into expanded memory for applications that need expanded. Such programs typically run without Windows (as DOS programs under Windows) or from Windows real mode only. A 286 does not use this because it uses memory on an expanded memory board. Such memory should be configured to use as much expanded memory as applications need. The rest can be converted to extended memory.

The performance of such Windows programs as Ami Pro comes from the performance of Windows. Windows 286 and Run-time can only use available conventional memory and 64K or less of extended memory for program operation. Windows 3.x gives better performance, especially in standard or enhanced modes. There it can use extended memory for program operation. You should also get a fast processor, plenty of RAM (2MB at least for one program, 4MB or more for running more programs at once), and a fast hard disk for good Windows performance. A fast video adapter helps too. A 16-bit card with an accelerator is probably best. A hard disk should have at least a 28-millisecond access time, and a 16-bit disk controller is a good idea as well. IDE, ESDI, and SCSI controllers are generally faster than MFM controllers.

If you use DOS 5, replace the EMM386.SYS driver that comes with Windows 3.0 with the EMM386.EXE driver that comes with DOS 5, but use the one that comes with Windows 3.1 or later.

For best Windows performance, keep FILES= and BUFFERS= in CONFIG.SYS to reasonable values, such as FILES=60 and BUFFERS=10 (if you're using a disk cache such as SMARTDRV) or BUFFERS=20 (with no disk cache). If you have more than 8MB of memory, set up a RAM drive of 2 to 4MB where the TEMP files can be kept.

Keep more conventional memory available by loading drivers high. QEMM and QRAM can do this. DOS can too, although not as easily or well. Getting 600K or more free is good for running DOS applications under Windows.

If you run regular DOS applications in full-screen display instead of in sizable windows, you'll use less memory.

If you have DOS applications running the background, they use memory. If possible, don't select the PIF file setting Background.

If your Windows program won't run because there isn't enough memory, you may have eaten up some of that memory by running Windows twice. That is, when you tried to exit Windows you double-clicked on the DOS Prompt icon. Then when starting again you typed WIN instead of EXIT. To see if you did this, exit Windows by selecting Exit Windows from the File menu. At the DOS prompt type EXIT. If the Program Manager shows itself again, you were running a second session of Windows.

If HIMEM.SYS is not loading or installed correctly, you may not have enough memory available for Windows programs. Or you may have to close some other applications that are running.

Be sure to use the most recent version of EMM386.EXE.

For Windows, specify a value of 30 or less for FILES and 20 or less for BUFFERS. If you use SMARTDRV, use only 10 BUFFERS. Set LASTDRIV only for the drives you have, including RAM disks and network drives. Then set the STACKS=0,0 command. (The default is 9128 on a 286 and 386.) Each uses a lot of memory. If Windows locks, try removing the STACKS command altogether. Remove all INSTALL commands except for SHARE.EXE if you're using a network. That's a DOS 4 way of loading memory-resident programs, and you should be loading these high with DOS 5's LOADHIGH command or QEMM's LOADHI in AUTOEXEC.BAT.

Don't load unnecessary memory-resident programs with Windows. Each one you load subtracts memory from all Windows programs. Instead try running each in its own window, as a non-memory-resident program, if you can.

WordPerfect For Windows

When troubleshooting for Word Perfect for Windows version 5.1 (all release dates up to January 1992), you should know whether troubles occur in Windows Enhanced-386 mode or standard mode. You'll also need to know how much memory is available (Manifest can help with this) and the full contents of the AUTOEXEC.BAT and CONFIG.SYS files.

One of the ways to figure out what is wrong is to run "vanilla in regards to Windows." This means having only buffers, files, and memory manager (QEMM) statements in CONFIG.SYS. It can also help to try running in Windows standard mode, by starting Windows with the command WIN /S. Even more vanilla is only having FILES=30 and HIMEM.SYS in CONFIG.SYS, not using memory managers at all.

Sometimes it helps to remove TSRs and then add them back one at a time. This is especially true of TSRs such as Windows Environment overlays such as Norton's Desktop for Windows and HP's NewWave.

If there are extended memory conflicts, look for conflicts between network addresses, an EMS page frame, display memory, and the HMA area.

You can see how much memory is available by looking in ABOUT in the Program Manager of Windows. Here you can check on free memory and free system resources.

Listing all .INI files can help too, as well as getting a complete list of system TSRs.

To check expanded memory problems, you can try some of the startup parameters. Try starting with the /32 parameter. If this solves the problem, then keep using it as a permanent fix. If it does not, try the /NE parameter. If this works, then you should contact your Expanded Memory Manager maker because there is something wrong with the management of expanded memory.

If you start Windows in standard mode, using QEMM 5.11 as the extended memory manager in the CONFIG.SYS file, and then open WordPerfect for Windows and try to use the speller, you could see the error message

```
Not Enough Memory To Load WPCSPEL.DLL
```

This means you can't check spelling. To fix the problem, add the parameters

```
NS NO NT
```

to the QEMM statement in CONFIG.SYS.

If you're using QEMM 5.12 with and a SCSI controller card driver (for a hard drive controller), you could get a UAE when leaving WordPerfect for Windows 5.1. This can be solved with an update to the driver, such as Adaptec, the ASPI4DOS.SYS version 3.0 driver. The problem may also exist with QEMM 6.0. The new driver works with software that uses virtual memory, such as Windows 3.0 and QEMM 6.0.

There have been cases of slow printing and slow starting of WordPerfect 5.1 for Windows. This can come from slow hard disks, slow CPUs, or even slow graphics cards (when the sloth involves rewrites of the screen). But it can also come from lack of memory, because a utility was using all or most of extended memory even when it was not supposed to. You may need to set parameters for installing utilities to make sure they don't use all the extended memory. SuperPCK is one of these.

One way to test if this is a problem is to use the DOS MEM command. This tells how much conventional, expanded, and extended memory are available. More extended memory means faster Windows applications. However, QEMM and other memory managers treat any extended memory as extended or expanded. If you see a MEM listing that shows only expanded memory, QEMM or some other memory manager may be converting all memory at that moment to expanded memory. However, it will be converted back to extended as needed.

The error message

```
System Error: Cannot Read From Drive A
```

can come from a driver in high memory that conflicts with the BIOS. One example is the PCNFS.SYS driver that connects a PC to a Sun Microsystems network. This error can appear after sending a print job to a network printer. However, when you remove the driver from high memory, such as with QEMM, the error evaporates. Sometimes the same error can be fixed with a new graphics driver for Windows, one that won't conflict with the network driver.

The error

```
WPCSHAR1.DLL Not Found
```

can occur if you don't load QEMM first in CONFIG.SYS.

You could have a font display problem, such as in New Century Schoolbook 12pt not being able to see the capital Hs and the number 9s on screen. They will show when you use Reveal Codes and Print Preview. The way to cure this, to always see the Hs and 9s, is to add

```
EMMEXCLUDE=E000-FFFF
```

to the SYSTEM.INI file under the [386Enh] section.

You could get an error for accessing illegal memory or the computer could just freeze if you use QEMM 6.0 with WordPerfect for Windows. You can avoid this trouble by using this QEMM line in CONFIG.SYS

```
DEVICE=QEMM386.SYS RAM X=A000-C7FF NRH
```

This stops any use of the RAM statement so there is only about 32K for loading high. You can also try

```
DEVICE=QEMM386.SYS NRH
```

If you get a UAE when trying to enter WordPerfect for Windows 5.1, you could try specifying a minimum number of bytes for QEMM to use as expanded memory, and then run Windows in Enhanced-386 mode and then in standard mode.

The error

```
Shared Error Code Unable To Execute WPCDLL.EXE. Probable
Cause Insufficient Memory
```

can occur when running WordPerfect for Windows 5.1 with QEMM instead of HIMEM.SYS. Even booting after this with QEMM removed in favor of HIMEM.SYS causes the error

```
Cannot Find WPCSHAR1.DLL
```

To fix it, create an AUTOEXEC.BAT file with

```
C:\WPWIN
```
and
```
C:\WPC
```

in the path.

Another way to fix the

```
Shared Error Code
```

error is to remove applications from memory of to increase the FILES and BUFFERS in the CONFIG.SYS file.

UAEs can occur when entering WordPerfect for Windows if QEMM.SYS is used instead of HIMEM.SYS. If switching back to HIMEM.SYS fixes the trouble, you can check

- EXCLUDE statements
- LOADHI commands
- Conflicts with other device drivers
- How other QEMM was configured

You should use SMARTDRV.SYS when running WordPerfect for Windows and QEMM, or WordPerfect for Windows will run very slowly.

If there are problems, try running in standard mode rather than in Enhanced-386 mode. That is, start Windows with

```
WIN/S
```

If there are problems, try replacing QEMM with HIMEM.SYS as the memory manager. Also try running "vanilla" Windows, with only the following in CONFIG.SYS:

```
DEVICE=HIMEM.SYS
BUFFERS=something
FILES=something
```

If you need to call for technical support, have ready a list of all TSRs and programs running, of the memory manager and its version, and listings of the following files:

```
AUTOEXEC.BAT
CONFIG.SYS
WIN.INI
SYSTEM.INI
WPWP.INI
WPC.INI
```

If there's a problem in the Speller, File Manager, or Thesaurus, have listings of the .INI files for those too.

If you use the VSHIELD.EXE virus-checking program, you could have the problem of documents printing with garbage or ASCII characters that are out of place. Ways to fix this include the following:

- Add the /WINDOWS parameter to the VSHIELD command in AUTOEXEC.BAT.
- Remove VSHIELD.
- Remove the /NB parameter from the command line that loads VSHIELD.
- Remove XMSNETX or EMSNETX and use instead NET3/4/5 or NETX3.22 drivers.
- If you're on a Novell network, update to the latest IPX (version 3.04 or later).
- If NETBIOS is being loaded, remove it.
- Remove other TSRs.
- If you are using SuperPCKwik, remove it.
- Print to LPT1.0S2 or LPT1.DOS (for Windows 3.1). (Go into File|Select Printer|Setup|Port|File. Change the filename to LPT1.OS2. Change the port in Windows by going into Control Panel|Configure|Port and select LPT1.OS2 or LPT1.DOS (for Windows 3.1). This disables Windows special handling of output info to printer.)
- In the SYSTEM.INI file, exclude an address area from A000 to just above the highest addressed area being used by a program loaded in upper memory. With QEMM, check to see what is loaded into upper memory with the LOADHI utility.
- Remove any TSRs that speed up keyboard repeat rate.

If you get the error

```
Cannot Find WPCSHAR1.DLL
```

check the order of entries in CONFIG.SYS. QEMM or HIMEM should be on the first line, before anything else.

If sometimes what you type is not what appears on screen (for example, typing aaa shows as "ppp") take 386SMX out of CONFIG.SYS and use QEMM for memory management.

The error

```
General Failure Reading Drive C:
```

in enhanced mode while using Stacker and a SCSI hard drive can be fixed by excluding the SCSI BIOS and the driver memory areas in QEMM and the [386Enh] section of the SYSTEM.INI file. When troubleshooting a system running Stacker, troubleshoot as if Stacker isn't there, but remember that Stacker uses device drivers in CONFIG.SYS that must remain there.

Being exited to a D> prompt when using WordPerfect for Windows and QEMM can be solved by removing the DOS=HIGH command from CONFIG.SYS.

Lotus 1-2-3 3.1 Under Windows 3.0 or 3.1

When using Lotus 1-2-3 version 3.1 under Windows 3.x, you need enough RAM and disk space (referred to as application swap file space). (WYSIWYG is a 1-2-3 add-on program.)

In real and standard modes both 1-2-3 3.1 and Windows create swap files if needed. (Windows even creates swap files to run non-Windows programs.) Under enhanced mode, Windows creates a 386 swap file, but 1-2-3 uses Windows virtual memory and does not make its own swap file. (Exact swap file sizes depend on such factors as which video driver the PC is using, and on any drivers or TSRs loaded before Windows.)

	Real	Standard	Enhanced-386
Available RAM	1MB	1.5	2.0
Swap file space	1.625	1.625	2.25

You can use the Windows Help menu and its About Program Manager choice to see how much free memory is available. You need 3.4MB to start 1-2-3 3.1. To run 3.1 under Windows 3.x in Enhanced-386 mode on a 2MB PC, you may need to make a permanent Windows swap file of at least 2.5MB so there is enough disk space for Windows to use virtual memory. The Windows manual explains how to make a permanent swap file.

The swap file amounts don't include necessary disk space for temporary files made by Windows and Windows applications. A minimum of 2MB will meet most programs needs there.

In real and standard modes, 1-2-3 3.1 manages memory the same as under DOS. Its VMM virtual memory manager manages conventional, extended, and virtual memory. DOS environment variables let you control memory use. Any expanded memory is used for storing data. Expanded memory is not swapped to disk and can't be used by other applications running under Windows.

In real mode, though, Windows can't control how 1-2-3 3.1 uses extended memory. Any XMS settings in the 123.PIF are ignored. In standard mode the XMS settings limit the amount of extended memory available to 1-2-3 3.1.

Task switching (sometimes called task parametering) from 1-2-3 3.1 to another program under Windows differs from real to standard modes. In real mode when you leave 1-2-3, Windows writes conventional and video memory out to a swap file and suspends 1-2-3 operation. Any extended memory used by 1-2-3 is not available to other applications under Windows. In standard mode, when you leave 1-2-3, Windows writes the conventional, extended, and video memory used by it out to an application swap file and suspends 1-2-3 3.1 operation. The swapped-out memory, including extended memory, is available to other applications running under Windows.

If you see the error message "Cannot initialize resident segments" when you try to load 1-2-3 3.1 on a Windows 3.x system in Enhanced-386 mode, then some of the extended memory may be in use. 1-2-3 needs all 2MB of extended memory. To create a permanent swap file to help this solution, start by defragmenting the hard disk, which may make more space for the swap file. Then move TSRs and drivers out of memory, start Windows 3.x in real mode with WIN /R, close any applications including the File Manager so that only the Program Manager is running, and choose File menu and then Run. Type SWAPFILE, and choose OK. The Swapfile program looks for a contiguous space for the swap file. When it finds at least 2048K or more, it shows a dialog box with information on the size available. Use at least 2.5MB. Choose Create. Exit Windows and restart in enhanced mode by typing WIN.

If 1-2-3 won't load under Windows, remove drivers from CONFIG.SYS and TSRs from AUTOEXEC.BAT. One of these might be the SMARTDRV disk cache, which is not necessary for Windows (although it does make Windows faster). Remove SMARTDRV.SYS from CONFIG.SYS.

CGA for Windows display driver must be the primary display driver for 1-2-3 to run in a sizable window in Enhanced-386 mode. The PIF file to load 1-2-3 in a window should list the name of the 123DCF file that has CGA for Windows as the primary display driver followed by -M in Parameters. A PIF file set for Windowed Display Usage without the necessary reference in Parameters produces an error message.

CHAPTER EIGHTEEN

QEMM with Applications and Utilities

QEMM can greatly improve the way you run your application and utility programs and let you run more of them. This chapter gives you special tips you can use to manage memory and configure QEMM for smooth, optimum operation of many popular programs.

If you see the error message "Packed File is Corrupt," you probably ran a program in the first 64K of conventional memory that had been compressed with a utility such as EXEPACK. This is used by software developers to reduce the disk space of programs. Try using up more lower memory, such as by running a second copy of COMMAND.COM. (Type COMMAND /X where X is the program having trouble executing.)

WordPerfect 5.1

WordPerfect is the most popular word processor today. Version 5.1 needs a PC-compatible with at least 384K of RAM to run, but it runs better with at least 512K or even 640K of RAM. In fact, the more RAM available to WordPerfect the faster it can work. After all, WordPerfect keeps as much of a document in memory as it can, because things in memory move much faster than things that must be requested from, brought in, then pushed back out to disk. Any part of a document that doesn't fit in memory is kept on disk in a temporary or virtual file. The more memory, the smaller the virtual file, and the faster the processing.

To get more memory you can, of course, just add memory to the system. If you often receive the error message

```
Not enough memory
```

you can try these things:

1. Remove any TSR programs, including Shell (via a WordPerfect parameter).
2. Use a DOS extender or memory manager such as QRAM or QEMM to make more available conventional memory.
3. Reduce FILES= and BUFFERS= commands in CONFIG.SYS, but don't reduce FILES to less than 20.

WordPerfect can use LIM EMS 4.0 expanded memory (which can add up to 32MB to a PC). WordPerfect uses expanded memory in several ways. First it stores more of the active document in memory. Second it stores as much of the program as possible in memory, because it can also run faster when it doesn't have to swap parts in from disk. To use expanded memory with WordPerfect, however, you need a memory manager program such as QEMM or QRAM.

WordPerfect 5.1 adheres to the LIM 4.0 specifications more tightly than do some other programs. The unfortunate result of this is that some older EMS drivers don't work with it. These are the drivers you might find bundled with the expanded memory card, especially an older memory card, that does not meet full LIM 4.0 specifications. If you try to use WordPerfect 5.1 with expanded memory and such a driver, WordPerfect hangs when loading (that is, it freezes the computer and so not only cannot function but also prevents the computer from functioning until you reboot the system).

With the WordPerfect version 5.1 dated 11/06/89 or later, you can eliminate this problem by loading WordPerfect using the /NE startup parameter. That makes WordPerfect ignore expanded memory. This isn't the best solution, of course, because it means WordPerfect cannot benefit from the existence of expanded memory. But at least it lets you keep that expanded memory in the system for the use of other programs that don't have such driver troubles. Another solution is to get a new driver (look to memory-board companies).

WordPerfect often upgrades its software without changing the version number. This is called "slipstreaming". In other words, not all versions 5.1 are the same. When minor changes are made, the version number is kept but a date is added to it.

To start WordPerfect (to load it, that is), from the DOS prompt you type

```
WP /NE
```

with a space between the "WP" letters and the "/NE" characters. Then press Enter (or Return, whatever the key is called on your system).

If you have WordPerfect 5.1 dated 1/19/90 or later, you may use the /32 startup parameter to make WordPerfect use the older LIM 3.2 specification. This permits WordPerfect to work with older driver software, although you lose the advantages of LIM 4.0 (larger expanded memory and the ability to run programs from expanded memory, not just store data in it). To do this, start WordPerfect by typing

```
WP /32
```

then pressing Enter.

Another way around EMS troubles with WordPerfect is to use QEMM.

WordPerfect can also use extended memory that has been converted into expanded memory. On 286 systems this can mean 15MB more memory; on 386 and 486 systems up to 32MB more memory. Again, you need a memory manager such as QEMM to convert extended memory to expanded.

The WordPerfect Office shell can also use expanded memory. It uses this to swap programs.

WordPerfect 5.1 and QEMM 4.23 don't work well together—they can freeze a PC if the FRAME= parameter is on the QEMM.SYS line. The solution is to get a newer version of QEMM.

When using WordPerfect 5.1's View Document command in DESQview 386 2.22 and QEMM 5.0, you may need to change the memory for the window. Use the Set Memory Size command in DESQview to select 380K in the Change a Program screen of DESQview.

WordPerfect's /W parameter lets it use all the expanded memory available. Using just the /R parameter may give you the "Not Enough Expanded Memory" error message. Then you need to use /W as well. Using just /R means you need at least 708K—640K won't be enough to hold the entire .FIL file. (Remember that you cannot use all of expanded memory because some percentage will be used by the EMM.)

WordPerfect doesn't use extended memory directly. Its abilities to use memory beyond conventional were developed before extended memory standards existed.

Using the WP Library shell with the /32 parameter uses all of conventional memory and all but 32K of expanded memory.

You need at least two logical pages (32K) of expanded memory for WordPerfect 5.0 or 5.1 to use LIM 3.2 expanded memory. One is a dummy page to prevent data aliasing. For LIM 4.0, only one logical page is necessary, but having at least 64K is better for virtual files.

You can figure the minimum amount of expanded memory you need to use WordPerfect 5.1 with the /32 or /R parameter together with this equation:

```
(((SIZE OF WP.FIL + (16K-1)) / 16K) * 16K) +16K
```

where 16K = 16384. With the WP.FIL at 596,622 bytes (the 3/30/90 release), this works out to

```
(37.41 * 16K) + 16K
```

and rounding to a whole number of pages,

```
(37 * 16K) + 16K = 622592 = 608K
```

That much expanded memory can store the WP.FIL file and leave one page free for virtual files. Since running from the shell means WordPerfect can use only 88% of the available expanded memory (the shell uses 12%), you need 691K to get the 608K. Expanded memory only comes in 16K chunks, so you need the next higher multiple of 16K, or 704K.

If you get a message about not having enough expanded memory, use the equation.

Some boards, such as the AOX MicroMaster Board, have a cache that must be disabled to work with WordPerfect, DESQview 2.26, and QEMM 4.23.

If WordPerfect freezes when you try to save, retrieve, or list files or adjust setup parameters, and removing QEMM resolves the problem, it could be QEMM's parameters that are making the trouble, not QEMM itself. Try QEMM without parameters (see Chapter 6), and then try adding the NOXBDA parameter.

Get QEMM 4.23 or later for compatibility with WordPerfect.

Use BUFFERS if you don't have a disk cache, and especially if you don't have expanded memory. The best setting for BUFFERS depends on how much memory you have and how large the documents are; 25 to 35 should work in most systems.

With WordPerfect 5.10 and QEMM 5.12, your PC could freeze when you go to View Document, which uses the EGA graphics modes. If you have a TSR loaded high into the EGA video ROM area, the memory conflict causes problems. Be sure to exclude that area with an X=E000-EFFF parameter on the QEMM386.SYS line in CONFIG.SYS. The full parameters might be RAM X=E000-E7FF NOSH.

Using WordPerfect 5.10 and Norton Cache Version 6.0 together can cause problems. When you save a file to a full disk, get a "Disk Full" error, and then scroll to page 2 of the WordPerfect document, you may see garbage characters and the computer may freeze. With QEMM resident as well, the computer doesn't freeze, but you can get the Exception 13 error. The I/O cached by the Norton utility was damaged and then written to disk. To avoid this problem, set the Norton Cache parameter to NCACHE WRITE=0.

Other caches can have similar troubles. Consider using the DBF parameter, as explained in Chapter 6.

When using WordPerfect 5.10 release 06/29/90 with QEMM 6.0 and the Super PCKwik print spooler, use the Super PCKwik /J parameter. Otherwise the system may lock when you try to print a document.

As WordPerfect's SPELL.EXE has evolved, it has changed its method of interpreting information. Newer versions of WordPerfect running with QEMM 5.13 can freeze or have other trouble when working on a supplementary dictionary created with a WordPerfect 5.1 version prior to 4/27/91. You may see the error message "Exception Error 13." The fix is to disable QEMM, expand the supplementary dictionary, save it as a DOS text file, retrieve it into WordPerfect, and save it again. Then you should be able to run and expand the dictionary with QEMM resident.

WordPerfect, QEMM 6.0, and DOS 5.0 loaded into high memory can have trouble when used with a TSR such as PCQUOTE. WordPerfect won't start. The solution is to remove DOS from high memory.

These parts of WordPerfect can use expanded memory: file caching, generate, hyphenate, overflow (virtual) files, printing graphics, spell, and view document.

If you get the error message "Packed File Corrupt," check to see if you're using STEALTH with QEMM. Ironically, by opening more conventional memory, STEALTH makes it possible to use the first 64K segment of conventional memory for WordPerfect. That can cause problems because of a bug in the EXEPACK program that compresses WordPerfect during linking. One solution is to get Microsoft's LOADFIX.EXE program to run WordPerfect. Another solution is to use a newer version of WordPerfect that comes with a bug-free newer version of EXEPACK. (EXEPACK is a Microsoft program, not a WordPerfect program, so WordPerfect will charge you for this update.)

If you don't have enough file handles when running WordPerfect, you'll see an error message such as "Insufficient File Handles, Increase Number Of Files In CONFIG.SYS." You may not be using the QEMM FILES command properly. Remember that when loading files high using LOADHI and FILES.COM, you don't need an equal sign, as you would with the DOS FILES statement in CONFIG.SYS. A command such as

```
LOADHI /R:1 FILES +50
```

increases the number of files by 50.

If your PC locks while using WordPerfect and QEMM 6.0, try using the /NK parameter when starting WordPerfect. If that helps, it may mean that the QEMM line in CONFIG.SYS had the ST:X parameter, the STEALTH command to map the ROM BIOS address with RAM. Try removing the ST:X parameter to fix this problem.

WordPerfect works in a DESQview window, but you could have trouble when switching from its window to another window using a communications program such as IRMA. This can apparently stem from a RAM parameter on the QEMM386.SYS line. Try removing the RAM parameter and using the /NC and /NK parameters for WordPerfect.

If you have trouble with network operations, such as printing over a certain file size, receiving a "Network Device Fault Error, Not Ready Drive X: Retry, Cancel" message when you try to merge a file from the network with a local file, or getting a blank directory listing for a network drive, the reason may be a network card memory conflict . Check the QEMM386.SYS line in CONFIG.SYS to see if the network card's memory buffer is excluded. If not, QEMM may be putting its page frame in the same place the network card is putting its buffer. A parameter such as X=D000-D3FF does the trick for many network cards. You can test for this first by starting WordPerfect 5.1 with the /NE option. That tells it not to use expanded memory. If all works fine without expanded memory, then you could have a page frame conflict.

Expanded memory tips and traps

The /R parameter puts all of WP.FIL into expanded memory. This is great if you're running a network copy of WordPerfect from a network drive. But if you're running WordPerfect from your own hard disk, then using /R leaves little memory for caching document virtual files, thus slowing editing. /R needs the size of WP.FIL plus 80K.

/WS on releases after 6/20/90 tells WordPerfect to pause before dropping into editing and shows the amount of available conventional and expanded memory.

The minimum setting for conventional memory is 53. With the WP /W=120,512 setting, WordPerfect starts using 120K of conventional memory (after the 384K default) and 512K of expanded memory. WP /W=65 starts WordPerfect using only 65K more than the 384K default memory.

For more speed add expanded memory to your PC and then use the /R parameter with WordPerfect to load WP.FIL into expanded memory.

Opening a third editing screen eats up 8 to 14K more conventional memory.

You can save memory by decreasing the number of fonts selected in your .PRS file. Each font listed uses 73 bytes. Unmark the fonts you rarely use, then divide those fonts you use into smaller related groups.

If you don't need to use expanded memory, you can free about 4K of conventional memory by restarting WordPerfect with the /NE parameter.

When running under the Library or WordPerfect Office shell, WordPerfect uses all available conventional memory and half of the available expanded memory. Without the shell it uses all available conventional memory and 88% of available expanded memory. The /W=*,* parameter makes all expanded memory available to WordPerfect. (Running the Shell takes up 47 to 50K of conventional memory.) WordPerfect5.0 and 5.1 need at least 384K of conventional memory.

WordPerfect 5.0 can only access up to 1.5MB of expanded memory.

Extended memory tips and traps

Using HIMEM.SYS with any other memory manager will cause WordPerfect to hang.

For more speed create a RAM disk and then redirect the WordPerfect temporary files to it. Use the WordPerfect starting parameter WP /D-ramdriveletter

The /D=ramdriveletter parameter directs writing and reading of temporary program files, including virtual files, to a drive other than the shared drive that contains WP.EXE. Use this for RAM disk work.

Word

Word is a popular word processing program from Microsoft that uses expanded memory. Unfortunately, if you install QEMM 5.11 or earlier, run Windows 3.0, and then leave Windows, any program you then start that uses expanded memory reboots the PC.

You can solve this problem in one of three ways:

- Get a more recent version of QEMM, such as 5.12 or later.
- Start Word with the /X parameter, which disables Word's use of expanded memory.
- Use a different memory manager than QEMM, such as the HIMEM.SYS that comes with Windows.

Works

Microsoft Works combines spreadsheet, word processing, database management, and telecommunications modules in a single, inexpensive package.

Using QEMM 5.11 or earlier makes any program that uses expanded memory reboot the system after exiting Windows 3.0. If you run Works 2.0 immediately after exiting Windows, your PC reboots.

The solutions are:

- Get the latest version of QEMM (5.12 or later).
- Use the HIMEM.SYS extended memory manager that comes with Windows instead of using QEMM.

dBASE

dBASE IV 1.0 needs 516K of conventional memory. It does not support expanded memory directly, but you can use extra memory, including expanded memory, to help dBASE by turning it into a RAM disk. Then you copy the just over 2MB of dBASE system files to the RAM disk and execute dBASE from the RAM disk. You need 2.5MB of expanded memory to make a RAM disk large enough. You can do the same thing with RUNTIME files, although you need only about 1MB of expanded memory configured as a RAM disk.

dBASE IV 1.1 supports expanded memory to cache its own overlay and program files. It still uses some conventional memory.

To set up a RAM disk, you need a driver program such as RAMDISK.SYS or VDISK.SYS (these come with DOS). Then you put a line for the driver into CONFIG.SYS, such as

```
DEVICE=C:\DOS\VDISK.SYS /E 2500 512 128
```

Put this before the QEMM.SYS line if you want that memory reserved for a RAM disk before QEMM gets its hands on the memory. Then you copy the dBASE system to the RAM disk. It's best to set up a batch file that would do this and would later automatically copy all files back to your hard disk. (You want to protect against losing data that will vanish from the RAM disk when the computer is turned off.)

Use a line in AUTOEXEC.BAT such as SET TMP=C:\TMPFILES\ to tell dBASE to create its TMP files on your hard disk, or it may have trouble when it tries to put them on the nearly full RAM disk.

Paradox

Paradox is a relational database manager. If you get the error message "Insufficient Memory" when you try to load Paradox, you need to know that Paradox theoretically can run on a 1MB system but really needs 1.5MB as a practical minimum. Using the DOS CHKDSK or MEM commands, you can see how much memory is available. If less than 470K is available when you try to load Paradox, you can make more by unloading TSRs or by using QEMM (or DOS 5's LOADHIGH and DEVICEHIGH) to load some programs and drivers into upper memory.

If Paradox problems crop up just after installing QEMM 6, then try adding the parameter XST:F000 to the QEMM line in CONFIG.SYS. STEALTH might be the cause of the problems, and that parameter can sometimes fix them.

DESQview or DESQview-386 with Paradox can create problems. For example, when running Paradox 3.5 on an XT or AT, the DESQview overhead can be 135K. (ATs with an HMA and HIMEM.SYS or QEXT.SYS can push that DESQview overhead down to 75 or 80K.) There may not be enough room left for Paradox. To have as much memory as possible, follow this setup procedure:

1. Install Paradox by the manual.
2. Choose Open Window from DESQview's main menu.
3. When upgrading from Paradox 3.0 to 3.5, choose Paradox 3 from the file list, and then choose Change a Program. If installing Paradox for the first time, use Add a Program and select Paradox 3 from the menu to add that to the list. You'll be asked what directory holds Paradox 3.5. Type that in and press Enter. Choose Open Window and Change a Program. Enter the two-key code for Paradox 3.
4. In the Standard Parameters screen, type the program name and any batch file name you use to start Paradox, along with any options. Include the REAL parameter, because Paradox must run in real mode on either XTs or ATs.
5. Set Memory Size to 512.
6. Set Writes Text To Screen to Y.
7. Set Displays Graphics Info to Y.
8. Set Virtualize Text/Graphics to N.
9. Set Uses Serial Ports to N.
10. Set Requires Floppy to N.
11. Press F1 to see the Advanced Parameters screen.
12. Set System Memory to 0.
13. Set Max Program Size to 640.
14. Set Script Buffer Size to 1000.
15. Set Max Expanded Memory to 512 (or higher or blank).
16. Leave Close On Exit blank.
17. Set Allow Close Window Command to N.
18. Set Uses Math Coprocessor to Y.
19. Set Share CPU When Foreground to Y.
20. Leave Can Be Swapped Out blank.
21. Set Uses Its Own Colors to Y.
22. Leave Runs In Background blank.
23. Set Keyboard Conflict to 0.
24. Set Share EGA When Foreground to Y.

25. Set Protection Level to 0.
26. Exit (from Change a Program or Add a Program).
27. Start Paradox under DESQview.

On a 386 with DESQview and QEMM, Paradox can run in protected mode while other programs run at the same time. For a 386 machine, set up this way:

1. Install Paradox by the manual.
2. Choose Open Window from DESQview's main menu.
3. When upgrading from Paradox 3.0 to 3.5, choose Paradox 3 from the file list, and then choose Change a Program.
4. If installing Paradox for the first time, use Add a Program and select Paradox 3 from the menu to add that to the list. You'll be asked what directory holds Paradox 3.5. Type that in and press Enter. Choose Open Window and Change a Program. Enter the two-key code for Paradox 3.
5. In the Standard Parameters screen, type the program name and any batch filename you use to start Paradox, along with any options.
6. Set Memory Size to 440.
7. Set Writes Text To Screen to N.
8. Set Displays Graphics Info to Y.
9. Set Virtualize Text/Graphics to Y.
10. Set Uses Serial Ports to N.
11. Set Requires Floppy to N.
12. Press F1 to see the Advanced Parameters screen.
13. Set System Memory to 0.
14. Set Max Program Size to 640.
15. Set Script Buffer Size to 1000.
16. Set Max Expanded Memory to 512 (or higher or blank).
17. Leave Close On Exit blank.
18. Set Uses Math Coprocessor to Y.
19. Set Share CPU When Foreground to Y.
20. Leave Can Be Swapped Out blank.
21. Set Uses Its Own Colors to Y.
22. Leave Runs In Background blank.
23. Set Keyboard Conflict to 0.

24. Set Share EGA When Foreground to Y.
25. Set Protection Level to 0.
26. Exit (from Change a Program or Add a Program).
27. Start Paradox under DESQview.

If you need to run the DOS SHARE command, as for many networks, then start DESQview with the command line parameter /DT. This lets DESQview know SHARE is there.

Paradox 3.0 supports EMS 4.0 expanded memory. If it doesn't work well with your EMS driver, you can start Paradox 3.01 with the command line parameter

```
PARADOX3 -EMS3
```

to use EMS version 3.2. You will probably need this if you use expanded memory that was converted from extended by QEMM.

As explained in Chapter 15, QEMM386.SYS can replace the HIMEM.SYS and EMM386.EXE memory management drivers found in DOS 5. QEMM supports the DOS=HIGH command that pushes the DOS shell into the HMA. However, QEMM versions 5.11 and earlier do not recognize the UMB parameter that follows the DOS=HIGH command of DOS 5.

Intel's Aboveboard EMS driver can have some trouble with Paradox and DOS 5. For example, the installation program can test memory in a way that corrupts extended memory. One fix is to use QEMM instead of DOS 5's memory management abilities.

When using QEMM with Paradox, the EMS page frame must be free, otherwise Paradox cannot run in protected mode with an EMS emulator. You cannot use Stealth, because it uses an EMS page frame. If you don't leave the page frame free, you could see the error message "Machine is running an incompatible memory manager," even though the memory manager is compatible. It is just not in the right mode. Don't use the FRAME=NONE parameter.

Paradox 3.5 in protected mode is compliant with VCPI. QEMM 4.10 was the first QEMM compliant with VCPI. Versions 4.20 to 4.22 had problems running multiple VCPI programs (such as running multiple Paradox sessions under DESQview). QEMM 4.23 fixed those problems. Versions 5.10 and 5.11 added support of the Windows enhanced 386 mode, and 5.12 added the ability to use DESQview's Close Window command on a VCPI program to reclaim that program's memory.

If you have trouble running Paradox 3.5, QEMM, and PCKwick, try the following:

- Remove STACKS=0,0 from CONFIG.SYS. Set it to STACKS=X,128, where X is the number of sectors per track of PCKwick.
- Run PCKwick from expanded memory instead of extended memory (although QEMM seems to prefer PCKwick in expanded memory).
- Use the /X parameter for PCKwick for an alternate caching algorithm (this is not in the PCKwick manual).
- Use the /5 or /5* parameter for PCKwick Version 4 to put the track buffer into conventional memory (to solve memory conflicts).
- Use the /&U parameter with QEMM and let PCKwick load itself into high memory (instead of using LOADHI).
- Use the /L parameter with PCKwick 4 (to shut off the lending feature which is less effective with Paradox anyway).
- Try adding NOSORT and IA parameters to QEMM386.SYS line in CONFIG.SYS.

If you run Paradox under Windows and see a system integrity error message, there is a conflict in high memory. This conflict is probably between the EMS page frame that Windows enhanced mode makes for DOS applications and some adapters, such as a graphics adapter or network adapter. You could add EMMEXCLUDE to the SYSTEM.INI file of Windows. You could exclude C000-CFFF or A000-CFFF (remove these same addresses from QEMM's use). With QEMM you could try removing the DEVICE= statement for it from CONFIG.SYS.

The MACE disk cache seems to work with QEMM and Paradox only if it is loaded in CONFIG.SYS before QEMM.

Because Paradox 3.5 is VCPI but not DPMI compatible, it cannot run in protected mode while Windows is in enhanced mode.

QEMM can convert extended memory into expanded without an EMS page frame. QEMM does this with the FRAME=NONE parameter. If you use that parameter, you must run Paradox in real mode (its default mode). Don't force it into protected mode or the PC could hang.

Quattro Pro

The Quattro Pro spreadsheet program can use conventional, expanded, and extended memory.

It uses expanded memory to speed work on large spreadsheets or many spreadsheets handled simultaneously by loading those spreadsheets into memory instead of swapping them in and out from disk. The expanded memory can come from an expanded memory card (Quattro automatically recognizes the expanded memory from a card) or from an Expanded Memory Manager (EMM) such as QEMM. QEMM would use extended memory in the PC to emulate expanded memory. (Remember that extended memory only exists if the PC has a megabyte or more of RAM.)

Quattro works with most expanded memory cards with either LIM 3.2 or LIM 4.0 support. Using LIM 3.2 you can have up to 4MB of expanded memory; using LIM 4.0 gives up to 8MB of expanded memory.

But you can also provide Quattro Pro with extended memory that emulates expanded memory. Use memory above 640K to act like LIM 4.0 expanded memory using QEMM.

Quattro Pro can access the Paradox database management program (both are from Borland International). You do this by using Quattro's Paradox Access command. Before you can use that command, however, you must configure memory so that the two programs can share and lock files without conflicting over use of expanded memory.

To set this configuration, you must alter three files: CONFIG.SYS, AUTOEXEC.BAT, and PXACCESS.BAT. CONFIG.SYS and AUTOEXEC.BAT are DOS files (in the root directory) that contain settings the PC implements when you first turn on the computer. PXACCESS.BAT is a batch file that prepares Paradox for a program link and loads Paradox into memory. It is in the /QPRO directory.

Take these steps:

1. Set FILES=40 in CONFIG.SYS.
2. Add a SHARE line to AUTOEXEC.BAT (this installs a TSR program that lets Quattro Pro and Paradox share and lock files).
3. Make sure Quattro Pro and Paradox are installed and in separate directories.
4. Make sure the AUTOEXEC.BAT file has Quattro Pro and Paradox in its PATH statements.
5. Make sure that the Paradox working directory and private directory are different. (If they aren't, use Paradox's Custom Configuration program to choose the Defaults Set Directory command.)
6. Make sure PXACCESS.BAT has the right memory allocation arguments (arguments are the little parameters that come after the main command). There are two lines in PXACCESS.BAT for this work. The first has the SHARE command (a DOS command). If SHARE isn't in AUTOEXEC.BAT, putting it here ensures the programs can share files. If it was in AUTOEXEC.BAT, the PC just ignores this second occurrence. The second line has a statement such as this:

```
Paradox -qpro -leaveK 512 -emK 0
```

where

`Paradox`	loads Paradox into memory
`-qpro`	creates the Quattro-Paradox link, to let Paradox work in a multiuser setting, and sets aside at least 384K of conventional memory for Quattro Pro
`-leaveK 512`	allocates the first 512K of memory to Quattro Pro
`-emK 0`	allocates all expanded memory to Quattro Pro (Paradox cannot use it)

The particular allocations here are typical ones. You may need others, depending on the memory in your system. For example, if you have a 386 with 4MB of expanded memory managed by QEMM, use this line:

```
Paradox -qpro -leaveK 3000 -emK 0
```

A 286 with 4MB of expanded memory on a board could use

```
Paradox -qpro -leaveK 0 -emK 0
```

but if that memory were configured by QEMM as extended, the line would be

```
Paradox -qpro -leaveK 2000 -emK 0
```

Always set -leaveK so that it is greater than 512 but less than the total extended memory and 1024K less than total system memory.

If you want to run Quattro Pro under Windows 3.0's standard mode, there's no Windows way to allocate expanded memory.

Quattro Pro can use extended memory to store part of its program code. This is done through the built-in VROOMM (Virtual Runtime Object-Oriented Memory Manager) in Quattro Pro 3.0 and later. VROOMM puts Quattro's Object Cache in extended memory.

If you use Quattro's ability to work directly with Paradox and you're using QEMM, make sure QEMM is not converting all of extended memory as expanded. You need at least 640K of conventional memory and 1.4MB of extended to load the Access program that permits this.

When you use a high resolution video adapter such as CGA, EGA, VGA, or XGA, the extra memory addresses used can also be used by other software, such as EMS or network drivers. If those devices conflict with each other, you could have serious problems. To prevent problems, QEMM can be told to exclude the video memory from use. Full video ROM and VRAM memory runs from A000 to C7FF, but the video RAM probably uses only part of this.

Quattro can have trouble when used with a Paradise 16-bit VGA card and QEMM. One solution is to run the VGA card in 8-bit mode.

Lotus 1-2-3

1-2-3 is a spreadsheet program that comes in several versions: there is one for Windows, for network Servers, to use multiple megabytes of memory (versions 3.1 and later), and to run on PCs with less memory (versions 2.3 and 2.4).

For 1-2-3 versions 2.3 and 2.4, use QEMM or QRAM's LOADHI to put as many TSRs and drivers as possible into upper memory. That leaves more conventional memory free for 1-2-3. Version 2.3 needs 512K of memory; 640K with the WYSIWYG add-in.

QRAM needs the NOVIDEOFILL parameter for use with WYSIWYG.

If you have only 1MB of memory in your PC, 1-2-3 3.1 can use all of it. Unlike most applications, it uses not only the 640K of conventional but also the 384K of upper memory. It has a DOS extender built in. The disadvantage to this is that no other program can use that memory. This prevents such programs as QEMM's LOADHI from using that 384K. When you use most of the PC memory, 1-2-3 moves data or parts of programs in and out of memory, swapping them to disk.

Most systems with more than 1MB of memory let you configure that memory as extended or expanded memory. Lotus recommends that you choose extended for as much of the memory as possible, because this often runs faster than expanded memory.

If you use applications other than Lotus and these applications need expanded memory only, only as much of memory as those other programs need should be configured as expanded. Make the rest extended. When you have both kinds of memory, 1-2-3 stores the program in extended memory and puts data (the worksheets) in expanded memory. When expanded memory is full, any more data is put in extended memory. When there is no longer room in extended memory for data, it is swapped out to a hard disk file.

If you have a 386 system and use drivers that emulate expanded memory from extended, and if this memory is not in use, 1-2-3 automatically uses it as extended memory. But 1-2-3 uses only the amount of memory that the drivers control. This is usually set by a statement in the CONFIG.SYS file. To change the amount, you may need to change the driver switches. 1-2-3 works with such drivers only if they support VCPI (Virtual Control Program Interface). QEMM 4.2 or later does support VCPI. If you use Windows 3.0 in 386-enhanced mode, 1-2-3 uses the DPMI (DOS Protected Mode Interface) that comes with Windows for its memory allocation.

When using a graphics printer with 1-2-3 Release 2.3 in Windows 3.0 as a DOS application in real and standard modes, 1-2-3 displays in a full screen only. You cannot put it into a resizable window. In enhanced mode you can use the clipboard and resize the window, as long as WYSIWYG is not in memory or 1-2-3 is not displaying a graph. If you use WYSIWYG, you can display only as a full screen. Enhanced mode is the only mode that uses memory parameters and background operations such as HIMEM.SYS and QEMM 5.1.

When running 1-2-3 Release 3 in DESQview with QEMM 5.12 or earlier, don't close the window with the DESQview Close Window command. If you do, the memory that window used cannot be recovered. Use 1-2-3's own commands to quit, then you can deallocate the memory. One way to avoid this problem is to set the Allow Close Window command parameter to N. Better yet, get a version of QEMM newer than 5.12.

1-2-3 Release 3 is compatible with DESQview and QEMM because they all support VCPI. On a 286, 1-2-3 Release 3 says it needs 384K extended memory, but it can actually load on a system with a 1MB expanded memory board and 128K of extended memory with QEXT.SYS using 64K of that extended memory. Load QEXT.SYS first in CONFIG.SYS. Don't use extended memory with a cache or RAM disk. You don't need to disable expanded memory and convert it to extended, although the 1-2-3 documentation seems to suggest so. If there is 600K of conventional memory free and some extended memory, 1-2-3 can use the expanded memory as well. You can even run multiple copies of 1-2-3 under DESQview on a 286 if you have DESQview 2.26 or later and enough memory. On a 386, 1-2-3 Release 3 can allocate all memory from QEMM. You don't need to reserve any as extended before QEMM. In fact, any you reserve in advance is wasted on 1-2-3: it uses only reserved or only QEMM pool memory. When using from the pool, it uses as extended.

If you want to use the Allways add-in but using it hangs the computer with 1-2-3 2.2, then you can use the AWEMM parameter to disable Allways' use of expanded memory. This cuts into conventional memory, so it is probably better to use the QEMM parameter X=C600-C7FF to keep QEMM out of an area that Allways wants.

When using DESQview-386 with 1-2-3 3.0, you should configure all memory as expanded and use QEMM 4.2 or higher (because they support VCPI).

To run Release 3.1 under Windows, you need to run QEMM with the right configuration. Use QEMM 5.1 or later for Windows 3.0 or QEMM 5.12 for Windows 3.00a. Put the RAM parameter and the X=F000-FFFF parameter after the QEMM line in CONFIG.SYS. (RAM tells QEMM to give the HMA for Windows. EXCLUDE keeps QEMM out of an area of memory that Windows wants.) If you see the "VM Error 19" error message when you run Windows 3 in standard mode and start 1-2-3, then QEMM 5.1 needs the EMBMEM parameter to limit the amount of memory QEMM lets Windows lock. Put EMBMEM=1024 on the QEMM line in CONFIG.SYS. If the computer reboots when you start 1-2-3, then there is less than 1.6MB of RAM in the system. Get more memory by removing programs that run in the background but remove or shrink the SMARTDRV and closing other Windows applications.

If you see the message "123 cannot start because the driver set is invalid" you're probably using VIDRAM. 1-2-3 is checking its graphic abilities, and those are limited because VIDRAM is in action. You can run the 1-2-3 INSTALL program and delete the graphics entry. Then 1-2-3 can work. From the Advanced Parameters and Modify Current Driver Set selections, go to Graph Display. Press the Del key on the driver selected. Then press Esc and use Save Changes. Save the results under a different name, such as 123TEXT. Then to use VIDRAM and 1-2-3, start 1-2-3 with the command

```
123 123TEXT
```

Freelance Graphics

Freelance Graphics is a chart-making program. It supports EMS memory and works with QEMM 5.11 and later. Freelance automatically uses 64K of expanded memory if it is available as the program starts. You can't increase or decrease that use, although you can turn off support for expanded memory altogether. It automatically puts command prompts, chart style settings, device configuration, print parameters, and error message files into expanded memory. This doesn't increase drawing or charting space, but you do get more of that space if you use the Large version with expanded memory on hand. Expanded memory can also lead to faster printing.

Freelance Graphics can run in several different forms:

	with 64K EMS	without EMS
Freelance Graphics (FL)	395K	455K
Freelance Small(FL S)	384K	453K
Freelance Large(FL L)	458K	526K

Add 22K to any of these numbers if you use Grandview LT.

Use the X parameter to stop use of expanded memory.

TimeLine

TimeLine is a project management program. It lets you create schedules and analyze the people and resources necessary to accomplish a task.

TimeLine can run more efficiently with more memory. If possible, have at least 64K of extended memory so TimeLine can use the HMA (see Chapter 4 for details). You can use HIMEM.SYS or QEMM to manage the HMA.

Fast!

The disk caching program Fast! works with QEMM-386 and DESQview. However, the Advanced Update feature of version 3.10 is automatically disabled by QEMM 6.

Stacker

Stacker is a utility that compresses files on your disk drives so they take up less space, fewer megabytes. Then when any program asks for a file, Stacker automatically decompresses it so that it is useful again. This can effectively double the size of your disk drives, at the price of Stacker (which isn't much) and a small delay in getting a file on slow computers (which need the time to decompress). The overhead of decompression time is more than compensated for by the effective doubling of the disk's transfer rate. It also costs you a little memory—the memory taken by Stacker's program instructions.

If you can, get a 386 machine to use Stacker. On a plain 286 you'll hurt performance, and even on a 286 with the Stacker coprocessor, you'll lose some memory because a 286 isn't as good at remapping memory for the Stacker program instructions and buffers.

Stacker works with QEMM and QRAM, as well as with EMM386. Stacker detects QEMM and asks you during installation (of Stacker) if you want to cache part of Stacker in EMS (expanded) memory. If you answer yes, the Stacker drivers in conventional memory take up 14K instead of 26K. You can use OPTIMIZE to configure high memory to hold Stacker also. Stacker has buffers that need memory, too, typically expanded memory (either as itself or from emulated extended memory).

Stacker works by compressing all data into a single hidden file called STACVOL.XXX, where XXX is the first partition, and numbers from 000 to 999 are used for more partitions. Then Stacker installs a device driver through the CONFIG.SYS file. After that, whenever a program needs a file from disk, the Stacker driver intercepts the request and gets the information from the hidden file, decompressing it for immediate use. Stacker adds new drive letters, such as adding a drive D to a system that had only a C hard drive. The SSWAP program then switches drives C and D, so your batch files are not affected. You won't even know Stacker is operating—except for all that extra disk space, of course.

Watch to see that you're installing Stacker on all relevant drives.

If you use Stacker on a slow 286 machine, you should choose the coprocessor version, otherwise the additional overhead of immediately compressing and decompressing files could slow your computing. On a 386 machine you probably won't notice the overhead hurting performance. However, you do need to consider memory use. Stacker stores itself as a TSR in conventional memory. If you have expanded memory, either on an expanded memory board or as emulated expanded memory from an emulator such as EMM386, Stacker can use that to reduce its impact on conventional memory. The software-only version of Stacker can use 26K of RAM with expanded memory, while it needs 41K without any expanded memory. The coprocessor version requires 14K with expanded memory or 30K without expanded memory. The Stacker buffers also take memory.

On a 386 machine you can use QEMM to load Stacker into high memory and to emulate expanded memory for Stacker's buffers.

Quarterdeck technical support warns against loading SMARTDRV high when using Stacker, but people have reported doing this without problems.

Stacker's SSWAP.COM comes in several versions. For Stacker 2.0 running on a system optimized for QEMM, you could drop from 635K conventional to 569K. But SSWAP.COM's drive name swapping can confuse OPTIMIZE. You need to disable SSWAP's device line in CONFIG.SYS, reverse all drive names in AUTOEXEC.BAT before running OPTIMIZE, and then return them to the proper settings when OPTIMIZE is done.

To install STACKER 2 on a computer that has QEMM installed:

1. STACKER 2 automatically copies most of the files OPTIMIZE needs to the \QEMM subdirectory of the uncompressed drive. However, it doesn't copy TESTBIOS.COM and WINSTLTH.VXD, which it needs for STEALTH testing and for Windows 3 enhanced mode using STEALTH. You should copy them yourself from the compressed drive to the uncompressed \QEMM subdirectory.
2. Reboot and then run OPTIMIZE. All the drives should be set for it.
3. Edit CONFIG.SYS, adding back the SSWAP.COM line.
4. Edit AUTOEXEC.BAT, restoring the drive settings.
5. Reboot again.

To install QEMM on a drive that has STACKER:

1. Create a QEMM subdirectory on the uncompressed drive. Have QEMM386.SYS, OPTIMIZE.COM, LOADHI.SYS, TESTBIOS.COM, LOADHI.COM, BUFFERS.COM, RSTRCFG.SYS, MCA.ADL, WINHIRAM.VXD (on Micro Channel machines), WINSTLTH.VXD (if using Windows 3 enhanced mode).
2. Reboot and then run OPTIMIZE. All the drives should be set for it.
3. Edit CONFIG.SYS, adding back the SSWAP.COM line.
4. Edit AUTOEXEC.BAT, restoring the drive settings.
5. Reboot again.

SuperStor

SuperStor is a utility that compresses files on disk and then automatically decompresses them when they're needed. This saves disk space, effectively doubling (approximately) a disk's size at the price of a slight delay on slower computers when a file is first requested. It is sold by itself and as part of the DR-DOS 6 operating system from Digital Research.

There are reports that SuperStor doesn't load automatically and easily into upper memory or that it doesn't work once loaded there.

With QEMM 5.1, even when changing locations, loading order, and disabling Shadow RAM, SuperStor won't necessarily load high. With 6.02 it still won't load in all cases.

SuperStor versions 1.3h and later, dated 1/14/92 and later, load high in some systems. Older releases load some of the program high but leave about 20K in conventional memory.

PCKwik

The PCKwik disk cache improves disk performance. It offers two different caching approaches, one a generic, slower algorithm for deciding what stays in the cache, the other an advanced, faster algorithm.

STEALTH in QEMM 6.0 forces PCKwik to use its slower, generic caching algorithm. In fact, the same thing happens when running PCKwik with DESQview, and the SuperPCK/P display won't even admit it. You can also force the use of the generic algorithm without STEALTH by putting the parameter

/H- on the PCKwik command line. Any advanced parameters you chose earlier using the /H+ parameter on the PCKwik command line won't work, even if you type /D+, /O+, or /Q+. The PC runs slower than it might with these advanced parameters working.

Don't try to fix the problem by using any QEMM 6.0 parameters to force the advanced caching; you could lose hard disk data. QEMM 6.02 should solve some of the advanced parameter problems.

If you use a QEMM or DESQview version that isn't compatible with the advanced parameters, load PCKwik with the /H- /D- parameters. You can't get the advantages of the advanced options anyway, and if you choose to leave them out, you save some memory space because they won't even bother to load.

OPTIMIZE can have trouble with PCKwik, too. When PCKwik is loaded high, it takes a different amount of memory than when loaded low (into conventional memory). OPTIMIZE loads programs low when it is figuring out how much memory they want, so this change baffles it. The result could be that programs you try to load high after the disk cache may not be able to—some of their memory may be occupied. If you at least use the /T?8 parameter with PCKwik, you limit the cache's look-ahead memory and so restrict the memory the cache takes.

In general, you can avoid trouble by avoiding disk cache advanced parameters that include delayed writes. Such parameters can boost performance but always involve some additional risk of lost data.

Norton AntiVirus

The Norton AntiVirus program helps protect your PC from, and cure it of, computer viruses—programs that seek to copy themselves from one disk to another, one computer to another. Many viruses do more than just reproduce. They often damage your system, either accidentally by conflicting with other software or intentionally by erasing a disk drive or otherwise inflicting harm.

AntiVirus likes to be the first program loaded into your PC when you turn on the power, so it can check any other programs that try to load and see if they are infected. However, you can load AntiVirus high only if QEMM is actually the first program loaded.

The thing to do is to use AntiVirus's curative powers to make sure there are no viruses in your system, including on your QEMM disk. Then you can create a new CONFIG.SYS that loads QEMM and then, immediately after QEMM, loads AntiVirus and its protection abilities. That way only the MSDOS.SYS, IO.SYS, and QEMM386.SYS files load before AntiVirus.

Norton Utilities

The Norton Utilities is a collection of utility programs for the PC. One of those utilities is a disk cache called NCACHE. OPTIMIZE and NCACHE don't get along too well. Nor do NCACHE and LOADHI get along, because NCACHE does not consistently load into the same place in memory. For best results, try putting NCACHE into extended memory.

PC Tools

PC Tools is a collection of utilities for the PC. Many but not all of the utilities can be loaded high by QEMM.

Deskcon, Mirror, PC-Cache, and Vdefend can all load high, as can the SWAP programs.

Datamon and Commute load themselves high if there is space. (They need 300K each to initialize, however, so they won't load high by QEMM.) This can trouble OPTIMIZE, so before OPTIMIZE is done you may want to disable the load high feature by starting Datamon as

```
DATAMON /LOW
```

to make it load into conventional memory. Start Commute with

```
COMMUTE /NU
```

so it does not use any upper memory and loads into conventional.

Once OPTIMIZE is done, you could remove those parameters to let Datamon and Commute load into upper memory if they can find the room.

PC Shell and Desktop, however, need at least 400K to initialize before becoming memory resident. Upper memory never has more than 384K, and realistically not even that much, so they cannot fit into upper memory.

If you choose to run PC Shell or Desktop from AUTOEXEC.BAT, those programs appear during OPTIMIZE. Get out of them by pressing the F3 key so OPTIMIZE can do its work.

The PC-Cache program of PC Tools runs best from extended memory, especially if you use Windows or QEMM's STEALTH. If you must run PC-Cache from expanded memory, you could have trouble with PC-Cache's tendency to directly write to the page frame. To avoid the problem add this parameter to the QEMM line in CONFIG.SYS:

```
DISKBUFFFRAME=10
```

This uses more conventional memory but lets QEMM buffer direct writes to the page frame while using STEALTH or Windows 3. (The value 10 can be decreased to use less conventional memory or increased to improve system performance.)

If you're going to use OPTIMIZE or DESQview, you should also disable the Delayed Writes feature of PC-Cache with this parameter on the command line:

```
/WRITE=OFF
```

HyperCache, HyperDisk

HyperWare's HyperDisk disk cache is popular for making disk drives work faster, but it has had problems working with STEALTH in QEMM 6.0. As of version 4.30 it can corrupt files on disk, making them unreadable and unusable. And STEALTH mode disables HyperDisk's Advanced Update functions.

Version 4.31 of HyperDisk was intended to solve the problem on many systems and permit the Advanced Update functions with STEALTH. This works automatically; you don't need to manually select the QEMM VHI parameter.

Unfortunately, reports indicated that some PCs still couldn't use STEALTH and HyperDisk. If you have such troubles, you can try the following:

1. Make sure STACKS=0,0 is in your CONFIG.SYS.
2. Add the XST=F000 parameter to the QEMM line in CONFIG.SYS.
3. Add XI:- to the HyperDisk installation line. (This disables automatic STEALTH support.)

Above Disc

Above Disc uses a driver called ABOVE.EXE to emulate expanded memory in extended memory, or in some cases on a hard disk. This lets those without enough expanded memory operate as if they have lots, because hard disk space is typically much more available.

If ABOVE.EXE is used with HIMEM.SYS and with DOS=HIGH of DOS 5, or in some cases with just HIMEM.SYS, the computer can lock up on startup, beep uncontrollably, or reboot over and over. ABOVE.EXE can also cause problems with caching programs such as SMARTDRV.SYS and with memory managers such as QEMM.

The problems arise because ABOVE.EXE uses the HMA from 1024K to 1088K in extended memory. HIMEM.SYS also uses this area. When HIMEM.SYS loads DOS high, it is putting it into this area. That can conflict with ABOVE.EXE's attempt to use the HMA. But even when DOS is not loaded high, HIMEM.SYS may not work with ABOVE.EXE.

To avoid the conflicts, you can get an upgrade of Above Disc to version 4.1b or later. This should be compatible with DOS 5 and with QEMM.

Another fix, for earlier versions, is to install Above Disc with its hardware set to Normal IO 286/386 and under its Change Feature parameter to check EMS 4.0. You could still have problems if DOS is loaded high (with the line DOS=HIGH in CONFIG.SYS).

CHAPTER NINETEEN

QEMM with Networks

LANs (local area networks) are connecting more and more of the world's PCs. A LAN connection lets a PC easily and quickly exchange files and messages with other PCs. It also permits peripheral sharing—many PCs can use the same printer or large hard disk, spreading the cost. Finally, LANs are the foundation for cooperative programs, called groupware, that let many computer users work on the same project or data at the same time.

To connect to a LAN, a PC needs hardware and software. The hardware is a network interface adapter, typically on a circuit board that plugs into one of the PC's slots. (Some of the latest PCs have network interface hardware built in.) The software will be a network driver that communicates between the PC's operating system and the network operating system (typically installed on a central server computer).

LAN connections use PC memory in three ways. The adapter has a ROM that occupies memory addresses in upper memory. Many adapters also have RAM of their own. And then there's the software driver that must load into memory and remain there the entire time the PC is connected to the network.

These three memory needs of networks can overwhelm the PC. In fact, it may have been the network memory demand that pushed memory managers such as QEMM into the limelight. The adapter ROM isn't a major problem, as long as QEMM can find it and exclude those addresses from upper memory blocks. Sometimes it doesn't find the adapter, as detailed below. What's worse, many adapters have some RAM of their own. But on some adapters, such as some Ethernet cards (a popular network type), the RAM doesn't show up when QEMM first checks. The RAM only awakes after the card is up and running. Then it may conflict with some driver or memory-resident program QEMM has loaded into the same addresses. You have to find such RAM and exclude it manually (see Chapter 6 for details on the EXCLUDE parameter).

Most network adapter cards have ROM that must be excluded from UMBs. QEMM usually does this automatically. But many network adapter cards have RAM that QEMM won't find, which you must exclude manually.

The driver software can eat as much as 50 to 100K or even more from conventional RAM. When that is added to DOS's needs and another driver or two—such as a mouse driver—suddenly there isn't enough memory for most applications to run. Network drivers can be much larger than other typical drivers, and network drivers aren't as easy to unload. After all, if the point of the network is smooth and immediate transmission of files and messages, it is impractical to disconnect, change the drivers, compute, change the drivers, reconnect to the network to check for information, and so on.

Load network drivers high.

DESQview and Networks

The network adapter automatically puts its ROM (and RAM, if it has that) at some addresses in upper memory. You don't need to live with whatever addresses it chooses. After all, QEMM (or QRAM with EMS hardware) can remap these areas. Use QEMM or QRAM to ensure that the RAM and ROM are in optimal positions, such as creating the maximum contiguous free memory, so there's room for drivers and TSRs to load high (including the network driver).

Most expanded memory drivers are loaded before the typical network shell loads. The shell may then initialize a RAM buffer in upper memory at the same address used by the EMS frame. An application using expanded memory could then write over that network RAM buffer, crashing the PC, hurting the application's operation, or disrupting network access.

The best way to find a network card's ROM and RAM is to look to its documentation. If you cannot find the information you need there, call the network card or operating system makers technical support people. This saves you from having to hope that OPTIMIZE finds all ROMs and RAM in upper memory, or from having to do detective work with Manifest to find these potential memory conflicts.

Once you find the areas the network hardware and software need, exclude them from use by QEMM and STEALTH (see Chapter 6 for details on doing this). Typically, to exclude an area of upper memory from QEMM's reach, you put an EXCLUDE parameter at the end of the QEMM.SYS line in CONFIG.SYS, like this:

```
DEVICE=C:\QEMM\QEMM386.SYS X=XXXX-YYYY RAM ST:M
```

where XXXX-YYYY is the beginning and ending addresses of the RAM or ROM occupied space in memory, given in hexadecimal.

Typically you can then load the network shell in upper memory, using QEMM or QRAM.

Novell NetWare

Novell's NetWare is the most popular network operating system. It depends on several pieces of software in the workstation for initializing the network connection and redirecting any network requests from DOS to the network operating system. You can use LOADHI to put these drivers into upper memory.

NetWare puts a shell, a LAN driver, and a protocol driver into each workstation. The shell is a TSR that intercepts application requests and determines whether they should be handled by DOS or routed to the network file server to be serviced by NetWare. The LAN driver controls the network board. The protocol driver links the communication protocol to the LAN driver.

The shell file comes in three versions:

- NETx.COM, which loads into conventional memory
- EMSNETx.EXE, which loads into expanded memory (and some conventional memory)
- XMSNETx.EXE, which loads into extended memory

Earlier versions of these shell files had names specific to the DOS version, such as NET3 for DOS 3.x, NET4 for DOS 4.x. The current versions work with all versions of DOS.

There are two types of LAN and protocol drivers for NetWare: dedicated drivers and ODI drivers. Dedicated IPX drivers work with the IPX protocol from Novell. The IPX.COM driver supports only Novell's own IPX and SPX protocols. Open Data-Link Interface, or ODI, is Novell's route to supporting multiple protocols and drivers. ODI drivers aren't dependent on a particular media or protocol. They can use several protocols, such as IPX/SPX, AppleTalk, or TCP/IP, without adding more network boards. IPX drivers use slightly less RAM than ODI drivers, but they must be configured and linked using the WSGEN program, and a different driver must be made for each type of LAN card used. ODI drivers don't need to be configured and linked. However, not all LAN cards come with ODI drivers.

A typical QEMM-configured AUTOEXEC.BAT would have lines such as these:

```
C:\QEMM\BUFFERS=20
C:\QEMM\LOADHI /R:3 C:\QEMM\FILES+10
C:\QEMM\LOADHI /R:2 LSL
C:\QEMM\LOADHI /R:1 SMCODIWS
C:\QEMM\LOADHI /R:2 IPXODI
C:\QEMM\LOADHI /R:2 NETX
```

LAN Manager and PROTMAN

Microsoft's LAN Manager is one the challengers to Novell's NetWare network operating system. Although it is far behind Novell in popularity, Microsoft's clout in the market makes LAN Manager a powerful second-place program.

PROTMAN.DOS is the protocol manager for LAN Manager. (It is also used in 3Com's 3+Open network, as well as in some other LAN-Manager-derived networks.) PROTMAN is a device driver. It is typically the first network program loaded by CONFIG.SYS.

Some versions of PROTMAN.DOS, before 2.0x, needed only about 100 bytes of memory for themselves. But then they often grab about 32K more memory from the top of whatever area they're in for the code from the particular network that will call PROTMAN. Other DOS programs could accidentally grab this memory and so conflict with PROTMAN. This can crash the network in a number of ways: by being written over by a new program loaded into memory, by writing over itself, or even by writing over something beneath itself (when you load PROTMAN into a 16K area). This 32K grab by PROTMAN can also make trouble for

QEMM's LOADHI program. The LOADHI /GETSIZE parameter figures out how much memory is available when loading a TSR by writing its own signature throughout available memory. Use LOADHI /GS after loading PROTMAN, and PROTMAN's 32K could be overwritten with GS signatures. Exception 13 errors could result. Finally, OPTIMIZE relies on LOADHI /GS and so could crash when detecting what memory is available. Making detection difficult, it would probably crash when some other network driver is loaded after PROTMAN, though PROTMAN was the problem.

To avoid these problems, follow these steps:

1. Put the RAM parameter on the QEMM line.
2. Reboot.
3. Make sure the largest upper memory region is at least 33K. (Use Manifest to check.) If not, don't run OPTIMIZE with PROTMAN. Load high manually. That is, manually put LOADHI.SYS and LOADHI.COM on every CONFIG.SYS and AUTOEXEC.BAT line that has a program to load high. Don't LOADHI PROTMAN, though. Reboot.

Some 3Com cards on DECNET need not just 33K but as much as 48K for PROTMAN to load.

4. Don't let any programs allocate UMBs through the EMS. (Use the programs' own parameters.) That could trouble OPTIMIZE and cause a crash.
5. If you do have a 33K or larger upper memory area, run OPTIMIZE. When you see the DETECTION PHASE display, press the Esc key. Then press F1.
6. Edit CONFIG.SYS to delete all the LOADHI.SYS parameters on the PROTMAN line. That is, delete the /GS parameter and the label parameter. Leave the LOADHI.SYS command and any PROTMAN parameters.
7. Reboot. Let OPTIMIZE complete its work.
8. PROTMAN loads in conventional memory and uses only about 100 bytes of memory.

Token Ring Network Cards

Token ring adapter cards, such as the IBM Token Ring PS/2 Primary Adapter cards, have both RAM and ROM for upper memory addresses. There are two versions of the IBM card: one that uses 8K ROM and 8K RAM, and one that uses 16K ROM and 16K RAM. Here are some addresses that work for the cards. (They also work for other PS/2 adapter cards, such as ESDI hard disk controller cards.)

If 8K in size		If 16K in size	
ROM	**RAM**	**ROM**	**RAM**
C800 C9FF	C800 C9FF	C800 CBFF	C800 CBFF
CC00 CDFF	CA00 CCBF	CC00 CFFF	CC00 CFFF
D000 D2FF	CC00 CDFF	D000 D3FF	D000 D3FF
D400 D6FF	CE00 CFFF	D400 D7FF	D400 D7FF
D800 D9FF	D000 D1FF	D800 DBFF	D800 DBFF
DC00 DDFF	D200 D3FF	DC00 DFFF	DC00 DFFF
	D400 D5FF		
	D600 D7FF		
	D800 D9FF		
	DA00 DBFF		
	DC00 DDFF		
	DE00 DFFF		

The potential trouble with RAM buffers in network cards is that QEMM may not find them. (Sometimes it even misses the ROMs on some token ring cards.) That means you must find and exclude those addresses yourself to avoid memory conflicts.

Use the EXCLUDE rule as mentioned at the beginning of this chapter. The default location of token ring RAM is D800. The IBM PS/2 Reference Diskette can verify the RAM and ROM addresses. Use the Select View Configuration from the main menu.

If QEMM can't put a page frame for EMS in upper memory after you exclude the token ring buffer, it puts the page frame in conventional memory. That takes 64K away from other conventional memory uses. You could relocate the token ring ROM and RAM and relocate other adapters to get that 64K page frame back into upper memory. You may need to use parameters for the network shell or drivers to put them into upper memory and to let them know where the relocated ROM and RAM are. For example, the Novell NetWare ANET3 file may need to be told to see the new addresses. The IBM PC LAN may need the TOKRUI driver with a special parameter to tell it the address of the ROM and RAM. See the documentation for the way to do this.

Using an IBM Token Ring card on a computer other than a PS/2 means you have to change the parameters on parameter block 1 of the card to relocate the ROM address. See the documentation for details. Typical possibilities include the following:

Memory Location	Parameters 1 to 6 (F=OFF N=ON)	Don't use this location if your video display is
A800	N F N F N N	EGA or VGA
AA00	N F N F N F	EGA or VGA
AC00	N F N F F N	EGA or VGA
B000	N F F N N N	Mono, MGA or Hercules
B400	N F F N F N	MGA, Hercules
B800	N F F F N N	CGA ,EGA, MGA, Hercules, VGA
BC00	N F F F F N	CGA, EGA, MGA, Hercules, VGA
C000	F N N N N N	EGA or VGA
C200	F N N N N F	EGA or VGA
C400	F N N N F N	Extended Bios EGA or VGA
C800	F N N F N N	(XT Hard disk ROM)
CC00	F N N F F N	
D000	F N F N N N	
D400	F N F N F N	
DC00	F N F F F N	

TOPS network

TOPS, from Sitka, is a popular, inexpensive network operating system. It is generally compatible with QEMM (and with DESQview), using a variety of hardware connections, including AppleTalk and Ethernet.

However, there are some steps you should take to make sure it works well.

To use QEMM with TOPS, set the LAP driver's DMA to none. Do this for both ALAP and ELAP503. With a DMA setting of 1 or 3 you can crash the system when loading TOPS or NetPrint. This happens immediately with ALAP but can happen even with ELAP503, although more slowly and less dramatically. Accessing expanded memory seems to set the stage.

Use LOADHI to load the TOPS and NetPrint modules into high memory.

With QEMM 4.1, if you attempt to load a TOPS module high and it doesn't fit, and so you load into conventional memory, the TOPS functions cannot work. This doesn't happen with QEMM 4.2 and later.

Banyan VINES

Banyan's VINES network works with QEMM (and with DESQview). With QEMM (or with QRAM and EMS hardware), you can load Banyan's drivers high. You need at least one 112K area and two 64K areas to put them there.

BAN.EXE is a TSR that loads two other TSRs: NEBAN (the actual name depends on the network card you use) and REDIRALL (the redirector, which may have a name such as REDIR3). OPTIMIZE can't load BAN.EXE high because it needs a large memory area for initialization, but you can divide the Banyan programs into parts that will load into upper memory.

One way to do this is to create a new batch file, called something like START.BAT, with lines such as

```
C:
CD \BAN
BAN /NC
NEBAN
REDIRALL
Z:LOGIN
```

This START.BAT does the following

C:............................makes C the current drive

CD/BAN ....makes the Banyan directory current (that's where the Banyan program files are)

/NC........................makes BAN load without loading the network card driver and redirector. Ignore the "no network interface enabled" message.

Then replace the BAN.EXE line in AUTOEXEC.BAT with

```
@CALL START.BAT
```

Now run OPTIMIZE. The three TSRs for VINES load separately. OPTIMIZE has a better chance of loading them high when they are in smaller pieces. You may want to use STEALTH to make sure there's enough room in upper memory for all three programs.

Remember that if your network card has a RAM buffer (as often happens with cards such as those for token ring networks), you must exclude it from QEMM's use. Otherwise other memory uses may try to use that RAM's address.

Pathworks/DECNET

Digital Equipment's Pathworks network operating system is also referred to as DECNET. This is a multiplatform networking system from DEC, one of the world's largest computer companies.

Pathworks is compatible with QEMM (and with DESQview). But smooth operation does require a few customizing steps.

STARTNET.BAT is a batch file that starts Pathworks. It is 200 to 250 lines long. As of QEMM 6.0, the OPTIMIZE program can process a called batch file such as this. But OPTIMIZE has only about 9K of buffer space for holding AUTOEXEC.BAT, CONFIG.SYS, and any called batch files it handles. STARTNET.BAT is often larger than 9K. The result: OPTIMIZE cuts it short, truncating lines from the end of STARTNET.BAT so that it fits 9K.

To fight this (to keep all of STARTNET.BAT available to OPTIMIZE), you can delete the remark statements in STARTNET.BAT. (These are the lines that begin with REM.) Remarked lines help explain what a file is doing, or sometimes help keep temporarily unused lines on hand in the file. But they don't have any effect on the computing, except to take up space. So deleting them won't change anything. Remark statements make up about half of STARTNET.BAT, so deleting them should save you a lot of room.

Another way around this problem is to use the latest OPTIMIZE program, the one that comes with QEMM 6.02. This can handle files up to 20K instead of the older 9K limit.

When you use OPTIMIZE on called batch files, back those files up first. OPTIMIZE only backs up AUTOEXEC.BAT and CONFIG.SYS.

One of the batch files that STARTNET.BAT calls is EXECINFO.BAT. The last line of EXECINFO re-enters (calls) STARTNET.BAT like this:

```
\DECNET\STARTNET.BAT RUN
```

This isn't necessary and can make STARTNET loop endlessly. OPTIMIZE won't like that. It's unnecessary because after a Call, the PC returns to STARTNET anyway. So just REM this line out of existence (and save the resulting EXECINFO.BAT file to actually use).

DNNETHAT is about 50 to 55K. DNNETHLD loads DNNETHAT into EMS expanded memory, freeing 45 to 50K. But DNNETHLD assumes the page frame is saved and restored during each interrupt. EMS doesn't require this, and STEALTH doesn't allow it. A STEALTHed ROM is mapped into the page frame when the ROM is called upon. That may happen during an interrupt. STEALTH doesn't restore the page frame contents when it is done with such a ROM call. That makes trouble for DNNETHLD. Because DNNETHLD saves 45 to 50K and STEALTH can save 99K when using a DEPCA card, foregoing DNNETHLD and using STEALTH is the better idea. (EMSLOAD is another loading program that can put programs from STARTNET.BAT, such as DNNETHLD, into EMS memory. It has the same problems with the page frame and STEALTH that DNETHLD has.)

STEALTH can help give more high RAM when using Pathworks. It can help you load high as many of the 140K and more network drivers that Pathworks typically uses. Put the page frame at DC00, or wherever the DEPCA ROM starts. That will save 16K of memory. If the page frame isn't at DC00, or wherever the beginning of the DEPCA ROM is, then the DEPCA ROM must be STEALTH-excluded. Use XST=DC00 or XST=CC00, whichever represents the beginning of the DEPCA ROM.

The DEPCA cards have two typical configurations:

64K at D000
32K at D800

Both configurations use a 16K ROM at DC00. The rest is RAM buffer.

Put a page frame on top of the DEPCA ROM at DC00 gives back 16K that otherwise wouldn't be available. But it is only possible using STEALTH and therefore only with QEMM 6.0.

The REDIR command in Pathworks can be loaded into the HMA with the

```
/HIMEM:YES
```

parameter. That saves 33K of conventional memory, leaving only 9K in conventional memory. However, when you use DESQview you might want to avoid this touch, because only one program can use the HMA, and DESQview can load more than 33K of itself into the HMA. DESQview in HMA means a 63K savings; REDIR means only a 33K savings.

DNNETH is a driver that doesn't always work well with OPTIMIZE. The command

```
LOADHI/GS
```

(where /GS is the GETSIZE parameter) says that 128K is necessary to load DNNETH high. In fact, DNNETH needs only about 35K to load high. You can enter this information in the PARAMETERS menu of the second step of OPTIMIZE. Type 2 there. Then give an initial size for DNNETH of 35000.

LANtastic

LANtastic is an inexpensive peer-to-peer network from Artisoft. Peer-to-peer means it doesn't require a separate server for the main network software. Instead the communications are entirely among client PCs, any of which may also be a server.

The LANtastic Starter Kit includes two 2Mbps (megabit per second) LAN adapter cards, cable to connect them, terminators for the cables, and a disk with version 3.02 of the LANtastic NOS (Network Operating System). When using LANtastic 3.02 from the Starter Kit with DESQview versions 2.2 and 2.3 and with QEMM 4.2 to 5.1, you need to exclude the LAN adapter ROM at D800-DFFF. The LANtastic user guide has details on the placement of this ROM. However, if you use a 10Mbps Ethernet adapter instead of the adapter in the Starter Kit, you don't need this EXCLUDE. In fact, the Artisoft Ethernet adapters use neither ROM nor RAM, unless you select Novell compatibility, so you don't need to exclude anything on their account.

The LANBIOS.EXE program activates LANtastic in your PC. This program occupies only 2K of memory, but even that can be loaded high.

REDIR.EXE is the actual networking software that runs on each PC node or client. REDIR uses 11K, and it too can be loaded high.

SERVER.EXE is another LANtastic program. A PC that runs SERVER can be used as a file server, as well as operate as an independent client. SERVER needs 30 to 50K of memory, and it too can (most of the time) be loaded high.

LANtastic needs the DOS SHARE.EXE program loaded. That's where the network gets its file protection and locking. The parameters for running SHARE from AUTOEXEC.BAT can be

```
SHARE /F:4096 /L:200
```

SHARE can be loaded high as well.

Artisoft's LANtastic does not function properly with BUFFERS.COM loaded high.

When using LANtastic with 2Mbps LAN adapters, exclude D800-DFFF. With 10Mbps Ethernet adapters, this isn't necessary. Load high LANBIOS.EXE (2K), REDIR.EXE (11K), and SHARE.EXE, and if you use it to allow file server abilities, SERVER.EXE (30K to 50K).

CHAPTER TWENTY

QEMM with Hardware
PCs, Disk Drives, Displays, Keyboards, and More

The millions of QEMM users in this world have amassed a lot of experience using the program with a variety of systems and peripherals. This chapter describes some of the best-known incompatibilities and problems QEMM and your hardware could have, along with suggested solutions. The chapter is organized by hardware type in this order:

- Systems (computers, including particular BIOSes)
- Boards (memory and other plug-in boards)
- Disk drives
- Keyboards
- Displays

NEC PowerMate

QEMM 5.0 installed with the NEC PowerMate SX can cause continual reboots. This doesn't happen with QEMM 6.0 and later—they detect the PowerMate and work around the problem.

To avoid the trouble with QEMM 5.0, add the NOSH parameter to the QEMM line in CONFIG.SYS, like this:

```
DEVICE=C:\QEMM\QEMM386.SYS RAM NOSH
```

The other parameters may differ in your particular installation of QEMM. Whatever parameters you have, add NOSH at the end of the line.

NOSH is the acronym for no Shadow RAM. This tells QEMM not to use any unused part of the Shadow RAM. That doesn't stop your computer from using Shadow RAM. It just stops QEMM from using leftover parts. See Chapter 6 for details on the NOSH parameter. See Chapter 4 for details on what Shadow RAM is.

BSR Computers

Some owners of BSR computers have trouble installing MS-DOS version 5.0. After installation the computer may not start from the hard drive or from the floppy. To start the computer you must use a floppy from a previous version of DOS. Next use the SYS command to transfer the previous DOS to the hard drive, and copy the older COMMAND.COM from the floppy to the hard drive's root directory. Then copy all of the DOS floppy files to the hard drive. (If you want your old AUTOEXEC.BAT and CONFIG.SYS files, you can find them as AUTOEXEC.DAT and CONFIG.DAT on the DOS 5 Uninstall disk.) Finally, you back up the hard drive to floppies, and manually install the previous version of DOS on the hard drive.

The first fix to let DOS 5 work on the system is to turn off parameter 2 on parameter bank 1 of the computer. Unfortunately, that fix stops QEMM from working on the system. To get DOS 5.0 and QEMM, you should call BSR for a BIOS upgrade, and then install DOS and QEMM.

Altima NSX and DOS 5's EMM386

Altima's NSX 80386SX computer can have trouble with the DOS 5 EMM386.EXE device driver. Install EMM386.EXE and you may see this message:

```
EMM386 not installed—insufficient memory
```

even if you have lots of extended memory in the computer.

This problem comes from the Award BIOS "version 3.1 with a few changes" in the computer. One of the "changes" sets aside 4K of extended memory for Shadow ROM and 320K of extended memory for EMS expanded memory. This makes the BIOS different from PC standards. What's worse, you can't disable these changes—you're stuck with them.

The result: EMM386 won't work on the Altima system no matter how much extended memory you have.

The solution: Use QEMM instead of EMM386. It works with the nonstandard BIOS and can still do everything EMM386 might have to manage memory. (DOS 5's other memory management abilities, such as using HIMEM.SYS to load the DOS 5 kernel into the HMA, still work, but aren't necessary because QEMM does that too. It does all that HIMEM.SYS does.)

Toshiba 3100, PCKwik, and Windows

The Toshiba 3100 portable computer has trouble when running the PCKwik Power Pak utilities and QEMM with Windows. (This is surprising because both are bundled with the computer.)

The solution: Don't use PCKwik Power Pak and QEMM with Windows. Instead use Windows' own SMARTDRV.SYS disk cache in place of PCKwik's cache, and use Windows HIMEM.SYS instead of QEMM. Many users think this means they are living with a less capable cache and memory manager, but at least Windows works.

Toshiba 5100 and 5200

The Toshiba 5100 and 5200 portable computers are some of the most powerful portables on the market. They work with QEMM but need some special settings.

The default configuration for the 5100 does not offer any extended memory. Instead it has expanded memory and an expanded memory driver installed. When QEMM doesn't see any extended memory, it does not load, nor can it load drivers and TSRs high.

The solution is to run the Toshiba setup utility. In that program you can configure the memory as 640K of base memory, with the rest as extended memory. You don't need to create any expanded memory at this point.

Then edit the CONFIG.SYS file to remove the expanded memory driver line. It has a name such as EMM.SYS or EMM386.SYS. (If you can't find it, it may not be there, or you may need to look its name up in the manual.) Finally, install QEMM. It should load properly.

IBM PS/1

The IBM PS/1 is aimed at the home and small-business market. It is a PC-compatible, but it is newer and has some more sophisticated design features. The PS/1 works with QEMM (and QRAM) but requires some special setup steps.

First, the PS/1 boots from a ROM with built-in CONFIG.SYS and AUTOEXEC files. Because these are on a ROM, you can't change them. But as you know if you've read the earlier chapters of this book, QEMM (or QRAM) installs itself by inserting new lines in the CONFIG.SYS and AUTOEXEC.BAT files. What you need to do is choose the IBM DOS selection from the opening screen on the PS/1 (the first screen that appears when you turn the PS/1 on). Then choose Customize How System Starts from the menu.

At the prompt

```
Choose where the computer looks for the operating system
```

choose

```
Try Diskette First, Then Try Fixed Disk
```

the last parameter on the list. When you see the prompt at the bottom of the screen

```
When the System Starts From Built-in DOS the Following
Parameters Can be Set
```

choose the

```
From Disk
```

parameter for both the CONFIG.SYS and AUTOEXEC.BAT files. For

```
Disk to Read From
```

choose C.

Now your PS/1 boots from the CONFIG.SYS and AUTOEXEC.BAT files on the hard disk instead of from those unchanging versions found in the ROM.

Oops. You're not quite done yet. The CONFIG.SYS file on the hard disk has been set to Read-Only, so you can't yet add QEMM instructions to it. You need to change the CONFIG.SYS file's status to Read/Write. Do this with the DOS command:

```
C:\DOS\ATTRIB -R C:\CONFIG.SYS
```

(Type that string at the DOS prompt and then press the Enter key.)

The next step is to deal with the shell. There's a line in CONFIG.SYS that loads the shell (the program that makes DOS easier to use by adding menus to it). The shell gets in OPTIMIZE's way. You don't want to eliminate it, just take it out of operation for a bit. Find the line:

```
INSTALL=C:\DOS\SHELLSTB.COM C:\DOS\ROMSHELL.COM
```

and add the REMARK command

```
REM
```

in front of it (with a space between REM and the rest of the line) so it looks like this:

```
REM INSTALL=C:\DOS\SHELLSTB.COM C:\DOS\ROMSHELL.COM
```

Now the shell is neutralized, until you take the REM command out. (Remember to handle any CONFIG.SYS or AUTOEXEC.BAT editing with an editor or word processor that leaves only plain-text "ASCII" files.)

Now install QEMM with the standard QEMM process (see Chapter 1). Run OPTIMIZE.

After OPTIMIZE's first step, the installation halts. There's a bug in the PS/1 DOS that affects how batch files are executed. To get around it you need to edit the OPT2.BAT file. Its last line should be

```
@C:\QEMM\OPTIMIZE /SEG:XXXX /B:C C:\QEMM\LOADHI.OPT
```

or something close to that. After that line insert

```
VER
```

That's it. Now run the changed OPT2.BAT by typing

```
C:\OPT2.BAT
```

at the DOS prompt and then pressing the Enter key. OPTIMIZE finishes its work. You can then remove the REM from the shell command mentioned earlier. You're done. QEMM (or QRAM) is running in your PS/1.

Unless... Unless you have QEMM 6.0 and want to use STEALTH. A PS/1 can use STEALTH, but only if you use ST:F (see Chapter 6) or ST:M with the right EXCLUDE parameters. Also, the same bug that troubles OPTIMIZE when installing QEMM also shows up when running OPTIMIZE/STEALTH. You need to add the VER line to OPT1.TEXT and OPTAUTO.BAT after the first reboot, then run OPT1TEST, and then add VER to OPT2.BAT after the second reboot.

IBM PS/2

The PS/2 series of computers was IBM's follow up to the PC, XT, AT line. Not all PS/2 models are alike, but many added such sophisticated elements as the Micro Channel bus expansion slots.

PS/2s work with QEMM. For models 50 and 60 there is a special version called QEMM 50/60. The QEMM 50/60 memory management driver is not compatible with HIMEM.SYS (the XMS standard driver described in Chapter 4). QEMM-386's driver is compatible with XMS when you use the EXTMEM=64 parameter. QEMM-386 can convert extended memory, both off and on the motherboard, of Models 70 and 80 into LIM 4.0 expanded memory. QEMM 50/60 converts extended memory into expanded only for the Memory Expansion Parameter, XMA board, and boards completely compatible with them. It does not convert motherboard extended memory into expanded—such memory doesn't have the necessary hardware registers for tracking page frames.

If you wish to EXCLUDE E000 from STEALTH (XST=E000) on a Micro Channel bus machine, you must load the HOOKROM.SYS program as the first item in your CONFIG.SYS file, before QEMM386.SYS.

QEMM can't be used along with PS2EMM.SYS.

The IBM cache uses extended memory, not expanded. If you load it after QEMM, it won't see any extended memory, unless you reserve some for it. You can't fix the problem by loading IBMCACHE first, because QEMM's memory management confuses the system, leading to disk troubles. Load QEMM and use QEMM's EXTMEM or MEMORY parameters (see Chapter 6) to reserve as much of the extended memory that QEMM can't manage as you want in the cache. Then load IBMCACHE—it should use that memory. Use the same technique for other caches that want extended memory. (Expanded memory caches shouldn't have any trouble when loaded after QEMM.)

IBM AS/400

The IBM AS/400 terminal emulation setup is similar to that of a 5250 terminal. It takes two or three file references in CONFIG.SYS and two more loaded from the DOS prompt. Then there are other files you can load to get other terminal functions.

As of 1990 the drivers were these sizes (some get smaller in later releases): ECYDDX.SYS, 21K, and FSDD.SYS, 59K (for virtual drives, and ECYDDX.SYS must be loaded first, although in later releases the TSR STARTFLR does the same work). The TSRs were these sizes: E5250AH.COM, 8.2K (to manage terminal emulation hardware for the 5250 card—each different card for AS/400 connection requires a different managing TSR—sometimes WSEAH.COM is used instead) and STARTRTR.COM, 56K. STARTRTR needs 160K area in upper memory during loading, although it uses only 56K when loaded.

Some of the connection cards grab some RAM, such as 8K starting at CC00 or some other XC00 address. QEMM may not detect this RAM when installing, so you have to find it and exclude it yourself. You could use Manifest after loading E5250AH.COM to find the RAM. You could also add the parameter

```
/MX
```

to the E5250AH.COM line to limit the areas that E5250AH reaches in memory. (The X is the same as above—referring to the address of the 8K.)

The AS/400 STF utility doesn't always load high with QEMM 5 or 5.11. Although the LOADHI /GS parameter may report that STF needs only 26K or so to load, it sometimes doesn't load even when shown an area of 79K or so.

Some AS/400 drivers and TSRs can store themselves in expanded memory.

Some versions of STARTFLR may fail in a DESQview window when QEMM is installed and enabled.

When loaded high by QEMM 5, ECYDDX.SYS can fail and show the error message "Keyword invalid." Versions 5.11 and later don't have this trouble.

Micro Channel

The Micro Channel Adapter (MCA) is the new bus IBM introduced with the PS/2 computers. It replaces, for IBM, the Industry Standard Architecture (ISA) bus of the PC series of computers. Each bus is the set of signals that come from the computer's memory and processor to the slots. The slots are the places where you can plug in add-on boards, or cards, to add features such as memory, fax modems, or graphics processing to the computer.

The Micro Channel is more sophisticated and potentially more powerful than the older ISA bus (although it is rivaled by the competing, new EISA bus.)

QEMM (and QRAM) likes to know when it is operating on a Micro Channel machine. (Some companies other than IBM also make Micro Channel systems.) QEMM looks in its MCA.ADL file for any configuration information about Micro Channel plug-in cards, to figure out what memory addresses the computer and card wants (and which therefore QEMM cannot use).

If you use a Micro Channel computer that is not listed in the MCA.ADL file, QEMM gives you an error message. It wants you to find out about the high memory used by the network card, memory card, fax board, or other addition to the computer. If the card is new, Quarterdeck may not have added it to the MCA.ADL file yet.

To get the latest MCA.ADL file, you can

- Download it from the Quarterdeck BBS (310-314-3227, see Chapter 21 for details).
- Borrow one from a friend with a newer version of QEMM (or QRAM, it's the same file with all Quarterdeck products).
- If you can get by without an entire new file, you could call Quarterdeck technical support and have them mail or fax the details for your Micro Channel card. Then you'd use a word processor to edit your MCA.ADL file (as plain-text ASCII), adding the details to the file. You can insert them anywhere, although numerical order by Micro Channel ID numbers (in hexadecimal) is a good idea for organization.

Quarterdeck's example of this process is for an unknown Ethernet board, where you might get the message:

```
"Unrecognized Microchannel Adapter @5600"
```

Look to your MCA.ADL file and you see this:

```
5500    COREtape Controller
5502    CORE CNT-MCF Tape Controller
5606    Cabletron Ethernet Board E3010
 X X000XXXX /ARAM=C000-C3FF
 X X001XXXX /ARAM=C400-C7FF
```

```
  X X010XXXX /ARAM=C800-CBFF
  X X011XXXX /ARAM=CC00-CFFF
  X X100XXXX /ARAM=D000-D3FF
  X X101XXXX /ARAM=D400-D7FF
  X X110XXXX /ARAM=D800-DBFF
  X X111XXXX /ARAM=DC00-DFFF
```

The Cabletron board is 5600, which isn't in your MCA.ADL. Quarterdeck can tell you that this is the entry for 5600:

```
5600    Cabletron Ethernet Board E3020
  X X000XXXX /ARAM=C000-C3FF
  X X001XXXX /ARAM=C400-C7FF
  X X010XXXX /ARAM=C800-CBFF
  X X011XXXX /ARAM=CC00-CFFF
  X X100XXXX /ARAM=D000-D3FF
  X X101XXXX /ARAM=D400-D7FF
  X X110XXXX /ARAM=D800-DBFF
  X X111XXXX /ARAM=DC00-DFFF
```

When you insert this between 5502 and 5606, you'll have this:

```
5500    COREtape Controller
5502    CORE CNT-MCF Tape Controller
5600    Cabletron Ethernet Board E3020
  X X000XXXX /ARAM=C000-C3FF
  X X001XXXX /ARAM=C400-C7FF
  X X010XXXX /ARAM=C800-CBFF
  X X011XXXX /ARAM=CC00-CFFF
  X X100XXXX /ARAM=D000-D3FF
  X X101XXXX /ARAM=D400-D7FF
  X X110XXXX /ARAM=D800-DBFF
  X X111XXXX /ARAM=DC00-DFFF
```

```
5606    Cabletron Ethernet Board E3010
 X X000XXXX /ARAM=C000-C3FF
 X X001XXXX /ARAM=C400-C7FF
 X X010XXXX /ARAM=C800-CBFF
 X X011XXXX /ARAM=CC00-CFFF
 X X100XXXX /ARAM=D000-D3FF
 X X101XXXX /ARAM=D400-D7FF
 X X110XXXX /ARAM=D800-DBFF
 X X111XXXX /ARAM=DC00-DFFF
```

If Quarterdeck doesn't have the details for your card, you can send them information to let them develop the details. Send a copy of the file @XXXX.ADF from your adapter's software. (The value of XXXX depends on your card.) Quarterdeck will send the details back to you.

You may not even have a problem with QEMM and your unknown Micro Channel card. The details QEMM needs to know affect only the use of upper memory for loading device drivers and TSRs. If you don't load such things high, or are lucky enough not to overlap any of them with memory the card wants (and some cards don't use any memory), you'll never see a problem. In fact, QEMM may detect some or all of the memory used by the card anyway, using the same detection techniques it employs for standard bus PCs. QEMM then excludes those areas from its use so they won't conflict with high-loaded drivers and TSRs. In such a case you still see an "Unrecognized Microchannel Adapter" message when you run your PC, but it doesn't mean any trouble. You are given the parameter of not loading QEMM, but ignore that parameter and go ahead with loading if you haven't had any troubles.

Although you could avoid the message by using the parameter NOPAUSEONERROR, or NOPE, with the QEMM line in CONFIG.SYS, it's a bad idea because you wouldn't be told of any errors. Instead, just make your own temporary filler insertion for the MCA.ADL file. Edit that file to include an entry such as

```
XXXX  Waiting for a correct MCA.ADL entry from Quarterdeck
```

where XXXX is the number of your unrecognized adapter.

AboveBoard

Intel's AboveBoard is one of the more popular add-on memory boards. It supports most of the EMS 4.0 expanded memory specifications in hardware—the necessary abilities to let QRAM load drivers and TSRs high in an 8088, 8086, or 80286 PC. It can map EMS memory below the 640K mark, backfilling memory, and so is good for DESQvicw multitasking.

To use the backfilling ability, you must disable the motherboard's memory down below 640K, perhaps as low as 256K. Backfilling below that won't improve multitasking. Then use memory on the AboveBoard to fill in the 384K from 256 to 640K. (AboveBoard does not let you map any EMS memory pages into the video memory area.) Then specify MC (Map Conventional) as the parameter to the EMM.SYS driver that comes with AboveBoard.

Although D000 is a typical setting for a page frame, for QRAM's sake (and for DESQview's) place the page frame as low as possible in memory. C000 would be good. The AboveBoard Plus driver only maps memory above 640K as a single contiguous block, starting with the 64K page frame. Any other memory must be mapped directly above and contiguous with the page frame. (This restriction depends on the driver you have; later drivers may ease the restriction. Contact Intel for the latest driver.) In fact, AboveBoard was bundled with QRAM for a while, and the driver that came with it then defaulted to the lowest possible address for the page frame. If you manually use the CONFIG.SYS file assignment to set the page frame at C000, you get the lowest possible placement. After all, C000 is pretty low, and if that conflicts with the video ROMs or other devices—which it often does when set that low—the Intel driver detects those conflicts and then seems to place it higher, only as much as necessary to load.

Early versions of AboveBoard let you configure board memory only as extended memory in minimum units of 512K. That means if you want 64K of extended memory to support the HMA, such as to use QEXT.SYS to load part of DESQview into HMA, you must give up 512K of memory. However, the extra can be used as a disk cache or RAM disk. You can use the upgrade to configure memory in 128K units, or you can use other extended memory for the HMA if your system has it.

AboveBoard Plus won't map into the video memory area, so it may not save as much memory as you'd like.

Bus-Mastering Devices

Bus-mastering devices handle their own DMA (direct memory addressing). They don't use the computer's main processor, as other devices do. By eliminating the processor from the work, these devices are able to work much faster than those that don't bus-master. Many hard disk controllers work this way, especially SCSI (Small Computer Systems Interface) controllers, as do some network interface cards.

Unfortunately, bus-mastering can be incompatible with the virtual-86 mode of the 386 and 486 processors. The bus-mastering device can use absolute memory addresses and assume that the addresses remain constant, while the V-86 mode can quickly shift the address meanings when it pages from one virtual machine to another. That can crash or hang your computer. You could start your computer with a bus-mastering disk controller, run one DESQview application, and then crash when switching to another application. Using LOADHI with QEMM could also crash the system because the disk controller would grab an address from some area in memory that QEMM had remapped. Theoretically, such switches could simply cause wrong results due to changed data. However, the changes are commonly so large that they crash programs and system entirely, not just corrupting the results.

Some bus-mastering devices use standard DMA channels and won't have any trouble with QEMM, which can handle standard DMA.

The best solution, the most reliable with the highest performance, is to get a new driver from the bus-mastering device maker, a driver that supports the VDS (Virtual DMA Services) specification. Quarterdeck (and IBM, Microsoft, and some others) support VDS, and their programs that are compatible with it let a bus-mastering device find the real physical address of data when the processor is in V-86 mode. QEMM 5 and later support VDS.

If the bus-mastering device is a hard disk controller, the solution can be to use QEMM's DISKBUF=XX parameter to prevent QEMM-SCSI problems. XX is the number of kilobytes used for buffering the disk; 2 is enough for most systems, 10 offers more performance, and above 10 is probably a waste. DISKBUF loses a little conventional memory, but saves the trouble. If you check the documentation for your disk controller you'll often discover that it too has a driver parameter for buffering or for 386 operation. This might be a

```
/B:32
```

or

/V386

after the driver's name to set an area of buffers for DMA or to prepare for V-86 mode.

If you use Windows, you can call upon its SMARTDRV.SYS driver to double-buffer disk I/O.

A third solution is to see if your bus-mastering device can be configured to use the BIOS or one of the standard DMA channels that QEMM can handle. Check the bus-mastering device's manual.

HardCard

The HardCard plug-in hard disk drive makes it very easy to add a hard disk to a PC: you just plug it into a slot and then add the HardCard driver to the PC's software.

You can load the HardCard driver high with DOS 5 or QEMM commands. But you need QEMM 6.0 to do more than only exclude the HardCard's ROM, using an EXCLUDE parameter on the QEMM386.SYS line. You also need to add the XST=XXXX parameter (where XXXX is the address where HardCard is) to exclude the driver from STEALTH's work. Otherwise you may destroy the disk's FAT (file allocation table) when you write a file to disk, thereby losing all information on the disk.

Floppy-Disk Formatting

Having trouble formatting floppy disks? Maybe QEMM's STEALTH feature has disrupted the part of ROM that has some vital instructions for floppy formatting. This can happen when STEALTH is set with the ST:M parameter. The formatting of a 720K floppy can abort near the end. (Using the ST:F parameter doesn't usually bring on the same problem.)

The solution starts with finding out what happened. You can use QEMM's Analysis procedure, and you can use Manifest's interrupt listings to see what happened in memory. (Look especially at interrupt 13 of the First Meg Interrupts screen.)

To figure out the problem step by step, follow these instructions: Remove all QEMM parameters. In their place use just the ON parameter. (Back up CONFIG.SYS so you can return to the predetection configuration, and then edit the new CONFIG.SYS to change the parameters.) Reboot the PC, type QEMM RESET at the DOS prompt, and try to format a floppy. Then type QEMM ACCESSED MAP at the DOS prompt. You see a map of the system ROM that was last accessed. Look to the FN00 line. Write down the addresses of all "A"s in the map—areas that were accessed in the ROM's address space.

Now exclude those addresses on the QEMM line of CONFIG.SYS. (As in, EXCLUDE X=F800-FAFF, start with 00 at the end of the first address and end with FF at the end of the last address.) You may need more than one EXCLUDE to catch multiple "A"s in the map that aren't all in a row.

If you're using STEALTH, you may not want to just exclude these areas entirely. Instead you can use the ROM= parameter on them, such as ROM =F800-FAFF. Then add ROM parameters for other ROMs in the system, such as video ROMs.

Again, start the PC and try to format a floppy. If it still doesn't work, then you may not be able to use the ST:M parameter.

Konan TenTime Disk Controller

Some early versions of the Konan disk controller have a ROM and a RAM area that aren't always enabled. That means QEMM sometimes cannot find them when installing and so cannot exclude them from usable upper memory. If you have one of these controllers you need to find the RAM and ROM yourself, either by using Manifest or by looking in the controller's manual, and add appropriate EXCLUDE statements to your CONFIG.SYS file. (See Chapter 6 for details on EXCLUDE.)

Super-VGA Display Cards

Super-VGA display cards offer resolutions greater than VGA's top of 640x480 pixels. Some offer 1024x768, which makes for a much larger work area on screen or for far smoother images and text. However, using this super high resolution, the cards need more memory than simple VGA. They often use the area of upper memory officially reserved for text on a monochrome display (MDA). This region is the B000-B7FF area. QEMM usually finds this unused and provides it as an extra 32K of high memory for drivers and TSRs. If you use a super-VGA card, often for Windows in a high resolution mode, you will probably have to exclude this area from QEMM use. Add this line to QEMM:

```
X=B000-B7FF
```

XGA

The XGA video display adapter offers greater resolution and more colors than the older VGA adapter.

When using an XGA adapter with QEMM you may see a message such as "Unrecognized Microchannel Adapter 8FDB." To avoid this error you need to add this line to your MCA.ADL file:

```
8FDB   XGA Video Adapter /NT
```

(The NT parameter makes it so you won't see the QEMM logo corrupted on screen during boot-up.)

XGA cards have an adapter ROM. That ROM's address in memory can be set with the XGA Reference Diskette. QEMM detects the ROM and excludes it. QEMM 6 doesn't STEALTH the ROM because the ROM is not accessed by an interrupt. (See Chapter 6 for details on STEALTH operation.)

If you use Windows with an XGA adapter and QEMM, you may see an error message such as:

```
Cannot load enhanced memory manager
```

This can be caused by a bug in the Windows XGA driver, XGAVDD.386. This can't load if there is RAM in the first 4K area of the 32K region where the XGA ROM is located. On a PC with the XGA at D600-D7FF, the driver won't load if QEMM has put RAM at D000-D0FF. The fix: Exclude D000-D0FF in CONFIG.SYS with a line such as:

```
DEVICE=C:\QEMM\QEMM386.SYS RAM X=D000-D0FF
```

Alternatively, try using the default Windows VGA driver, *VDDVGA, instead of XGAVDD.386. You can still use XGA modes with this driver if you replace the line

```
DISPLAY=XGAVDD.386
```

in SYSTEM.INI with the line

```
DISPLAY=*VDDVGA
```

QEMM versions up to and including version 6.00 are not compatible with Windows in standard mode and XGA video modes. They may work for awhile, but then they can crash and reboot the PC. Use VGA mode or QEMM 6.01 or later.

Keyboards

Do you have a "sticky Shift key" with QEMM installed? That is, do the Shift, Control, or NumLock keys sometimes act as if they're pressed even though they're not?

This can be a result of a program that is intercepting signals for interrupt 9—the interrupt for keyboard input. Some TSRs do this, especially those that pop up when you press a hotkey combination. Other TSRs that monitor or accelerate keyboard action also grab interrupt 9. Some applications even do it, looking for keyboard input that tells them what to do. If the keyboard input isn't important to them, they pass it on to whatever device had it before interrupt 9. Several programs in a row may be grabbing, inspecting, and releasing keyboard input this way. Eventually the input should reach the ROM BIOS, the central worker for keyboard input.

Before the AT, PCs would read keyboard input by inspecting the keyboard port, resetting the keyboard, and then inspecting the keyboard port again (where another key could have been pressed). Since the AT the process is more complicated: disable the keyboard (so another key cannot be pressed during the keyboard read, although this is done in thousandths of a second so the user doesn't have to wait), read the keyboard port, reset the keyboard, and re-enable the keyboard (so a new key can be pressed). If there's a PS/2 mouse, that must be disabled too.

To stay away from such interrupt 9 trouble, programs can use interrupt 15, Function 4F, to read the keyboard.

Some of the trouble arises because a new key may be placed in the keyboard port to read before the PC has set itself up to read that port. QEMM makes this worse by slowing down the system, both by its own code and by putting the processor into virtual-86 mode. QEMM also confuses the situation by controlling port 64. This one port both is part of the keyboard reading process and controls the state of the A20 address line (which QEMM must watch because A20 controls access to the first 64K of extended memory, the HMA).

All of this is particularly likely to lead to a new key input before the old one is processed through interrupts if you have one of the 101-key keyboards made after 1987. They have separate number and cursor keypads, and the cursor pad keys generate up to 12 interrupts (6 on the way down and 6 more on the way up) when pressed with NumLock on. Some of those interrupts tell that there is an UpShift or DownShift key, and if one of those interrupts is lost during the cascade of interrupts, the PC continues to think the Shift key is pressed even when it is not.

The IGNOREA20 parameter for QEMM tells QEMM not to trap port 64. Because that is also the port for the keyboard controller chip, this also tells QEMM to ignore the keyboard.

There are several solutions. First, just tap the sticky Shift key. This sends a new set of interrupts that should alert the PC to the real keyboard condition. You may also get a new keyboard. Some have their own processors to evenly pace keyboard input to the PC. Some have setup parameters, such as A20 settings that can avoid the trouble mentioned here.

If that isn't enough, you can track down and eliminate the TSR that is confusing the interrupt chain. If you want more detail, you can use Manifest to see which programs are grabbing interrupt 9. Check the Interrupts screen of the First Meg display. Press F3 to see a list of interrupts by number.

But if that isn't reliable enough, or if you want to keep that TSR, you can use the QEMM IA parameter. Add IA to the end of the QEMM line in CONFIG.SYS, like this:

```
DEVICE=C:\QEMM\QEMM386.SYS otherparameters IA
```

IA keeps QEMM from affecting keyboard input. It tells QEMM not to trap the manipulation of the ports of the 8042 keyboard controller chip.

On Micro Channel computers, QEMM doesn't monitor port 64. Instead if monitors port 92 to watch the A20 line. So on a PS/2, using IA won't affect keyboard work.

CHAPTER TWENTY ONE

Getting Help and Support

Quarterdeck offers technical support—help in using QEMM. This chapter explains all the ways you can get this help.

Technical support includes

- Answers to questions about how the programs work
- Advice in using the programs
- Help in correcting any problems with the programs
- Upgrades to the most recent versions of programs

You can reach technical support by

- Calling
- Faxing
- Writing a letter
- Sending E-mail
- Sending an on-line bulletin board message
- Probably by showing up in person

This chapter explains how to do each of those, along with the relevant telephone numbers and addresses.

If you're in an incredible hurry, try these numbers now:

Telephone: 310-392-9701 (USA)
Fax: 310-314-3217 (USA)
BBS: 310-314-3227 (USA)
On CompuServe: GO PCVENB

Getting Ready For Support

To get tech support help with your program, follow these steps:

1. Register (if you haven't already done so)
2. Find your program's serial number and version
3. Write down the particulars of your problem (use the Problem Report in the Passport booklet, or fill out the list that follows this section)
4. Have Manifest installed in your PC (if you can, this helps in analyzing the trouble)
5. Then contact Quarterdeck

To get support, you must first register your program. Do this by filling in and sending in the Quarterdeck Product Registration Card that comes in the program box.

Register your program to be eligible for support. Registration also puts you on the lists for notification of product updates and new products. Notify Quarterdeck when you change your address if you want updates to reach you.

Once you're registered (or have at least sent the card) you can contact Quarterdeck's experts. Before you contact them, however, you should prepare yourself. They'll need to know more than just "it doesn't work." To help you as accurately and quickly as possible they'll need to know:

- Product (such as QEMM, QRAM, Manifest)
- Version # (of product)
- Serial # (of your product, see the next section for help in finding the #)

- Computer
  - Make/Model
  - Processor
  - Memory
  - Total
  - Extended (amount)
  - Expanded memory board (maker, amount on it)
- Mouse (Make)
- Network (Make and version)
- Display
  - Make/Model
  - Adapter (and how much video RAM on it)
- Disk Drives
  - Number of Diskette Drives
  - Make/Capacity
  - Number of Hard drives
  - Make/Capacity
- Modem (Make and which port it is connected to)
- DOS (Make/Version)
- Memory-resident programs (TSRs) and device drivers loaded
- Contents of your AUTOEXEC.BAT file (you can use Manifest to see this)
- Contents of CONFIG.SYS file (you can use Manifest to see this)
- Problem description (results, such as error messages or crash)
- Steps to recreate problem (what you did before it happened)

Serial numbers

Since February 13, 1992, the program's serial number is on the original disk or on the upgrade invoice (ready to be stuck on a disk if you like). This includes QEMM 6 and QRAM 2.

For versions before that, the serial number typically is on the back of the product upgrade manual or folder, on a small rectangular sticker.

Keep the number handy so you'll always know it when you call for support. Quarterdeck suggests you write it into the Passport support policies booklet.

Here are some details on finding serial numbers for the various programs:

- **DESQview 386 2.26:** on the rectangular sticker on the lower-right-hand corner of the back of the red DESQview 386 manual.

- **DESQview 2.26:** on the rectangular sticker on the lower-right-hand corner of the back of the gray booklet, "DESQview 2.26 Upgrade Booklet," which is enclosed with the main DESQview manual.

- **QEMM-386 5.0:** on the rectangular sticker on the lower-right-hand corner of the back of the red folder, "Quarterdeck Expanded Memory Manager 386," which holds the QEMM and Manifest manuals.

- **QEMM 50/60 5.0:** on the rectangular sticker on the lower-right-hand corner of the back of the purple folder, "Quarterdeck Expanded Memory Manager 50/60," which holds the QEMM 50/60 and Manifest manuals.

- **Manifest 1.0:** on the rectangular sticker on the lower-right-hand corner of the back of the blue folder, "QEMM-386," which holds the QEMM and Manifest manuals.

- **QRAM 1.0:** on the rectangular sticker on the lower-right-hand corner of the back of the green folder, "QRAM," which holds the QRAM and Manifest manuals.

On earlier versions of the programs you should look in these places:

- Lower-right-hand corner of the back of the manual
- On the original disk
- Lower-right-hand corner of the upgrade booklet
- Lower-right-hand corner of the DESQview 386 box
- Some versions of DESQview that were packaged with AST hardware boards do not have serial numbers

Support Levels

Now that you have all that information noted, you need to know your Support Level, so you know which methods you're authorized to use when contacting Quarterdeck. (The more you pay, the more ways you have.)

There are five levels of support for Quarterdeck programs: no support, Standard Passport, Extended Passport, Priority Passport, Developer Passport, and Corporate Passport. Standard comes free with the purchase of a Quarterdeck program. The other levels add to Standard but cost you extra.

No support

If you don't register your program because you made an illegal copy from someone else's original, you aren't officially entitled to support. You can get one technical support call's worth of help and can probably get some other, non-Quarterdeck help after that, but you should feel badly about asking for such a dole. (That's my recommendation, anyway, not an official statement from Quarterdeck.)

Standard Passport

This level of support is free when you buy a Quarterdeck program and register it. You get free, unlimited telephone, fax, mail, and bulletin board support for 90 days from the date of your first request. Standard level is meant to help you through installing and learning your program.

Extended Passport

This support level extends the length of time you may use the phone, fax, or mail of Standard Support. It extends the support to one year, letting you make up to 15 calls, faxes, or mailed questions during that year. (Technically it also extends the 90-day Limited Warranty on the disks your program came on. This warranty is useless, however, because it only protects the $4 disk, not the $50 to $500 software on it.) Extended Passport also gives you special prices on Quarterdeck upgrades and advance notice of those upgrades.

Priority Passport

Like Extended, this support level extends your support and your Limited Warranty to a full year, and it gives you advance notice and special prices on upgrades. But instead of the 15 contacts allowed by Extended, you're given up to 25 contacts.

The key to Priority Passport isn't the numbers, however, it's the line jumping. This support level gives you priority over Standard and Extended support callers. You immediately move to the front of the waiting line when calling, faxing, or writing for help. You get priority even when using the BBS (Bulletin Board System—a computer with a program that will automatically answer modem calls and respond to the calling computer), because you're able to reach more notes, utilities, and samples. Priority also gets you first availability on upgrades and access to written technical support white papers on frequently asked support questions.

Quarterdeck Offices Around the World

Quarterdeck Office Systems Inc.
150 Pico Blvd.
Santa Monica, CA 90405
USA
Tel: 1-310-392-9701
Fax: 1-310-314-3802
BBS: 1-310-314-3227
Compuserve: Email 76004,2310
Forum GO QUARTERDECK
BIX: Email QOS.REP2
Forum JOIN DESQVIEW
MCI Mail: Quarterdeck

Quarterdeck Office Systems Canada Inc.
70 York Street, Suite 1220
Toronto, Ontario M5J 1S9
Canada
Tel: 1-416-360-5758
Fax: 1-416-360-4885

Quarterdeck Office Systems UK Ltd.
Widford Hall, Widford Hall Lane
Chelmsford, Essex CM2 8TD
United Kingdom
Technical support:
Tel: 44-71-973-0663
Fax: 44-71-973-0664
BBS: 44-71-973-0661
Q/FAX: 44-71-973-0665
Product Information:
Tel: 44-24-549-6699
Fax: 44-24-549-5284
BBS: 44-24-526-3898

European Headquarters
Quarterdeck International
B.I.M. House, Crofton Terrace
Dun Laoghaire, Co. Dublin
Ireland
Technical support:
Tel: 353-1-2844-144
Fax: 353-1-2844-380
BBS: 353-1-2844-381
Q/FAX: 353-1-2844-383
Product Information:
Tel: 353-1-2841-444
Fax: 353-1-2844-380

Developer Passport

This level of support is for a software developer or systems integrator. It permits up to 20 calls to special, highly-technical support and API (Applications Programming Interface) specialists. It also opens up a special part of the BBS with code samples and utilities for developers. Developer support also brings the Limited Warranty extension to one year, free technical support white papers on frequently asked support questions, and advance notice and discounts on upgrades.

Quarterdeck Office Systems S.A.R.L.
4, Rue du General Lanrezac
75017 Paris
Technical support:
Tel: 33-1-44-09-03-40
Fax: 33-1-44-09-00-69
BBS: 33-1-44-09-01-07
Q/FAX: 33-1-44-09-00-81
Product Information:
Tel: 33-1-44-09-03-91
Fax: 33-1-44-09-03-47

Quarterdeck Office Systems GmbH
Willstatter Strasse 15
D-4000 Dusseldorf 11
Germany
Technical support:
Tel: 49-211-59-79-040
Fax: 49-211-59-79-060
Q/FAX: 49-211-59-79-065
Product Information:
Tel: 49-211-59-79-00
Fax: 49-211-59-41-26

Quarterdeck Office Systems Middle East Ltd
1 Souliou Street, Suite 103
Strovolos, Nicosia
Cyprus
Product Information and Support:
Tel: 357-2-311-630
Fax: 357-2-311-560

Quarterdeck Office Systems S.A.
Gran Via de les Courts
Catlanes, 617 10-3A
08007 Barcelona
Spain
Product Information and Support:
Tel: 34-3-412-29-45
Fax: 34-3-412-44-41

Corporate Passport

This level of support permits an unlimited number of calls from up to six designated employees. The calls go directly to senior technical support representatives who specialize in the corporate support. In fact, there will be specific tech support people and a direct line assigned to your company.

Corporate passport also gives priority access to the bulletin board and free copies of all white papers. Advance notice, first availability, and special prices on upgrades are also part of the deal.

International Support

This is not a different level of support, but a different source. The international support sites (offices, phones, fax, BBS) are staffed by experts with knowledge of local systems, not just of US systems. There are also international editions of the Quarterdeck programs.

Telephone Support

The easiest way to get help is to call the Quarterdeck tech support line. If you're prepared with the necessary information mentioned earlier in this chapter and can afford the call, here's the main number for the US:

310-392-9701

Remember that you have to call during open hours, which for the US are

8 AM PST - 5 PM PST or PDT Mon-Thurs
10AM PST - 5 PM PST or PDT Friday

Other numbers work if you have other support levels or are outside the US.

If you can fax or BBS for support instead of calling, you may pay a lower phone bill and you'll certainly make life easier for Quarterdeck. But they know that sometimes you need the information right now.

Fax Support

Quarterdeck's fax line is open 24 hours a day, unlike the voice answer line, which has limited hours (noted above).

You have two choices when faxing questions: You can fax a question and wait for an individualized response (Quarterdeck's tech support people can call or fax you back during their business hours); or you can use the Q/FAX service anytime and receive immediate faxed answers to common QEMM and QRAM questions.

To fax for an individual response, fax to this number (in the US):

310-314-3217

Here's how Q/FAX works:

1. Using your fax machine, type the Q/FAX number: 310-314-3214.
2. If you don't yet have the master list of fax answers, then when you hear the computer answer, type 100 and then the pound sign (#). When the Q/FAX computer says to, press the Start/Copy or Receive button on your fax machine. Q/FAX then faxes you the latest master list of fax answers.
3. Once you have the master list, choose the topic closest to your needs from that list.
4. When you hear the computer answer this time, type the number of the answer you need and then type the pound sign. You may order as many as three faxed answers each time you call. When the Q/FAX computer says to, press the Start/Copy or Receive button on your fax machine. You'll immediately receive the answers you want.

If you make a mistake when typing fax numbers, press the asterisk key (*) and type the number again.

BBS Support

Quarterdeck maintains a bulletin board system (BBS) to provide helpful information. This BBS is a program running on a computer, with that computer connected by a modem to a telephone line. It is available 24 hours a day, 7 days a week. Your answers won't appear immediately if a Quarterdeck support expert isn't on line at that moment and ready to answer, but they can come back quickly.

If you have a computer, modem, and telecommunications program, you can use the Quarterdeck BBS. Just have your program dial this number (in the US):

310-314-3227

and then follow the menus that appear. The BBS can help you through

- reading messages about QEMM and other programs
- sending your own requests for information or help
- downloading white papers about QEMM details
- downloading utility programs that could help your computing

The first time you call you'll be able to read Quarterdeck news and bulletins, read messages left for public viewing, download technical documents, and register as a BBS user. Once registered you have other services you can use, such as joining the technical and API conferences, leaving messages for other users, and getting into other file directories. (The access you have also is set by the passport support level you've paid for.)

When you want to send an individual E-mail message about QEMM, send it as a message to

```
SYSOP
```

(short for System Operator).

If you're a telecomm pro, you should know that the communications setup is 8 data bits, 1 stop bit, no parity. There are five modems for it, each a Courier HST able to move data at up to 14,400 bps. The BBS handles ASCII downloads as ASCII, XMODEM, YMODEM, Kermit, or XMODEM CRC. It handles binary (program) downloads through XMODEM, YMODEM, or ZMODEM protocols.The BBS will tell you how large the files you select are and approximately how long it will take to download them.

Many of the files you can download have been compressed with the PKZIP program. (Compressed files move through the phone line faster.) They have a filename extension of .ZIP, as in the following sample list from the BBS:

```
DVOPEN.ZIP/Bin  Bytes:  45798, Count:  111, 28-Feb-92
XGA.ZIP/Bin     Bytes:   1935, Count:  126, 27-Feb-92
WINFLO.ZIP/Bin  Bytes:  11591, Count: 4474, 25-Nov-91(29-Jan-92)
STEALT.ZIP/Bin  Bytes:   7643, Count: 3876, 16-Sep-91(29-Jan-92)
QRAM.ZIP/Bin    Bytes:   6464, Count:  785, 11-Dec-91(29-Jan-92)
PCT7.ZIP/Bin    Bytes:   3053, Count: 2071, 11-Nov-91(29-Jan-92)
DRDOS6.ZIP/Bin  Bytes:   5270, Count: 1041, 11-Dec-91(29-Jan-92)
```

To expand them so you can use them, first download the PKUNZIP program, then download the files you want, and then type (at a DOS prompt)

```
PKUNZIP FILENAME
```

replacing FILENAME with the name of the file you want to decompress. (If you use PKUNZIP, you should send in the shareware registration fee for it, as noted in the PKUNZIP itself.)

Some other programs are compressed with the ARC.EXE program, which you may also download. (These have a filename extension of .ARC.)

If you're having trouble reading mail messages about QEMM or downloading files, get on-line help for the BBS by typing H and pressing Enter.

Other Bulletin Boards

Quarterdeck's isn't the only BBS that has information about QEMM. A number of bulletin boards, many maintained just by enthusiastic individuals, some by companies for their own tech support, have discussions about DESQview, QEMM, and other related programs. Look to the tech support department for your computer, your applications, and any other pieces of computer hardware or software you have. Ask them if they have a BBS. You can also ask a local user group for recommendations.

SmartNet

SmartNet is a collection of many interconnected BBS systems. Some, but not all, carry a DESQview forum. Those that do daily update each other, so that messages or responses appearing on one will appear on the others.

The central system is the Sound of Music BBS (SOM). This has more than 1.5GB of disk storage, including more than 10,000 files for users to use.

Regional hubs call SOM every night to exchange new messages received that day. The hubs then exchange information with individual local BBSs. Quarterdeck can send technical bulletins, upgrade information, and answers to SOM, and they propagate out to the all participating BBSs on the SmartNet.

The DESQview product support conference on SmartNet covers QEMM, QRAM, and Manifest, as well as DESQview.

SmartNet Bulletin Boards

Sound Of Music	516-536-5630	Oceanside, NY
Oasis BBS	613-236-1730	Ottawa, ONT, CANADA
PC Connect	416-733-9052	Toronto, ONT, CANADA
Rose Media	416-733-2285	Toronto, ONT CANADA
Chips+ Connection	714-760-3265	Newport Beach, CA
DPS	310-459-6053	Pacific Palisades, CA
Easy Access BBS	415-829-6027	San Ramon, CA
Hideaway BBS	916-961-1042	Sacramento, CA
LAX Lighthouse	213-673-4745	Inglewood, CA
Little Angels PCBoard	213-387-5901	Los Angeles, CA
SeaHunt BBS	415-344-4348	Burlingame, CA
The CHARISMA BBS	415-349-6576	Foster City, CA
The HIDEAWAY	916-961-1042	Sacramento, CA
The Higher Powered BBS	408-737-9447	Sunnyvale, CA
The Hotline	818-567-6564	Burbank, CA
The Network 2000	415-474-4523	San Francisco, CA
The PC GFX Exchange	415-337-5416	San Francisco, CA
West Los Angeles BBS	310-838-9229	West Los Angeles, CA
Twin Peaks BBS	303-651-0225	Longmont, CO
HH Info-Net	203-738-0306	New Hartford, CT
Boston Gas BBS	617-235-6303	Wellesley, MA
Channel 1	617-354-8873	Cambridge, MA

You can get on the SmartNet through one of the local systems or by calling directly to the central Sound of Music BBS. Have your modem dial

516-536-8723

You can use this free for 90 days. After that you must pay a subscription. Also, free access is only at 1200 or 2400 bps. For the faster 9600 bps access, you must subscribe.

Travel Online	314-625-4054	St. Louis, MO
The Odyssey	201-984-6574	Morris Plains, NJ
Apollo III BBS	716-894-7386	Buffalo, NY
HI TECH NetWork	212-769-4734	New York, NY
PharmStat BBS	718-217-0898	Bayside, NY
The Big Apple BBS	516-536-1546	Rockville Centre, NY
The Invention Factory	212-431-1194	New York, NY
Blue Lake	503-655-0842	West Linn, OR
Chemeketa OnLine	503-393-5580	Salem, OR
The Underdog PCBoard	215-788-6647	Croydon, PA
Data World BBS	615-966-3574	Concord, TN
Tejas	713-681-1920	Houston, TX
The Abend BBS	713-771-2802	Houston, TX
Ye Olde Bailey	713-520-1569	Houston, TX
Arlington Software	703-532-5568	Falls Church, VA
Data Bit NETWork	703-719-9648	Alexandria, VA
Springfield Bypass	703-941-5815	Springfield, VA
The Midnite Rider	703-591-5744	Fairfax, VA
Poverty Rock	206-232-1763	Mercer Is., WA
Poverty Rock PCBoard	206-367-2596	Seattle, WA
Real Batchin'	206-391-2330	Issaquah, WA
Starfinder I	206-277-1689	Renton, WA

Dial into one of these BBSs, preferably one that's a local call for you, sign on, and then look for the DESQview conference. There should be some good QEMM information there—maybe you can even help answer someone else's question.

FidoNet

FidoNet is a lot like SmartNet—it is a collection of independent BBS systems all over the world. Each night the various Fidos exchange messages. You may ask your questions on the local Fido-running BBS PC, and get your answer back soon after that.

Go On-Line For Support

Typically, bulletin boards are small systems, run by companies or individuals. You also can use on-line services and E-mail networks to get to Quarterdeck. These are run by companies as commercial services or are interconnections of many smaller networks and individual systems. Some of the on-line systems offer only electronic mail, so you must send individual E-mail messages to the Quarterdeck representatives. Others offer E-mail and forums, so you can send individual messages or you can post messages that anyone can read. This is better, generally, because a public message can get an answer from a Quarterdeck expert and from any other subscribers to the system who might have some advice or similar experience. This is the Quarterdeck Office Systems/Electronic Technical Support effort. It is "semi-formal," meaning they could discontinue it at any time, but it's a wonderful resource for as long as it lasts (there are no signs it will stop soon).

Quarterdeck representatives answer E-mail messages sent to their addresses on

- CompuServe
- BIX
- MCI Mail
- SmartNet (mentioned above)
- FidoNet (mentioned above)

You can get answers on those services if you're a subscriber. You also can get answers on those services if you use some other service that can exchange E-mail with one of the above, as described in the "E-mail" section later.

CompuServe

CompuServe is an on-line information service that includes electronic mail; forums for discussing issues, computers, and other subjects; shopping; databases; financial information; and more. To use CompuServe you need a PC or ASCII terminal, a modem, a telecommunications program, a phone line, and a subscription to the service. You can find the subscriptions at almost any computer store. They also come free with many modems and telecommunications programs.

Two programs—TAPCIS and AUTOSIG—can automate CompuServe for you. Both are available through CompuServe itself.

Quarterdeck has technical support experts who monitor the CompuServe information service for public questions (in a Quarterdeck forum) and E-mail questions. There are many ways you can send a message to these experts. One is to have a CompuServe account and send a message directly. Send it to the CompuServe address:

76004,2310

Another is to have access to some other E-mail service that passes messages on to CompuServe (these are explained in a later section).

To discuss QEMM or other Quarterdeck products with both Quarterdeck experts and other QEMM users, type

```
GO QUARTERDECK
```

when you're hooked up to CompuServe. The first time you do this you are asked to join the PCVENB forum. It's free, so you may as well. After that, type

```
MES BRO SEC:1
```

to browse through the messages in Section 1. Read the messages that relate to your QEMM use. Quarterdeck representatives also monitor the IBM SIG (Special Interest Group) on-line to help answer questions.

To learn the various CompuServe commands type

```
HELP
```

You also can download certain files—some are information, some are programs. To download a file, type

```
LIB 1
```

and then

```
BRO
```

You see a list of the files. Then type

```
HELP
```

to get details on the downloading process.

Besides the PCVENB Section 1, you can get information on DESQview in the Multitasking section of the IBMSYS forum, Section 4.

You can even fax messages to Quarterdeck headquarters, using the CompuServe service. You don't even need a fax machine (but you do need a CompuServe account).

To send a fax to Quarterdeck using CompuServe, choose the CompuServe E-mail, and make this the address you send to:

Fax 310-314-3217

BIX

BYTE magazine is one of the most popular magazines about personal computing. *BYTE* started its own information service called BIX, for BYTE Information eXchange.

BIX offers both discussion areas and E-mail. Quarterdeck operates its own vendor support conference on BIX, which you can reach with the command

```
JOIN DESQVIEW
```

at the main BIX prompt. You may also use the BIX keyword

```
VS.QOS
```

(In fact, if you use that keyword for Quarterdeck Office Systems, you might get in on one of the special deals offered occasionally that could save you $14 off the BIX registration fee.)

To send an E-mail message to a Quarterdeck expert on BIX, address the message to

```
QOS.REP2
```

You can register for BIX by calling (with your modem) the registration line:

800-225-4129
(in MA call 617-861-9767)
(international call NU 1-31-069-015-7800)

When you reach the "login" prompt, type

```
BIX
```

At the "name" prompt, type

```
BIX.VILLE
```

BIX has a search feature that can dig through hundreds or thousands of messages to find the ones of most interest to you. Simply type

```
SEARCH WORDTOSEARCHFOR
```

(replacing WORDTOSEARCHFOR with whatever subject you want to know more about) and BIX finds and lists for you all messages in a conference that contain that search word. You may then select messages from the list and read them.

MCI Mail

MCI Mail is one of the most popular commercial E-mail services. Once you've registered for it, you pay only for the messages you send on it. These messages can be to other MCI Mail subscribers (such as Quarterdeck), to other E-mail users (via the Internet, as explained below), or even to those without computers. That is, MCI Mail prints your E-mail, stuffs it into an addressed envelope, and lets the US postal service deliver it the old-fashioned way.

You can dial into MCI Mail with your modem using an 800 number, such as

800-234-6245

Then you use the MCI Mail commands to send messages or to read messages waiting for you. Send Quarterdeck messages to

```
QUARTERDECK
```

(That's easy!) If you need help once on-line, type

```
HELP
```

Internet

The Internet is a worldwide collection of connected computers. Many other E-mail systems use the Internet as a common exchange point for E-mail, so knowing how to send a message through the Internet can be vital to you if you're not on one of the other on-line services. It's important even if you are.

Once you learn Internet addressing, you can send messages from any one of these networks to any other. Because Quarterdeck support experts monitor BIX, CompuServe, FidoNet, and MCI Mail, you'll probably want to know how to get from the other networks to those.

Here are some tips:

From Internet or UUCP or UseNet

- From Internet or UUCP or UseNet to CompuServe, send to

  ```
  76004,2310@COMPUSERVE.COM
  ```

Networks Connected to the Internet

AppleLink ....Apple Computer's network
BitNet ....an international academic network
BIX ....the BYTE Information eXchange, a service created by *BYTE* magazine
CompuServe ....a commercial on-line information service
Connect ....a commercial on-line service
EasyNet ....Digital Equipment's network
Envoy-100 ....a commercial E-mail service in Canada
FidoNet ....a widespread network of Fido bulletin board programs running on PCs
GeoNet ....the GeoNet Mailbox Systems commercial on-line service
MCI Mail ....a commercial E-mail service
NASA Mail ....the National Aeronautics and Space Administration's own E-mail system
SI Net ....Schlumberger's own information network
Span ....the Space Physics Analysis Network, which includes HEPnet
SprintMail ....a commercial E-mail service, which used to be called Telemail

- From Internet or UUCP or UseNet to MCI Mail, send to

  `QUARTERDECK@MCIMAIL.COM`

- From Internet or UUCP or UseNet to BIX, send to

  `QOS.REP2@DCIBIX.DAS.NET`

From Connect

- From Connect to CompuServe, send to

  `CONNECT ID: DASNET`

  and make the first line of the message

  `\76004.2310@COMPUSERVE.COM\@DASNET`

- From Connect to MCI Mail, send to

  `CONNECT ID: DASNET`

  and make the first line of the message

  `\QUARTERDECK@MCIMAIL.COM\@DASNET`

- From Connect to BIX, send to

  `CONNECT ID: DASNET`

  and make the first line of the message

  `\QOS.REP2@DCIBIX.DAS.NET\@DASNET`

From SprintMail

- From SprintMail to CompuServe, send to

  ```
  [RFC-822=76004.2310(a)COMPUSERVE.COM@GATEWAY]
  INTERNET/TELEMAIL/US
  ```

- From SprintMail to MCI Mail, send to

  ```
  [RFC-822=QUARTERDECK(a)MCIMAIL.COM@GATEWAY]
  INTERNET/TELEMAIL/US
  ```

- From SprintMail to BIX, send to

  ```
  [RFC-822=QOS.REP2(a)DCIBIX.DAS.NET@GATEWAY]
  INTERNET/TELEMAIL/US
  ```

From AppleLink

- From AppleLink to FidoNet, send to

  `QOS.TECH@DAWGGON/FIDONET.ORG@INTERNET#`

- From AppleLink to CompuServe, send to

  `76004.2310@COMPUSERVE.COM@INTERNET#`

- From AppleLink to MCI Mail, send to

  `QUARTERDECK@MCIMAIL.COM@INTERNET#`

- From AppleLink to BIX, send to

  `QOS.REP2@DCIBIX.DAS.NET@INTERNET#`

From BitNet

- From BitNet to FidoNet, send to

  `QOS.TECH@DAWGGON.FIDONET.ORG`

- From BitNet to CompuServe, send to

  `76004.2310@COMPUSERVE.COM`

- From BitNet to MCI Mail, send to

  `QUARTERDECK@MCIMAIL.COM`

- From BitNet to BIX, send to

  `QOS.REP2@DCIBIX.DAS.NET`

From EasyNet

- From EasyNet to FidoNet, using VMS, use NMAIL to send to

  `NM%DECWRL::\QOS.TECH@DAWGGON.FIDONET.ORG\`

- From EasyNet to FidoNet, using Ultrix, send to

  `QOS.TECH@DAWGGON.FIDONET.ORG`

- From EasyNet to CompuServe, using VMS, use NMAIL to send to

  `NM%DECWRL::\76004.2310@COMPUSERVE.COM\`

- From EasyNet to CompuServe, using Ultrix, send to

  `76004.2310@COMPUSERVE.COM`

- From EasyNet to MCI Mail, using VMS, use NMAIL to send to

  `NM%DECWRL::\QUARTERDECK@MCIMAIL.COM\`

- From EasyNet to MCI Mail, using Ultrix, send to

  `QUARTERDECK@MCIMAIL.COM`

- From EasyNet to BIX, using VMS, use NMAIL to send to

  `NM%DECWRL::\QOS.REP2@DCIBIX.DAS.NET\`

- From EasyNet to BIX, using Ultrix, send to

  `QOS.REP2@DCIBIX.DAS.NET`

From Envoy

- From Envoy to CompuServe, send to

  `[RFC-822=\76004.2310(a)COMPUSERVE.COM\]`
  `INTERNET/TELEMAIL/US`

- From Envoy to MCI Mail, send to

  `[RFC-822=\QUARTERDECK(a)MCIMAIL.COM\]`
  `INTERNET/TELEMAIL/US`

- From Envoy to BIX, send to

  `[RFC-822=\QOS.REP2(a)DCIBIX.DAS.NET\]`
  `INTERNET/TELEMAIL/US`

From GeoNet

- From GeoNet to CompuServe, send to

  `DASNET`

  and make the subject line

  `76004.2310@COMPUSERVE.COM!SUBJECT`

- From GeoNet to MCI Mail, send to

  `DASNET`

  and make the subject line

  `QUARTERDECK@MCIMAIL.COM!SUBJECT`

- From GeoNet to BIX, send to

  `DASNET`

  and make the subject line

  `QOS.REP2@DCIBIX.DAS.NET!SUBJECT`

From NASA Mail

- From NASA Mail to CompuServe, send to

  ```
  POSTMAN
  ```

  Make the subject whatever you like, and make the first line of your message (what you write just after the Text: prompt)

  ```
  To: "76004.2310@COMPUSERVE.COM"
  ```

- From NASA Mail to MCI Mail, send to

  ```
  POSTMAN
  ```

  Make the subject whatever you like, and make the first line of your message (what you write just after the Text: prompt)

  ```
  To: "QUARTERDECK@MCIMAIL.COM"
  ```

- From NASA Mail to BIX, send to

  ```
  POSTMAN
  ```

  Make the subject whatever you like, and make the first line of your message (what you write just after the Text: prompt)

  ```
  To:"QOS.REP2@DCIBIX.DAS.NET"
  ```

From SI Net

- From SI Net to Compuserve, send to

  ```
  M_MAILNOW::M_INTERNET::\76004.2310@COMPUSERVE.COM\
  ```

  or to

  ```
  M_MAILNOW::M_INTERNET::COMPUSERVE.COM::76004.2310
  ```

- From SI Net to MCI Mail, send to

  ```
  M_MAILNOW::M_INTERNET::\QUARTERDECK@MCIMAIL.COM\
  ```

  or to

  ```
  M_MAILNOW::M_INTERNET::MCIMAIL.COM::QUARTERDECK
  ```

- From SI Net to BIX, send to

  ```
  M_MAILNOW::M_INTERNET::\QOS.REP2@DCIBIX.DAS.NET\
  ```

  or to

  ```
  M_MAILNOW::M_INTERNET::DCIBIX.DAS.NET::QOS.REP2
  ```

From Span

- From Span to CompuServe, send to

```
AMES::\76004.2310@COMPUSERVE.COM\
```

- From Span to MCI Mail, send to

```
AMES::\QUARTERDECK@MCIMAIL.COM\
```

- From Span to BIX, send to

```
AMES::\QOS.REP2@DCIBIX.DAS.NET
```

Upgrades

Quarterdeck is always developing new versions of the programs, adding power and eliminating bugs.

When a new version with significant changes is released, it is called an update and is given a new version number, such as from 4.0 to 5.0 or from 6.0 to 6.1. When a version is released without such major changes, it is called a compatibility update. These have number changes to the second digit after the decimal, such as 6.01 to 6.02. Generally they are intended to provide compatibility with some new popular program or computer. (QEMM may not have been compatible as it was.) Quarterdeck decides when to issue compatibility releases based on the number of technical support calls it receives about the product and on the sales of the product. You won't be automatically notified of compatibility updates.

You should get the latest version of your program for the most complete compatibility with any hardware and other programs you might use. Getting the latest also buys you new features, such as the STEALTH feature of QEMM 6.0.

There is no set schedule for new releases, but you will be notified if you've registered. (You did register, didn't you?)

However, new versions aren't free. To pay for the development and manufacturing costs, Quarterdeck does charge you, though not as much as if you were buying the program for the first time. You can order compatibility updates for just a shipping and handling cost, or you can receive them free when you have Extended, Priority, Developer, or Corporate level support.

Training and DESQaway

Quarterdeck offers training in its memory management products and DESQview. These DESQaway courses range from beginning level to advanced, for everyone from the novice installing the program to the expert looking for optimum network configurations. Anyone attending a course finds

- reference materials (a Quarterdeck-produced manual)
- computers (Quarterdeck supplies the hardware and software)
- instructors (this is not video training, but real live stuff)
- a free copy of Manifest (the memory analysis utility, described elsewhere in this book)

For details on training, call 800-LEARN DV (800-532-7638).

The courses

These were the courses in 1992:

- PC-Intro/DOS
- Intro to Memory Management
- Advanced Memory Management/QEMM
- Intro to DESQview
- Advanced DESQview
- DESQview/X
- DESQaway Retreat

The PC-Intro/DOS class and the DESQaway Retreat are for those with little or no knowledge of PCs.

The other introductory courses are for people who know only a little about PCs, perhaps understanding a half dozen DOS commands (Copy, Del, Format, CD, MD, and so on) and the purpose (and basic contents) of the PC's CONFIG.SYS and AUTOEXEC.BAT files.

The advanced courses are for people who configure PCs by editing BAT and SYS files. These courses are also geared to those who have completed the introductory courses. Typical enrollees are consultants, programmers, network administrators, and value-added resellers (VARs).

Intro to Memory Management covers hardware and software schemes to free memory. Conventional, extended, and expanded memory are grist for the class. It tells when extended is preferred over expanded. You'll see how to load TSRs and device drivers into high RAM to free conventional memory for applications. The course teaches using Manifest to see what memory is doing and then QEMM, QRAM, LOADHI, and OPTIMIZE to find and set the best use of memory. To get the most from the class, enrollees should be familiar with basic PC operations and DOS commands.

Advanced Memory Management/QEMM describes how to install QEMM to optimize memory use. It covers the Analyze, OPTIMIZE, and Manifest QEMM utilities and delves into network (finding the best address for a network adapter), video, and misbehaving applications troubles. It also covers using QEMM with DOS 5 and Windows 3. To get the most from this course, enrollees should have taken Intro to Memory Management or have otherwise come to understand conventional, extended, and expanded memory.

Intro to DESQview tells how to install the DESQview program, how to open programs within DESQview, how to switch among those programs, how to display more than one program at a time, how to move information between programs, and how to best configure DESQview. Along the way it explains multitasking and task switching with an eye to how much memory you need to handle these, and what sort of processor chip makes them possible. To get the most from the course, enrollees should know basic PC operations and DOS commands, and ideally know a bit about memory (such as what is taught in the Intro to Memory Management course).

Advanced DESQview digs deeper into the configuration parameters that tell DESQview how to use memory, allocate graphics resources, and run the processor most efficiently. This includes the Change Program screen with its allocation of conventional and expanded memory for programs, optimization of graphics programs, letting programs run in background, and using terminal emulators. Fine-tuning DESQview with hardware such as networks, modems, and tape backups is part of the course, which also tackles advanced subjects such as mixed text and graphics, working with Windows, running communications in the background, screen bleed-through, network issues, losing screens when switching, and handling memory-use conflicts. To get the most from the course, enrollees should know something about memory and about DESQview, either independently or from the introductory memory and DESQview courses.

The DESQview/X class explains what this latest version of DESQview is and how the X Windows technology in it can connect workstations and PCs. Naturally it also covers installation, networking, and resource sharing.

Course locations

These were the cities where courses were presented in 1992:

- Los Angeles (Santa Monica)
- New York
- Boston
- Miami
- Washington, D.C.
- Denver
- Chicago
- Detroit
- St. Louis
- Houston
- Minneapolis
- Philadelphia
- Phoenix
- Seattle
- Salt Lake City
- San Francisco
- San Jose
- Dallas/Fort Worth
- Toronto
- Ottawa
- Montreal
- Calgary
- Vancouver
- London
- Paris
- Dusseldorf

There are other places to get trained.

Perhaps the most luxurious is the DESQaway Retreat, which teaches the basics of DOS, DESQview, WordPerfect, 1-2-3, and Time Line in a week spent at a vacation spot such as Point Reyes National Seashore or Palm Springs. The classes are no larger than eight students, and each has their own PC for the twice-daily training sessions.

Training is also available on site. An instructor can come to a company's site or to a conference center. The instructors investigate the company's specific uses of PCs and Quarterdeck programs in advance so they can tailor the material to the site, with relevant examples.

DESQaway instructors and Quarterdeck Technical Support experts can be called to a company's site not just to provide training but to help install, configure, and optimize Quarterdeck software.

Video

Quarterdeck offers a 90-minute VHS video on memory management, with three lessons by Gary Saxer focusing on memory basics, optimization, and use. It covers QEMM, QRAM, MANIFEST, and DESQview.

DESQaway sites for training and office services

Finally, there are the DESQaway offices. Quarterdeck needed sites for its training sessions because not all could take place within company walls. Quarterdeck executives also believed the market for temporary offices—equipped with com-

DESQaway Offices

DESQaway Los Angeles
Edgemar
2445 Main Street
Santa Monica, CA 90405
Tel: 1-310-314-4280
Fax: 1-310-314-4276
Contact: Orla Buckley

DESQaway London
Clareville House
26-27 Oxendon St.
London SW1Y 4EL
Tel: 44-71-973-0988
Fax: 44-71-973-0981
Contact: Elaine Pinkster

DESQaway New York
Rockefeller Center
1270 Avenue of the Americas
New York, NY 10020
Tel: 1-212-314-4280
Contact: Maricela Gabb

DESQaway Paris
4 Rue du General Lanrezac
75017 Paris
Tel: 1-44-09-03-91
Fax: 1-44-09-03-47
Contact: Susan Lurachi

DESQaway Toronto
70 York Street
Toronto, Ontario M5J 1S9
Tel: 1-416-360-5758
Fax: 1-416-360-4885
Contact: Cambria Ravenhill

DESQaway Dusseldorf
Willstatter Strasse 15
D-4000 Dusseldorf 11
Tel: 49-211-597900
Fax: 49-211-594126
Contact: Chris Granderath

puters for those who needed some PC time but didn't need or couldn't afford full time—was growing. So they decided to create DESQaway training centers. These offices offer both training and business services. The training covers QEMM, QRAM, and DESQview, naturally, but also takes in WordPerfect, Lotus 1-2-3, dBASE, Paradox, and other programs. Special classes cover troubleshooting systems and programs. Quarterdeck expects traveling executives, small business owners, sales representatives, and conference organizers to use the facilities.

Each office has

- desks with PCs (386s with word processor, spreadsheet, and other software)
- photocopiers, fax machines, and laser printers
- a conference room
- a newsstand with computer magazines from around the world
- audio and video recorders and players
- refreshments
- personnel to explain and operate the above

You can duck into a DESQaway office to

- Make a copy.
- Use a PC.
- Make a call. (You get your own phone with private number and a personal voice-mail box: you record the outgoing message and retrieve received message 24 hours a day, remotely. Calls are logged for you. The offices are set up with a discounted international calling service to England, Ireland, France, and Germany. The discount may soon apply to calls and faxes to other parts of Europe and to Canada.)
- Send a fax or receive a fax. (Received faxes are sorted into private fax boxes and are then available 24 hours a day, and only to you.)
- Receive a parcel. (The parcel boxes are accessible 24 hours a day.)
- Get technical support on Quarterdeck programs.
- Demonstrate a product.
- Give an interview.
- Hold a meeting or give a seminar (in the conference room).

- Pay to have word processing or other secretarial chores done.
- Take a class (one of the DESQaway training courses mentioned above).

Costs

There are no long-term leases or contracts for DESQaway services. You pay as you go. You can use anything from an hour to a year's time in the office, paying for the equipment time you use, the telecomm charges, and the labor. Registered Quarterdeck program owners can receive a 10% rate reduction.

DESQview User Magazine

All of the standard PC magazines—such as *PC Magazine, PC World*, and *PC Computing*—review new versions of QEMM and contain hints on using it. But for the most focused information, you can look to *DESQview User Magazine*, a quarterly published in the UK. This has regular articles on QEMM, DESQview, and other Quarterdeck products.

DESQview User Magazine
Widford Hall, Widford Hall Lane
Chelmsford, Essex CM2 8TD
Tel: 44-0245-496699
Fax: 44-0245-495284
Editor in Chief: Andrew Ward

Utilities

There are some useful utilities available on the Quarterdeck BBS and on disks from Quarterdeck and the *DESQview User Magazine*. For example, the Issue 3 Support Disk from *DESQview User Magazine* offers QTEST, a utility to tell you whether QRAM can help on your PC, as well as a disk cache program and other utilities. The Issue 4 Support Disk contains technical notes on using Windows 3 with Quarterdeck programs. All of the support disks from the magazine contain lots of useful utilities for DESQview owners.

Quarterdeck White Papers and QWHITE.COM

Quarterdeck publishes white papers with information from the tech support staff. Each covers a single topic about QEMM, QRAM, DESQview, or other Quarterdeck programs. The white papers change as they are periodically updated to cover the latest changes in software. With some of the software support levels, you automatically get these papers. Otherwise you need to call the Quarterdeck BBS and download them, or use Q/FAX (see the "Fax support" section) to receive them. Quarterdeck also offers a DESQview program—QWHITE.COM—to let you read the papers from disk.

APPENDIX A

QEMM Installation

QEMM is easy to start, as Chapter 1 explains. But it is a deep program, with many parameters. This appendix tells you how to choose among those parameters.

This appendix is a detailed description of the automatic installation process. When you're ready to improve on this installation, to learn about QEMM and then to flex that knowledge, turn to Chapter 3. (Skim Chapters 4 and 5 if you need a review of memory terms.)

Quick use of QEMM comes just from having a 386 or 486 system, putting the QEMM disk into the floppy drive, typing A:INSTALL, and then confirming all of QEMM's default suggestions by pressing Enter when asked. Follow the instructions on screen. That's it!

Here's the QEMM installation process in detail:

1. Have a PC-compatible computer with a 386, 386SX, 486, 486SX, or compatible microprocessor. (Ask when you buy, or have a knowledgeable friend tell you if your PC has such a main chip.)

2. Have the DOS operating system software running on that PC (any MS-DOS, Compaq-DOS, or PC-DOS version from 3 to 5).

3. Have a hard disk on that PC. (You can install QEMM on a floppy-based system, as explained in Appendix C. But because any PC needs a hard disk for good performance, and hard disks are inexpensive these days, I will assume you have a hard disk.)

4. Have at least 384K of extended memory in that computer (the amount typically found in a PC with 1MB of RAM).

5. You may have any other software you want installed on the hard disk, including applications such as WordPerfect or Lotus 1-2-3, and operating system extensions, such as Windows and DESQview.

6. Turn on your PC. Watch it warm up and wait until the DOS prompt, typically something like

   ```
   C>
   ```

   appears on the screen.

7. QEMM comes on a single disk. On the front label is a serial number. Write this number down here:

   Serial Number:________________________

   You'll need the serial number when asking questions of Quarterdeck technical support experts, as explained in Chapter 21. If you don't have the serial number because you've copied the disk, you can find it in a later installation display (as noted below). If you don't have the serial number because this isn't really your copy of QEMM, think about how little QEMM costs (less than $100 nearly everywhere) versus how much it can do for your PC and how happy you'll be to have a serial number if some scruffy program gives you memory trouble at some point.

   Write your serial number down—it'll ease life later.

8. Put the QEMM disk into your PC's floppy disk drive A. (If you have a single floppy drive, it is A. If you have two, one of them is A, probably the one on top. If that doesn't help, ask that knowledgeable friend for help again.)

9. Type

```
DIR:A
```

and press Enter. You'll see something like the display in Figure A-1.

```
C>a:dir
Bad command or file name

C>dir a:

 Volume in drive A is QEMM386-602
 Volume Serial Number is 2F6E-0DC9
 Directory of A:\

INSTALL  EXE     77490 11-13-91   6:02a
QEMM386  QIP    251366 11-13-91   6:02a
        2 file(s)     328856 bytes
                      400384 bytes free

C>
```

Figure A-1. QEMM files on disk

You can see from this that there are only two files on the QEMM disk: INSTALL.EXE and QEMM386.QIP. From these, though, you get a whole bunch of programs and files that make up QEMM. They are all compressed into the single QEMM386.QIP file so they fit neatly on a single disk. The INSTALL.EXE file is a program that creates the appropriate QEMM directory on your hard disk, decompresses the QEMM files from QEMM386.QIP, and copies those files to the QEMM directory. Then it even installs the fundamental QEMM commands in your AUTOEXEC.BAT and CONFIG.SYS files, where they automatically take charge of memory each time you turn on your PC.

10. From the C> prompt, type

```
A:INSTALL
```

and press Enter. You'll see the display of Figure A-2 (which shows your serial number). As the display says, press the Esc key to quit at this point, or press the Enter key to continue installation.

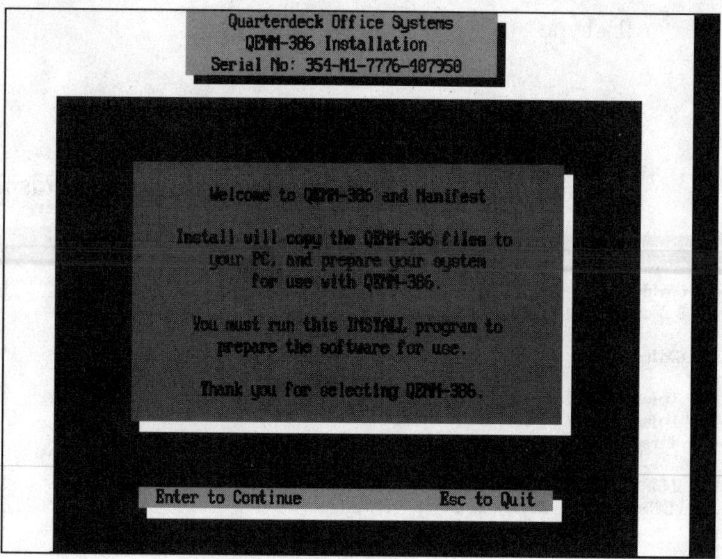

Quarterdeck Office Systems
QEMM-386 Installation
Serial No: 354-M1-7776-407958
Welcome to QEMM-386 and Manifest
Install will copy the QEMM-386 files to
your PC, and prepare your system
for use with QEMM-386.
You must run this INSTALL program to
prepare the software for use.
Thank you for selecting QEMM-386.
Enter to Continue
Esc to Quit

Figure A-2.
Serial Number display

11. You'll be asked for your Owner Information at this point. Type your name and address to imprint them on the QEMM floppy. Then anyone using your floppy is reminded from whom they got QEMM (and may be prompted to buy their own copy). If the floppy has been "ownerized" before, you can just press Enter at this point.

12. Where do you want to put QEMM on your hard disk? Unless you have some special reason to put it elsewhere, just go with the default directory

```
C:\QEMM
```

as shown in Figure A-3. Press Enter to confirm this direction.

If you want it in another directory, type that directory name and press Enter.

QEMM now asks you to confirm where the files are coming from, and where they are going to on the hard disk (the destination path). Press Enter to confirm these choices.

13. QEMM does its most important work by putting commands into the CONFIG.SYS file. This file is created by DOS and altered by many

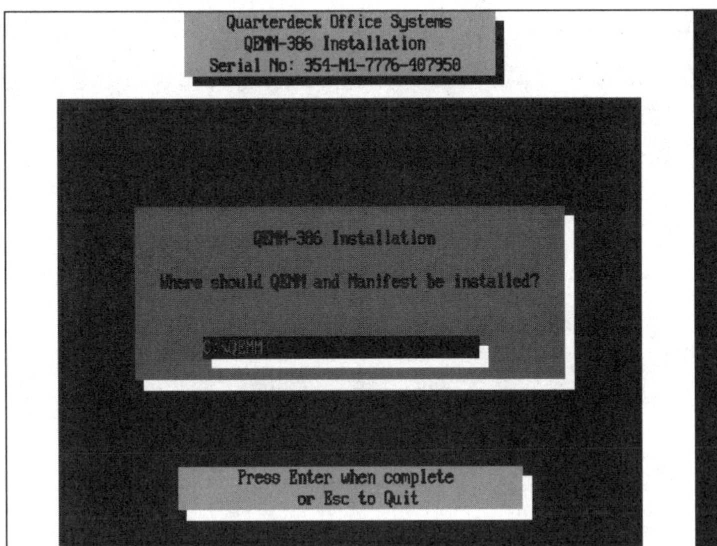

Figure A-3. Changing the directory

programs you put into your PC. (See Chapter 4 for details on CONFIG.SYS.) CONFIG.SYS should be in the root directory, that is, the main directory of your hard disk. This is the directory symbolized by the DOS backslash prompt, as in

```
C:\
```

If the file is not in the root directory, QEMM can't find it immediately. If that happens, QEMM asks you where it is:

```
Where is your boot drive for CONFIG.SYS to be updated?
```

Press the letter for the disk drive that has DOS and the CONFIG.SYS file. If that's too confusing, ask your knowledgeable friend for help or call Quarterdeck.

14. Now comes the default choice. QEMM is smart enough to do a good job setting up for your PC. It makes some choices, called the defaults, for various memory parameters. If you want to just try those—I strongly suggest you do—press Enter at the display of Figure A-4.

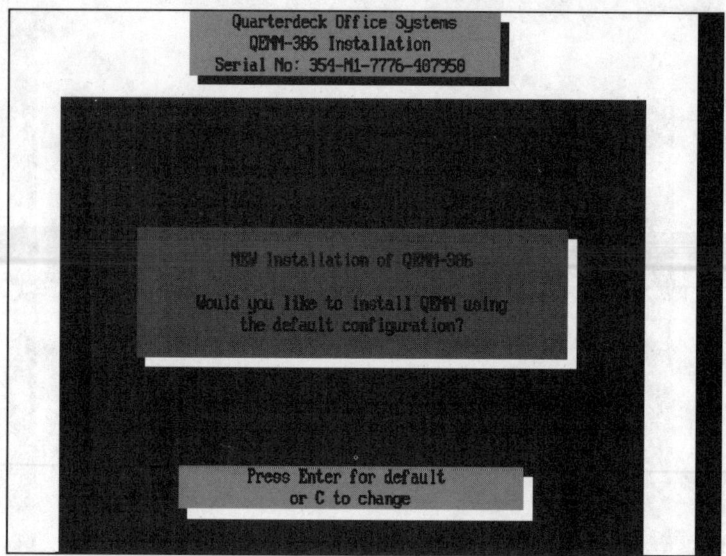

Figure A-4. Choosing the defaults for QEMM

If you don't want the defaults, if you want to try your hand at perfecting QEMM operation, instead press C for Change. You'll see the display of Figure A-5. To understand the parameter settings here, look to Chapters 5 through 14.

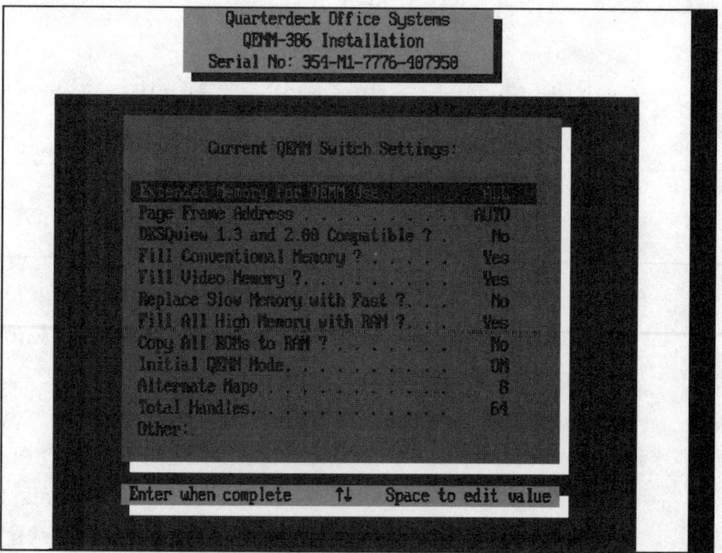

Figure A-5. Changing from the defaults in QEMM

15. Again QEMM asks if you want to stick with its default ideas. Press Enter to agree.

16. Finally QEMM's INSTALL program starts decompressing files and putting them in place. It lets you know about how long the process will take (about a minute on my PC) and shows you the files as they are copied.

17. As it installs, QEMM looks to see if you have Windows on your hard disk.

    If you do, it alters the Windows SYSTEM.INI file so that Windows works smoothly with QEMM. (This is true as of QEMM version 6.) If it does not find Windows, it tells you so. You can then press W to tell it where Windows is hiding on the hard disk, or just remember that this Windows alteration will be necessary later. (You can do it later by running the QWINFIX program any time after you install Windows.) Press Enter to continue installing QEMM.

18. The display in Figure A-6 alerts you that QEMM has been installed. The READ.ME file offered to you is a collection of details and news that are too recent to be in the QEMM manual. Unless you're in a breakneck hurry (in which case you can always read READ.ME later)

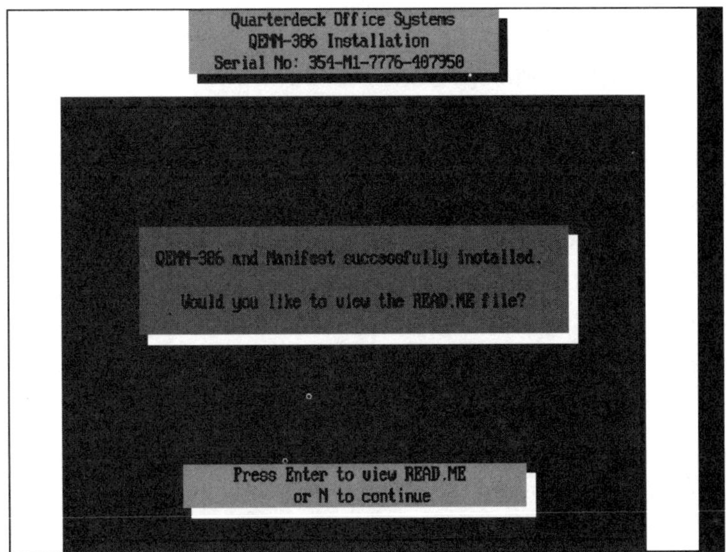

Figure A-6.
What you see when QEMM is done installing

take a minute now to scroll through READ.ME. Press Enter to do so, N to hurry on without.

19. When reading, press PgUp and PgDn or the UpArrow and DownArrow keys to scroll through the READ.ME file. Figure A-7 shows an example page. When you're done reading, press Enter again.

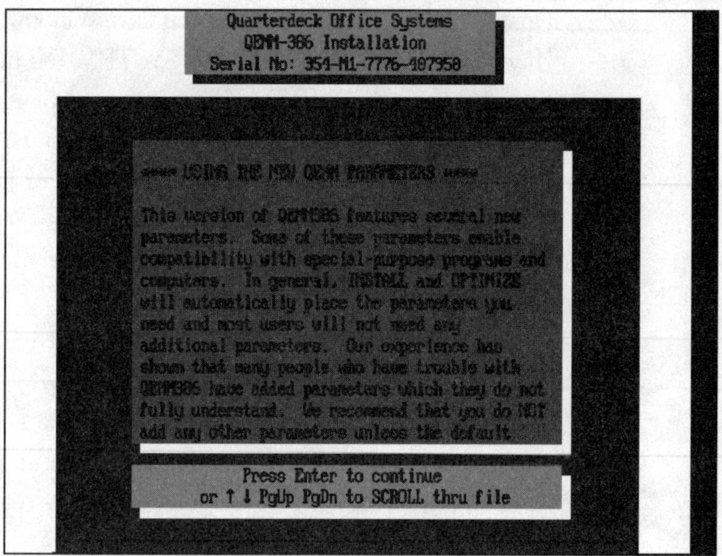

Figure A-7. Example of a READ.ME file page

20. Now installation is really complete—sort of.

Remove the QEMM floppy from drive A.

As the screen in Figure A-8 tells you, you need to reboot your PC to have QEMM operate. (The PC only reads the QEMM instructions from the CONFIG.SYS and AUTOEXEC.BAT files when your PC is turned on, or rebooted.)

However, even going that far isn't enough. You'll want to run the OPTIMIZE program to see the true default setup for QEMM.

With QEMM version 5 you need to reboot the PC, change to the QEMM directory, and run the OPTIMIZE program yourself by typing

```
OPTIMIZE
```

and then pressing Enter.

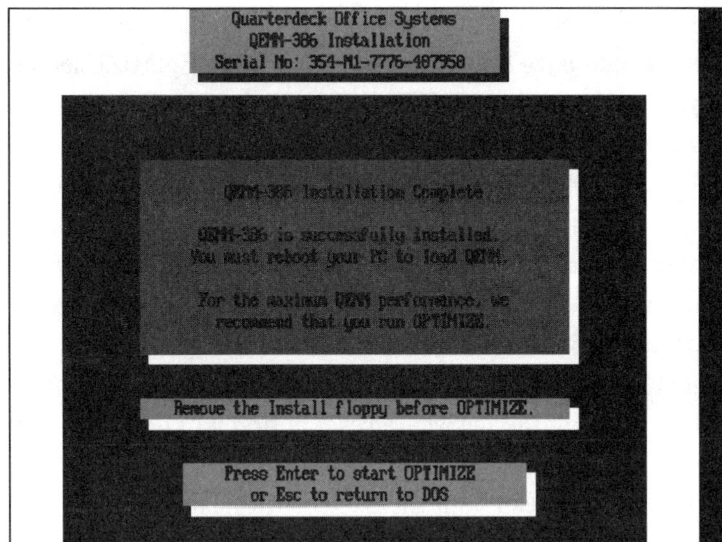

Figure A-8.
Your instructions on rebooting for OPTIMIZE

With QEMM version 6 you can start OPTIMIZE automatically just by pressing Enter from Figure A-8. That's what I advise.

21. OPTIMIZE starts with the display of Figure A-9. This program guesses and tests all the ways you could use QEMM's ability to move driver and utility programs from precious conventional memory to newly set

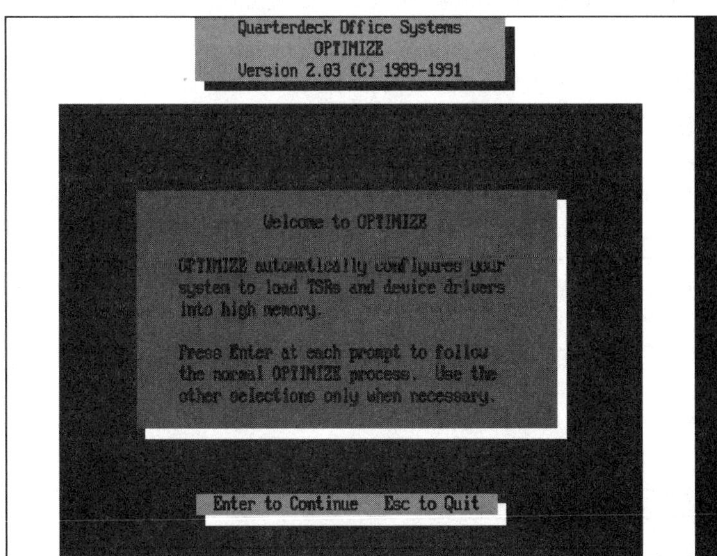

Figure A-9.
OPTIMIZE starts

up upper memory blocks (that QEMM set up!). You don't have to be a memory whiz and have hours to tinker if you let OPTIMIZE loose. However, you can improve on OPTIMIZE's results if you learn about memory and experiment with QEMM.

Press Enter to let OPTIMIZE work, or press Esc to quit using it.

As OPTIMIZE runs it examines memory to see how large its parts are and where they are, it examines your programs to see how much memory they need, and then it logically plays with the programs to fit as many as possible into the least memory. To do this it must reboot the PC to get QEMM working. (Some computers require that you actually reboot by pressing the hardware reset button for OPTIMIZE, or by turning the power off completely. Leave it off for 10 seconds, then turn it back on. Others can do it themselves with a software equivalent of the Ctrl-Alt-Del key combination that starts the PC working from scratch without turning the power off—a warm reboot.)

Your original CONFIG.SYS and AUTOEXEC.BAT files are saved as CONFIG.QDK and AUTOEXEC.QDK, just in case you want to get back to your original setup. If you quit OPTIMIZE at any point, these files are put back into practice immediately.

22. After it has thoroughly experimented, OPTIMIZE reports its analysis to you. You'll see a display that says something like

```
Analysis Complete
```

OPTIMIZE has tried all combinations of loading X resident programs into X high RAM regions. The best configuration found was:

Resident programs loaded high:	XX
Conventional memory used:	XX
High RAM used:	XX
Largest free block of high RAM:	XX
Total free high RAM:	XX
Total combinations:	XX

The "X"s stand for numbers that depend on your particular PC's amount of memory, programs to use, and so on.

At this point you can continue with OPTIMIZE's suggested defaults, its best-guess memory setup (by pressing Enter), or you can try your hand at some parameters (by pressing O).

23. The parameters are:
    1. Display the region layout.
    2. Modify the data collected during the detection phase and rerun the analysis.
    3. Play "what-if" with the order in which you load TSRs. Your configuration files won't change.

    Press 1 to see the details on the memory setup, press 2 to modify the data, and press 3 to change the TSR loading order. See Chapter 4 to understand these terms and Chapters 5 through 14 for details on using the parameters.

OPTIMIZE does not include conditionally executed programs in its analysis. If you have IF EXIST... IF ERRORLEVEL..., or IF %VARIABLE%=, remove them from your AUTOEXEC.BAT and any batch files it calls. Set up for the most likely configuration.

24. The final phase of OPTIMIZE takes the defaults and puts them into CONFIG.SYS and AUTOEXEC.BAT. Press Enter to continue with this. Then you'll see a report that OPTIMIZE has completed its work, and that some amount more memory, from a few kilobytes to hundreds, is free for your DOS programs to run within.

25. Press Enter and you are back at the DOS prompt, ready to compute, with QEMM installed and handling extended, expanded, and high memory. Most times you won't even know it is there, although you may notice how much faster and easier your PC can run and how it can handle some programs that wouldn't fit before. Sometimes QEMM's work is obvious, other times it is more like insurance—not apparent until you really need it.
26. To see the changes to CONFIG.SYS and AUTOEXEC.BAT you can

start the Manifest utility by typing

```
MFT
```

at the DOS prompt for the QEMM directory and then pressing Enter (see Chapter 4 for details), or you can change to the root directory of your hard disk and type

```
TYPE CONFIG.SYS
```

and press Enter, then

```
TYPE AUTOEXEC.BAT
```

and press Enter. CONFIG.SYS will have lines such as

```
DEVICE=C:\QEMM\QEMM386.SYS RAM
```

while AUTOEXEC.BAT will have lines such as

```
C:\QEMM\LOADHI/R:4 C:\QEMM\BUFFERS=15
```

The particulars of these lines depend on your programs, memory, and PC.

For details on improving your QEMM installation, see Chapter 6.

APPENDIX B

QRAM Installation

QRAM is easy to start, as Chapter 1 explains. But it is a deep program, with many parameters. This appendix tells you how to choose among those parameters.

This appendix is a detailed description of the automatic installation process. When you're ready to improve on this installation, to learn about QRAM and then to flex that knowledge, turn to Chapter 3. (Skim Chapters 4 and 5 if you need a review of memory terms.)

Quick use of QRAM comes just from having an 8088, 8086, or 286 system (and adding a LIM EMS 4.0 expanded memory board to any of the above for yet more benefits), putting the QRAM disk into the floppy drive, typing A:INSTALL, and then confirming all of QRAM's default suggestions by pressing Enter when asked. Then you can run the OPTIMIZE program as advised by the screen instructions. That's it!

Here's the QRAM installation process in detail:

1. Have a PC-compatible computer with an 8088, 8086, 80286, or compatible. (Ask when you buy, or have a knowledgeable friend tell you if your PC has such a main chip.)

2. Have the DOS operating system software running on that PC (any MS-DOS, Compaq-DOS, or PC-DOS version from 3 to 5).

3. Have a hard disk on that PC. (You can install QRAM on a floppy-based system, as explained in Appendix C. But because any PC needs a hard

disk for good performance, and hard disks are inexpensive these days, I will assume you have a hard disk.)

4. For an 80286 computer, have some extended memory. For an 8088 or 8086 computer, have an EEMS or EMS 4.0 expanded memory board with some expanded memory or a Chips & Technologics NEAT, LEAP, or SCAT Shadow RAM. See Chapters 4 and 5 for explanations of these items.

5. You may have any other software you want installed on the hard disk, including applications such as WordPerfect or Lotus 1-2-3 and operating system extensions such as Windows and DESQview.

6. Turn on your PC. Watch it warm up and wait until the DOS prompt, typically something like

   ```
   C>
   ```

   appears on the screen.

7. QRAM comes on a single disk. On the front label is a serial number. Write this number down here:

   Serial Number:____________________________

   You'll need the serial number when asking questions of Quarterdeck technical support experts, as explained in Chapter 21. If you don't have the serial number because you've copied the disk, you can find it in a later installation display (as noted below). If you don't have the serial number because this isn't really your copy of QRAM, think about how little QRAM costs (a good deal less than $100 nearly everywhere) versus how much it can do for your PC and how happy you'll be to have a serial number if some scruffy program gives you memory trouble at some point.

Write your serial number down—it'll ease life later.

8. Put the QRAM disk into your PC's floppy disk drive A. (If you have a single floppy drive, it is A. If you have two, one of them is A, probably the one on top. If that doesn't help, ask that knowledgeable friend for help again.)

9. Type

```
DIR A:
```

and press Enter. You'll see something like the display in Figure B-1.

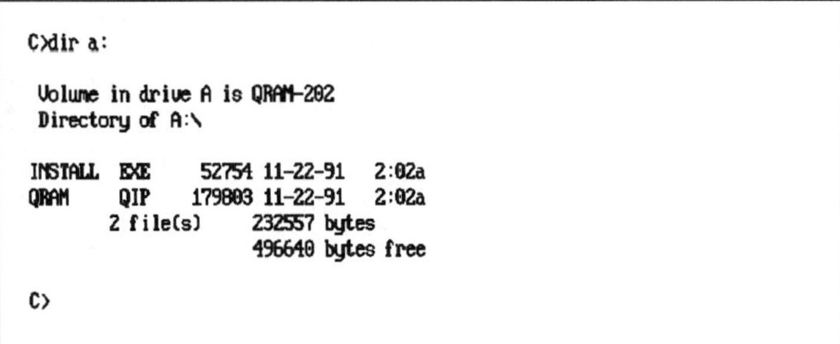

```
C>dir a:

 Volume in drive A is QRAM-202
 Directory of A:\

INSTALL  EXE     52754 11-22-91   2:02a
QRAM     QIP    179803 11-22-91   2:02a
        2 file(s)     232557 bytes
                      496640 bytes free

C>
```

Figure B-1.
QRAM files on disk

You can see from this that there are only two files on the QRAM disk: INSTALL.EXE and QRAM.QIP. In fact, QRAM is a whole bunch of programs and files, but they are all compressed into the single QRAM.QIP file so they fit neatly on a single disk. The INSTALL.EXE file is a program that creates the appropriate QRAM directory on your hard disk, decompresses the QRAM files from QRAM.QIP, and copies those files to the QRAM directory. Then it even installs the fundamental QRAM commands in your AUTOEXEC.BAT and CONFIG.SYS files, where they automatically take charge of memory each time you turn on your PC.

10. From the C> prompt, type

```
A:INSTALL
```

and press Enter. You'll see the display of Figure B-2 (which shows your serial number). As the display says, press the Esc key to quit at this point, or press the Enter key to continue installation.

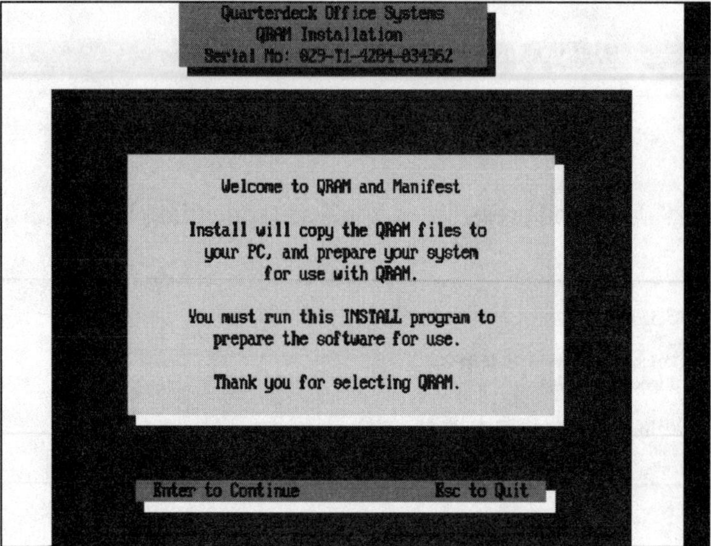

Quarterdeck Office Systems
QRAM Installation
Serial No: 029-T1-4284-034362
Welcome to QRAM and Manifest
Install will copy the QRAM files to
your PC, and prepare your system
for use with QRAM.
You must run this INSTALL program to
prepare the software for use.
Thank you for selecting QRAM.
Enter to Continue
Esc to Quit

Figure B-2. Serial Number display

11. You'll be asked for your Owner Information at this point. Type your name and address to imprint them on the QRAM floppy. Then anyone using your floppy is reminded from whom they got QRAM (and may be prompted to buy their own copy). If the floppy has been "ownerized" before, you can just press Enter at this point.

12. Where do you want to put QRAM on your hard disk? Unless you have some special reason to put it elsewhere, just go with the default directory

    ```
    C:\QRAM
    ```

    as shown in Figure B-3. Press Enter to confirm this direction.

    If you do want it in another directory, type that directory name and press Enter.

    QRAM now asks you to confirm where the files are coming from and where they are going to on the hard disk (the destination path). Press Enter to confirm these choices.

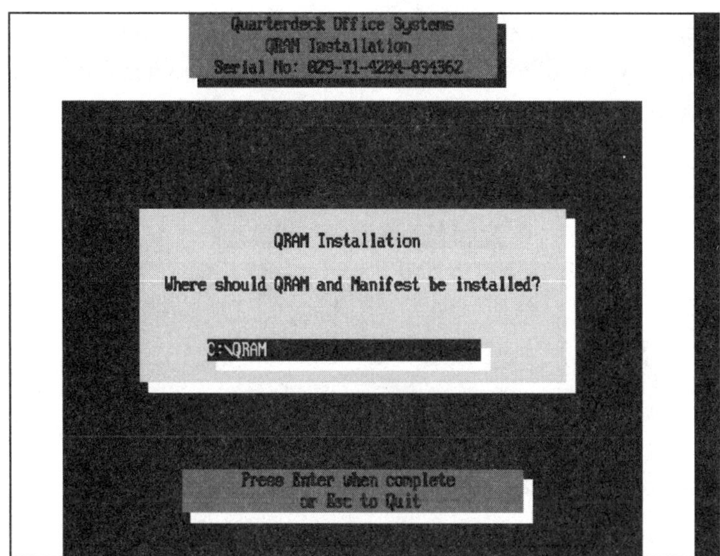

Figure B-3. Changing the directory

13. QRAM does its most important work by putting commands into the CONFIG.SYS file. This file is created by DOS and altered by many programs you put into your PC. (See Chapter 4 for details on CONFIG.SYS.) CONFIG.SYS should be in the root directory, that is, the main directory of your hard disk. This is the directory symbolized by the DOS backslash prompt, as in

    ```
    C:\
    ```

    If the file is not in the root directory, QRAM can't find it immediately. If that happens, QRAM asks you where it is:

    ```
    Where is your boot drive for CONFIG.SYS to be updated?
    ```

    Press the letter for the disk drive that has DOS and the CONFIG.SYS file. If that's too confusing, ask your knowledgeable friend for help or call Quarterdeck.

14. Now comes the default choice. QRAM is smart enough to do a pretty good job setting up for your PC. It makes some choices, called the

defaults, for various memory parameters. If you want to just try those—I strongly suggest you do—press N at the display of Figure B-4. If you don't want the defaults, press Enter.

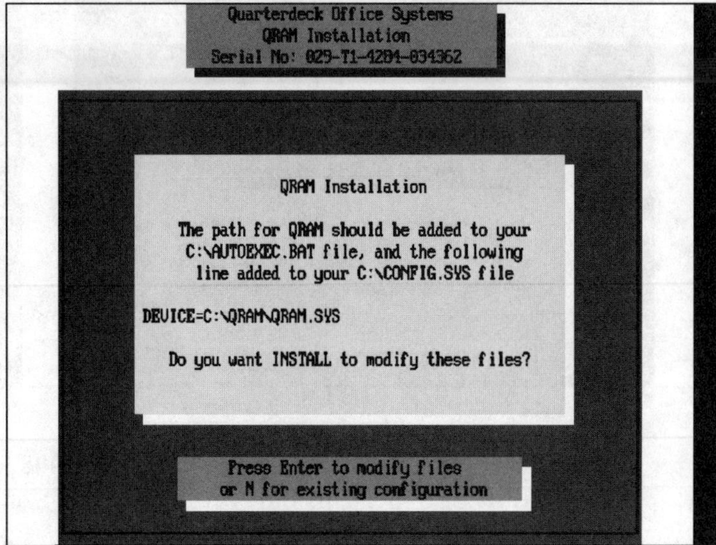
Quarterdeck Office Systems
QRAM Installation
Serial No: 029-T1-4201-034362
QRAM Installation
The path for QRAM should be added to your
C:\AUTOEXEC.BAT file, and the following
line added to your C:\CONFIG.SYS file
DEVICE=C:\QRAM\QRAM.SYS
Do you want INSTALL to modify these files?
Press Enter to modify files
or N for existing configuration

Figure B-4. Choosing the defaults for QRAM

15. Finally QRAM's INSTALL program starts decompressing files and putting them in place. It lets you know about how long the process will take (about a minute on my PC), and shows you the files as they are copied.

16. The display in Figure B-5 alerts you that QRAM has been installed. The READ.ME file offered to you is a collection of details and news that are too recent to be in the QRAM manual. Unless you're in a breakneck hurry (in which case you can always read READ.ME later), take a minute now to scroll through READ.ME. Press Enter to do so, N to hurry on without.

17. When reading, press PgUp and PgDn or the UpArrow and DownArrow keys to scroll through the READ.ME file. Figure B-6 shows an example page. When you're done reading, press Enter again.

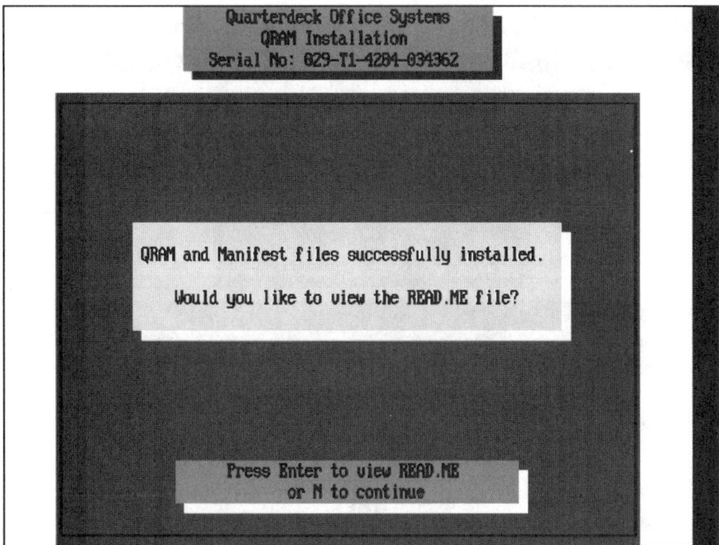

Figure B-5. What you see when QRAM is done installing

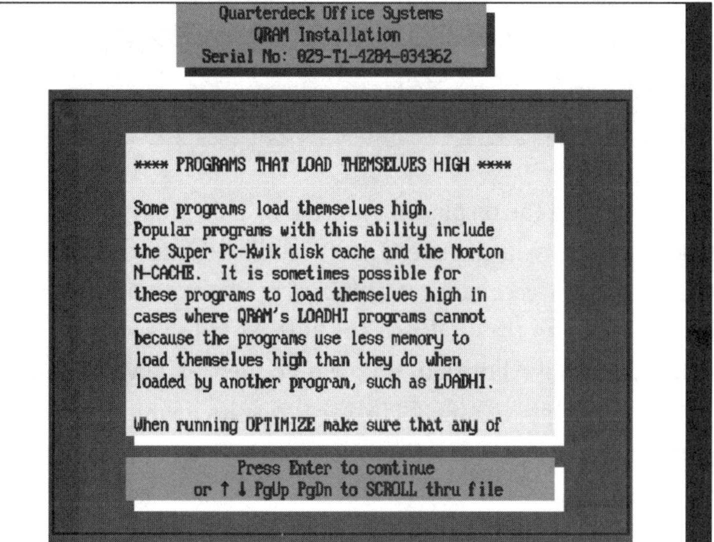

Figure B-6. Example of a READ.ME file page

18. Now installation is really complete—sort of.

    Remove the QRAM floppy from drive A.

    As told in Figure B-7, you need to reboot your PC to have QRAM actually operate. (The PC reads the QRAM instructions from the CONFIG.SYS and AUTOEXEC.BAT files only when your PC is turned on or rebooted.)

However, even going that far isn't enough. You'll want to run the OPTIMIZE program to see the true default setup for QRAM.

You can start OPTIMIZE automatically just by pressing Enter from Figure B-7.

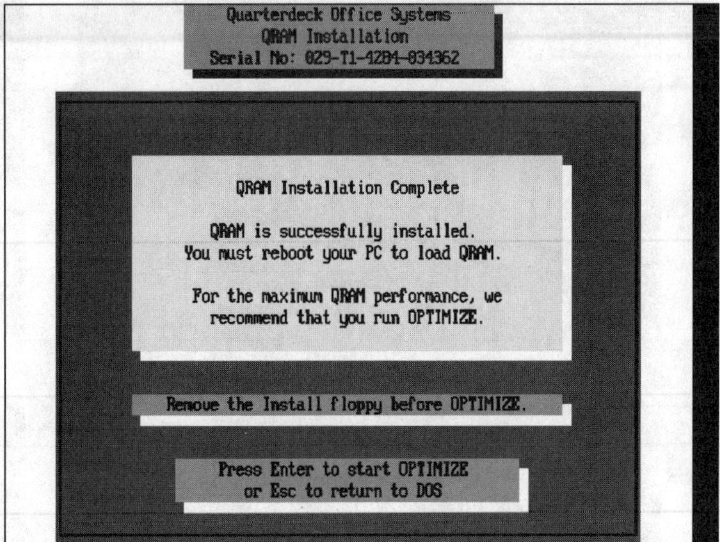

Quarterdeck Office Systems
QRAM Installation
Serial No: 029-T1-1204-034362
QRAM Installation Complete
QRAM is successfully installed.
You must reboot your PC to load QRAM.
For the maximum QRAM performance, we recommend that you run OPTIMIZE.
Remove the Install floppy before OPTIMIZE.
Press Enter to start OPTIMIZE
or Esc to return to DOS

Figure B-7. Your instructions on rebooting for OPTIMIZE

19. OPTIMIZE starts with the display of Figure B-8. This program guesses and tests all the ways you can use QRAM's ability to move driver and utility programs from precious conventional memory to newly set up upper memory blocks (that QRAM set up!). You don't have to be a memory whiz and have hours to tinker if you let OPTIMIZE loose. However, you can improve on OPTIMIZE's results if you learn about memory and experiment with QRAM.

    Press Enter to let OPTIMIZE work, or press Esc to quit using it.

    As OPTIMIZE runs it examines memory to see how large its parts are and where they are, examines your programs to see how much memory they need, and then logically plays with the programs to fit as many as possible into the least memory. To do this it must reboot the PC to get QRAM working. (Some computers require that you actually reboot by pressing the hardware reset button for OPTIMIZE or by turning the power off completely. Leave it off for 10 seconds, and

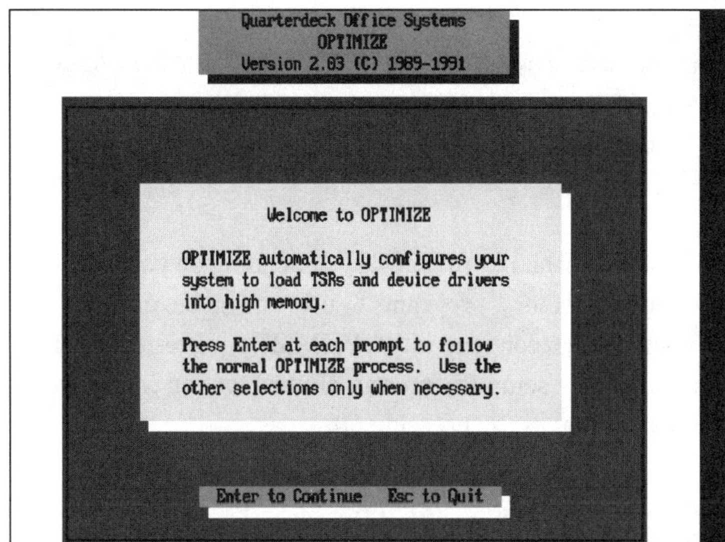

Figure B-8. OPTIMIZE starts

then turn it back on. Other PCs can do it themselves with a software equivalent of the Ctrl-Alt-Del key combination that starts the PC working from scratch without turning the power off—a warm reboot.)

Your original CONFIG.SYS and AUTOEXEC.BAT files are saved as CONFIG.QDK and AUTOEXEC.QDK just in case you want to get back to your original setup. If you quit OPTIMIZE at any point, these files will be put back into practice immediately.

20. After it has thoroughly experimented, OPTIMIZE reports its analysis to you. You'll see a display that will say something like:

```
Analysis Complete
```

OPTIMIZE has tried all combinations of loading X resident programs into X high RAM regions. The best configuration found was:

Resident programs loaded high:	XX
Conventional memory used:	XX
High RAM used:	XX

Largest free block of high RAM:	XX
Total free high RAM:	XX
Total combinations:	XX

The "X"s stand for numbers that vary depending on your particular PC's amount of memory, programs to use, and so on.

At this point you can continue with OPTIMIZE's suggested defaults, its best-guess memory setup (by pressing Enter), or you can try your hand at some parameters (by pressing O).

21. The parameters are:
    1. Display the region layout.
    2. Modify the data collected during the detection phase and rerun the analysis.
    3. Play "what-if" with the order in which TSRs are loaded. No changes will be made to your configuration files.

    Press 1 to see the details on the memory setup, press 2 to modify the data, and press 3 to change the TSR loading order. See Chapter 4 to understand these terms and Chapter 6 for details on using the parameters.

OPTIMIZE does not include conditionally executed programs in its analysis. If you have IF EXIST..., IF ERRORLEVEL, or IF %VARIABLE%=, remove them from your AUTOEXEC.BAT and any batch files it calls. Set up for the most likely configuration.

22. The final phase of OPTIMIZE then takes the defaults and puts them into CONFIG.SYS and AUTOEXEC.BAT. Press Enter to continue with this. Then you'll see a report that OPTIMIZE has completed its work and that some amount more memory, from a few kilobytes to hundreds, is free for your DOS programs to run within.

23. Press Enter and you are back at the DOS prompt, ready to compute, with QRAM installed and handling extended, expanded, and high memory on an 80286 or expanded memory on an 8088 or 8086 machine with an EMS board. Most times you won't even know it is there, although you may notice how much faster and easier your PC can run and how it can handle some programs that wouldn't fit before. Sometimes QRAM's work is obvious, other times it is more like insurance—not apparent until you really need it.

24. To see the changes to CONFIG.SYS and AUTOEXEC.BAT, you can start the Manifest utility by typing

```
MFT
```

at the DOS prompt for the QRAM directory, and then pressing Enter (see Chapter 5 for details), or you can change to the root directory of your hard disk and type

```
TYPE CONFIG.SYS
```

and press Enter, then

```
TYPE AUTOEXEC.BAT
```

and press Enter. CONFIG.SYS will have lines such as

```
DEVICE=C:\QRAM\QRAM.SYS
```

while AUTOEXEC.BAT will have lines such as

```
C:\QRAM\LOADHI MOUSE.SYS
```

The particulars of these lines depend on your programs, memory, and PC.

For details on improving your QRAM installation, see Chapter 6.

APPENDIX C

Installing Without a Hard Disk

You can use QEMM (or QRAM) on PCs that don't have hard disks. The minimum you need is a floppy disk drive on the PC for the QEMM installation disk, and another disk drive to install the files too. This can be a hard disk on another PC, a network disk, another floppy disk drive, or even a RAM disk.

First you run INSTALL to install QEMM to the other disk drive. Then you copy the QEMM files from that disk to the startup floppy of your destination PC.

Start INSTALL, and when asked

```
Where Should QEMM and Manifest be Installed?
```

answer

```
X:\QEMMDISK
```

where X is whatever the letter that designates the other drive (network, RAM, floppy, or whatever). The other drive can even be on another computer, where you install QEMM to that computer and then copy the files to a startup floppy you carry back to the first computer.

When INSTALL is done, don't run OPTIMIZE. Copy the new QEMM files to your startup floppy. If you've installed to a network hard disk, pull out the QEMM disk and put the network startup disk into the single floppy drive. Create a QEMM directory on the network startup disk and copy all files from the

X:\QEMM directory to the A:\QEMM directory. Commands such as

```
MD QEMM
CD QEMM
COPY X:\QEMM\*.* *.*
```

will do the trick. If you get the message "Not enough memory" for the copy operation, copy only the QEMM file itself, as here:

```
COPY X:\QEMM\QEMM*.SYS *.*
```

If you install to a floppy, you could install to your startup disk (or a copy of it, which is safer). If you didn't, copy the files to the startup disk. If you installed to a RAM disk, copy the files to your startup floppy, without rebooting (that would lose all files in the RAM disk). If you installed to the hard disk of another computer, then copy the files there to your own PC's startup disk.

Then you must create a CONFIG.SYS file that will tell your floppy-only PC about QEMM. Put this line

```
DEVICE=A:\QEMM\QEMM386.SYS RAM ST:M
```

in CONFIG.SYS.

APPENDIX D

Troubleshooting

The QEMM and QRAM manuals offer some basic troubleshooting hints, which are summarized here.

1. **Want to load TSRs and drivers high.**
   Use the RAM parameter, and then use the LOADHI command.

2. **Want more processing speed.**
   Use the ROM parameter (to copy ROMs into faster RAM).

3. **Want more memory.**
   Use the INCLUDE parameter to tell QEMM which part of high RAM to make available.

4. **System crashing.**
   Use the EXCLUDE parameter to keep QEMM from mapping memory over some vital hardware it didn't recognize.

5. **Troubles with network.**
   Use the ADAPTERRAM or ADAPTERROM parameter to tell QEMM where network adapter RAM and ROM is. (These parameters work like EXCLUDE.)

6. **Troubles with Compaq PC.**
   Use the NOCOMPAQFEATURES parameter to shut off all Compaq-specific parameters, including COMPAQEGAROM (which relocates video ROM), COMPAQHALFROM (which splits the system ROM in

half to make the redundant half useful as high memory), or COMPAQROMMEMORY (which speeds the system by using reserved addresses for shadowing ROMs and for loading TSRs and drivers).

Some older programs don't find extended memory, even though it is there. Such programs may not follow the XMS specification for using extended memory. Use the EXTMEM=X parameter to set aside X kilobytes of extended memory that won't be converted into expanded memory.

7. **Want to limit QEMM's use of extended memory.**
   Use the MEM=X parameter to tell QEMM not to use X kilobytes of extended memory.

8. **Want to move page frame (because some hardware is at its proposed address or because the entire reserved memory area is too crowded).**
   Use the FRAME=X parameter, where X is the beginning address of the page frame. (X is NONE if you don't need a page frame.)

9. **Want to prevent a small program from monopolizing the HMA.**
   Use the HMAMIN parameter to set a lower limit on the amount of HMA a program can request and actually get rights to the HMA.

10. **Want to prevent any program from using the HMA.**
    Use the NOHMA parameter.

11. **Want to experiment with QEMM parameters.**
    Use the PAUSE parameter. This pauses the display when outputting messages, so you can press Esc to stop QEMM from installing with its new parameters.

12. **Want to know if interrupt troubles are making your computer run slowly.**
    Use the WATCHDOG parameter with WD=1 for a PS/2 or WD=2 for a Compaq Deskpro 386.

13. **Want to use DOS 5's EMM386 for expanded memory management but QEMM for extended memory management.**
    Use the NOEMS parameter.

14. **Want to use DOS 5's HIMEM.SYS for extended memory management but QEMM for expanded memory management.**
    Use the NOXMS parameter.

15. **Don't want to see the message that hardware isn't in the MCA.ADL file.**
    Use the NOPE parameter.

16. **Have a SCSI hard disk controller that does bus mastering and DMA.**
    Use the DISKBUF parameter.

17. **Have a program that wants to regulate the length of DMA transfers.**
    Use the DMA=XXX parameter.

18. **See a message of "Insufficient DOS Buffers."**
    Use the HANDLES= parameter to specify more.

19. **Typing on the keyboard sends out inappropriate results.**
    Use the IGNOREA20 parameter (although this also disables HIMEM.SYS).

20. **Want to multitask many programs.**
    Use the MAPS= parameter to specify at least one map per program, plus one original map.

21. **PC has trouble when backfilling memory below 640K.**
    Use the NOFILL parameter.

22. **Want to save 4K of memory.**
    Use the NOROM parameter so the 4K reboot page won't be mapped.

23. Program reboots itself when it's loading.
Use the NOROMHOLES parameter (to disable QEMM's attempt to detect and use holes in the ROM).

24. Troubles with Shadow RAM.
Use the NOSHADOWRAM or NOSH parameter.

25. Get parity errors using Windows 3, a PS/2 Model 80, a Compaq Deskpro, an Inboard PC, or an early ALR computer.
Use the NOSORT parameter to sort memory by speed.

26. Troubles when using a very large memory cache or a Northgate Tower PC or when running Windows in enhanced mode.
Try the NOTOPMEMORY parameter.

27. Troubles when using Mountain tape backup or an Inboard AT that won't run Windows in enhanced mode or have Norton Disk Doctor.
Use the NOVIDEOFILL parameter.

28. Troubles with a Tandy 4024, 1046SX, Grid 386, or Quantum IDE drives.
Use the NOXBDA parameter.

29. Using old version of DESQview (version 1.3 or 2.0).
Use the OLDDV parameter.

30. Troubles with a communication program—it hangs.
Use the TA parameter (which you should only have to use with QEMM versions before 5).

31. Have a nonstandard 8042 keyboard controller.
Use the UNUSUAL8042 or U8 parameter.

32. **Have a 286 that was turned into a 386 with a lot of unusual extended memory in it.**
    Use the UNUSUALEXT parameter.

33. **Have a program that writes directly into the page frame using BIOS-level calls (such as PC-Cache, Norton 5.0's N-Cache, and Compaq's Cache) and want to use EMS memory, not XMS, for the cache.**
    Use the DISKBUFFRAME parameter.

34. **Have loaded HIMEM.SYS to handle XMS calls and don't want QEMM to make XMS calls.**
    Use the DONTUSEXMS parameter.

35. **Recently upgraded from DOS 3.3 to DOS 4, and Lotus 1-2-3 2.2 is not working under DESQview.**
    Use the DOS4 parameter.

36. **Want to multitask PageMaker 4.0 and Autocad in Windows, but Autocad can't find memory it needs.**
    Use the EMBMEM parameter to set the maximum amount of memory that programs can use by the XMS specification.

37. **Want to EXCLUDE an area but want to use STEALTH.**
    Use the EXCLUDE parameter, which does not stop ROM relocation by STEALTH.

38. **Have a program that won't start because it detects that an interrupt is not pointing to the system BIOS.**
    Use the EXCLUDESTEALTHINT or XSTI parameter.

39. **The video is not displaying properly when using STEALTH.**
    Use the FASTINT10:N or F10 parameter.

40. Don't have a 64K contiguous area above 640K for the page frame, but want to use EMS and don't want to put the page frame below 640K.
Use the FORCEEMS parameter (but this only works with programs that can use a partial page frame).

41. Don't have a 64K contiguous area above 640K for page frame and don't want to put it below 640K.
Use the FRAMELENGTH=X or FL parameter to tell QEMM to assume a page frame with X pages (cannot be used with STEALTH).

42. Want accurate analysis of memory though using STEALTH.
Use the FORCESTEALTHCOPY:Y or FSTC parameter (but only for troubleshooting—remove it when configuring for real).

43. Troubles when using STEALTH.
Use the FRAMEBUF:N or FB parameter to turn off the breaking up of disk reads into the page frame and disk writes from the page frame.

44. Have XT and DOS 2.01 where QEMM doesn't work.
Use the IOTRAP=64 parameter.

45. Have a PS/2 on a network and want to include some high memory areas, but have a mix of QEMM-386 and QEMM-50/60 PCs on the network.
Use the INCLUDE386 parameter, which works just like INCLUDE but can be added to the MCA.ADL file as a QEMM-386-specific switch that won't be found as a parameter by QEMM-50/60 or QRAM.

46. Have a 10Net network.
Use the LOCKDMA parameter to keep interrupts disabled during DMA.

47. Never run Windows 3 in any mode but real, and want to save 1K conventional memory.
Use the NOWINDOWS3 parameter.

48. **Want system to run faster, don't use Windows, and have memory chips from many sources.**
Use the SORT:Y parameter to sort memory use by speed. (This is the default anyway.)

49. **Want more high memory to use.**
Use the STEALTH parameter ST:X, where X is M for mapping or F for the frame method.

50. **Have a laptop with the Suspend/Resume feature and QEMM keeps crashing when the laptop is turned on or off.**
Use the SUS parameter or SUS:XX, where XX is 2, 72, 73, or 77.

51. **Have a disk cache that works with QEMM 6 and STEALTH and would like to try the cache's advanced feature.**
Use the VIRTUALHDIRQ:N parameter.

52. **Have trouble running Windows in enhanced mode, and can't seem to find two files with a .VXD extension.**
Use the VXDDIR= parameter to tell QEMM where WINHIRAM.VXD and WINSTLTH.VXD are.

53. **Have PC on which STEALTH doesn't work, and have discovered that one specific section of the ROMs should not be stealthed.**
Use the XST= parameter to exclude those ROMs.

APPENDIX E

Things to Know
Before Contacting Tech Support

Record as many of these things as you can before calling Quarterdeck for technical support. It'll savc cvcrybody time. If you don't know them, use Manifest (see Chapter 5).

Serial # (on your QEMM or QRAM) ______________________

Hardware

- Computer
  - Make/model ______________________
  - Processor ______________________
- Memory
  - Total ______________________
  - Extended (amount) ______________________
  - Expanded memory board ______________________
- Mouse (make) ______________________
- Network (make) ______________________
- Display
  - CRT Make/model ______________________
  - Adapter Make/model ______________________

Disk drives

- # Diskette drives—Make/capacity ______________________
- # Hard drives—Make/capacity ______________________
- Controller—Make/model ______________________

Modem

- Make ______________________
- Other boards in system (scanner, voice mail, sound) ______________________

  ____

Software

- Quarterdeck product—Version # ______________________
- DOS—make/version ______________________
- Memory-resident programs/device drivers loaded ______________________

  ____
- Contents of AUTOEXEC.BAT file ______________________

  ____

  ____
- Contents of CONFIG.SYS file ______________________

  ____

  ____

Problem description ______________________

____

____

____

____

Steps to recreate problem ______________________

____

____

____

____

APPENDIX F

Hexadecimal Numbers

PCs are built on base-2 arithmetic, because electronics are most reliable when they deal with only two values, on and off. These two values can be represented as 0 and 1, the basis of the binary system. Memory addresses are represented as 0s and 1s as well.

Unfortunately, accurately remembering long strings of 0's and 1's is difficult. For example, an address in video memory might have the address 1100011111110000. Imagine dealing with many such numbers and not making any mistakes repeating them!

Fortunately, there's a simple translation from base 2 into base 16, or hexadecimal arithmetic. After all, 16 is a direct, exponential multiple of 2. That is, 2 to the fourth power, or 2*2*2*2=16. Almost magically the result is that each set of four numerals in a base-2 value can be translated into a single base-16 numeral.

Base 16 has 15 numerals and 0. From 0 to 9 it uses the same numerals as our regular base-10 or decimal arithmetic: 0,1,2,3,4,5,6,7,8,9. But then instead of moving to 10 (meaning 1 times the value 10 and 0 times the value 1), base 16 keeps using single numerals. Instead of using some complicated shapes or symbols, base 16 just borrows some of our letters, which normally do not have any mathematical meaning. For 10 in decimal, base 16 uses A. For 11 it uses B; for 12, C; for 13, D; for 14, E; for 15, F; and then for 16 it uses 10—meaning 1 times 16 and 0 times 1. (Just as in decimal, each place in a numeral means another exponent level. The number 111 in decimal means 1 times 100, 1 times 10, and 1 times 1. In hexadecimal 111 means 1 times 256 (16 times 16), 1 times 16, and 1 times 1.)

This is a lot to gobble in one sitting. But the result is that the binary number 1100011111110000 is just C7F0 in hexadecimal.

You could also translate that value into decimal, but it wouldn't make a lot of sense to do so. As you'll see throughout this book, computers work in binary or hexadecimal more naturally than in decimal, for addressing certainly. The values 640K and 1024K are common memory measurements. Hexadecimal values are clean, even numbers, such as A000 and 10000. In decimal those same addresses would be 655360 and 1048576, which are not so clean and even.

So if you're working with tiny hexadecimal (or just hex for short) numbers, here's a translation table:

Decimal	Binary	Hexadecimal
0	0	0h
1	1	1h
2	10	2h
3	11	3h
4	100	4h
5	101	5h
6	110	6h
7	111	7h
8	1000	8h
9	1001	9h
10	1010	Ah
11	1011	Bh
12	1100	Ch
13	1101	Dh
14	1110	Eh
15	1111	Fh
16	10000	10h
17	10001	11h
18	10010	12h
19	10011	13h
20	10100	14h

Notice the "h" put after a hexadecimal number. You don't have to put that there, especially if you're only using hexadecimal numbers, but it is a good idea if you're dealing in a mix of decimal and hexadecimal numbers. After all, the symbol 12 means different things in decimal and hexadecimal, and if you don't use an "h" to tell people you're talking hex, errors can result.

Now the numbers previously listed probably aren't too useful for memory addressing: they're too small. So here's a table of more typical translations for the work you'll do addressing ROMs, video buffers, and other such stuff of QEMM and QRAM concern.

Kilobytes of memory	Decimal	Hexadecimal	In the 64K Segment
1K	1024	400	0
2K	2048	800	0
4K	4096	1000	0
8K	8192	2000	0
16K	16384	4000	0
32K	32768	8000	0
64K	65536	10000	1
128K	131072	20000	2
256K	262144	40000	4
384K	393612	60000	6
512K	524288	80000	8
640K	655350	A0000	A
704K	720896	B0000	B
736K	753664	B8000	B
768K	786432	C0000	C
832K	851968	D0000	D
896K	917504	E0000	E
960K	983040	F0000	F
1024K	1048576	100000	

QDPMI

DPMI, the DOS Protected Mode Interface, is a software specification. Programs that follow its rules can work in harmony when using protected mode and extended memory on 386 and 486 systems. DPMI offers more flexibility than the older VCPI standard. It was created by a consortium including Quarterdeck, Borland, IBM, Intel, Lotus, Microsoft, Locus, Phar Lap, Phoenix, and others.

Protected-mode multitasking environment programs, memory managers, and operating systems that contain DPMI functions are DPMI hosts. Protected-mode applications that request DPMI functions, either directly or indirectly, are DPMI clients. DOS applications using DPMI clients can run in many operating environments—including DOS, DR DOS, Windows, OS/2, UNIX, and DESQview—if a DPMI host is present. The first DOS applications to support DPMI are Microsoft's C/C++ Development System for Windows version 7, Borland's C++ version 3, and Intel's Code Builder Kit version 1.1. Windows 3.1 includes its own DPMI host.

QDPMI, the Quarterdeck DPMI host, is a companion program to QEMM-386. QDPMI fully implements version 0.9 of DPMI, including DOS extensions and virtual memory. It gives mode switching and extended memory management to DPMI clients. QDPMI runs at a higher privilege level than the clients, using hardware to enforce the supervisor/user protection mode. That way QDPMI supports central virtual memory and fully controls client programs' address spaces and hardware access. DESQview-386 and DESQview/X can run multiple QDPMI clients simultaneously, each with its own virtual memory.

Because Windows 3.1 has its own DPMI host, when QDPMI sees Windows 3.1 start, QDPMI retires to let Windows provide DPMI services.

QDPMI is so new that few people have experience with it yet. Therefore, most of this section is taken directly from the Quarterdeck documentation.

Installation

QDPMI is available free to registered Quarterdeck software users. They can download it from the Quarterdeck BBS (see Chapter 21) along with its documentation. Compuserve, BIX, Genie, Internet, SmartNet (through the Sound of Music board), Rimenet (through Running Board), and FidoNet will all have the program as well. To order it on disk with a manual from Quarterdeck for $30, call 800-354-3222. (Passport Support subscribers can get it free.)

You must install QEMM-386 before you install QDPMI. Next run the QDPMI installation program, INSTALL, on the QDPMI disk. Type

```
INSTALL
```

and press Enter.

If you have an LCD or gas-plasma display or a monochrome monitor, run INSTALL with the /M parameter for better viewing by typing

```
INSTALL /M
```

If you downloaded QDPMI, it will be as a file called QDPMIZIP.EXE. This is a compressed file that automatically decompresses itself. Just type

```
QDPMIZIP
```

and press Enter. Then you can type

```
INSTALL
```

You'll see several screens asking for information. From your answers, INSTALL automatically sets up the AUTOEXEC.BAT and CONFIG.SYS files to load and configure QDPMI.

The first question is, which directory do you want to copy QDPMI files to. The default is the QEMM directory—and there is rarely a reason to choose any other.

Next you are asked if you want to provide virtual memory support for each DPMI client, as in Figure G-1.

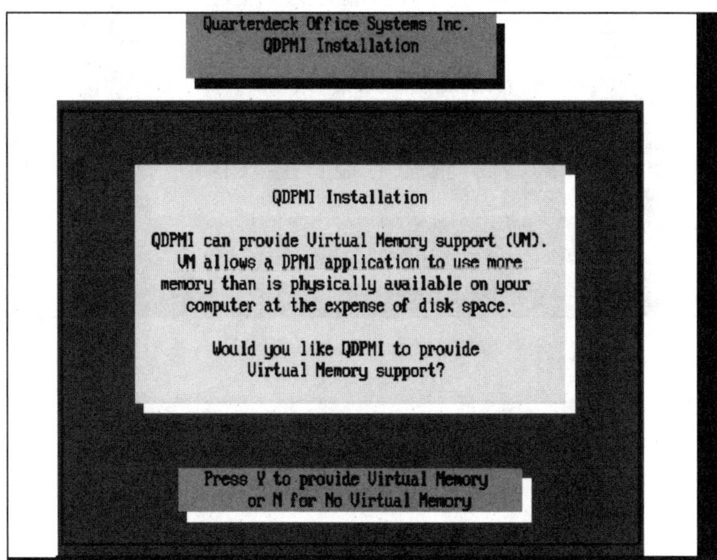

Figure G-1. Choosing virtual memory support when installing QDPMI

Answer yes to specify how much disk space to allocate. The default is 1024K per DPMI client. This makes a virtual swap file. Then you are asked if that file should be automatically deleted when the application is done, to save on disk space (at the expense of some time spent deleting). Finally you are shown the changes this INSTALL makes to your CONFIG.SYS and AUTOEXEC.BAT files, as in Figure G-2.

Now run OPTIMIZE to configure QEMM for this latest change to your PC. (See Chapters 1 and 14 for details.) Then reboot your PC.

To see if QDPMI is working, type

```
QDPMI
```

at the DOS prompt, and you'll see a screen showing the current status, as in Figure G-3.

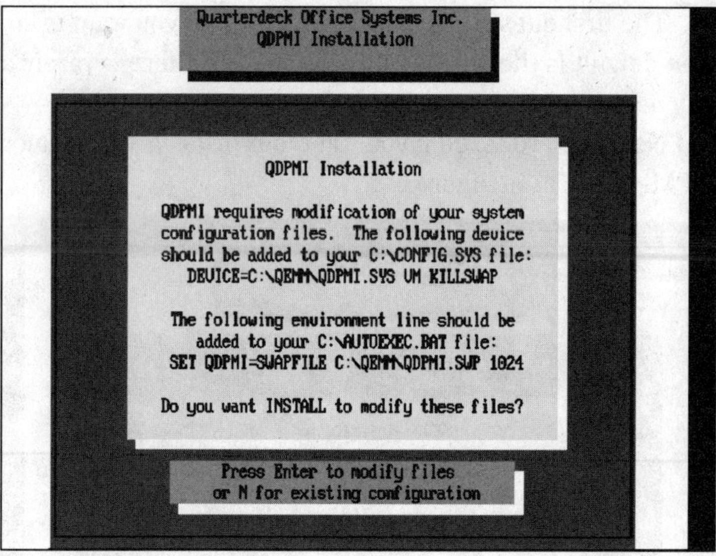

Quarterdeck Office Systems Inc.
QDPMI Installation
QDPMI Installation
QDPMI requires modification of your system configuration files. The following device should be added to your C:\CONFIG.SYS file:
DEVICE=C:\QEMM\QDPMI.SYS VM KILLSWAP
The following environment line should be added to your C:\AUTOEXEC.BAT file:
SET QDPMI=SWAPFILE C:\QEMM\QDPMI.SWP 1024
Do you want INSTALL to modify these files?
Press Enter to modify files
or N for existing configuration

Figure G-2. The changes QDPMI INSTALL makes to CONFIG.SYS and AUTOEXEC.BAT

Figure G-3. Status screen for QDPMI

```
C>cd qemm

C>qdpmi

QDPMI: Quarterdeck DPMI Host V1.0

   DPMI 0.9 Services are...ON
   DPMI Virtual Memory is..ON
   Auto Swap Deletion is...ON
   Extender Checking is....ON

C>
```

Virtual Swap Files

Virtual swap files are central to QDPMI operation. When a DPMI client initializes, QDPMI tries to make a swap file with name and size taken from the QDPMI environment variable. (In DESQview, each task or window can have its own unique set of QDPMI switches and environment variables.) If the file is there, its size is changed to equal the specified value. If there isn't such a variable for name or size, the file is opened as QDPMI.SWP, with a size of 2MB in the directory from which QDPMI.SYS was loaded. Each successively opened DPMI program needs its own swap file, and this is named with a successive digit after the environment variable name, such as QDPMI01.SWP.

The KILLSWAP option can delete a swap file when the DPMI client terminates.

The default STACKS=9,128 DOS resource setting may not be enough for some QDPMI applications. They may need a setting of STACKS=9,256 in CONFIG.SYS.

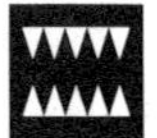

QDPMI can support 16- or 32-bit DPMI clients. In 32-bit support, all bits of the processor's 32-bit registers should be preserved. Some drivers and TSRs, such as Novell's LAN WorkPlace for DOS version 4.01 and the TCPIP.EXE program, don't preserve them. Run the TSR LWPFIX.COM after loading TCPIP.EXE to prevent erratic behavior.

Parameters

QDPMI is actually two programs: QDPMI.SYS and QDPMI.COM. The .SYS version loads as a driver from CONFIG.SYS (as DEVICE=C:\QEMM\QDPMI.SYS). The .COM version can be used at the DOS command line. Both offer a variety of parameters, as explained in this section.

The parameters set options. You type the parameter on the same line as the QDPMI command, after a space. Many parameters also have abbreviations. So you can get the effect either with

```
QDPMI parameter
```

or

```
QDPMI P
```

where "P" is the abbreviation for the parameter. Set the QDPMI parameters with the following commands:

- `DPMI`
  or
  `ON`
  turns DPMI services on (which is the default).

- NODPMI
  or
  OFF
  turns DPMI services off.

- VMON
  or
  VM
  turns QDPMI virtual memory on (which is the default).

- VMOFF
  or
  NOVM
  turns QDPMI virtual memory off.

- KILLSWAP
  or
  KLSW
  tells QDPMI to delete a clients virtual memory swap file when that client terminates (which is the default).

- KEEPSWAP
  or
  KPSW
  tells QDPMI not to delete a virtual memory swap file when a client terminates.

- EXTCHKON
  or
  XCHK
  tells QDPMI not to get in the way of incompatible DOS extenders (which is the default).

- `EXTCHOFF`
  or
  `NOXCHK`
  tells QDPMI not to worry about getting in the way of incompatible DOS extenders.

Environment Variable

As mentioned above, QDPMI looks to its environment variable to know what to name and how big to make the virtual swap files for client applications. You put that information into the environment variable with the command

```
SET QDPMI
```

followed by the variables and values. You can do this at the DOS prompt when you want to change the environment variable setting, but more typically you put it in the AUTOEXEC.BAT file so it automatically loads when you start your PC.

You don't have to set the environment variable. Default values automatically appear.

You can specify the environment variables in any order. They are all optional.

The variables are described in the following sections:

- `MAXMEM XXXX`
  The maximum kilobytes of physical memory reserved by QDPMI. This can be up to the memory in the system—which is the default (all memory, or as much as the current DESQview partition will allow). The memory is allocated from VCPI, XMS, extended, and conventional memory, in that order. QDPMI uses memory for code, data, page tables, and the memory requested by the DPMI client application. MAXMEM settings that are larger than possible are automatically trimmed settings that are possible. MAXMEM must be greater than or equal to MINMEM, or it is changed to be so.

- `MINMEM XXXX`

  The physical kilobytes of memory reserved by QDPMI when a DPMI client initializes. The least possible is 140K, and the default depends on the particular system. Any lower setting automatically is expanded to meet those requirements.

The difference between MAXMEM and MINMEM is the memory QDPMI manages dynamically, offering it to other applications, such as DPMI clients, when it is available. Dynamic memory is managed VCPI memory only.

- `MAXLOW XXXX`

  The maximum kilobytes of conventional memory to be reserved by QDPMI for use as its memory resources. The default is 0. Any nonzero setting lets QDPMI allocate conventional memory for its memory pool, but QDPMI uses conventional memory only if expanded and extended memory are insufficient for MINMEM.

- `SWAPFILE filename XXXX`

  Filename is the name of the virtual memory swap file QDPMI will use. XXXX is the size in kilobytes. Size can be up to 64MB or the free space on the disk. The default is QDPMI.SWP at 2MB.

MAXMEM plus the virtual swap file size is the amount of virtual memory available to QDPMI clients.

APPENDIX H

Startup Disk

Whenever you're experimenting you should create a Startup disk. This is a floppy with the minimum amounts of DOS on it to start your PC. Once you have such a Startup disk, you won't be in danger from any configurations you try with hard disk files that could fail to start or could immediately crash the PC. Without a Startup disk, if you configured your DOS on the hard disk (especially the CONFIG.SYS and AUTOEXEC.BAT files) so they failed to start the PC, you'd have no way to eliminate those failed files. You'd have to borrow for a startup disk from someone else's PC or from a tech support person.

To make a Startup disk, put a blank floppy (or one that you don't mind erasing) into the floppy drive (probably drive A), and type

```
format a: /s
```

and press Enter. (Be sure to put a space between the a: and the /s.) This will format (erase and prepare for new files) the floppy, and then put the basic system DOS files (that's the /s part) onto it.

You'll see a message such as

```
System Files Transferred
```

Now copy the current CONFIG.SYS and AUTOEXEC.BAT files to it. Use the commands

```
copy c:\config.sys a:
```

and

```
copy c:\autoexec.bat a:
```

and press Enter after each one. Now pull that floppy out and label it as "Startup disk".

Now test that Startup disk. First make sure the file COMMAND.COM is on it. Put the floppy in the A: drive and type

```
dir a:command.com
```

and then press Enter. If the PC says the file is there, along with its size, the disk is OK. If the PC can't find the file, try making the disk again, and be sure you use the /s parameter. Now test some more by turning your PC off, putting the Startup disk into the floppy drive, then turning the PC on. If it is able to boot (start) properly from the floppy, ending up at the DOS prompt (probably a:) then the disk is fine. If not, try making it again from scratch. (See a DOS book if you want more DOS details.)

Now make another one, just the same. Label that "Startup disk (backup)" with a date.

You're set.

Glossary

A-20 handler. The A-20 address line handles the HMA area of extended memory beyond the first 1024K of memory. To get to that extended memory, your computer needs a program to handle the A-20. HIMEM.SYS does this, as does QEMM.

adapter. An adapter is the intermediate stage between programs or computer pieces that makes one understand the other. Adapters can be software or hardware, although more often they are hardware. Most peripherals hooked to a computer, such as a disk drive or display screen, need an adapter to communicate with the computer.

address. A location in memory, typically given in hexadecimal.

address line. A wire coming out of a microprocessor or computer that gives one of the signals necessary to specify an address in memory.

address space. The total amount of memory a microprocessor can reach.

algorithm. A program; a computer's recipe for doing something.

alternate maps. Computers with the right hardware (386, 486, or EMS board) can remap addresses to move programs and data about in memory, changing addresses as you work. When this is done, the computer needs to use alternate maps to remember the previous address setups so it can return to them. These maps can be in software, but that is slow. For true multitasking they should be in hardware—chips made to remember other mappings of memory.

AT-class. A computer based on the 286 or better (386 or 486) processor.

AUTOEXEC.BAT. A file in the root directory of a PC running DOS. This batch (.BAT) file is read automatically when the PC starts running, and the programs and commands in it are automatically executed. QEMM and QRAM put some of their commands into AUTOEXEC.BAT.

backfill. An EMS memory card or a 386 or 486 chip can map expanded memory into conventional memory addresses to bring the total of conventional memory to the 640K maximum. This is backfilling. Such backfilled memory is better for multitasking than standard conventional memory is, although you may need to disable some conventional memory to do so.

background. A multitasking system has one program that runs in the foreground, and all other programs run in the background, operating but only partially or not at all visible on screen.

batch file. A file on disk with a .BAT extension to its name. Type that name and press Enter, and DOS tries to execute as a list of instructions.

BIOS. The basic input/output system set of routines in ROM chips. These are the most fundamental programs for the computer.

BIOS data area. An area of RAM memory where the BIOS routines keep their working knowledge of how the PC is running.

binary. Base-2 arithmetic, entirely of 1s and 0s, that computers run on.

bit. The smallest piece of information in a computer, just a 1 or a 0.

board. A circuit board; a set of electronic chips and circuits that is part of a computer or peripheral.

boot. To start a computer; comes from the expression "lift by its own bootstraps."

buffer. An area of memory used to keep the most frequently used or most recently used information from some other source.

BUFFERS. A DOS implementation of buffers, to keep the most recently used information from disk.

byte. The least information you can use to represent typical letters and numbers; consists of 8 bits.

cache. An area of memory used to keep the most frequently used information from another area of memory in order to speed operation (similar to a buffer).

caching. Using a cache.

capacitor. An electronic device that holds a charge of electricity—the basis for most RAM chips that hold their information of 1s and 0s as charges in tiny capacitors.

CGA. Acronym for Color/Graphics Adapter. One of the early standard video display adapters for the PC.

CEMM.SYS. Compaq's Expanded Memory Manager driver.

CMOS. Acronym for complementary metal oxide silicon. A way of making RAM chips so the chips use very little power. Most PCs have a little CMOS memory, with a battery attached, for holding their configuration information.

COMMAND.COM. The fundamental DOS program that watches what you type on the command line and tries to do it for you.

command line. The line on screen where you type PC commands.

Compaq. A popular maker of PCs. Compaq PCs have some specific features that sometimes call for different memory management methods. See Chapter 6 for the handful of QEMM parameters that deal specifically with Compaq.

CONFIG.SYS. A file in the root directory of a PC running DOS. This system driver (.SYS) file is read automatically when the PC starts running, and the programs and commands in it set the system's configuration. QEMM and QRAM load themselves from lines in CONFIG.SYS.

conventional memory. The memory addresses from 0 to 640K. This is where most program instructions sit while a program is operating (see Chapter 4 for details).

converted. *See* LIMULATOR.

coprocessor. A secondary microprocessor chip that speeds execution of particular work, such as graphics or mathematics.

CPU. Acronym for central processing unit. The electronic circuits that make up the central brain of the computer. Most personal computers have a single microprocessor chip for a CPU. This chip controls what information is pulled in from disk, stored in memory, added, subtracted, compared, stored, displayed, and so on.

crash. When a PC dies—the screen blanks, shows random information, or freezes so you cannot affect it from the keyboard—you say that PC has crashed.

dd. *See* device driver.

default. The automatic choice, unless instructed otherwise.

device driver. A program that helps DOS understand some peripheral or other program.

DEVICEHIGH. A DOS 5 command for loading device drivers into high memory.

DIP. Acronym for dual in-line package. The common package for a memory chip. The plastic or ceramic package has two parallel rows of metal legs protruding. You plug these into sockets in a memory board.

directory. An area of a disk set aside with a name for holding related files. You may create and destroy directories, as well as directories within directories, known as subdirectories.

disable. To turn off.

disk cache. A cache that uses some RAM to hold the most frequently used information from disk and so makes apparent disk operation much faster.

display. The screen that shows what the computer is doing.

document. A file for an application such as a word processor or spreadsheet.

DOS. Acronym for disk operating system. The fundamental software that runs on almost all PCs and determines memory handling and management.

DOS environment. A set of variables that DOS uses to know its own configuration.

DOS extender. A piece of program that programmers can build into applications, so those applications can then switch into protected mode and reach extended memory.

DOS resources. The FILES, BUFFERS, and other such memory uses that DOS offers.

DPMI. Acronym for DOS Protected Mode Interface. The successor to the VCPI standard for letting DOS-extender programs get along when reaching protected mode and extended memory.

DRAM. Acronym for dynamic RAM. The most common kind of RAM memory chip.

driver. *See* device driver.

8088/8086. The Intel 8088 and 8086 or compatible microprocessor chips, which have the same memory handling abilities. They can reach 1MB of memory and can run only in real mode. Although QEMM can't run on 8088/8086 machines, QRAM can if those machines have an EMS 4.0 expanded memory board or a Chips & Technologies chip set.

80286. *See* 286.

80386. *See* 386.

80486. *See* 486.

EEMS. Acronym for Enhanced Expanded Memory Specification. A competitor to LIM EMS 3.2 and quite similar to LIM EMS 4.0. A now-obsolete expanded memory specification that allowed for greater multitasking and use of expanded memory than the original LIM EMS 3.2 specification.

EGA. Acronym for Enhanced Graphics Adapter. The successor to the CGA as a video display adapter standard for PCs. Now made obsolete by VGA and the following XGA.

EMM. Acronym for Expanded Memory Manager, a program to manage expanded memory.

EMM386.EXE. DOS 5's Expanded Memory Manager, in the form you can run from the command line.

EMM386.SYS. DOS 5's Expanded Memory Manager, in the form you can load from CONFIG.SYS.

EMS. Acronym for Expanded Memory Specification, the standard rules for handling expanded memory.

Enhanced-386 mode. The Windows mode that uses the 386 or 486 chip's mapping abilities for true multitasking. Requires at least 2MB of extended memory and has the most trouble with QEMM.

EXCLUDE. A QEMM parameter that can stop QEMM from mapping memory into some addresses, in case those addresses have some other use—such as an adapter—that would create a conflict.

expanded memory. A type of memory that avoids the DOS limits on direct addressing (see Chapter 4) by switching in and out of a page frame (again, see Chapter 4). Used to store both data and programs. Ruled by the LIM EMS specification. *See also*, LIM and EMS.

Expanded Memory Manager. A program to manage expanded memory.

extended memory. A type of memory useful to PCs with 286, 386, or 486 processors. Extended memory is at addresses above 1024K (1MB). Most DOS programs cannot use extended memory directly, but can when aided by special memory management utilities such as QEMM.

FCBS. Acronym for file control blocks. A DOS resource used more in earlier versions of DOS but still used by networking systems. FCBS take up some memory, but that memory use can be controlled by QEMM's FCBS.COM program.

filename. The name given a piece of information or program on disk, with up to eight characters followed by a period and up to three characters of filename extension.

FILES. A DOS resource that tells how many files can be open for use at once. A larger FILES means more use of memory, but this can be controlled with QEMM's FILES.COM program.

footprint. The size of a program in memory.

foreground. A multitasking system has one program that runs in the foreground and can be seen on screen, and other programs that run in the background, operating but only partially or not at all visible on screen.

486. An Intel 80486 or 486SX or compatible microprocessor chip. The 486 offers everything the 386 does but runs faster. This includes real, protected, and virtual-86 mode operation.

GB. Short for gigabyte. A thousand megabytes.

handle. A reference name or number given to a computer resource, such as a handle for an expanded memory page.

hang. *See* crash.

hexadecimal. Base-16 arithmetic, a system of counting often used in place of the binary arithmetic that computers run on (see Appendix E).

high DOS. The memory addresses from 640K to 1024K.

high memory. The memory addresses from 640K to 1024K.

high memory area. The memory addresses from 1024K to 1086K, an area of extended memory that can be used by one program as a form of conventional memory when managed by QEMM or HIMEM.SYS. Also referred to as the HMA.

HIMEM.SYS. The DOS 5 program for managing extended memory and the HMA.

HMA. *See* high memory area.

INCLUDE. A QEMM parameter for mapping memory to some area that was overlooked or left out before.

interupt. A computer mechanism for stopping in the middle of one operation to take care of another. Interrupts use a small amount of memory.

K. Short for kilobyte, a thousand, or more precisely 1024, bytes of memory.

kernal. The central part of an operating system.

kilobyte. *See* K.

LAN. Acronym for local area network. A set of hardware and software that allows PCs to directly communicate with one another, sharing messages, files, and programs.

LASTDRIV, or LASTDRIVE. A DOS resource that specifies the last allowable drive letter name for a disk drive.

LIM EMS. The Lotus Intel Microsoft Expanded Memory specification. The original version was 3.2, which was able to reach 8MB for storing data. Version 4.0 followed the EEMS standard in allowing up to 32MB and use for both storing data and programs.

LIMULATOR. A program such as QEMM that can convert extended memory into LIM EMS expanded memory.

LOADHIGH. A program statement that relocates a program or device into high memory.

loading high. Memory managers such as QEMM and QRAM can free conventional memory for use by standard programs. One way they do this is to take small driver and TSR programs from conventional memory and instead load them high—that is, put them into unused areas of high memory at addresses from 640K to 1024K.

local area network. *See* LAN.

mappable. Memory addresses that could have memory mapped into them by a memory manager and the right hardware.

MB. Short for megabyte, a thousand kilobytes.

MCA. Acronym for Micro Channel Adapter. A computer bus invented by IBM for connecting a computer to peripherals.

memory board. A circuit board with memory chips on it. You can plug memory boards into many PCs to increase the PC's amount of memory.

memory manager. A program such as QEMM that controls the use, access to, and assignment of memory in a PC.

memory map. A diagram of memory.

memory-resident. A program that remains in memory after it has stopped working, unlike standard programs that load into memory, work, then dump out of memory, freeing that memory for other uses.

Micro Channel. *See* MCA.

microprocessor. A chip that is the focus of a PC, that performs the fundamental calculations and manipulations of information.

modes. Processors run in various modes—real, protected, or virtual-86—that let them reach different amounts of memory. Programs can have modes too, such as Windows 3.0's real, standard, and enhanced modes.

motherboard. The main circuit board in a typical PC. The motherboard holds the CPU (microprocessor) as well as some memory, disk controllers, display controllers, and so on.

MS-DOS. Acronym for Microsoft DOS. The most common version of the disk operating system.

multitask. Run more than one program at a time.

nanosecond. A billionth of a second. This tiny slice of time is used to measure how quickly memory chips can release or accept information. Typical memory chips operate in from 50 to 150 nanoseconds.

network. *See* LAN.

network adapter. A piece of hardware that lets a PC connect to a LAN.

ns. *See* nanosecond.

page. A 16K piece of memory mapped through the expanded memory page frame (which typically holds four of these pages).

page frame. A 64K area of memory addresses through which programs reach to expanded memory. *See also*, page.

parameter. A code name for an option. QEMM and QRAM have parameter codes that let you control just how memory is managed.

PC compatible. A computer that can run programs and use peripherals built for the IBM PC and its DOS operating system.

PC-DOS. IBM's version of DOS.

pixels. A single dot of light on the computer screen is a pixel (short for picture element).

protected mode. An operating mode for the 286, 386, and 486 processors that permits access to 16MB of memory.

RAM. Acronym for random access memory. The name given to the most common types of memory chips. (The name comes from their ability to accept or divulge any bit of information in any order—some other memory types must work sequentially.) When people ask how much memory a computer has, they almost always mean RAM.

RAM-cram. Having too many programs to fit into the 640K limit of conventional RAM.

reading. Getting information from a memory device.

real mode. An operating mode for any PC microprocessor that can reach only 1MB of memory.

reboot. To start the PC over. A cold reboot is turning the power off and then on again. A warm reboot is pressing the Ctrl, Alt, and Del keys all at once.

reserved memory. Memory addresses from 640K to 1024K, officially reserved for computer system functions such as the BIOS ROM and various adapter ROMs.

resolution. The number of pixels on the screen. A higher resolution means more pixels, a more realistic picture, and more legible text.

ROM. Acronym for read-only memory. The type of memory chip used for permanent programs in a PC, such as the fundamental BIOS the PC uses to communicate with disk drives and the keyboard. ROM chips always retain their information, even if the PC is turned off.

root directory. The main directory on a disk.

Shadow RAM. RAM put into reserved memory addresses, to which the various ROMs are then copied for improved performance. As explained in Chapter 6,

Shadow RAM can conflict with QEMM's approach to reserved memory addresses.

SIMM. Acronym for single in-line memory module. A set of 8 or 9 memory chips soldered together in a single strip for easy insertion in a PC.

single tasking. Running one program at a time.

slots. The spots inside a PC into which you can plug new circuit boards, such as for adding memory to the computer.

SRAM. Acronym for static RAM. A more expensive but faster type of RAM chip than a DRAM.

standard mode. A Windows 3 operating mode that doesn't require a 386 chip but offers more access to extended memory than Windows real mode.

system ROM. The ROM chip holding the BIOS and other basic system software.

task switching. Moving quickly from one program to another, even if those programs aren't actually running simultaneously (which would be multitasking).

386. An Intel 80386 or 386SX or compatible microprocessor chip. The 386 offers real, protected, and virtual-86 mode operation, and has built-in memory mapping abilities. Its abilities are also in the 486 processors.

top memory. A memory use found in some Compaq computers (see Chapter 4 for details).

TSR. Acronym for terminate-and-stay-resident. A type of program that stays in memory even when it isn't running, unlike typical DOS programs that are covered over with new software or erased from memory when they are done running. Because TSRs stay in memory, they are more immediately useful, but their residence also means they take up memory that then is not available to other programs. *See also*, memory-resident.

286. An Intel 80286 microprocessor chip, or a compatible chip. The 286 can reach up to 16MB of memory. It offers real and protected mode operation but does not have the virtual-86 mode or mapping abilities of the 386 and 486.

UMB. Acronym for upper memory block, an unused part of upper memory in a PC (memory from addresses 640K to 1024K). Note that not all UMBs are unused. DOS cannot use UMBs, but a memory manager such as QEMM can, loading high device drivers and TSRs.

upper memory. The memory addresses from 640K to 1024K. *See also*, high memory.

upper memory block. *See* UMB.

V-86. *See* virtual-86 mode.

VCPI. Acronym for Virtual Control Program Interface, a set of rules for DOS-extended programs that use protected mode, virtual-86 mode, and extended memory (see Chapter 4 for details).

VGA. Acronym for video graphics adapter. The standard video display adapter after EGA.

video adapter. Circuitry that adapts the PC to a particular display.

video buffer. An area of RAM memory, typically in the lower part of reserved memory addresses, that holds information to be sent to the display screen.

video memory. *See* video buffer.

VIDRAM. A program that can take unused video buffer and use the addresses for standard conventional memory tasks.

virtual-86 mode. An operating mode of 386 and 486 processors that permits multiple 1MB spaces to run side by side for multitasking and for protected program's from bothering each other's memory use. QEMM uses V-86 mode.

wait state. A delay inserted into a computer's reading and writing of memory when the microprocessor is faster than the memory (see Chapter 4).

wildcard. A symbol used to mean "anything here," such as the DOS wildcard *, which can stand for any character in a filename.

Windows. A program from Microsoft that gives DOS more memory management and the ability to use pull-down menus (see Chapter 16).

writing. Sending information to memory.

XMS. Acronym for Extended Memory Specification. The rules (now in version 2.0) for controlling extended memory.

Index

H

I

K

L

M

V

W

X

ORDER FORM

To Order:

Return this form with your payment to M&T Books, 411 Borel Avenue, Suite 100, San Mateo, CA 94402 or **call toll-free 1-800-533-4372 (in California, call 1-800-356-2002).**

ITEM #	DESCRIPTION	DISK	PRICE
		Subtotal	
		CA residents add sales tax ____%	
		Add $4.50 per item for shipping and handling	
		TOTAL	

Charge my:
- ❑ **Visa**
- ❑ **MasterCard**
- ❑ **AmExpress**

❑ **Check enclosed, payable to M&T Books.**

CARD NO. ____________________

SIGNATURE ____________________ EXP. DATE ____________________

NAME ____________________

ADDRESS ____________________

CITY ____________________

STATE ____________________ ZIP ____________________

M&T GUARANTEE: If your are not satisfied with your order for any reason, return it to us within 25 days of receipt for a full refund. Note: Refunds on disks apply only when returned with book within guarantee period. Disks damaged in transit or defective will be promptly replaced, but cannot be exchanged for a disk from a different title.

2950